Growing Up Between Two Cultures

Problems and Issues of Muslim Children

A volume in
Research in Multicultural Education and International Perspectives

Series Editors
Rumjahn Hoosain and Farideh Salili,
The University of Hong Kong

Research in Multicultural Education and International Perspectives

Rumjahn Hoosain and Farideh Salili, Editors

Growing Up Between Two Cultures

Problems and Issues of Muslim Children

edited by

Farideh Salili and Rumjahn Hoosain
The University of Hong Kong

INFORMATION AGE PUBLISHING, INC.
Charlotte, NC • www.infoagepub.com

Library of Congress Cataloging-in-Publication Data

Growing up between two cultures : problems and issues of Muslim children /
edited by Farideh Salili and Rumjahn Hoosain.
pages cm. -- (Research in multicultural education and international
perspectives)
Includes index.
ISBN 978-1-62396-619-5 (paperback) -- ISBN 978-1-62396-620-1 (hardcover) --
ISBN 978-1-62396-621-8 (e-book) 1. Muslims--Non-Islamic countries. 2.
Muslim children. 3. Muslim children--Education. 4. Muslim youth. 5.
Muslim youth--Education. 6. Muslims--Cultural assimilation. 7. Ethnicity.
8. Group identity. I. Salili, Farideh. II. Hoosain, R. (Rumjahn)
BP52.5.G76 2014
305.23088'297--dc23

                                                            2014002398

Printed in the United States of America

CONTENTS

v

PART III: ISSUES RELATED TO
IDENTITY FORMATION OF MUSLIM CHILDREN

PART IV: THE ROLE OF GENDER IN
ACCULTURATION AND IDENTITY FORMATION

PART V: EXPERIENCES OF MUSLIM YOUTHS GROWING UP
IN A NON-MUSLIM COUNTRY

PREFACE

Farideh Salili

In a book titled *The Clash of Civilizations and the Remaking of World Order,* Samuel P. Huntington (1997) argued that "the central and most dangerous dimension of the emerging global politics would be conflicts between groups from different civilizations" (p. 13). The events that followed the tragedy of 9/11 in the U.S. appear to support the above argument. What emerged in post-9/11 is a feeling of hostility, suspicion and distrust by Americans as well as other Western non-Muslim nations towards Muslim people. The 9/11 tragedy caused by a few terrorists brought the old animosity between Christians and Muslims to the fore. Muslims are frequently isolated, profiled as security risks, and looked at with suspicion. Some Western countries have placed restrictions on Muslim women wearing head covering and have codified legal regulation to ban them. In France for example, a law passed in recent years prohibits women from wearing head covering in state schools. In Quebec, a controversial bill called the Charter of Quebec Values is before the national assembly. The controversial aspect of this bill is about religious accommodation which bans displaying all kinds of religious symbols at work and in schools. This bill if passed will ban people from showing any symbols of their religion at work in public institutions including schools, hospitals, and government offices. To most Muslims this

Growing Up Between Two Cultures: Problems and Issues of Muslim Children, pp. ix–xi
Copyright © 2014 by Information Age Publishing

represents intolerance of Muslims and places in particular Muslim girls and women at a disadvantage. There are many Muslim women who will be affected by this bill in a significant way. Those who follow more conservative Islamic faith feela need to wear Hejab (head covering). If this bill passes, the law will effectively prevent many Muslim women from working in public places. Recently, in Montreal there are reports of attacks on Muslims since the proposal of the Charter: within 2 days there was an attack on a Muslim family, vandalism at a Turkish bath which is a spa frequented by Muslim women, and a woman wearing Hejab was harassed in a public bus.

There are many debates and conferences on the topic of veiling women in Western Europe. There are concerns about the well being of veiling women. Veiling is seen as a "form of social control," and the debates are driven by efforts to free these women from "their oppressive communities or even from themselves" (Amir-Moazemi, 2010, p. 192). However, the well being in this case means liberating women and by the Western standard this means freedom for youth to experience youthful sexuality. Experiencing freedom to engage in youthful sexuality is seen as a necessary step to becoming physically and psychologically healthy adults. For example, one aspect of freedom for women in France is superficially defined as "lying in the beaches with naked breast" (L'Express 2004, cited in Amir-Moazami, 2010, p. 192). However, from the standpoint of these veiling women who appear to be well educated and present in these debates, freedom and the touchstone to their adulthood is trying to please God, doing their religious duties and cultivating piety. To avoid temptations of sexual activities prior to matrimony is important to them. It is interesting to note that veiling very often does not come from their families. Mothers of these girls are often without Hejab.

In such a hostile environment, Muslim children and youths try to sort out their identities and are facing dilemma of negotiating between accepting the values taught by their parents, their clans, and established institution of Islam with those of the society in which they live. The central theme of this book is how Muslim children and youths cope and develop their unique identities in the midst of the conflicts that exist between Islamic and Western civilizations and the hostilities of post-9/11. Contributors to this volume have discussed their views, experiences and research findings. Muslim youths appear to have different reactions to this so called Islamophobia in the West. Depending on their national culture, spoken language and upbringing as well as other factors, they may use different strategies to cope . Some hide their religion, others convert out of Islam, or become atheists or agnostics, and yet some youths return to Islam in a way that they had not before. This seems to be particularly true of Arab Muslims in the United States. According to Bayoumi (cited in Bayat & Herrera, 2010), in order to survive in a hostile climate, "young Arab Muslims were compelled to come to terms with their religious identity" (p. 21), because everyone defined them as Muslims in post-9/11. Instead of hiding their religion, they visibly embrace the religion and redefine and educate themselves as Muslims. "They embraced the religion because in a hostile climate, their survival depended on establishing a recognition that is okay to be young Muslim, and American" (p. 21), as did the veiling young women in Europe.

The degree to which children and youths experience problems in integrating and defining their identities in a non-Muslim country appears to depend on many factors. The national culture, the country of origin, their native language, and whether the children or youths are brought up in a liberal Muslim home as well as other factors are important in defining youth identity. These factors can be summed up in terms of congruence and continuity between values the youths learn at home and those of the society in which they live. The more congruent the less problems they have in adjusting their identities.

REFERENCES

Amir-Moazami, S. (2010). Avoiding "youthfulness": Young Muslims negotiating gender and citizenship in France and Germany. In L. Herrera & A Bayat (Eds.), *Being young and Muslim: New cultural politics in the global south and north.* (pp. 189-205). London, England: Oxford University Press.

Bayat, A., & Herrera, L. (2010). Introduction: Being young and Muslim in neoliberal times. In L. Herrera & A Bayat (Eds.), *Being young and Muslim: New cultural politics in the global south and north* (pp. 3-26). London, England: Oxford University Press.

Huntington, S. P. (1997). *The clash of civilizations: Remaking of world order.* New York, NY: Touchstone.

PART I

INTRODUCTION

CHAPTER 1

GROWING UP
BETWEEN TWO CULTURES

Issues and Problems of Muslim Children

Farideh Salili and Rumjahn Hoosain

INTRODUCTION

Muslims have always lived in the West, but since mid-19th century there has been a steady growth in the numbers of Muslim immigrants to the West. These numbers have drastically increased in the past 2 decades, as many Muslims left their home countries for better lives, better education, or as war refugees and exiles to escape repressive regimes. Recent statistics show that the number of Muslims in Europe has grown from 2.6 million in 1990 to 44.1 million in 2010, and is projected to exceed 58 million by 2030. The number of Muslims living in the Americas has similarly increased, and in 2009, 4.6 million Muslims lived in America (Pew Research Center's Forum on Religion and Public Life, 2011).

Muslim children born or raised in non-Muslim countries have to face many challenges and issues growing up. They have to cope with two different cultures and two languages, the language and culture of home and that of the school and the society in which they live. They also have to cope with demands of their religion which require them to dress and behave in certain ways, which can be very difficult in a secular Western country.

While much has been published on Islam and the West, not many research articles or books exist on Muslim children growing up in the West. The purpose of this book is to explore problems and issues facing Muslim children in non-Muslim Western countries. To better understand these difficulties, the present chapter will first introduce readers to Islam as a religion and a way of life. It aims at providing a background for chapters that follow.

TENETS OF ISLAM

Muslims believe that there is one God (deity) who is benevolent and compassionate and the source of all Creation, and Mohammad is the last prophet of God. He was sent to guide humanity by carrying God's message through the *Qur'an*. Like other Abrahamic religions it believes in the day of judgment and divine revelation, and advocates love and peace for mankind.

> The *Qur'an*, which is the holy book for Muslims, contains 114 chapters (called Suras). Muslims believe that it is the pure word of God, unadulterated over 14 centuries. It deals with issues that affect human beings in their earthly lives; issues like piety, upright human conduct, worship, the creation of a just and virtuous society and the practice of ethics. (Islam Guide, 2013)

The tenets of Islam are referred to as the five Pillars of Islam. They are: (1) the testimony of faith (i.e., "There is no true god (deity) but God (Allah), and Muhammad is the Messenger (Prophet) of God"), (2) prayer: Muslims pray five times daily (morning, mid-day, afternoon, evening, and night) to achieve inner peace and have direct link with God, (3) giving "Zakat" (support of the needy by giving a certain percentage of one's belonging in money to needy people), (4) fasting during the month of Ramadan (for the purpose of spiritual self-purification by cutting oneself from worldly comfort to experience how needy people feel), and (5) the pilgrimage to Makkah at least once in a lifetime for those who are able.

Muslims are to follow the Divine Laws of Shari'a which guide every aspect of their lives.

> Shari'a law is collections of "Hadith" (memories of what prophet Mohammed said and did during his life passed on orally and in writing by those close to him) regarded by traditional Islamic schools of jurisprudence as important tools for understanding the Quran and in matters of jurisprudence. "Hadith"

were evaluated and gathered into large collections during the 8th and 9th centuries. These works are referred to in matters of Islamic law and history to this day. The largest denominations of Islam, Sunni, Shi'a, and Ibadi, rely upon different sets of "Hadith" collections. (https://en.wikipedia.org/wiki/Hadith)

Islam has two main schools of thought—the Shi'a and the Sunni. The Sunnis believe that after Muhammad's death Abu Baker, a friend of Muhammad, was selected by the community as Leader. The Shi'as believe that the Prophet Muhammad had appointed Ali, his cousin and son-in-law, as his successor (that the leadership was through divine succession). Roughly, 10% of the world's Muslims are Shi'a. There are also a number of branches of Shi'a and Sunni. Both the Sunnis and the Shi'as have the same major beliefs and pray in the same way. "The differences are mainly theological and jurisprudential" (Islam Guide, 2013).

ISLAM AND THE WEST

Islam is the fastest growing religion in the world. One out of every five people in the world is a Muslim. Yet, Islam is also the most misunderstood religion. The presence of Muslims in the West has impact on both civilizations, and just as in any coming together of cultures, beliefs, and attitudes, it has the potential for good as well as ill. Islam has contributed to Western civilization in significant ways.

> They have made substantial contributions to the development of science, medicine, mathematics, physics, astronomy, geography. and literature. Muslims like Avicenna and Averroes have played major roles in the advancement of science in the West. Many crucial systems such as the Arabic numerals, algebra, the first map of the globe and navigational maps were developed by Muslims and adopted by the medieval Europeans. (Wikipedia-Dictionary. com-Answers.com-Merriam Webster)

There has long been conflicts and hostilities between Western Christians and the Islamic world. The Crusader wars are but one example. After a long period of relative peace between peoples of the two religions, recently (in the last 40 years), the presence of Muslims in the West, particularly in North America and Western Europe has led to increasing social and other conflicts, often reported in the forefront of the news. Terrorist incidences of some extremists particularly taint the view towards all Muslims. With millions of Muslims now living in the West, the old dichotomy of Muslims and the West is revived. Specially after the events of 9/11, there is rising negative attitudes and hostilities directed at Muslim people. Correspondingly there is increasing hostility towards the West by Muslims who perceive their human rights being ignored and taken away, and increasingly sense negative attitudes of Western people towards them.

Demographic Background of Muslim People in the West

Muslim youths live in societies where their Western counterparts often know little about Islam beyond what they see on television or in movies. Muslims are often seen by Westerners as one people, ignoring their geographic and demographic backgrounds. Like people of the other religions, Muslims living in the West have varied ethnic, cultural, and religious backgrounds. They come from every country where Muslims live, and now usually live in major metropolitan areas in the West. Los Angeles, for example, is symbolic of this diversity. The largest number of Muslims in Los Angeles come from South Asia, Iran, and the Arabic speaking countries. The largest groups are from South Asia (i.e., Bangladesh, India and Pakistan). The second largest group are Iranians, followed by Arabs.

Muslims living in North America are more affluent, and on average more educated than average Americans. Those living in Europe are generally from less well-off backgrounds and many live in slums and ghettoes in the cities. Depending on cultural and ethnic backgrounds, different interpretations of the *Qur'an* are also followed. Muslims coming from Arab countries and those from other countries such as Pakistan and Afghanistan who follow Arab interpretation of the *Qur'an* are generally more conservative than those who are for example from Iran and Turkey, sometimes causing conflicts among various groups. Arabs consider themselves speakers of the same language as that of the *Qur'an*, and are sometimes impatient towards Muslims who speak other native languages. "And there are tensions between American born Muslims, mainly of African descent and Muslim Immigrants" (Tirmazi, Husain, Mirza, & Walsh 2011, p. 58). There are as many followers of traditional Islam as are more liberal Muslims.

There are also generation differences and different manners of response to the new environment. For example, while many first generation Muslims are traditional, their children growing up in the West become westernized. Many immigrants and their children going to North America like "the freedoms that America offers and become less observant of religion (some even convert out of Islam)." Youths often act out "what they could not fully express in their own countries" (Tirmazi et al., 2011, pp. 59–60).

There are also those who become more religious. The tragic event of 9/11 has changed the social fabric of American culture.

Subsequent events, such as the ongoing wars in Afghanistan and Iraq. the continued Israeli-Palestinian conflict, military focus in Pakistan, fighting Alquaida and Osama Bin Laden and other isolated incidents involving Muslims have all resulted in Muslim being looked with suspicion in Western countries, including the United States. (Tirmazi et al., 2011, pp. 59–60)

Westerners in general have little knowledge about Islam and have difficulties understanding the "distinct" Islamic religion and culture. Hence, they often prefer Muslims to assimilate into mainstream western societal norms and values rather than "integrate as Muslims." (Tirmazi et al., 2011)

Since 9/11, the interest in Islam and Muslims increased dramatically, but not necessarily in a positive manner. Young Muslims often become target of profiling by authorities. This "Islamophobia" has made psychosocial adaptation and acculturation of youth in the new country difficult and has resulted in public debates among Muslims about their adopted new country and their ethnic identity. The feelings of alienation can have the following effects: (1) many Muslims have decided to defend Islam and have become more committed to their faith, (2) others have developed a sense that they do not belong in the new country (Abdo, 2006), and (3) others like some Ismai'lis have tried to hide their religious identity (see Chapter 7). Still others have converted to other religions or call themselves agnostics or atheists.

Many Muslim youths have actively turned to Islamic teachings and follow its way of life, and many become active in promoting the religion (Bayoumi, 2010). Some learn to be "Khateeb" (Speakers on Islam, promoting the religion). There are many Muslim youth organizations and mosques teaching young children about their religion and training them to become "Khateeb" (Fitzsimon, 2011).

Challenges Muslim Children Face to Perform Their Religious Duties

To follow the practical aspects of their religious duties strictly, Muslim children or youths living in a non-Muslim country face many challenges. For example, they need to find a way to pray five times a day when attending school in an area which by Muslim standard is considered clean (e.g., on a prayer rug). And there are the ritual of washing and cleanliness that must be observed prior to prayer. Boys from the age of 12 and girls from the age of 9 are required to follow laws of Shari'a which require them to dress modestly and protect their chastity. This is interpreted by conservative Muslims to mean that girls should cover themselves from head to toe in the presence of the opposite sex who are not their immediate family. No physical contacts, even shaking hands, are permitted with the opposite sex. Muslims are required to avoid eating meat that are considered unclean (e.g., pork) or that has been produced in an un-Islamic way (i.e., the meat which is not Halal). Even such everyday behavior as using the toilet is prescribed (i.e., Muslims should use water to wash themselves when using the toilet and not just rely on toilet paper). During the fasting month of Ramadan, they cannot eat from dawn to the evening and thus have to cope with hunger during the time they are in school. These are some practical examples of challenges they face outside their home environment in order to perform their strict religious duties.

There are also other social and emotional problems that they face, such as being ridiculed or harassed by their non-Muslim peers and being isolated because of their appearance. It is easy to see the problems that Muslim children from traditional conservative families are faced with in a secular non-Muslim country.

CHILDREN GROWING UP IN THE WEST

Parents of Muslim children, regardless of their background, expect their children to show respect and obedience towards them. They want them to work hard in school and achieve in their academic work. They want them to follow their own cultural tradition which is that of the old country and behave accordingly. They fear that their children learn from their Western peers to be disrespectful, disobedient, self-indulgent, and proud. Many religious "Muslims see Western customs touching on family relations and position of women as morally corrupt and endangering their way of life. Their worries include family honor, divorce, abandonment of faith, and intermarriage" (Pipes & Duran, 2002, p. 12). Some religious Muslims try to control their children's moral behavior by sending them to Islamic schools (see Chapter 13). However, as Pipes and Duran state, this does not protect them from the influences of the rest of society or "solve the problem of uncoolness." Some girls who are forced by their parents to wear long and loose dresses secretly carry tighter clothing to change on reaching school. They pretend to be dieting to lose weight in the month of Ramdan (Pipes & Duran, 2002). On the other hand there are also children of nonobservant Muslims who have discovered "a range of attraction in Islam—morality, discipline, even plain old fashionedness. The younger generation rediscovers Islam as the religion of its heritage and take it up with various degrees of strictness" (Pipes & Duran, 2002, p. 12).

An important worry of religious parents is related to their teenage daughters. Following strict Islamic tradition men and women are not allowed to mingle lest they engage in sexual activities before marriage. Just when Western girls are discovering their sexuality, many Muslim girls are made to wear head covering and loose clothing. Some families cloister their daughters and if possible guard them with family members. Others behave as if they still live in their old countries as far as girls and sex are concerned, leading to tension in the family (Pipes & Duran, 2002). There are some publicized incidents of what is called honor killing of girls who have embraced Western ways with regards to dressing and relation with boys, by the father or brother.

The restrictions on meeting Muslim girls often lead men to look for non-Muslim women for companionship and sex, leading to marriage with non-Muslim women. Whereas a man can marry a non-Muslim woman, marriage of a Muslim woman with a non-Muslim man is strictly forbidden in Islam. Muslims are developing novel ways, like "summer camps, social for singles, and advertisements for marriage. But even these Muslim institutions have a difficult time keeping boys and girls apart" (Pipes & Duran, 2002, p. 13).

There are, however, many enlightened and modern Muslim families where men and women meet before marriage.

Development of Identity in Muslim Youths

As the above account shows, Muslim youths today experience more intense challenges in the process of acculturation and psychosocial adaptation to their new environment than youths with other religions. Against this background, children born to Muslim immigrants or raised in the new country from early childhood have to develop an identity that can adapt and negotiate with both the culture of home and that of society in which they live. The very young children may not be aware that there are any differences between them and their non-Muslim peers until they are older and someone ask them where they come from. It is when peers question them or tell them they are foreigners that they find out they are from a different country (Baiza, 2011). Subsequently increasingly they notice differences such as looks, language, and other characteristics of their ethnic identity. The physical appearance of many Muslim children and youths who are visible minorities poses an extra difficulty, when compared with for example those from eastern Europe. According to Erikson (1968), teenagers have to resolve "identity crises" or "confusion," "which is a transition period from childhood to adolescence when the self is in need of a "central perspective" and direction, and where the hopes and anticipations of adulthood are realized" (Erikson 1958, p. 12). "The crisis occurs when a gap emerges between the young person's burgeoning identity and the parentally given identity. The successful resolution of the identity crises occurs through the adolescent "having integrity and continuity, and ... keeping the internal and external world aligned to each other" (Rattansi & Phoenix, 2005, cited in Baize, 2011, p. 83). Here, integrity refers to "one's psychological needs and interests and defenses with the cultural milieu in which one resides" (Hendry, Mayer, & Kloe, 2007, p. 183). In the case of Muslim adolescents, integrity is achieved through maintenance of continuity with the identity given to them by their parents and the culture of the country in which they now live. In a study of Ismai'li immigrants from Afghanistan living in Germany, Baiza (2011) found that many teenagers when asked where they come from, considered themselves 50% German and 50% Afghani.

In the construction of teenage identity besides ethnicity, religion, and language are also important. Religion, language, and ethnicity connect one to other members of one's community and become part of who one is. Immigrant Muslims are from many different countries and different denominations, and whether passage through adolescence is smooth or difficult can depend on their background. For example, a Muslim adolescent from a liberal minded Iranian family living in the West will have little difficulty negotiating his/her home identity and the identity adopted in the Western country. But an adolescent from an ultrareligious Pakistani family or from an Arab country will have a more difficult time doing so. In matters of following the stricter Islamic code of behavior, such as wearing head covering or performing prayers, it is more difficult for the adolescent to align home culture and values to the one in the school and society at large. This is particularly so if people of the adopted country have negative attitudes towards Muslims and view them with suspicion.

ABOUT THIS BOOK

This volume is presented in four broad areas related to issues and challenges that Muslim children and youths face growing up in non-Muslim and Western countries. Part I explores demographic characteristics and acculturation issues faced by Muslim students. King, Abuzayyad-Nuseibeh, and Nuseibeh (Chapter 2) apply transformatiive learning models to examine social and educational issues that Muslim parents face raising their children in United States. The study reveals that Middle Eastern parents have to deal with many challenges ranging from "eating limitations, to dating habits and clothing to morality, and more."

> Parents with teenagers have additional challenges. They find that important factors that help families cope with these challenges are: recognizing the

problem and facing it, adjusting their expectations, and understanding that they are living in a different culture than the one in which they were raised.

They show that Middle Eastern parents experience transformative learning and use intercultural competency skills to deal with "challenges and concerns about social and educational issues of raising their children and teens in the United States." In Chapter 3, Shifa Hussain tries to identify demographic characteristics and acculturation issues faced by Muslim students. The study finds "that male students had greater intensity of acculturation issues than the female Muslim adolescents." In addition, language spoken at home has an important effect. Students whose spoken language at home were Urdu and Arabic had greater acculturation issues than those who speak English at home. Further, the length of time parents lived in the U.S. appears to be inversely related with their adolescent's experience of acculturation issues. Country of birth seems to have an impact as well. In Chapter 4, Myra Daniel focuses on the extent of problems Muslim children face in schools in United States. Learners face issues related "to mismatch between culture that their parents had inculcated in them and the norm of the main stream culture". Conflicts are rooted in religious, cultural, and familial perspectives, and result in learners' unsuccessful understanding of their teachers' expectations.

Part II examines issues that are related to the identity formation of Muslim children. Antonette and Tahoun in Chapter 5 discuss how the sociocultural identities of Muslim children are shaped by conflict "between the culture of religious communities (i.e., Ummah) in which their parents participate and the expectation of the American Public School System." In the time of crisis such as the tragic events of 9/11, Muslim children as well as non-Muslims realize how the Ummah and the discrimination practiced in American Public Schools shape American Muslim identity. Deborah Stilles and Osman Ozturgut in Chapter 6 explore development of prosocial behavior among Muslim adolescents living in Norway and Singapore. They find that "regardless of their religious and ethnic background, both groups espouse prosocial values and show positive identity development, and ideal aspirations." But both groups of adolescents in this study have very supportive environment and may not be representative of all Muslim youths in those countries. In Chapter 7, Hafiz Printer reviews research conducted on experiences of second generation Ismai'li youths growing up in Canada, in order to understand how these youths view their own religious and ethnic identity. It is found that children who face discrimination avoid calling themselves Muslims in order to fit in the Canadian society and avoid discrimination, while those who are not asked about their religion consider themselves Muslim.

Part III examines the role of gender in acculturation and identity formation. In Chapter 8, Khalid Arar investigates equity and social justice discourse in educational institutions in developing societies. In his study among Arab high schools in Israel, he finds that "although official rhetoric supports an equitable society within the school, the influence of the traditional environment supports a covert inequitable culture that strives to maintain patriarchal norms." Delia Omerbasic in Chapter 9, examines how Muslim women and refugees are considered as weak and homogeneous. A feminine postcolonial perspective is used to explore "what it means to be a young Muslim woman with refugee status by considering the intersection of gender and religion with race, class, age, ethnicity, nationality, and language." The author also suggests the use of "digital space through which women can negotiate their hybrid identity and interrupt some of the deficit oriented discourse" through which they are characterized. In Chapter 10, Liza Hoffman presents the findings of a study conducted among Bosnian Muslim girls living in the United States. The narratives presented show that "adolescent women idealize a bicultural identity and succeed in various degrees with cultural code-switching."

Part IV explores experiences of Muslim youths growing up in a non-Muslim country. In Chapter 11, Dodds, Albert, and Lawrence use "computerized illustrated paired comparison task to examine the local Australian and Somali children's perceived strength and school related skills as well as those attributed to them by their parents or guardians." The findings show that most Somali's perceived strength and skills are similar to those of their Australian counterparts. "Somali children were choosing personal preferences from among the values held out to them by their own Somali heritage as well as the mainstream Australian culture." Chang-Ho Ji in Chapter 12 explores the relationship between subjective well-being and personal religiosity among American Muslim youths. The chapter also examines the "moderating effect of gender between faith maturity and subjective well-being." It is found that American Muslim youths are very religious and relatively happy about their life in the United States. The moderating effect of gender hypothesis is also supported by the study. Finally, in Chapter 13, Farah Ahmed, in a small-scale qualitative study explores experiences of British Muslims growing up in England and the problems they face. As an alternative, she suggests "Islamic schools as a parental response to difficult childhood experiences of their children in mainstream British schooling."

In this book we have discussions about the problems and issues Muslim children have, growing up in a new culture in different continents: Asia, Europe, and North America. In many ways, what they experience is unique in history. Their situation involves a combination of ethnic, religious, and cultural factors intensified by the political problems in Palestine and the

Middle East. It is this combined baggage that weighs on top of the usual problems of adapting to a new environment. The intensity of feelings outside their home can rise to such pitch that there was a report of a Sikh being mistaken for a Muslim and killed in the street soon after September 11. Added to the intensity of feelings from outside of home, the intensity of feelings and attitudes at home can be just as strong if not more so, epitomized by the occasional reports of honor killing. It is this interaction of difficulties from inside and outside the home, from a whole range of attitudinal, cultural, religious, and other factors which make growing up a Muslim child in a non-Muslim Western culture so challenging. This calls for understanding and help from educators, parents, and all others who have a stake in seeing these children adapt and do well.

REFERENCES

Abdo, G. (2006, August 27). American Muslims aren't as assimilated as you think. *Washngton Post*, p. B30.

Baiza, Y. (2011). Religion, language or ethnicity? Hybridized identity among the Ismai' li youth of Afghanistan in Germany. In F. Ahmad & M. S. Seddon (Eds.), *Muslim youth: Challenges, opportunities, and oxpectations* (pp. 78–98). New York, NY: Continuum International Publishing Group.

Bayoumi, M. (2010). Being young, Muslim, and American in Brookling. In L. Herrera & A. Bayat (Eds.), *Being young and Muslim: New cultural politics in the global south and north* (pp. 161–177). London, England: Oxford University Press.

Erikson, E. H. (1958), *Young man Luther: A study in psychoanalysis and history.* London, England: Faber & Faber.

Erikson, E. H. (1968). *Identity youth and crises.* London, England: Faber & Faber.

Fitzsimon, A, (2011). Training Muslim youth to be "Khateebs". In F. Ahmad & M. Siddique Seddon (Eds.), *Muslim youths: Challenges, opportunities and expectations.* New York, NY: Continuum International Publishing Group.

Hadith (n.d.). *Wikipedia.* Retrieved from http://en.wikipedia.org/wiki/Islam

Hendry, L. B., Mayer, P., & Kloep, M. (2007). Belonging or opposing? A grounded theory approach to young people's cultural identity in a majority/minority social context. *Identity: An International Journal of Theory and Research*, 7(3), 181–204.

Islam Guide. (2013). Chapter 3, *General information on Islam.* Retrieved www.islam-guide.com

Pew Research Center's Forum on Religion and Public Life. (2011, January). *The future of the global Muslim population.* Washington, DC: Author.

Pipes, D., & Duran, K. (2002). Muslim immigrants in the United States. *Center for Immigration Studies.* Retrieved from http://www.Danielpipes.org/441/faces-ofamerican-Islam-immigration.

Rattansi, A., & Phoenix, A. (2005). Rethinking youth identities: Modernist and postmodernist frameworks. *Identity: An International Journal of Theory and Research, 5*(2), 97–123.

Tirmazi, M.T., Husain, A., Mirza, F. Y., & Walsh, T. R. (2011). Understanding Islam and the Muslims. In F. Ahmad & M. S. Seddon (Eds.), *Muslim youth: Challenges, opportunities, and expectations* (pp. 57–78). New York, NY: Continuum International Publishing Group. Retrieved from www.islamicity. com/education/understandingislamandmuslims/

PART II

DEMOGRAPHIC CHARACTERISTICS AND ACCULTURATION ISSUES

CHAPTER 2

RAISING CHILDREN AND TEENS OF MIDDLE EASTERN BORN PARENTS IN THE UNITED STATES

Issues and Problems of Muslim Children

Kathleen P. King,
Heba AbuZayyad-Nuseibeh, and Hasan Nuseibeh

ABSTRACT

This chapter presents recent research among Middle Eastern born parents (MEBPs) living in the southeastern United States, who have raised children into their teenage years. This research applies adult learning models (transformative learning (Cranton, 1994; King, 1997; Mezirow, 1990) and intercultural competency (Gertsen, 1990; Han, 2012)) to examine three major research questions regarding the social and educational issues of raising these Muslim children and teenagers.

Growing Up Between Two Cultures: Problems and Issues of Muslim Children, pp. 17–38
Copyright © 2014 by Information Age Publishing

INTRODUCTION

What is it like to be a Middle Eastern born expatriate living in the south-eastern United States? Consider the following experiences.

- Living in a foreign country which does not accept or respect your faith.
- Walking the streets where your women are often scorned because of their dress.
- Being bombarded by media and confrontations which insult your moral values.
- Functioning in a community which often wants to keep you outside.

These are just a few of the daily conflicts Middle Eastern born (MEB) expatriates experience as they seek to make a life for themselves and their families, temporarily or permanently, in the United States.

What urgency could make MEB expatriates endure such alienation? Often MEB people seek higher education, work for foreign firms, or a new life for their families in the United States. Yet in the midst of the struggle to succeed and thrive, they know they cannot assimilate completely without surrendering a great deal of their faith and heritage.

In the United States, life post-9/11 has been especially difficult for MEB people as they seek to function in their work, social and private world without interference by the dominant culture (Livengood, & Stodolska, 2004; Peek, 2003). Certainly, physical and verbal abuse was most prominent for the first year post-9/11, but hard feelings, scapegoating and cultural stereotypes have not changed or disappeared quickly. The Muslim focused antagonism was fueled further and deeper by the media-focused chase for Osama bin Laden. Considering society's collective memory, the aftermath of 9/11 has been long lived and negative for Muslims residing in the United States and beyond. In the U.S. 21st century thus far, the Middle Eastern born adult, the Muslim, has been the person of disdain and distrust.

Certainly, all American expatriates and immigrants have dealt with being the "outcast" in the first generations in the country, but the MEB people carry a much greater burden than Judeo-Christian expatriates and immigrants. Because of recent historical events they are judged guilty by culture and faith, even though the faith of such extremist terrorists is unlike theirs.

This cultural conflict is the context in which many MEB parents (MEBPs) are raising youngsters and teenagers in the United States. Their culture, religion and families represent the fears and counterculture of many Americans. Yet the MEBPs seek ways to preserve their faith and culture amidst a Western world that often disdains them, but at the same time, in their view, is far below their own moral standards. A storm of confusion is too weak a phrase to describe this swirling conflict of judgment, values, morals and faith. "Hurricane" more appropriately fits the power of the onslaught to MEBP's values and the threats to their next generation's moral foundation. In the midst of this "hurricane," many MEBPs are nonetheless raising youngsters and teens in the United States. We believe their experiences offer essential insight into human determination, survival and ingenuity.

The study discussed in this chapter uniquely addresses (1) the perspective transformations which parents experience as expatriates raising children in a contradictory culture, and (2) the potential concurrent intercultural competencies develop. Specifically, the study examines the challenges in raising *and* educating their children and teenagers; and MEBPs suggestions for successfully raising children to navigate both Middle Eastern culture and Western Culture.

The three major research questions regarding social and educational issues addressed in this research are: (1) What are the challenges and opportunities which Middle Eastern born parents (MEBPs) face in raising children and teenagers in the United States? (2) What are the challenges and opportunities which MEBPs face in educating children and teenagers in the United States? And (3) What do MEBPs suggest for successfully raising children to navigate both Middle Eastern culture and Western culture?

RELATED LITERATURE

Two models, transformative learning (Cranton, 1994; King, 1997; Mezirow, 1990) and intercultural competency (Gertsen, 1990; Han, 2012), frame this research study to provide new insight into the experiences of MEBPs parents and their children.

Transformative Learning

The research and literature of transformative learning have explored a wide scope of topics over the years since its inception in 1978 (Mezirow). Transformative learning is an adult learning theory which identifies 10 stages adults engage in as they make sense of and navigate difficult, even distressing, cognitive, moral and value dilemmas. The result of a completed transformative learning process is that one's world view, perspective is radically changed and one experiences a perspective transformation.

It must be clarified; however, that there are several critical conditions for transformative learning in informal, formal and self-directed learning sessions. It is unethical to "force" someone into a perspective transformative (Cranton, 1994; King, 2005, 2009). One never understands the breadth, depth and nuances of differing social and cultural norms; therefore, we can never truly comprehend the risks one might assume when choosing perspective transformation. In addition, as a basic individual right, one should never presume to decide that another should be put at risk with their family, social or cultural group, or other possibilities. Transformative learning is not always a positive mountain top experience of cognitive revelation. Instead, as indicated in the warnings above, there can be very difficult, even dangerous, consequences of questioning norms, beliefs, and values, much less when choosing to separate from them.

What transformative learning offers is a powerful framework to understand the conflicts (known in the transformative learning literature as disorienting dilemmas) which adults encounter, and how they build coping strategies to navigate them. In the case of this study of MEBP raising children and teenagers in southeastern United States, these coping strategies are the reason for the choice of transformative learning as a framing theory. Not only is the very focus of this study one of disorienting dilemmas, but the solution finding experience is decidedly one of coping and navigating many factors. Perhaps, for this reason one of the early studies of transformative learning was related to intercultural competence (Taylor, 1994). Taylor used transformative learning to examine the experience of living in another country and making sense of different norms, values and practices. We propose that in a way, this study triples the scope of much prior research. First, by not only examining how MEBP cope with the host culture, but also, second, how their children and teens do the same, and then, third, how the parents and children together navigate the challenges of the children and teens' development. We expect transformative learning will help understand and illuminate the narratives which describe all three of these experiences.

Intercultural Competence

The literature of intercultural competency has developed over many years to describe the skills and characteristics needed for people to be able to successfully negotiate among cultures different from their own (Han, 2012; Taylor, 1994). Intercultural competency skills include cross-cultural awareness, respect, strong observational skills, and many more (Hannigan, 1990). Models of intercultural competency extend across many dimensions to explain how one develops the skill/trait (Kim & Ruben, 1988; Lustig & Koester, 2003).

One purpose of this study was to determine if MEBPs who raise their children and teens in the southeastern United States reveal evidence of intercultural competency. Much like transformative learning, in this research intercultural competency is essential in three different dimensions: (1) MEBPS coping with the host culture, (2) children and teens coping with the host culture, and (3) MEBPS needing to effectively guide children and teens through the host culture challenges and opportunities. Given the described complexity of the situation, the researchers expect to contribute to the literature by posing new observations of the theory in general and for these specific situations.

RESEARCH METHOD

A multiple, sequential data gathering approach and qualitative research provided extensive data through snowball sampling, focus groups and follow-up questionnaires in this study (Johnson & Christiansen, 2010). Studying the experiences of MEBP raising children and teenagers in a secular culture necessarily included many discussions about different perspectives, values, and challenges. Qualitative research was the best choice for this study because it afforded the opportunity for participants to share their experiences and insights, respond to follow up questions, and provide details (Creswell, 1998, 2003).

Participants

Seven Middle Eastern born adults who are parents (MEBP) of Muslim children or teenagers and who live in the southeastern United States participated in this study. The participants were recruited through a snowball sampling technique (Johnson & Christiansen, 2010). The initial phone calls provided opportunities for our limited relevant contacts to suggest other individuals who might be interested and qualified (MEBP) to participate in the study. All phone conversations were conducted by the researcher who is a MEBP, is part of the local Arab expatriates' community, and is fluent in Arabic language and culture.

We were concerned to explicitly and authentically exercise efforts to protect the identity of the participants, and foster more open discussion. Therefore, once the participants arrived for the focus group, we asked them to select pseudonyms for themselves. This strategy allowed the session's audio transcription to include their pseudonyms and preserve greater confidentiality. All original records of participant names were kept confidential. All publications and presentations use the participants' pseudonyms.

Procedures

Once the participants were identified, the co-researcher, who is also a Middle Eastern born parent, invited them to attend a focus group session. We reasoned that since at this time a southeastern U.S. culture is not entirely Muslim friendly, having a Muslim person extend the invitation would be considerate and helpful in building a greater sense of safety and comfort for the participants. The focus group was held at the local University during the early evening, midweek.

The focus group discussion was audio recorded and then transcribed by the researchers for analysis. In addition, we used a postsession questionnaire for participants to share additional comments which they thought of after the event, or which they wished to share privately with the researchers, rather than in the small focus group. These questionnaires were collected at the end of the focus group session.

Analysis

The free response data analysis of the questionnaires included transcription and coding. Qualitative data was analyzed via constant comparison coding for emergent themes, and frequency of occurrences, and via memoing (Creswell, 2003). Using robust and multiple forms of qualitative analysis (memoing, constant comparison, and frequencies of responses for instance) provides for deeper analysis of data rather than a single method is able (Johnson & Christensen, 2010; Onwuegbuzie, & Teddlie, 2003). Decreasing subjectivity in coding is a challenge, using at least two researchers to rate all qualitative data greatly reduced this issue. In order to increase the efficacy of the qualitative coding, inter-rater reliability strategies and calculations were used. (Creswell, 1998; Onwuegbuzie, & Teddlie, 2003).

FINDINGS

The study consisted of four MEBP couples (one of the MEB men was married to an Muslim U.S. woman) that are living in the southeastern United States. One of the couples was only represented by the husband, because his wife and children were living in her original country in the

Middle East along in order to raise the children based in the Middle Eastern culture. Therefore, the total participants in this study were seven: four males and three females.

All the participants have higher education levels that vary from a college bachelors to doctorate degree level. All the participants had lived in the United States for 20 years or more and are from different countries in the Middle East as illustrated in Table 2.1.

Table 2.1.   Demographic Information of Participants

Pseudonym	Gender	Education Level	Country	# of Years Living in the Unites States
Lou	Male	Master's	Jordan	30 years
Amal	Female	College BA	Syria	Almost 20 years
Irbed	Male	Doctorate	Jordan	25 years
Omar	Male	Master's	Palestine	35 years
Sara	Female	Master's	U.S. Muslim Married to MEB husband	50 years
Tina	Female	College BA	Jordan	20 years
Gus	Male	College BA	Jordan	29 years

Research Questions

This section reveals findings related to the three major research questions of this study.

(1) What are the challenges and opportunities which Middle Eastern born parents face in raising children and teenagers in the United States?

The participants of the study discussed a number of challenges. Many of those challenges stem from the many differences between the United States and the Middle East including culture, religion, political system, food habits, educational system, and so forth.

Cultural Differences

One of the most important challenges the MEBPs identified was dealing with the image that many people in the United States have of Muslims and Arabs. MEBPS usually need to help their children deal with this image, and to teach them how to explain to their friends and classmates the differences in the culture. One parent described this sense of difference by saying, "I think it's hard for them [the children] to have [a] different religion, for them to be in a small group that have different religion is a challenge for them [to be a minority]"

In this study, one of the most frequently recurring issues for MEBPS was regarding helping their children understand and explain the headscarf that many Muslim women wear. For instance, sometimes teenage girls may wear their headscarf to school, or for boys their mothers or sisters may visit their school and be wearing the headscarf, which raises many questions among the child's peers.

MEBPs tend to compare their Muslim community childhood with that of their children, and they see the differences in even the smallest things. One of the parents commented that there was a difference between the way her children speak to her and how she used to speak to her parents as a child. In the Middle East the relationship between parents and children tends to be more formal than the United States, and this formality demonstrates greater respect for parents. Therefore, it takes time for MEBPs to understand the cultural gap and to realize that the less formal way children speak to their parents in the United States does not imply less respect towards parents, but may merely be another cultural difference.

Cultural Versus Religious Differences

Another issue that surfaces when MEB parenting in the United States is the need for parents to differentiate between which part of their past way of life comes from culture and which part comes from religion. As one parent points out,

> There are two areas that I have concern [for] as far as raising children in the United States: what is the [the] differentiation between religion and culture, because the way we were raised back home everything was a culture which is supposedly been taken out of religion. [This reasoning] is not the real fact, the real fact is we follow certain criteria and certain conducts that we thought was (sic) a religious conducts or had a religious basis, but it was not actually based on religion. So these are some of the issues that we're facing with our children is that they do differentiate between culture [basis] and real religion basis in the United States.

As described below, such questioning was something the MEBPs did not entertain in their home culture. Therefore, this struggle and debate is a new challenge facing the expatriates.

While many Muslim MEBPs usually try to protect their children's religious identity and habits, they tend to be more flexible towards cultural adaptations, which do not conflict with religion. However, it can be challenging for parents to discern which of their habits and ideas are rooted in religion and which come from different cultures.

Moreover, in many cases MEBP did not always learn the logic behind habits and rules and this fact makes the differentiation even more difficult. As one parent said "because growing up in that culture, you didn't get a chance to ask. Not because you were not allowed to ask, but it was part of the culture, and embedded in the culture." The MEBPS also said that in many cases they need to be able to explain to their children the logic behind what they ask them to do, and what they ask them not to do. As another MEBP explains, "because at that age [teenagers] there is always a why, where, and what question."

Such cultural and religious debate issues arise on a daily basis for MEBPs raising children in the southeastern United States. For example, Muslims are not allowed to eat pork, and because pork meat is popular in many forms in the United States (bacon, deli pork, barbeque, some meatballs, pepperoni, barbeque, etc.), it can be challenging for both children and parents to make sure that food eaten outside the home has no pork meat. In this case, MEBPs need to teach their children to ask about the food they are offered in school cafeteria, parties, and other social gatherings. In addition, often MEBPs need to communicate this restriction to the staff at the school cafeteria, parents of their children's friends, and so forth.

National and Religious Identity

National and religious identity is another issue that is of importance to many MEBP, and it becomes more challenging as their children grow up. Therefore, many MEBP worry about finding the most effective ways to pass on their identity to their children while allowing them to adapt to the American culture. As one parent says, "Well for me I think the biggest challenge is basically having the identity of the kids, what are they, are they Americans? Are they Jordanians? Are they Arabs? Are they not? So that was the main challenge that we face."

MEBPs try to guide their children through this transition while simultaneously not being viewed as a minority. Needless to see achieving all these goals at once can be challenging.

Parent-Child Relationships

Although the nature of relationships between parents and children in the United States can be a challenge to many MEBPs, it can also be seen as an opportunity because (1) the less formal and more open kind of discussions between parents and children in the United States makes communications and exchange of opinions and experiences easier, and (2) it reduces the barrier between parents and their children. One parent describes this greater communication, "[we] used the meal times as a forum to discuss Islamic tradition and practices such as diet, wearing decent clothes." These parents identified meal times as an opportunity to introduce these topics and discuss them with their children.

Also, some parents found an opportunity in participating in school activities to interact with their children in their school environment and to communicate with teachers and other school staff. This strategy also helped improve the communication between parents and their children. One parent said,

> we were involved in the schools, so we had the chance to became friends with the teachers and explain things to them, and sometimes they would invite us to come and educate the friends, you know the kids in the classrooms. So we would go and explain to them about the Middle Eastern culture, about the Islamic culture, the Islamic religion—I am sorry, and things like that, so it helped, I think it helped boost the kids' egos.

Another parent mentioned that when they started going on camping trips with their children, their children started seeing their parents as friends, which improved the level of trust between them. This shift in parent-child relationships helped them eventually face the challenges in a smarter way. As the parent said,

> One of the things that we did when our children were in the school was, for example our boys were in cub scouts. So if were not a hundred percent sure how this overnight trip is going to go with these little kids, or if were not sure what kind of food they going to feed them, we often participated in that with our children all the time until they were older and were able to. Then [at that age] they knew the difference: this is what's acceptable and this is what's not acceptable.

Many parents saw living in the United States as a unique opportunity for their children to broaden their interests and knowledge. They found a great advantage with their children having friends from different cultural backgrounds and with different views and interests. They saw that this diversity of experience and friendships improved their children's character. However, other parents expressed concern that their children were not able to mix well with others since they are from outside their culture, and did not know how to deal with that situation.

Teenage Years

Many parents noticed that when their children became teenagers additional challenges were introduced. However, they believe those challenges were related to the psychological and physiological changes which all teenagers experience. As expected, their children argued more about every rule, and wanted more explanation for every difference in culture which can both be attributed to increased individuation and ego development at this age.

One particular challenge MEBPs face is the more restrictive rules in the Arab and Islamic culture towards relations between the sexes outside marriage. A parent commented,

> In the Middle Eastern culture we do not date; there isn't such a thing as dating. So when boys and girls get to be at a certain age and they're going to public school [here in the United States] and then they look at all their friends and they're having boyfriends and girlfriends, you see, they start questioning why they can do this, why can't we?

This situation creates an even greater challenge for MEBPs to explain their religious beliefs and rationale to their teenagers, because the U.S. raised children are urged to be involved in such dating relations, and the surrounding society (non-Arabs) in general sees this as acceptable. Some MEBPs address this challenge by putting more effort into building trust with their children, standing by everything they say, and being consistent. As one parent shared, "Gaining the ultimate level of trust with your kids when they trust you they can listen to you. When they don't trust you, they don't care what you say."

Also, the MEBPs advised that it's helpful to try to know about their children's friends, start a relationship with those families, and learn about their environments. That is, continuing to be involved in their children and teenagers' lives.

(2) What are the challenges and opportunities which MEBPs face in educating children and teenagers in the United States?

Many people do not realize that there are major differences in school systems between the United States and the Middle East (ME). One of those differences is the role of parents in the education of their children. While in the ME parents have a less active role in their children's education, parents in the U.S. are expected to be partners with the schools. The participants consider that they have to go to the U.S. schools often. These visits have many different purposes including meeting with teachers, signing students up for activities, helping with fund raising, and so forth. Until parents understand the different role of parents in the school systems, it can be a challenge for them to take this responsibility. Quoting one parent,

> We grew up under a different system, and you know we attended school like great school in a totally different system. In our culture, parental involvement was not really a big thing, whereas here especially in elementary the

parents are there. I am involved with my kids before sixth grade; it seems like I was at school every day, not because they are in trouble, but because you know schools do things. You know there is PTA, there are carts- you know you go read to the kids, things like that you know. In the Middle eastern educational system that doesn't exist, or at least it did not exist when I was there.

Some of the interviewed parents chose to send their children to Islamic private schools in the U.S. where their teachers were either from the same culture or understood the Arab and Islamic culture in a better way. This choice made the parents' task much easier in enriching their Arab identity while insuring that their children stayed in touch with the American culture and the English language. In addition, these schools helped in teaching Islamic religion and Arabic language, which is a challenge for parents sending their children to American public schools. As one parent said "Our kids at a certain age went to private Islamic school. So some of these challenges that happen to kids in public school, they did not happen in private school."

(3) What do MEBPs suggest for successfully raising children to navigate both Middle Eastern culture and Western culture?

The interviewees suggested that MEBPs can do many things to help navigate both cultures. First MEBPs can start by reeducating themselves about their own culture and religion. They may need to be able to question themselves about things that they always took for granted as children. They also need to learn to distinguish between culture and religion; and they need to learn the logic behind certain rules and practices (i.e., head scarves, eating restrictions, chastity, etc.).

Also MEBPs need to educate themselves about the U.S. culture, and how it is different from their own culture. This fact is especially true related to parenting, child rearing, and school. These areas may be entirely different in the American culture and the MEB people may not have encountered these particular differences until they are parents.

Dialog and communication between parents and children is also very important. Some of the MEBPs participants described how some of the issues at first seemed like a challenge, but became an opportunity for them to improve their communication and level of trust with their children. They know now that these opportunities will eventually help the children in identifying with their parents' culture and can help them as parents communicate better the logic behind the different ways of life and rules to their children.

"Reaching beyond the home" is also important according to the participants. They described how getting more involved in their children's school lives and participating in school activities helped improve understanding of children and MEBPs. Another helpful strategy was allowing their children to see them as friends, in order to improve communication. This latter point is a great shift from the way in which the MEBP were raised, but needed in this situation.

Patterns of Interventions

This section describes patterns of interventions MEBPs used to help raise their Muslim children in the U.S. culture.

Community Support

A few MEBPs mentioned resources where they found support from the community. They might attend events that discussed the very parenting issues with which they were dealing: lectures that are targeted to new Muslim parents in mosques, conventions held by Muslim organizations, focus groups, and finally talking with other parents who have been through the same experience. Several parents shared their experiences in this area. A parent shared,

> In our case, most of the time if we needed support in any of these issues it actually came out sometimes from the community itself like the mosque where they carry out what's called "Halaqa." It's like discussion group ... so when we used to attend these it gives you the knowledge on how to ... face these challenges with your kids if you ever come into big question about certain criteria or certain areas weather it's cultural, or religious.

Another parent shared that she used to talk to other MEBPs and learn from their experiences and get their impact about how to deal with such issues. She also said, "We used to talk to other parents who had the experience before us." A second parent added to this the point, "They [other parents] will enlighten you on how they dealt with it [the same kind of problems]."

Ultimately as mentioned earlier, one of the easiest and most comprehensive solutions that some parents choose is to send their children to Muslim schools which provide an Islamic education, and support from the teachers and school staff where they interact with people from the same culture and religion.

Family Communications

All MEBPs agreed that the first step in having a happy family was by supporting each other, communicating, and exchanging thoughts to find the optimal solutions for their children. Building and communicating with their children was vital. Discussions are where children learn reasons for values, actions, and decisions also build a foundation of respect. The following quotes illustrate this finding.

One parent shared, "Listen to them [your children] with an open mind, accept what they're saying to you and try to make a discussion." Another parent shared, "With my kids, I will not answer any question unless I am a 100% sure this is the answer. Otherwise I have no problem to tell [sic] them I don't know."

Teenage Years

Another difficult solution that some parents choose when their children reach teenage years is either for the entire family to move to an Arab country, or to divide their families so that the mother and children would live in a ME country. If the father is unable to move his career to a new country, parents take this action to raise the teenagers in a more conservative culture during what they believe to be the most sensitive time of their moral development. This strategy also offers their children an opportunity to improve their Arabic language skills and embrace their Arab identity.

For example, one of the MEBP couples in this study decided to send the wife and their teenagers to live in a Middle Eastern country. They made this decision in order for the teenage children to enhance their Arab and Muslim identity. However, in order to accomplish these goals, the father travels back and forth between the United States and this Middle Eastern country regularly to maintain the family unit.

One parent described how he chose this option, "I took my kids home.... I decided to take them for three to four years to educate in the Middle East for the two reasoning which I mentioned earlier, which is identity and get them to believe and interact with the culture." Another group participant asked, "How is it working?" He answered, "It's working perfect, they are learning Arabic."

Divergent Opinions Regarding ME Relocation

Some of the MEBPs participants pointed out that sometimes there are other costs in choosing that part of the family move to a Middle Eastern country. For instance, the teenagers experience many adjustments as they entire the ME culture and society fulltime including culture shock in the beginning. Consider the many differences they encounter from being raised in the United States. A major issue is that they will experience such a different educational system of academics, discipline and expectations. Amidst all these different systems and expectations, not all children will thrive; some may experience deterioration in their moods, academic achievement, or other areas. From experience, these MEBPs believe that ultimately there is a positive impact on personality and psychological development of their children adapting to a different culture than the one in which they were raised. And while the children learned how to face different kind of difficulties, some parents found that their children appreciated living in the U.S more, and they had fewer challenges with them. Read for example what participants state about this issue.

"So far its working, the relationship between us is getting very strong between us, they understand now both cultures."

Another parent shared, "We had a positive impact when they [his kids] went back there. It made them realize that we're really living in a better environment here [United States] that the challenges here, the way that we are exposed here are much better than the way it's back there."

Other MEBPs indicated that the choice for part of the family to relocate creates whole new sets of challenges for the children. These MEBPs believe that they are better off dealing with the challenges in the United States, keeping their families united, and continuing their careers and businesses. The following quotes illustrate this experience and perspective. "The challenges in here [US] are less than the challenges in the Middle East." Another parent added to the negative point of returning to the ME,

> In there [in the ME] there is no privacy, anybody can ask any question and it's up to you to answer them smartly or honestly. Our kids in here [US] they are very honest: they are very straight forward, they don't know how to lie, and they don't know how to cheat. However, in there [ME] if you cheat, then you are smart.

Surely, the MEBPs experiences and comments above illustrate the complexity of choosing between relocation to the ME or staying the United States. This difficult decision is just one of countless examples of the challenges MEBPs must address raising their children and teens in the United States.

DISCUSSION

Transformative Learning

Examples of transformative learning (TL) experiences among MEBPs abound in this study. In this analysis at least five major disorienting dilemmas were identified: (1) cultural versus religious debate, (2) national and religious identity, (3) different educational systems for parents and children, (4) coping with influence of children's friends, and (5) returning home to ME. The pathways taken once encountering such dilemmas depends on many factors for all people (King, 2009). In this study, among the MEBPs it is evident their prior experiences, values and beliefs were pivotal deciding points. This section examines each of the TL experiences described above and the coping strategies employed.

Several of the MEBPs shared examples of cultural vs. religious debates as disorienting dilemmas. The specific topics ranged from eating limitations to dating habits, and clothing to morality, and more. Overall, these issues were significant struggles for the parents because they had been raised where the dominant culture had been Muslim and no questions needed to be asked. Now their youngsters were confronted with different behaviors and choices; therefore, they pose many "new" questions. In the case of food limitations, parents developed several strategies including modeling the correct choices to their children (camping with them and their friends), to instructing the children directly, and visiting the school administrators and dining room staff. The new TL perspective was not to eat pork, but rather how to successfully navigate a society that does eat pork and is many times unaware of Muslim diet observances.

In the area of coping with the different educational systems, MEBPs again encounter territory they did not walk through as children and teenagers with their parents. As their children reach the P–6 grade school years in the United States, the MEBPs were at first puzzled by the expectations to participate in their child's formal education. While initial confusion no doubt included inquiries, discussions and potential plans, this disorienting dilemma seems to have provided a springboard for integrating their world into the new. Some of the parents began to present cultural, national and religious information with classrooms and schools, while others participated in the parent groups, and classroom support. Rather than being pushed to the margins, these MEBPs found ways through their transformative perspective to become part of their children's world.

Intercultural Competence

The theme of intercultural competence (IC) is interwoven throughout the accounts of these MEBPs raising children in the southeastern United States. Whether they are determining how to navigate childrearing issues their parents did not, coping with entirely different educational systems or having to uphold their religious beliefs and values in a more liberal society, they have to do so with IC deftness. In his research, Taylor (1994) viewed intercultural competence individuals' ability to adapt and become effective across cultures.

Looking at two frameworks for identifying the essential components of IC offers many overlaps. Campinha-Bacote (2002) identified five components: (1) cultural awareness, (2) cultural skill, (3) cultural knowledge, (4) cultural encounter, and (5) culture desire. While, Lister (1999) developed a taxonomy for cultural competent professionals including: (1) cultural awareness, (2) cultural knowledge, (3) cultural understanding, (4) cultural sensitivity, and (5) cultural competence.

Specific IC components as evidenced in the accounts and documented in this research include building cultural awareness skills, cultural knowledge, navigating cultural encounters, cultural sensitivity and cultural desire. It must be remembered that while ICC is needed among all expatriates, those of a different culture and value system raising children in a host culture have high stakes for intercultural competency.

Successful Interventions

All the MEBPs participating in this study agreed that the most important factors that help families cope with the challenges of living between two cultures are: first, recognizing the problem and facing it, adjusting their expectations, and understanding that they are living in a different culture than the one in which they were raised. These differences have many implications and challenges with which MEBPs have to cope. Their children will interact and be exposed to the different dominant culture and it will affect them in many ways. There is an inherent conflict which has to be resolved frequently and in many ways as the children are exposed to the dominant culture and yet their MEBPs come from a different culture and want them to live by these different values.

The MEBPs indicate that much communication, discussion, and explanation is needed in this cross-cultural child rearing situation, even though this was not an issue for their parents. During their developmental years, they lived in the same culture as their parents and in many cases they did not need to question any of the dominant values.

For success in MEBPs raising children in U.S. culture then the first key would be for parents to build strong communication channels with their children and establish a high level of trust among them. The MEBPs must also be prepared to explain and justify everything to their children; they should be open-minded for the many questions and discussions they will have throughout the child rearing years.

Another decision MEBPs need to make is whether they want to send their children to Islamic schools, or to public schools. If they choose the latter, they know they will have several additional responsibilities: work more to help their children connect with their Muslim culture, maintain a higher level of communication with their public school staff, be cautious about peer pressure in public school, and develop a good mix of friends with the same and different cultural backgrounds. At the same time, MEBPs will need to monitor the effect of peers on their children to avoid trouble.

Teenagers introduce additional challenges for all parents, but especially MEBPs. While some MEBPs may choose to send one parent with their teenagers to a Middle Eastern country to keep them away from influences the parents want to avoid, this adds its own challenges. At the same time, if MEBPs choose to keep their teenage children in the United States, it's important to continue building trust and communication with them and keeping a closer eye on their teenager's behavior and that of their friends. Other suggestions include several different options: try to involve the teenagers in healthy activities, or limit the freedom of their teenage children. However, all the MEBPs agreed that parents cannot and should not try to impose ideas on their children. Instead, the preferred approach is to discuss questions and issues and challenge their children to grow into better people.

SIGNIFICANCE OF THE STUDY

Ultimately, this study seeks to inform MEBPs of effective perspectives and strategies for raising their children in southeastern U.S. culture. Moreover, it should provide strategies and concepts for host people (e.g., Americans) to be more interculturally aware and build greater understanding of intercultural competency. As our society expands to more global dimensions of daily interactions, such learning is needed and may be applied in many different ways. In addition, this research contributes to the theoretical and best practices literature of both transformative learning and intercultural competence continuing the connection of these theories, but scaffolding further the complexity of consideration and potential academic dialogue.

LIMITATIONS OF THE STUDY

The first limitation of this research is the small number of participants. While it provides insight into experiences and perceptions of the Arab Middle East, one cannot draw any conclusions from this research in relation to all Muslim populations with different national cultural backgrounds. Arab Middle Eastern people are generally more conservative and literal in their interpretation of the Koran. In future research, a broader sample of MEBPs from different regions would be beneficial for more complete understanding of interventions and perspectives.

Moreover, considering the specifics of these many MEB subcultures, reveals likely differences in the values and intervention methods studied in this research. For example, families of more conservative Muslim beliefs may try to protect their children from interacting with others that can influence them; on the other side of the spectrum some parents are less observant of their religion, language and other aspects of the culture. The more liberal Muslims may allow their children to not adopt or retain anything from their parents' culture. In comparison, to these two extremes, the sampled MEBPs were interested in gaining from both cultures. We fully realize that such a reciprocal approach may not represent the full spectrum of the Muslim subcultures.

Finally, this study was conducted in southeastern U.S. which is a strong Christian conservative culture. MEBPs in other sections of the United States may have different experiences as the clash with culture might not be as dramatic. In this study, the conservative community in which the participants reside is metropolitan, but still not as liberal and diverse as found in other metropolitan areas of the United States. While more liberal communities might present greater challenges for MEBPs, more diverse communities may be less demanding environments.

RECOMMENDED FUTURE RESEARCH

Certainly, the final point above leads to the recommendation that future research is needed in different U.S. communities which vary with diversity and across the conservative-liberal spectrum to identify whether this study has unique results. Moreover, future studies are needed which include larger samples and MEBPs from other countries in order to represent and examine similarities and differences among subcultures and nations. Finally, it would be valuable to include MEBPs who were of different Muslim subcultures according to their religious beliefs. Such studies would help us better understand the unique variations that different MEBPs experiences and coping strategies while raising children in a host Western culture.

CONCLUSION

It is a great challenge for MEBPs to raise children in the midst of a society which has negatively biased beliefs about your culture and religion. Moreover, the drastic differences between the context and way in which the MEBPs were raised and the situation they face raising their children, provides little guidance and much frustration. Results of this study reveal that the participating MBEPs experience transformative learning and utilize intercultural competency skills as they navigate these specific, serious challenges and concerns about social and educational issues of raising their children and teens in the United States. From seeking to differentiate cultural and religious issues, to being involved in the society, maintaining their religious practice, building strong communication and relationships with their children, and more MEBPs continue to carve a life in a foreign culture in which their families can value their beliefs and uphold their religion.

ACKNOWLEDGMENT

The authors greatly appreciate the contribution of Gerene Thompson to this study. Thank you for your gracious and professional support.

APPENDIX A
FOCUS GROUP QUESTIONS

Let's get to know one another as we discuss this topic. Can we go around the room and each person share their names (pseudonyms) and how many children they have, along with the ages of the children? Please also tell us how long you have lived in the southeastern United States (FL, GA, AL, etc.)

What challenges do you face as MEBP who raise children in the southeastern United States?

How have you addressed these challenges with your children?

What have been the results of these interactions?

What challenges do you face as MEBP who raise teenagers in the southeastern United States?

How have you addressed these challenges with your teenagers?

What have been the results of these interactions?

What support have you sought during these times?

If you have experienced great conflict raising children and/or teenagers in the southeastern United States, have you returned home? Why or why not?

What recommendations would you share with other MEBP about raising children in the southeastern United States?

What recommendations would you share with other MEBP about raising teenagers in the southeastern United States?

APPENDIX B
POSTSESSION QUESTIONS

What is your pseudonym?

_____

What is your gender?   male   female
What is your highest level of education?

____ HS	____ Technical Diploma
____ College BA	____ Master's
____ Doctorate	____ Postdoctorate
____ Other	

What country are you from? _____
How long have you lived in the United States?_____

Do you have any additional comments you have thought of after leaving the event which you would like to share with the researchers on the questions or general topic discussed during our group meeting? If so, please use the space below and on the reverse.

Do you have any additional comments you would like to share in writing with the researchers on the questions or general topic discussed during our group meeting? If so, please use the space below and on the reverse.

REFERENCES

Campinha-Bacote, J. (2002). The process of cultural competence in the delivery of Healthcare Services: A model of care. *Journal of Transcultural Nursing 13*(3), 181–184.

Cranton, P. (1994). *Understanding and promoting transformative learning.* San Francisco, CA: Jossey-Bass.

Creswell, J. (1998). *Qualitative inquiry and research design.* Thousand Oaks, CA: Sage.

Creswell, J. (2003). *Research design* (2nd ed.). Thousand Oaks, CA: Sage.

Gertsen, M. C. (1990). Intercultural competence and expatriates. *The International Journal of Human Resource Management, 1*(3), 341–362.

Han. P. (2012). Developing global workforce: An integrative intercultural effectiveness model for international human resource development. *Proceedings of the Adult Education Research Conference.* Las Vegas, NV. Retrieved from http://www.adulterc.org/Proceedings/2012/papers/han.pdf

Hannigan T. P. (1990). Traits, attitudes, and skills that are related to intercultural effectiveness and their implications for cross-cultural training: A review of the literature. *Intercultural Journal of Intercultural Relations, 13,* 89–111.

Johnson, R. B., & Christensen, L.B. (2010). *Educational research* (4th ed.). Thousand Oaks, CA: Sage.

Kim, Y. Y., & Ruben, B. D. (1988). Intercultural transformation. In Y. Y. Kim & W. B. GudyKunst (Eds.), *Theories in intercultural communication* (pp. 299–321). London, England: Sage.

King, K. P. (1997). Examining learning activities and transformational learning, *International Journal of University Adult Education, 36*(3), 23–37.

King, K. P. (2005). *Bringing transformative learning to life*. Malabar, FL: Krieger.

King, K. P. (Ed.). (2009). *Handbook of evolving research approaches in transformative learning: The Learning Activities Survey* (10th anniversary edition). In *Series: Adult education special topics: Theory, research and practice in lifelong learning*. Charlotte, NC: Information Age Publishing.

Lister, P. (1999). A taxonomy for cultural competence. *Nursing Education Today 19*, 313–318.

Livengood, J. S., & Stodolska, M. (2004). *The effects of discrimination and constraints negotiation on leisure behavior of American Muslims in the post-September 11 America*. Emmitsburg, MD: National Emergency Training Center.

Lustig, M. W., & Koester, J. (2003). *Intercultural competence: Interpersonal communication across cultures* (4th ed.). Boston, MA: Allyn & Bacon

Mezirow, J. (1978). *Education for perspective transformation: Women's re-entry programs in community colleges*. New York, NY: Teacher's College, Columbia University.

Mezirow, J., & Associates. (1990). *Fostering critical reflection in adulthood*. San Francisco, CA: Jossey-Bass.

Onwuegbuzie, A. J., & Teddlie, C. (2003). A framework for analyzing data in mixed methods research. In A. Tashakkori & C. Teddlie (Eds.) *Handbook of mixed methods in social and behavioral research* (pp. 351–383). Thousand Oaks, CA: Sage.

Peek, L. A. (2003): Reactions and responses: Muslim students' experiences on New York City campuses post 9/11. *Journal of Muslim Minority Affairs, 23*(2), 271–283.

Taylor, E. W. (1994). Intercultural competency: A transformative learning process. *Adult Education Quarterly, 44*(3), 154–174.

CHAPTER 3

EXTENT OF ACCULTURATION EXPERIENCES AMONG HIGH SCHOOL MUSLIM STUDENTS IN THE UNITED STATES

Shifa Podikunju-Hussain

ABSTRACT

Muslim high school students often face bicultural issues, unknown to American peers. Muslim students often deal with a "home culture" and a "school culture" and lead double lives, which can be a source of additional stress while making the transition from childhood to adulthood. This study explored the extent of acculturation issues experienced by Muslim students by using the Muslim Youth Acculturation Rating Questionnaire which is a questionnaire that was developed by the author for use in this study. A higher score on the MYARQ reflected greater extent to which the respondent experienced acculturation problems. Therefore, lower MYARQ scores are associated with higher acculturation (i.e., lesser extent of acculturation problems) while higher scores imply lower acculturation (i.e., greater extent of acculturation problems). This was a descriptive study based on a nationally representative geographic sample of high school students in the U.S.

Growing Up Between Two Cultures: Problems and Issues of Muslim Children, pp. 39–88

The students were systematically selected based on the criteria of being Muslim. Results from the 144 respondents indicated statistical significance in three areas. Boys had higher scores on the MYARQ than the girls, Urdu and Arabic speakers had higher scores than English and Other speakers, and the longer the length of residence for respondent's father and mother, the higher the respondent's scores. The results from this study support previous research findings. However, new information also was found which may have potential impact on the study of acculturation trends especially among Muslim youth living in America.

INTRODUCTION

High school is a period of choices and decisions that can impact future education and career plans in the adolescent's life. During this time students learn to become independent of their parents and voice their own opinions and choices (Carter, 1999). Muslim high school students often face bicultural issues, unknown to American peers. For example, American adolescents as a whole may have the freedom or flexibility to make their own choices in high school curriculum and postsecondary careers whereas such behavior is often more restricted in the Muslim family. Muslim students often deal with a "home culture" and a "school culture" and lead double lives, which can be a source of additional stress while making the transition from childhood to adulthood (Carter, 1999; Ghuman, 2003). The study in this chapter seeks to identify the related demographic characteristics and the extent of acculturation issues faced by Muslim students. It explores the extent of acculturation issues experienced by Muslim students by using the Muslim Youth Acculturation Rating Questionnaire (MYARQ) which is a questionnaire that was developed by the author for use in this study. The questionnaire is made up of 10 demographic questions, and 31 attitudinal questions that address different issues that may impact acculturation, as found in the related literature regarding immigrants, South Asians, Arabs and Muslims. A higher score on the MYARQ reflected greater extent to which the respondent experienced acculturation problems. Therefore, lower MYARQ scores are associated with higher acculturation (i.e., lesser extent of acculturation problems) while higher scores imply lower acculturation (i.e., greater extent of acculturation problems).

REVIEW OF LITERATURE

A wide variety of potentially influencing factors (i.e., issues) have been associated with acculturation processes among an equally wide variety of groups engaged in acculturation. Demographic variables typically associated with acculturation effectiveness over different age levels include gender, age, specific ethnicity, number of years in the country, parental characteristics such as number of years in the country, and language spoken in the home (Berry, Phinney, Sam, & Vedder, 2006b). There are, however, many other issues that might influence an individual's acculturation process, including those associated with perceptions and interpretations of gender roles, belongingness, interpersonal relations (i.e., dating), peer relations, religiosity, and individuation.

The Muslim population in America is made up of different ethnic groups; therefore it is critical that both cultural and religious worldviews are considered when working with this group. Gender roles, individuation, interpersonal relationships and dating, religiosity, belongingness, language, perceived discrimination and length of residence are considered important factors of interest in the literature review as having important effects in the acculturation process.

Cultural conflict is a current concern for American society in general and the education profession in particular as the number of immigrant families increases rapidly in the United States (U.S.) (Ying, 1998). According to one estimate, first-generation immigrants and second-generation children exceed 60 million, or 24% of the total population of the U.S. (U.S. Bureau of the Census, 2003). Almost one in four Americans under age 18 is an immigrant or a child of a recent immigrant and the proportion keeps growing (U.S. Bureau of the Census, 2003). The issues and problems that arise from linguistic, religious, cultural values, and other differences impact not only the immigrant families themselves, but also societal and cultural subsystems and social and other institutions in the U.S. (Ying, 1998). In particular, the problems and issues associated with assimilation of immigrants into American society impact school systems throughout the U.S.

The review of the literature highlight Berry's theory of acculturation and the research associated with acculturation. Acculturation is the process of adapting to a new cultural context (Berry, 1998; Berry & Sam, 1997; Berry, Trimble, & Olmeda, 1986; Redfield, Linton, & Herskovits, 1936). Issues related to acculturation that arise affect both parents and their children. However, it is important to acknowledge that there is diversity within and among immigrant groups, and therefore there also is diversity in their respective methods of and experiences in acculturation. Nonetheless, there also are common themes evident among most families engaged in acculturation (Dugsin, 2001).

In the U.S., Muslims are comprised of three groups: (a) immigrants, including both naturalized citizens and resident aliens; (b) American citizens who have converted to Islam; and (c) those born to either of these groups (Numan, 1992; Project MAPS, 2001). The Pew Research Center's Forum on Religion and Public Life (2011) projects the estimated population for Muslims in the U.S. will more than double, rising from 2.6 million in 2010 to 6.2 million in 2030. A review of the literature yielded some information about acculturation issues among South Asian and Arab populations in the U.S.. Therefore, given that the largest percentage of Muslims in the U.S. come from South Asian and Arab countries (Pew Research Center, 2007; Pew Research Center's Forum on Religion & Public Life, 2011), that literature and research on South Asians and Arabs allow some inferences about acculturation issues among Muslim families in the U.S. In particular, it yields some insight into the cultural and religious worldviews of U.S.-resident Muslims, particularly in regard to differences and similarities within and among various Muslim subpopulations in the U.S.

Scope of the Problem

The cultural adaptation, sometimes called "generation" gap between all parents and their children, widens (at least for a while) as young children mature developmentally and is particularly evident for children in adolescence. However, cultural adaptation (i.e., acculturation) among Muslim youth in the U.S. is especially difficult because of the combination of societal, familial, and developmental issues involved. Interestingly, children of immigrant parents generally acculturate to the majority culture at a faster rate than do their parents (Sodowsky, Kwan, & Pannu, 1995; Szapocznik & Kurtines, 1993; Ying, 1998). These children's rapid acculturation is seen in their quicker ability to speak English as a primary language, faster adoption of Western values and lifestyles, and earlier socialization into mainstream society (Sodowsky et al., 1995). Conversely, immigrant parents are more likely to hold onto their native language, cultural values, and lifestyles despite the demands and pressures to socialize into mainstream society (Sodowsky et al., 1995; Ying, 1998).

In particular, Muslim immigrants' views of Americans are largely derived from the media (Hedayat-Diba, 2000). For example, the Western cultural values of individuality; independence; "natural" developmental separation from family; and openness of sexual expression are viewed as morally corrupt at best, and sinful at worst by most Muslim adults (Hedayat-Diba, 2000). Muslim parents also feel a religious obligation to protect their children and families from cultural values different from their own (i.e., traditional Muslim family values). Therefore, their children often experience having to "betray" their parents while they try to assimilate into the majority culture. Conversely, other children feel that they betray themselves and their own personal growth and freedom while they "protect" their parents' way of life (Hedayat-Diba, 2000).

Parents of Muslim youth often experience anxiety and frustration in their interactions with their children. Typically, they come from backgrounds where they did not question their parents or their elders who made career or personal life choices for them (Ibrahim & Ohnishi, 1997). These parents must cope with raising their children in a new culture with which they are not familiar while they try to raise their children as if they were in their home culture. Parenting in such a context causes conflict and frustration for both child and parent. It is evident that most Muslim parents are trying to find a balance between their own cultural and religious standards and mainstream social norms so that their children will be successful (Ibrahim & Ohnishi, 1997). In effect, they want to "do the right thing" both according to the dictates of their culture and to the dictates of the larger society. There is a personal perspective in their attempts because among traditional Asian immigrants including Muslims, a child's choices and successes are a direct reflection of the parents' position in the community (Sodowsky et al., 1995).

Many immigrant youth appear to oppose their family's native values and lifestyles, and seek instead to assume Western, American mainstream values and lifestyles (Lee, Choe, Kim, & Ngo, 2000). Interestingly, many Asian immigrants,which may include Muslim parents, recognize that they themselves and their children need to adopt certain Western-oriented behaviors for all to be successful in society and for the children to be successful in school (Ying, 1998). Nonetheless, intrafamilial differences in perspectives and approaches to children's acculturation often are a major source of family conflict.

As the ethnic minority populations increase, counselors, teachers, and other mental health professionals are becoming more aware of the psychological and social effects of family conflicts on students and their families (Ying, 1998). Within the counseling setting, Asian American students attribute psychological distress to their relationships with their parents (Lee, 1997). School counselors often find that their role includes helping students adjust to the school environment (Myrick, 1997). However, they often find that they lack sufficient knowledge of Muslim populations (Carter, 1999) to provide effective interventions.

This study expects to identify the extent of acculturation issues faced by the Muslim student in the acculturation process and their related demographic characteristics. The demographic variables that were used in this study include gender, age, specific ethnicity, number of years in the country, parental characteristics such as number of years in the country, and language spoken in the home. In addition, other issues that might impact an individual's acculturation process such as perceptions and interpretations of gender roles, belongingness, interpersonal relations (i.e., dating), peer relations, religiosity, and individuation were also used to understand the participants' experience of acculturation.

METHOD

The purpose of this study is to identify the demographic characteristics and the extent to which high school-age Muslim students experience different issues presumed to be associated with the acculturation process. This section provides a description of the methodology for the study, including delineation of the relevant variables, population, sampling procedures, instrumentation, research procedures, and data analyses.

Relevant Variables

The independent variables addressed in this study include the responding student's gender, age, country of birth, ethnicity, number of years in the U.S., father's number of years in the U.S., mother's number of years in the U.S., primary language spoken in the home, origin of religion and type of high school. Gender was self-reported by the respondent as male or female. Respondent students also self-reported their respective current age in years and country in which they were born. Ethnicity was self-reported by the student as Indian, Arab, African American or Other. Responding students also self-reported the numbers of years the student, student's father, and student's mother, respectively, have lived in the U.S. Principal language spoken in the home was self-reported by the responding students as English, Urdu, Arabic, or Other. Origin of religion was reported as Muslim By Birth or By Conversion. The dependent variable addressed in this study is the responding student's total score on the Muslim Youth Acculturation Rating Questionnaire (MYARQ) (see Appendix F).

Population

The sample for this study was drawn from the population of American Muslim students attending public, private, and Islamic high (secondary) schools in the U.S. The U.S. Census Bureau does not collect data on religious identification or affiliation. Therefore, there are no official estimates of the Muslim population in the U.S census bureau data, and all reports of the Muslim population in the U.S. are estimates from other sources (Pew Research Center, 2007; Pew Research Center's Forum on Religion & Public Life, 2011). According to the latest estimates by Pew Research Center's

Forum on Religion & Public Life (2011), the population of Muslim children under the age of 15 in the U.S. amounts to only 13.1% of the total Muslim population (i.e., 340, 600). This number is projected to more than triple to 1.8 million in 2030 (Pew Research Center's Forum on Religion & Public Life, 2011).

About 65% of adult Muslims in the U.S. were born in another country (Pew Research Center, 2007; Pew Research Center's Forum on Religion & Public Life, 2011). Of the 35% American-born Muslims, 21% are converts to Islam and only 14% were Muslims born in other countries (Pew Research Center, 2007). Twenty one percent of the American-born (or 7% of all Muslims in the U.S.) are second-generation, with one or both parents having been born outside of the U.S. The 65% who were born outside of the U.S. come from at least 68 different nations (Pew Research Center, 2007).

Thirty five percent of all foreign born Muslim Americans emigrated from the South Asian region, including Pakistan, Bangladesh, India, and Afghanistan (Pew Research Center's Forum on Religion & Public Life, 2011). An additional 19.7% arrived from the Arab region, including Arabic-speaking countries in the Middle East and North Africa (Pew Research Center's Forum on Religion & Public Life, 2011). In terms of specific countries, Pakistan and Bangladesh were the top countries with 28.5% of the foreign-born Muslims in the U.S. (Pew Research Center's Forum on Religion & Public Life, 2011).

This study was focused in states reported to have the highest Muslim populations (Kosmin & Lachman, 1993) among state residents, including California (0.6%), New York (0.8%), New Jersey (0.6%), Illinois (0.4%), Pennsylvania (0.3%), Texas (0.2%), Michigan (0.3%), and Massachusetts (0.4%). More recent statistics (Association of Statisticians of American Religious Bodies, 2012) concur with the listed states having comparable rankings of Muslims in the state populations.

Sampling Procedures

The sample for this study included (self-identified) American Muslim students currently enrolled in public, private, and Islamic high schools in the U.S. Several different approaches were used to identify, contact, and solicit participation from these students.

The primary method used to obtain participants was solicitation of assistance from secondary school counselors in public high schools in the U.S. The American School Counselor Association (ASCA) provides an (updated annually) online member directory of elementary and secondary school counselors that includes the state in which they are located and their e-mail addresses. This directory is available to all ASCA members, and was used for initial contact with potential assisting secondary school counselors in the nine states that have the highest Muslim population.

Secondary school counselors, identified from the ASCA directory, were sent an e-mail inviting them to participate in this study (see Appendix A). Those responding affirmatively to the request were e-mailed the flyer as well as asked if they would like a packet of flyers sent to them via the U.S. postal service. As per the requirements stipulated by the Institutional Review Board, each counselor was asked to include in his/her reply that the school's administration had approved for the flyer to be distributed to the Muslim students. The participating school counselors were asked to distribute the flyers to Muslim students known to them and to request that each student thus identified take the flyer home to her or his parent(s). All school counselors expressed that they did not want the flyers mailed to them, as they did not have more than a range of ten to twenty Muslim students that they knew of in their schools. The flyer (see Appendix B) contains information about the study, an invitation for the parent of the student to contact the primary researcher via e-mail to get the URL address and the personal identification number (PIN) needed to allow their student to participate. The primary researcher had an automatic response set up at her e-mail that replied immediately to any parental e-mail asking for the study's URL and Pin number. The URL address conveyed the informed consent for the parent (see Appendix C). Insertion of the provided PIN at the Informed Consent website (a) represented informed consent by the parent(s) for the student to participate in the study and (b) allowed the student to access the questionnaire MYARQ. The student gave his/her Child's Assent (see Appendix C) by typing in YES, and then proceeded to respond to the 31 survey items and 10 demographic questions of the MYARQ. Students who were 18 or older did not need to get parental involvement and instead inserted the PIN number as their consent to participate in the study.

A paper version of the questionnaire was also made available for those who requested it.

Another sampling procedure included contacting Islamic centers and mosques in the states with the highest Muslim populations and Florida via e-mail to disperse information about the study. The centers contacted were identified from directories provided by the leading Muslim organization in North America, the Islamic Society of North America (ISNA). ISNA is "an association of Muslim organizations and individuals that provides a common platform for presenting Islam, supporting Muslim communities, developing educational, social and outreach programs and fostering good relations with other religious communities, and civic and service organizations" (Islamic Society of North America, n.d. para. 2). The directories provide the names, addresses, and telephone numbers of mosques and

Islamic centers that have registered with ISNA. The centers are listed alphabetically by states. Only the metropolitan centers in the states with high Muslim populations (as listed previously) were contacted for participation.

The request to the respective centers involved distribution of an announcement to adult mosque attendees to invite parents of adolescent Muslims to encourage their respective children to participate in the study (see Appendix D). An e-mail request sent to the director of an Islamic center requested information about the study which was attached to the end of the e-mail (see Appendix E) to be forwarded (e.g., via a listserv) to adult members of the center. Also, the director was requested to post a paper copy of the study's invitation at gatherings at the center (e.g., Friday afternoon prayers). This method also solicited interest from Islamic school directors who were interested in the participating in the survey.

Resultant Sample

Shavelson (1996) provided a convenient method, and table, for determining desired minimal sample size. He also indicated that an alpha level of .05 (α = .05) and a power level of .90 (β = .90) are common values for social science research, with β = .90 actually being a relatively stringent criterion. The remaining item needed to determine a suitable minimal sample size is the size of the difference between means (i.e., effect size) in standard deviation units (Δ). The effect size value can be determined a priori only on the basis of intuition, that is, in consideration of the ramifications of making incorrect decisions. For this research, the effect size was set at Δ = .25 because it is a relatively stringent criterion. Applying these values to the table provided in Shavelson (1996, p. 640), the minimum sample size for this study should be 168.

Survey Development

The Muslim Youth Acculturation Rating Questionnaire (MYARQ, see Appendix F) was developed for the purposes of this research and used to allow American Muslim youth to indicate the extent to which they have experienced various acculturation issues. The original version was an online questionnaire. During the data collection phase, several Islamic centers and some parents requested paper copies of the MYARQ. Therefore, the paper version of the survey was created for those who requested it. The (attitudinal) subsection requires respondents to use a Likert scale to indicate the extent to which they agree with the respective statements (which reflect various acculturation issues) as they apply to the respondent.

The attitudinal subsection of the MYARQ is preceded by a subsection that asks respondents to provide the personal (i.e., demographic) information investigated in the study.

The demographic questions asked for the respondent for his/her gender (male or female, age (write-in value), ethnicity (Indian, Arab, African American, Other), country of birth (U.S., other), primary language spoken at home (English, Urdu, Arabic, Other), number of years lived in the U.S. (born in the U.S., write-in value), number of years father has lived in the U.S. (write-in value), number of years mother has lived in the U.S. (write-in value), type of Muslim (by birth, by conversion), and type of high school (public high school, private high school, Islamic high school, other). These variables were chosen for this study as being pertinent variables related to acculturation from the literature (Berry et al., 2006b).

The attitudinal items (i.e., acculturation issues) in the MYARQ were derived from the professional literature. The items themselves are declarative statements intended to reflect the essence of a particular acculturation issue that has been presented in the professional literature. The attitudinal subsection of the MYARQ includes items to address six types of acculturation issues: (a) gender roles, (b) interpersonal and peer relations, (c) religiosity, (d) individuation from family, (e) belongingness, and (f) perceived discrimination. The items are statements relative to the respective acculturation issues. The item response choices are: (SA) Strongly Agree, (A) Agree, (U) Undecided, (D) Disagree, and (SD) Strongly Disagree. The MYARQ is presented in Appendix F.

Shown in Table 3.1 are primary sources for each of the items in the attitudinal subsection of the MYARQ.

In order to inhibit response sets, positive and negative wordings, and associated forward ($SA = 1, A = 2, U = 3, D = 4$, and $SD = 5$) and backward ($SA = 5, A = 4, U = 3, D = 2$, and $SD = 1$) item response weightings are used such that higher scores indicate that the issue is more problematic for the respondent. The MYARQ total score is achieved by summing the respective item response weights. For the 31 items of the MYARQ attitudinal section, the highest possible score is 123 and the lowest possible score is 63. The assumption that this study makes with the response sets is that the higher the total score, the more problems the respondent has with regard to acculturation issues.

Prior to initiation of the sampling procedures for the study, a pilot study was conducted with between eight American Muslim parents and youth in the Alachua County, Florida, area. Solicitation of participants for this pilot study was made through a local Islamic center. The purpose of the pilot study was to determine if the participant solicitation and online participation procedures are fully functional; data from the pilot study was included in the final data set for this study.

Table 3.1.   Referenced Issues for the MYARQ

Issues and MYARQ Item Numbers	Reference(s)
Religiosity	
Muslim youth should attend Mosque and weekend religious school (#22)	Ghuman (2003); Hedayat-Diba, 2000
Muslim youth should celebrate Christmas (#17)	Ghuman (2003); Hedayat-Diba, 2000
Muslims should be allowed to practice their daily prayers in school or at work (#19)	Carter (1999)
Muslims should eat Halal Muslim/Ethnic food all the time (#10)	Ali, Liu, & Humedian (2004); Carter (1999); Roysircar (2003)
Gender Roles	
Muslim girls and boys are treated the same in family (#14)	Ali, Liu, & Humedian (2004); Ghuman (2003); Hedayat-Diba (2000); Shaw, 2000; Talbani & Hasanali (2000)
Muslim men make all the important decisions (#15)	Ali, Liu, & Humedian (2004); Ghuman (2003); Hedayat-Diba (2000); Shaw, (2000); Talbani and Hasanali (2000)
Muslim women should be allowed more personal freedom (# 6)	Faragallah, Schumm, & Webb (1997); Musleh (1983); Shaw, (2000); Talbani & Hasanali (2000)
Muslim women should stay home and take care of family (#11)	Faragallah, Schumm, & Webb (1997); Musleh (1983).
Muslim women should work outside the home (#16)	Faragallah, Schumm, & Webb (1997); Musleh (1983).
Belongingness	
Muslim students should change their names so that others can say it easily (#3)	Ghuman (2003)
Muslim youth are uncomfortable socializing with White Americans (#4)	Ghuman, (2003), Kim, Brenner, Liang, & Asay (2003)
Muslims should wish they lived in a Muslim country, not America (#23)	Ghuman (2003)

(Table continues on next page)

Table 3.1.   (Continued)

Issues and MYARQ Item Numbers	Reference(s)
Belongingness	
Muslims are not happy living in America (#25)	Berry, Phinney, Sam & Vedder (2006a)
Muslims' closest friends are Muslim (#20)	Berry, Phinney, Sam & Vedder (2006a); Kim, Brenner, Liang, & Asay (2003)
Muslims should have Muslim and American/non-Muslim friends (#27)	Berry, Phinney, Sam & Vedder (2006a)
Individuation From Family	
The interests of family should come before personal interests (#12)	Ali, Liu & Humedian (2004); Berry, Phinney, Sam & Vedder (2006a); Brilliant (2000); El-Islam, (1983); Hedayat-Diba (2000); Ibrahim & Ohnishi, 1997; Sodowsky, Lai & Plake (1991)
Muslim children should always obey their parents (#9)	Ali, Liu & Humedian (2004); Berry, Phinney, Sam & Vedder (2006a); Brilliant (2000); El-Islam, (1983); Hedayat-Diba (2000); Ibrahim & Ohnishi, (1997)
Muslim children should look after their parents in their old age (#21)	Ali, Liu & Humedian (2004); Berry, Phinney, Sam & Vedder (2006a) Brilliant (2000); Hedayat-Diba (2000); Ibrahim & Ohnishi, (1997)
Muslim parents always do what is best for their children (#13)	Ali, Liu & Humedian (2004); Berry, Phinney, Sam & Vedder (2006a) Brilliant (2000); Hedayat-Diba (2000)
Muslim boys should live with their parents until they marry (#29)	Ali, Liu & Humedian (2004); Berry, Phinney, Sam & Vedder (2006a);
Muslim girls should live with their parents until they marry (#30)	Brilliant (2000); Hedayat-Diba (2000)

(Table continues on next page)

Table 3.1. (Continued)

Issues and MYARQ Item Numbers	Reference(s)
Interpersonal/Peer Relations	
Muslims boys and girls should be allowed to go out on group dates (#7)	Ghuman, (2003); Timimi, (1995); Wakil, Siddique, & Wakil (1981)
Marriage should be arranged by my family (#8)	Adudabbeh, 2005; Ghuman, (2003); Timimi, (1995); Wakil, Siddique, & Wakil (1981)
It is acceptable for Muslim girls and boys to talk to each other (#31)	Ali, Liu & Humedian (2004); Hedayat-Diba (2000); Talbani and Hasanali (2000); Timimi, (1995); Wakil, Siddique, & Wakil (1981)
Muslims should marry within their ethnic group (#1)	Adudabbeh, (2005); Ghuman, (2003); Sodowsky, Lai & Plake (1991); Wakil, Siddique, & Wakil (1981)
Muslim teenagers should behave like "American students" to be more successful in school (#2)	Ghuman, (2003); Wakil, Siddique, & Wakil (1981)

Data Analyses

Two major but different types of data analyses were conducted using Statistical Package for the Social Sciences (SPSS 16). Differences in MYARQ Total scores based on (a) gender, (b) country of birth, (c) ethnicity, and (d) primary language spoken in the home, and (e) type of high school were examined using one way Analysis of Variance (ANOVA). Post hoc multiple comparisons for ethnicity, primary language and type of high school were done using Least Significant Differences (LSD) and Bonferroni. The relationships among MYARQ Total scores and (a) respondent's age, (b) respondent's number of years in the U.S., (c) respondent's father's number of years in the U.S., and (d) respondent's mother's number of years in the U.S. were examined using nonparametric pairwise correlations. For those analyses that were statistically significant, univariate Analysis of Variance were done to examine any significant interaction effects. Cronbach's alpha was computed to establish an internal reliability coefficient for the MYARQ Total Score.

Methodological Limitations

A methodological limitation for this study is the participating students have no direct incentive to respond to the MYARQ or to respond to it openly, honestly, or completely. However, receiving the MYARQ materials from school counselors, who by virtue of their positions in schools should be viewed as helpful and caring adults, should impart to potential respondents that the survey and research are important and legitimate. In addition, the requirement for parental permission for participation necessarily means that parents must be aware of their children's participation and may serve to motivate their children to respond to the MYARQ. This could also possibly affect the respondents to provide socially desirable responses. Most important, however, is the realization among most American Muslims that there is great need for better understanding of them and of their lives by the general population of the U.S., which should serve as a strong motivation to participate in the study.

A similar limitation applies to the participating school counselors. That is, they too do not have any direct incentive to assist with the study. However, most practicing school counselors, as dedicated professionals, recognize the need for and value of substantive research that has good potential for application in the school counseling profession. Therefore, it is likely that those school counselors who agree to participate will do so to the best of their respective abilities.

RESULTS

The purpose of this study was to determine demographic characteristics and the extent to which high school-age Muslim students experience different issues believed to be associated with the acculturation process in the United States. Demographic characteristics and data are presented in Table 3.2. Next, the results of analyses of differences in MYARQ total scores by gender, ethnicity, country of birth, primary language, Muslims by birth or conversion and type of high school attended total are provided. Finally, the relationships among MYARQ total score and age and number of years lived are provided.

Table 3.2. Respondents' Demographic Characteristics

Variable	*Percentage (N)*
Gender	
Male	35% (50)
Female	65% (94)
Ethnicity	
South Asian	40% (58)
Arab	43% (62)
African American	5% (7)
Other	12% (17)
Country birth	
U.S.	68% (96)
Other	32% (46)
Primary language	
English	57% (82)
Urdu	9% (13)
Arabic	23% (33)
Other	11% (16)
Origin of Religion	
Birth	96% (137)
Conversion	4% (5)
Type of High School	
Public	67% (96)
Islamic	24% (34)
Private	7% (10)
Other	2% (3)

Demographic Characteristics

The total number of respondents was $N = 144$ (see Table 3.2). However, data from only 143 were used because of incomplete data from one of the respondents. Of the 143, 35% were male and 65% were female. In regard to ethnicity, 40% indicated they were of South Asian descent

(Indian, Pakistani, or Bangladeshi); 43% indicated they were of Arab descent (Egyptian, Iraqi, Yemeni or Lebanese); 5% indicated they were African American; and 12% indicated they were of "Other" ethnicity (which included American, Turkish, Albanian, Iranian, and Multi/Biracial). For their country of birth, 68% of the respondents were born in the United States, while 32% were born in another country. Two of the respondents did not provide this information. In regard to primary language spoken at home, 57% indicated English, 9% indicated Urdu, 23% indicated Arabic, and 11% indicated another language (including Turkish, Farsi, Swahili, and Albanian).

In regard to origin of religion, 96% indicated they were Muslim by birth, and the remaining 4% were Muslim by conversion. Two of the respondents did not provide this information. In regard to type of high school attended, 67% indicated public schools, 24% indicated Islamic high schools, 7% indicated private high schools, and 2% indicated "Other" (e.g., home-schooled). One respondent did not report this information. Response frequencies for the 31 attitudinal items MYARQ is shown in Appendix G.

The average age of the respondents was 15.84 years. The average number of years that the respondents had lived in America was 13.16 years. The average number of years that the respondents' father had lived in America was 14.70 years. The average number of years the respondents' mother had lived in America was 12.95 years (see Table 3.3).

Table 3.3. Respondent's Age and Length of Residence and Respondents' Parents length of Residence

Variable	N	M	SD	Minimum Years	Maximum Years
Age	143	15.84	1.27	13.0	18.0
Years in U.S	142	13.16	4.58	1.0	18.0
Years Father	132	14.70	14.52	0.0	57.0
Years Mother	125	12.95	13.15	1.0	60.0

Response Summary

SPSS software was used for all data summarizations and analyses. The alpha level was $p = .05$ for all analyses. For the 144 participants, their mean MYARQ total score was 93.09 ($SD = 11.29$) (see Table 3.4). SPSS Boxplot and Stem Leaf analyses of the respondents' total scores showed that the sample had a relatively normal distribution of MYARQ total scores.

Table 3.4.   MYARQ Total Score Response Means

Respondents	Mean Score	Lowest Score	Highest Score
144	93.09 (SD=11.29)	64	114

MYARQ Total Score Based on Respondent Gender

The MYARQ Total Score by gender showed males with an average score of 96 and females with an average score of 91.5 (see Table 3.5). An independent samples t-test found that male respondents had a statistically significant higher MYARQ total score mean than did the female respondents ($t = 2.28$ ($df = 142$; $p = .024$) (see Table 3.6).

Table 3.5.   MYARQ Total Score Means by Gender

	Gender	N	Mean	STD	STD Error Mean
Total Score	M	50	96	10.5772	1.4958
	F	94	91.5426	11.4118	1.1770

Table 3.6.   Independent Samples *t* Test for MYARQ Total Scores by Gender

		Levenes's Test for Equality of Variances		t test for Equality of Means					95% Confidence Interval of the Difference	
		F	Sig.	t	Df	Sig. (2-tailed)	Mean Difference	Std. Error Difference	Lower	Upper
Total Score	Equal variances assumed	.183	.669	2.288	142	.024	4.4574	1.9483	.6060	8.3089
	Equal variances not assumed			2.342	106.876	.021	4.4574	1.9034	.6841	8.2308

MYARQ Total Score Based on Respondent Ethnicity

The MYARQ Total Score data by ethnicity showed South Asian students had a mean score of 91.74, the Arab students had a mean score of 95.40, the African American students showed a mean score of 91.14 and the "Other" group of students had a mean score of 90.06 (see Table 3.7). A one way analysis of variance compared respondent MYARQ total score means by ethnicity (see Table 3.8) and showed no significant difference based on ethnicity ($F = 1.64$ ($df = 3,140$) $p = 0.182$).

Table 3.7.   MYARQ Total Score Means by Ethnicity

	N	Mean	STD Deviation	STD Error	Lower Bound	Upper Bound	Minimum	Maximum
					95% Confidence Interval for Mean			
South Asian	58	91.74	11.74	1.54	88.65	94.83	68.00	114.00
Arab	62	95.40	1.05	1.40	92.59	98.21	65.00	114.00
African American	7	91.14	7.73	2.92	83.99	98.29	83.00	103.00
Other	17	90.06	11.03	2.67	84.38	95.73	64.00	109.00
Total	144	93.09	11.29	.94	91.23	94.95	64.00	114.00

Table 3.8.   One Way Analysis of Variance for MYARQ Total Score by Ethnicity

	Sum of Squares	df	Mean Square	F	Sig
Between Groups	619.988	3	206.663	1.642	.182
Within Groups	17,621.838	140	125.870		
Total	18,241.826	143			

MYARQ Total Score Based on Respondent Country of Birth

The MYARQ Total Score data by country of birth showed those students who were born in the U.S. has a mean score of 93.09 while those who were born in another country had a mean score of 93.30 (see Table 3.9). An independent samples t-test compared respondent MYARQ total score means by country of birth (see Table 3.10) and found no statistically significant difference in MYARQ total score means based on country of birth ($t = -0.11$ ($df = 140$; $p = .916$).

Table 3.9. Means for MYARQ Total Score by Country of Birth

	COBIRTH	N	Mean	STD Deviation	STD Error Mean
Total score	United States	96	93.0938	11.1119	1.1341
	Another Country	46	93.3043	11.2128	1.6532

Table 3.10. Independent Samples *t* test on MYARQ Total Score by Country of Birth

		Levenes's Test for Equality of Variances		*t* test for Equality of Means					
								95% Confidence Interval of the Difference	
		F	Sig.	*t*	Df	Sig. (2-tailed)	Mean Difference	STD Error Difference	Lower	Upper
Total Score	Equal variances assumed	.026	.871	.105	140	.916	–.2106	1.9984	–4.1616	3.7404
	Equal variances not assumed			.105	88.079	.917	–.2106	2.0048	–4.1948	3.7736

MYARQ Total Score Based on Respondent Primary Language Spoken in the Home.

The MYARQ Total Score data by primary language spoken in the home (see Table 3.11) revealed the mean score for students who spoke English as 89.81. Students who spoke Urdu at home had a mean score of 99.46 while the Arabic speaking group had a mean score of 98.00. The group "Other" had a mean score of 94.56. A one way analysis of variance compared

MYARQ total score means across categories of primary language spoken in the respondent's home(see Table 3.12) and found that $F = 6.521$ ($df = 3,140$) $p = 0.000$. Subsequently, a Least Significant Difference (LSD) and Bonferroni post hoc comparison (see Table 3.13) revealed that primary home language of English and "Other" language were not statistically significant from each other and that the primary home languages of Urdu and Arabic were not statistically significant from each other. However, the primary home languages of Urdu and Arabic were statistically significant from the primary home language of English.

Table 3.11. Means for MYARQ Total Score by Primary Language in the Home

	n	Mean	STD Deviation	STD Error	95% Confidence Interval for Mean		Minimum	Maximum
					Lower Bound	Upper Bound		
English	82	89.8171	1,178.5866	1.2795	87.2712	92.3629	64.00	114.00
Urdu	13	99.4615	12.3397	3.4224	92.0047	106.9184	71.00	114.00
Arabic	33	98.0000	8.4668	1.4739	94.9978	101.0022	75.00	113.00
Other	16	94.5625	8.2054	2.0514	90.1901	98.9349	78.00	106.00
Total	114	93.0903	11.2945	.9412	91.2298	94.9508	64.00	114.00

Table 3.12 One Way Analysis of Variance for MYARQ Total Score by Primary Language in the Home

	Sum of Squares	df	Mean Square	F	Sig.
Between Groups	2,236.402	3	745.467	6.521	.000
Within Groups	16,005.424	140	114.324		
Total	18,241.826	143			

Table 3.13. Post Hoc LSD and Bonferroni Comparison of MYARQ Total Score by Primary Language in the Home

	(I) PRIMLAN	(J) PRIMLAN	Mean Difference (I-J)	Std. Error	Sig.	95% Confidence Interval	
						Lower Bound	Upper Bound
LSD	English	Urdu	−9.6445(*)	3.1919	.003	−15.9551	−3.3339
		Arabic	−8.1829(*)	2.2042	.000	−12.5408	−3.8251
		Other	−4.7454	2.9222	.107	−10.5228	1.0320
	Urdu	English	9.6445(*)	3.1919	.003	3.3339	15.9551
		Arabic	1.4615	3.5012	.677	−5.4606	8.3836
		Other	4.8990	3.9924	.222	−2.9942	12.7923
	Arabic	English	8.1829(*)	2.2042	.000	3.8251	12.5408
		Urdu	−1.4615	3.5012	.677	−8.3836	5.4606
		Other	3.4375	3.2572	.293	−3.0023	9.8773
	Other	English	4.7454	2.9222	.107	−1.0320	10.5228
		Urdu	−4.8990	3.9924	.222	−12.7923	2.9942
		Arabic	−3.4375	3.2572	.293	−9.8773	3.0023
Bonferroni	English	Urdu	−9.6445(*)	3.1919	.018	−18.1869	−1.1020
		Arabic	−8.1829(*)	2.2042	.002	−14.0820	−2.2839
		Other	−4.7454	2.9222	.640	−12.5661	3.0753
	Urdu	English	9.6445(*)	3.1919	.018	1.1020	18.1869
		Arabic	1.4615	3.5012	1.000	−7.9087	10.8317
		Other	4.8990	3.9924	1.000	−5.7858	15.5838
	Arabic	English	8.1829(*)	2.2042	.002	2.2839	14.0820
		Urdu	−1.4615	3.5012	1.000	−10.8317	7.9087
		Other	3.4375	3.2572	1.000	−5.2798	12.1548
	Other	English	4.7454	2.9222	.640	−3.0753	12.5661
		Urdu	−4.8990	3.9924	1.000	−15.5838	5.7858
		Other	−3.4375	3.2572	1.000	−12.1548	5.2798

* The mean difference is significant at the .05 level.

MYARQ Total Score Based on Respondent Muslim Belief Origin

Because such a small proportion of the respondents had become Muslim by conversion, the data were insufficient to allow appropriate data analysis.

MYARQ Total Score Based on Respondent Type of High School Attended

The MYARQ Total Score data by type of high school showed the mean for public school students was 92.92, for private schools was 89.00 and the mean for Islamic schools was 93.50 (see Table 3.14). The data from respondents of private (4.00) and public high schools (1.00) were combined as there were so few respondents who attended private schools that were not Islamic schools (2.00). A one way analysis of variance compared respondent MYARQ total score means by school type (see Table 3.15) and found that there was not a statistically significant difference in MYARQ total score means based on school type ($F = 0.223$ ($df = 2,140$; $p = 0.801$).

Table 3.14   Means Description of MYARQ Total Score and Type of School Attended

	n	Mean	Std. Deviation	Std. Error	95% Confidence Interval for the Mean		Minimum	Maximum
					Lower Bound	Upper Bound		
1.00	106	92.9245	12.1167	1.1769	90.5910	95.2581	64.00	114.00
2.00	34	93.5000	8.3130	1.4257	90.5995	96.4005	78.00	113.00
4.00	3	89.0000	10.8167	6.2450	62.1299	115.8701	77.00	98.00
Total	143	92.9790	11.2547	.9412	91.1185	94.8395	64.00	114.00

Table 3.15   One Way Analysis of Variance for MYARQ Total Score and Type of School

	Sum of Squares	df	Mean Square	f	Sig.
Between Groups	57.041	2	28.520	.233	.801
Within Groups	17,929.896	140	128.071		
Total	17,986.937	142			

MYARQ Total Score Among Respondent Characteristics

A univariate ANOVA examined the relationship between respondent gender and primary language spoken in the home and revealed a significant main effect for primary language ($F(3, 136) = 5.78, p < .001$) although the gender ($F(1, 136) = 1.88, p = .17$), and the gender by primary language interaction were not significant ($F(3,136) = .384, p = .77$).

MYARQ Total Score and Respondent Age

Because the range of respondent ages was restricted, a Spearman rank order (rho) correlation was computed (see Table 3.16) to determine the relationship between MYARQ total score and respondent age. Spearman's rank correlation coefficient is a technique which can be used to summarize the strength and direction (negative or positive) of a relationship between two variables. The result will always be between 1 and minus 1. For this analysis, it was found that $rho = -0.006$ ($df = 143; p = .947$). The negative correlation found signified that when age increased, the MYARQ Total score decreased. The negative correlation here is very weak (0.006) as a Spearman correlation of zero indicates that there is no relationship.

MYARQ Total Score and Respondent Years in the United States

A Spearman correlation was computed (see Table 3.16) to determine the relationship between MYARQ total score and respondent length of residence in the United States. For this analysis, it was found that $rho = -0.024$ ($df = 142, p = .776$). The negative correlation here means that when length of residence in the U.S. increased, the MYARQ Total Score decreased. A lower MYARQ Total score signifies more integration and less acculturation problems.

MYARQ Total Score and Respondent's Father's Years in the United States

A Spearman's rank correlation was computed (see Table 3.16) to determine the relationship between MYARQ total score and respondent's father's length of residence in the United States. It was found that $rho = .296$ ($df = 132; p = .001$). The positive correlation here signifies that when respondent's father's length of residence in the U.S. increased, the MYARQ Total Score also increased.

MYARQ Total Score and Respondent's Mother's Years in the United States

A Spearman's rank correlation was computed (see Table 3.16) to determine the relationship between MYARQ total score and respondent's mother's length of residence in the United States. It was found that $rho = .217$ ($df = 125; p = .015$). The positive correlation here signifies that when respondent's mother's length of residence in the U.S. increased, the MYARQ Total Score also increased.

**Table 3.16.   Spearman Correlation Coefficients of
MYARQ Total Scores With Respondent Age, Length of
Residence, Respondent's Father's Length of Residence, and
Respondent's Mother's Length of Residence**

		Total Score	AGE	YRS LIVED	YRSF	YRSM
Spearman's rho	Correlation Coefficient	1.000	–.006	–.024	.296(**)	.217(*)
	Sig. (2-tailed)	.	.947	.776	.001	.015
	N	144	143	142	132	125
	Correlation Coefficient	–.006	1.000	.434(**)	.064	.054
	Sig. (2-tailed)	.947	.	.000	.470	.553
	N	143	143	142	131	124
	Correlation Coefficient	–.024	.434(**)	1.000	.255(**)	.408(**)
	Sig. (2-tailed)	.776	.000	.	.003	.000
	N	142	142	142	131	124
	Correlation Coefficient	.296(**)	.064	.255(**)	1.000	.786(**)
	Sig.(2-tailed)	.001	.470	.003	.	.000
	N	132	131	131	132	122
	Correlation Coefficient	.217(*)	.054	.408(**)	.786(**)	1.000
	Sig.(2-tailed)	.015	.553	.000	.000	.
	N	125	124	124	122	125

**Correlation is significant at the .01 level (2-tailed)

*Correlation is significant at the .05 level (2-tailed)

Finally, a Cronbach's Coefficient Alpha was calculated to determine the internal consistency of the MYARQ. It was found to be 0.70 for the MYARQ Total Score for this group of respondents which is considered adequate in most social science research situations (Heppner, Kivlighan, & Wampold, 1992).

DISCUSSION

The primary purpose of this study was to determine the extent to which high school age Muslim students experience various acculturation issues that have been presented in the professional literature. In addition, differences in the extent to which they experienced the various issues based on gender, ethnicity, country of birth, primary language, origin of religion and type of high school attended were examined, as were the relationships between the extent to which they experienced those issues and the number of years that the respondent and each of the respondent's parents have lived in America. The extent to which the respondents experienced acculturation issues was made operational as the total score on the Muslim Youth Acculturation Rating Questionnaire (MYARQ).

Although much research has been done about acculturation for immigrant adults (e.g., Amer, 2005; Berry, Kim, Minde, & Mok, 1987; Berry, Kim, Power, Young, & Bujaki, 1989; Phinney, 1990; Sam & Berry, 1995), and some for immigrant youth (e.g., Berry et al., 2006b; Ghuman, 2003; Portes & Rumbaut, 2001), little attention has been focused on the cultural adaptation of Muslim youth (Alghorani, 2003; Hedayat-Diba, 2000). However, Muslim youth face a distinct acculturation process because of their "allegiance" to both traditional cultural values and religious beliefs and the social influences of their American peers. Additionally, since the historic events of September 11, 2001, Muslims have had to endure intense scrutiny as members of the greater American society. These unique stressors impact the acculturation process of Muslims, especially adolescents who also are experiencing other developmental changes and engaging in identity development. Therefore, this study surveyed Muslim adolescents to determine the extent to which they experience various acculturation issues presumed to be common in the acculturation process. Presented forthwith are the interpretations, conclusions, limitations, and recommendations that evolved from this research.

Interpretations

A higher score on the MYARQ reflected greater extent to which the respondent experienced acculturation problems. Therefore, lower MYARQ scores are associated with higher acculturation (i.e., lesser extent of acculturation problems) while higher scores imply lower acculturation (i.e., greater extent of acculturation problems). The lowest possible MYARQ score was 63 and the highest possible score was 123. For this study the lowest total score by a respondent was 64 and the highest score was 114.

The first finding addressed differences in MYARQ Total Score based on gender. There was a statistically significant difference in mean MYARQ total score, with male respondents having a higher mean score than female respondents. This result indicates that male Muslim adolescents had greater intensity of acculturation issues than the female Muslim adolescents.

A second major finding of this study was that the mean difference for primary language spoken in the home was statistically significant. The primary difference was among respondents from homes in which Urdu and Arabic were the main languages spoken at home and those in which English was the main language spoken at home, with students in the former having greater intensity of acculturation issues than in the latter.

The third major finding in this study was that of the positive and statistically significant correlations between the number of years that both the respondent's father and mother had lived in the U.S. and MYARQ Total Score. Apparently, parental duration in the U.S. is inversely associated with their adolescent's experience of acculturation issues.

Statistically significant differences were not found for MYARQ Total Score based on ethnicity, country of birth, and type of high school.

The variable "country of birth" was included to investigate whether there were differences based on being born in the U.S. While a majority (68%) of the respondents was born in the U.S., many of them had not lived in the U.S. their entire lives; the total number of years lived in the U.S. for the respondents were often different than their actual age. Presumably, discontinuity of time lived in the U.S. could have impacted the intensity of their experiences with acculturation. However, there was not a statistically significant difference for this variable.

One of the initial assumptions of this study was that public school students have greater exposure to mainstream America, and therefore would be a more accurate representation of the average or typical Muslim adolescent in America. Islamic school students' educations follow strict Islamic rules, which include segregation of the sexes, wearing a school uniform, intense study of religion, and daily prescribed prayers (Alghorani, 2003). Therefore, it would be easy to assume that these students have had a completely different experience of daily school, interpersonal, religious, and social life than the public school students. However, there were no statistically significant differences in intensity of acculturation experience based on school type.

CONCLUSIONS

The variables examined in this study were developed from the literature on theory and research related to acculturation of immigrants. In particular,

Berry's theory of acculturation states that demographic variables such as age, gender, ethnicity, length of residence, and parents' length of residence have been shown as possible sources of variation in the acculturation process (Berry & Sam, 1997). Intercultural variables such as language proficiency and use, social contacts, perceived discrimination and family relationship values have been researched within the context of Berry's theory, and found to have substantive relationships with acculturation process level of adaptation (Berry et al., 1989; Berry, Phinney, Kwak, & Sam, 2006a).

Berry's (1980) theory of acculturation includes that all issues are applicable to all persons experiencing the acculturation process. Further, for adolescents in immigrant families, acculturation attitudes are shaped by families, peers, their school experiences, and other adults with whom they interact (Phinney, Berry, Vedder, & Liebkind, 2006b). Thus, differences in preferences for acculturative change are dependent on contextual factors, any discrimination that they may experience, and personal characteristics (Phinney et al., 2006b). Because both the nature and extent of the acculturation issues with which a person is confronted change over time (Berry et al., 2006a), it is important that research on adolescents be conducted before they become adults. This study therefore contributes to the research and theory associated with the literature on acculturation of adolescent immigrants.

The result of gender difference in acculturation found in this study is in accord with the research of Berry et al. (2006b) and Ghuman (2003) who also found acculturation differences based on gender. Interestingly, Berry et al. (2006b) found in their study of acculturation, identity, and adaptation of immigrant youth living in 13 societies around the world that immigrant boys had slightly better psychological adaptation than immigrant girls, but there was poorer sociocultural adaptation for girls. Psychological adaptation in their study included factors such as life satisfaction, self-esteem, and psychological problems and sociocultural adaptation included factors such as school adjustment, and behavior problems. They concluded that "girls are more likely to internalize problems and have higher levels of depression, whereas boys are more likely to externalize problems and act out (Phinney, Berry, Sam, & Vedder, 2006a, p. 221). Girls tend to prefer a more integrative approach to acculturation which in turn may cause conflict with parental values. Tradition Muslim values lean towards protection of girls and prefer daughters to remain close to the home and family before marriage (Phinney et al., 2006a).

Ghuman's (2003) study on South Asian youth living in four Western countries reported that girls had the most to gain from accepting the norms and practices of gender equality, especially when the cultural and religious norms within their family did not allow for them to be treated the same as the boys. This may explain why the girls in the present study scored lower on the MYARQ (which implies lesser intensity of problems) because they stand to gain more by adopting Western values with regard to gender equality and treatment from others.

In regard to primary language spoken in the home, previous research (Swaiden, Marshall, & Smith, 2001) has shown that among Muslims in the United States, the more frequent the use of native language, the greater the desire to retain native culture and remain "separated" from mainstream American culture. Ghuman (2003) found that Muslims in particular in his study were more dedicated to learning, speaking, and keeping their primary language than the other religious groups. Similarly, Berry et al. (2006) concluded that Muslim immigrant youth were the largest group among the ethnic profile groups in which the orientation was toward high ethnic identity, ethnic language proficiency and usage, and ethnic peer contacts.

Language proficiency speeds the acculturation process (Swaiden et al., 2001), a proposition supported by the respondents in this study having higher scores MYARQ scores being the ones who were primarily speaking languages other than English at home.

Previous research by El-Badry and Poston (1990), El-Sayed (1986), and Musleh (1983) found a positive relationship between length of residence and acculturation success for Arab immigrants to the U.S. immigrants who had been in the U.S. for a shorter period suffered more problems than immigrants who had been in the U.S. for longer periods of time (Penaloza, 1994; Swaiden et al., 2001). However, apparently the potential acculturation adaptation benefits derived from longer residence in the U.S. is not transmitted directly, or at least uniformly, from parents to their children. A possible explanation is that, in general, the basic religious and cultural values of Muslims espouse the authority of the father in the household. Further, gender roles are clearly defined and hierarchical. Therefore, the father usually makes all the important decisions in the household, which could include the amount of contact the family has with the larger society, the activities in which the children are involved in at school or outside of school, and the interpersonal relationships allowed for the children and/ or the family in general.

Another plausible explanation for this finding may be the repercussions for Muslims in general following the events of September 11, 2001. September 11 has dramatically altered the way Muslims live in the U.S. (Abdo, 2006). In the "post-9-11 era," Muslims have become more religious and more conservative because they feel an urgent need to embrace their beliefs and to establish an Islamic identity as a unified community. For example, Abdo (2006) reported that there are more mosques, more women wearing headscarves, and more Muslims taking time to perform their daily prayers at work than in the decade prior to September 11, 2001.

And finally, most of the previous studies that showed a positive relationship between length of residence and acculturation success were conducted in the 1980s and 1990s. Acculturation success may have had different influences based on the historical events preceding that time. Now, however, Muslims are more frequently "keeping to their own ethnic groups" because of distrust and anxieties related to national and media propaganda against Muslims. On September 11, 2001, the respondents in this study were only between 6 and 11 years of age. After that date, their parents may have tried to "protect" their children more by keeping them separated from the larger society and the onslaught of negative stereotyping of Muslims. Abdo (2006) reported that young Muslims who were born or raised in the U.S. are often more observant of Islamic practices than their parents. Therefore, the respondents in this study may have had more intensity of acculturation issues regardless of how long their parents have lived longer in the U.S.

With regard to the lack of significant difference based on ethnicity, it is important to recognize that not all Muslims are alike. In the world at large, Muslims are comprised of several ethnic groups, but in the U.S. they are primarily comprised of three main groups: South Asian Muslims, Arab Muslims, and African Americans Muslims (Pew Research Center, 2007, Pew Research Center's Forum on Religion and Public Life, 2011). Considering that these three groups are vastly different in primary language, cultural mores, and historical background, it was expected that there would be differences in the intensity of their acculturation issues as well. However, that was not the case in this study. There is no readily apparent explanation for this lack of difference.

Most recent studies of Muslims (e.g., Ahmed, 2004; Ghuman, 2003; Mansour, 2000) have been focused only on one ethnic group (Arab or South Asian) or on other mental health issues (such as identity development, religiosity, or depression), and therefore did not address acculturation issues across different ethnic groups. An exception was Berry et al. (2006b) who investigated ethnicity as a variable in the acculturation process of immigrant youth in 4 of 13 different countries in their study. They concluded that there were strong differences in ethnic orientation and ethnic behaviors, and in turn in predicted adaptation outcomes. Therefore, the present study was distinctive in investigating potential differences in intensity of acculturation issues based on ethnicity, and also in not finding differences based on ethnicity.

The correlation between age and MYARQ score was not statistically significant. Berry et al. (2006b) found no age differences in acculturation adaptation in their study. They suggested that age may have been confounded with age of arrival which was not studied with their participants. Therefore, although it might seem reasonable to suggest that older students would have less intense experiences in acculturation, apparently that is not the case.

A basic issue in acculturation research is whether immigrants experience an essentially linear change from complete identification and involvement with their original ethnic culture to more or less complete identification and involvement with their new host culture (Berry, 1980). Berry et al. (2006b) found that change was not a linear progression, that is, that with longer residence, adolescents are more likely to be bicultural and integrated rather than assimilated. The majority of the respondents in this study were born in the U.S. It is possible that there was not a statistically significant correlation because they had already integrated and become bicultural to a large extent.

Generalizability Limitations

The purpose of this survey research was to gather information from high school age Muslim students about their experiences of issues in their acculturation process. The initial plan was to access the high school students by contacting high school counselors and Islamic centers to disseminate information about the study by means of a flyer. The flyer requested that parents contact the researcher for the link to the online survey (with the password provided as the informed consent for their child to take the online survey). Therefore, high school counselors who were members of the American School Counselor Association (ASCA) and resided in the nine states with the largest Muslim populations (i.e., California, Florida, Illinois, Massachusetts, Michigan, New Jersey, New York, Pennsylvania, and Texas) were contacted via e-mail. Islamic Centers in the same nine states also were sent e-mail information about and participation requests for the study. However, collectively these processes generated only twenty respondents over a 3-month period, even though a reminder e-mail was sent to the school counselors and Islamic centers every month. Therefore, thereafter "snowball sampling" was used to increase the response rate. Snowball sampling is deliberate sampling that typically proceeds after a study begins and takes place when the researcher asks participants to recommend other individuals to participate in the study (Creswell, 2002). This method helped to increase the final sample to 144. Although the desired sample size was not fully achieved, this sample is sufficient for valid data analyses, and substantial relative to the restricted population from which it was drawn (Creswell, 2002).

Another adjustment to the proposed procedures was to provide a paper version of the survey for those participants who requested it. The third adjustment was an addition to the type of high school attended by the respondents. Initially, it was intended that only students from public high schools would be sampled, based on the assumption that those Muslim students who were "main-streamed" adolescents would face the common acculturation issues. However, feedback and interest from parents and directors of Islamic schools who received the information about the study from their Islamic centers suggested that students in Islamic schools also experienced acculturation issues frequently. Therefore, students from public, private, and Islamic schools all were included in the study. Again, although this was a change from the original plan, the inclusion of students from Islamic high schools in effect allowed the sample to represent an even broader sample of Muslim adolescent students.

It was anticipated that the gender ratio among respondents would be approximately 50:50. However, the gender ratio for the sample was 65% female and 35% male. It may be that more females than males responded to the MYARQ as they tend to be more accommodating than males. However, while females are to some extent overrepresented among the respondents, there were sufficient numbers of respondents for each gender to allow valid gender difference analyses.

Recommendations

This study is among the few that have investigated the acculturation experience of immigrant adolescents, and that has specifically examined the acculturation experiences of Muslim immigrant and second-generation adolescents post-September 11, 2001, in the U.S. Some of the results from this study are supported in previous literature but the new results found may be especially pertinent for future studies.

Existing acculturation theory takes into account the importance of gender and primary language as impacting the acculturation process. However, from this study, it is recommended that theory also take into account how Muslim parents' length of residence is associated with acculturation of adolescents. While most immigrant parents achieve a higher degree of acculturation with a longer stay in the host country, Muslim parents may be seeking to shield their adolescent children from having similar experiences. September 11, 2001 has greatly impacted the level of attention that has been given to discrimination against Muslims in the professional. Further research to explore the extent of the problems experienced by Muslims relative to this tragic event is greatly needed to understand the full impact on their lives.

Clearly more studies in this regard are needed. In particular, studies having larger sample sizes and/or samples from different populations are needed to broaden the basis of cultural knowledge about adolescent Muslims in the U.S. Collaboration among Muslim educators, counselors, and local leaders is highly recommended to systematically specify and study pertinent acculturation issues. Also, more research is needed on the psychometric properties of the MYARQ; specifically, the subscales of the MYARQ can be further developed using factor analyses. Further research is also recommended in comparing immigrant Muslims pre-September 11 and post-September 11. This could identify more clearly the acculturation experiences for Muslims related to this important event in America.

A strong recommendation is made for including Muslims as a distinct group within multicultural education and training. The Muslim population is growing rapidly in the United States (Bagby, 1994; U.S. Department of State, 2001; Pew Research Center's Forum on Religion and Public Life, 2011). Such training should include the differential experiences of immigrant Muslim adults and second generation Muslim children. Increasing and correcting the information about Muslims in the American society in general and acknowledging their unique issues would help Muslims have better acculturation experiences.

SUMMARY

Muslims are fast becoming a significant and common component of the American society. However, there is not yet enough accurate information about this population in general, and about the youth of this population in particular. This study sought to determine the extent to which Muslim adolescents are experiencing acculturation issues in the U.S. and to investigate some variables associated with their acculturation experiences. In many respects, the results from this study support previous research findings. However, new information also was found. Therefore, further research is highly recommended to explore the nature of acculturation among Muslim adolescents.

APPENDIX A
INVITATION TO SCHOOL COUNSELORS

Dear Colleague,

My name is Shifa Hussain. I am a doctoral candidate in the Department of Counselor Education at the University of Florida. You may remember me from the April, 2007 issue of ACA's *Counseling Today* that featured the article Muslim "Teens Leading Double Lives" for which I was interviewed. As a high school counselor for over 8 years, I have worked in a variety of roles and with diverse populations, including Muslim students and parents. My dissertation research is entitled, "Acculturation issues of Muslim high school students in the United States." It involves American Muslim high-school-age students responding to an online and survey about acculturation issues they may be facing. It should take the students approximately 10 minutes to respond.

I am writing to ask if you would assist my research by distributing information about my research and survey to any Muslim students in your school. All you are asked to do is to contact any Muslim students in your school *known to you* and give each of them a flyer to take home to their parent(s). The flyer for the parent is attached for your perusal and for sharing with the appropriate school administration for approval of distribution of the flyers.

Please reply to this e-mail stating your interest and willingness to participate in this study. I also request for you to please <u>include in your reply your school administration's approval for this flyer to be distributed to the Muslim students</u>. I will send an appropriate number of flyers about the research via the U.S. postal service as soon as possible. The flyer is intended for distribution to the parent(s) of each Muslim student, so each student contacted should be asked to take the flyer home to his/her parent(s). If more convenient, you can print the flyer and give to your student to take home to his or her parent.

This study is funded in part by the by the Association for Spiritual, Ethical, and Religious Values in Counseling (ASERVIC), a division of the American Counseling Association.

I would appreciate your response to this e-mail.

Respectfully,

Shifa Podikunju Hussain

Shifa Podikunju Hussain, MEd, EdS,   Larry Loesch, PhD, NCC
Doctoral Candidate   Professor, Counselor Education
University of Florida   University of Florida
shifaph@ufl.edu or 352-339-4588

APPENDIX B
INFORMATIONAL FLYER FOR PARENTS OF AMERICAN
MUSLIM HIGH SCHOOL STUDENTS

I*n the tradition of greeting in the Muslim faith,*
Assalaamu Alaikum
(Peace be upon you)

Dear Respected Parent,

My name is Shifa Podikunju Hussain. I am a doctoral candidate in the school counseling program in the Department of Counselor Education at the University of Florida. I write to request your help in my research on adolescent Muslim students living in the U.S.

My doctoral dissertation research is entitled**, "Acculturation Issues of Muslim High School Students in the United States."** This study received funding in part from the Association for Spiritual, Ethical, and Religious Values in Counseling, a division of the American Counseling Association. The major research activity is completion of an approximately 10-minute, online survey by high school-age Muslim students. I am contacting you because you are the parent of a student eligible to participate in my study, and your consent is need for your student to participate.

As an American Muslim and a high school counselor for more than 8 years, I have worked with Muslim and other bicultural teens who face issues associated with adaptation to mainstream American society. I am aware that parents often feel overwhelmed when faced with the deluge of cultural differences that affect their children in schools and in society. This study is intended to be a foundation of discovery for actual issues that young Muslims face growing up in America. *I am interested in learning about Muslim high school students' opinions in topics such as relationships with peers including Muslims and non-Muslims, the roles of boys and girls in family life growing up in America, how Muslims are treated in America, and how connected Muslim boys and girls feel growing up in America.*

The results from this study should be helpful to educators, parents, children, and educational professionals in ways beneficial to all. It also may be that this research will help alleviate some of the misconceptions that the larger society may have about Muslims living in America. *If you have any other questions or would like to contact me regarding this study or the survey, you can welcome to call me at 352-339-4588 at any time, or my supervising professor at the University of Florida, Dr. Larry Loesch at 352-392-0731, extension, 225.*

This study is not connected to your school and will not impact the academic standing of your student in any way. The school is asked to only distribute this informational flyer to Muslim students known to the school counselor.

Muslim high school age students from across the United States are being requested to participate in this research by completing an approximately 10-minute online survey.

If you are willing for your child to participate in this 10-minute survey, please e-mail me at hussain.shifa@gmail.com for information on the survey website address and the Personal Identification Number (PIN) needed to participate. All participants receive the same standard PIN number and therefore cannot be identified by this PIN. Use of the PIN number is part of the informed consent process. **By providing the URL and PIN to your child, you are acknowledging informed consent for your child to participate in my search**. You may withhold consent simply by not providing this information to your child. This procedure has been approved by the Institutional Review Board of the University of Florida (**Protocol #2007-U-1056**).

I would appreciate your participation in this pioneering study on the acculturation issues faced by the Muslim children growing up in America.

I thank you in advance for your generous participation and your contribution to the literature on Muslims and their needs in America.

In the tradition of the Muslim faith,
Jazakallahu Khair,
(May God grant you good)

Shifa Podikunju Hussain, MEd, EdS,   Larry Loesch, PhD, NCC
Doctoral Candidate   Professor, Counselor Education
University of Florida   University of Florida
shifaph@ufl.edu or 352-339-4588

APPENDIX C
ONLINE PARENTAL CONSENT

Dear Respected Parent,

I am a doctoral candidate in the school counseling program in the Department of Counselor Education at the University of Florida under the supervision of Dr. Larry Loesch.

The purpose of this study is to find out how Muslim high school students feel about acculturation issues related to growing up in the United States. The results from this study should be helpful to educators, parents, children, and educational professionals in ways beneficial to all. It also may be that this research will help alleviate some of the misconceptions that the larger society may have about Muslims living in America. There are no known risks to your child.

This study is not connected to your school and will not impact the academic standing of your student in any way. The school is asked to only distribute this informational flyer to Muslim students known to the school counselor.

Muslim high school age students from across the United States are being requested to participate in this research by completing an approximately 10-minute online survey. With your permission, I would like to ask your child to participate in this research.

The survey asks the child to choose whether they agree or disagree with statements that the research literature has stated as relating to acculturation issues of ethnic and religious minority groups. **I am interested in learning about Muslim high school students' opinions in topics such as relationships with peers including Muslims and non-Muslims, the roles of boys and girls in family life growing up Muslim in America, how Muslims are treated in America, and how connected Muslim boys and girls feel growing up in America.**

The e-mail you received contains **a standard personal identification number (PIN)** that allows access to the survey. Use of the PIN number is part of the informed consent process. **By entering the PIN to your child, you are acknowledging informed consent for your child to participate in my search.** You may withhold consent simply by not providing this information to your child. This procedure has been approved by the Institutional Review Board of the University of Florida (protocol # 2007-U-1056).

There is no compensation for participation in the study. Your child's participation in this study is completely voluntary. Your child does not have to answer any question that s/he does not wish to answer. **No school personnel will know if your child participated or not, and choosing not to participate will in no way affect your child's academic standing.**

The individual student responses will be anonymous as there are no personal identifiers in the survey. Results will be kept confidential to the extent provided by law through a numerical coding system. Only group results will be shared with the doctoral committee and any future research publications and presentations. If you are interested to learn more about the results of this study or have any other questions, you may contact me (shifaph@ufl.edu) or my supervisor, Dr. Larry Loesch, at lloesch@coe.ufl. edu. Questions or concerns about your child's rights as research participant may be directed to the IRB02 office, University of Florida, Box 112250, Gainesville, FL 32611, (352) 392-0433.

Shifa Podikunju Hussain MEd. EdS,
Doctoral Candidate
University of Florida
shifaph@ufl.edu or 352-339-4588

Larry Loesch, PhD, NCC.
Professor, Counselor Education
University of Florida

I have read the procedure described above. By entering the PIN number, I voluntarily give my consent for my child to participate in Shifa Podikunju Hussain's study of acculturation issues of high school Muslim students in the United States.

Enter PIN here

CLICK to go to next page

Online Child's Assent

My name is Shifa Podikunju Hussain and I am a doctoral student at the University of Florida. I am trying to learn about how high school Muslim students feel about growing up Muslim in America. Muslim high school age students from across the United States are being requested to participate in this research by completing an approximately 10-minute online survey.

There are no known risks to participation. The results from this study should be helpful to teachers, parents, children, and other educational professionals in ways beneficial to all. It also may be that this research will help lessen some of the misconceptions that the larger society may have about Muslims living in America. You do not have to take part in this study or answer any question that you don't want to. No one will know who you are as the students are not asked for their personal information. Only group results will be shared with the researchers involved and presented as such. **No school personnel will know if you participated or not, and choosing not to participate will in no way affect your academic standing.**

Your parents have given their permission for you to participate. Would you be willing to participate in this study?

YES [Click to continue]

NO [Click to end]

APPENDIX D
PARENTAL INFORMED CONSENT (PAPER VERSION)

Dear Respected Parent,

I am a doctoral candidate in the school counseling program in the Department of Counselor Education at the University of Florida under the supervision of Dr. Larry Loesch.

The purpose of this study is to find out how Muslim high school students feel about acculturation issues related to growing up in the United States. The results from this study should be helpful to educators, parents, children, and educational professionals in ways beneficial to all. It also may be that this research will help alleviate some of the misconceptions that the larger society may have about Muslims living in America. There are no known risks to your child.

This study is not connected to your school and will not impact the academic standing of your student in any way. The school is asked to only distribute this informational flyer to Muslim students known to the school counselor.

Muslim high school age students from across the United States are being requested to participate in this research by completing an approximately 10-minute online/paper survey. With your permission, I would like to ask your child to participate in this research.

The survey asks the child to choose whether they agree or disagree with statements that the research literature has stated as relating to acculturation issues of ethnic and religious minority groups. **I am interested in learning about Muslim high school students' opinions in topics such as relationships with peers including Muslims and non-Muslims, the roles of boys and girls in family life growing up Muslim in America, how Muslims are treated in America, and how connected Muslim boys and girls feel growing up in America.**

There is no compensation for participation in the study. Your child's participation in this study is completely voluntary. Your child does not have to answer any question that s/he does not wish to answer. **No school personnel will know if your child participated or not, and choosing not to participate will in no way affect your child's academic standing. Your child should enclose the survey in the envelope that is attached to the survey, in order to ensure confidentiality, before giving it back to the school counselor or the assigned personnel at the Islamic Centers.**

The individual student responses will be anonymous as there are no personal identifiers in the survey. Results will be kept confidential to the extent provided by law through a numerical coding system. Only group results will be shared with the doctoral committee and any future research publications and presentations. If you are interested to learn more about the results of this study or have any other questions, you may contact me (shifaph@ufl.edu) or my supervisor, Dr. Larry Loesch, at lloesch@coe.ufl.edu. Questions or concerns about your child's rights as research participant may be directed to the IRB02 office, University of Florida, Box 112250, Gainesville, FL 32611 (352) 392-0433.

Shifa Podikunju Hussain, MEd, EdS,   Larry Loesch, PhD, NCC
Doctoral Candidate   Professor, Counselor Education
University of Florida   University of Florida
shifaph@ufl.edu or 352-339-4588

PARENT KEEPS THIS PAGE

PLEASE RETURN THIS PAGE TO:
SHIFA P. HUSSAIN,
2901 SW 13th Street, #217,
Gainesville, FL 32608

Parental Informed Consent

I have read the procedure described above. I voluntarily give my consent for my child, _____, to participate in Shifa Podikunju Hussain's study of acculturation issues of high school Muslim students in the United States. I have received a copy of this description.

Parent's signature_____Date_____

Child's Assent

My name is Shifa Podikunju Hussain and I am a doctoral student at the University of Florida. I am trying to learn about how high school Muslim students feel about growing up Muslim in America. Muslim high school age students from across the United States are being requested to participate in this research by completing an approximately 10-minute online/paper survey.

There are no known risks to participation. The results from this study should be helpful to teachers, parents, children, and other educational professionals in ways beneficial to all. It also may be that this research will help lessen some of the misconceptions that the larger society may have about Muslims living in America. You do not have to take part in this study or answer any question that you don't want to. No one will know who you are as the students are not asked for their personal information. Only group results will be shared with the researchers involved and presented as such. **No school personnel will know if you participated or not, and choosing not to participate will in no way affect your academic standing.**

Please enclose the survey in the envelope that is attached to the survey, in order to ensure confidentiality, before giving it back to the school counselor or the assigned personnel at the Islamic Centers.

Your parents have given their permission for you to participate. Would you be willing to participate in this study?

Child's Signature_____Date_____

APPENDIX E
REQUEST TO ISLAMIC CENTERS TO
HELP DISSEMINATE RESEARCH INFORMATION

Assalamu Alaikum
(Peace be upon you)

Dear Respected Islamic Center Director,

My name is Shifa Podikunju Hussain. I am a doctoral candidate in the Department of Counselor Education at the University of Florida. I am writing to request your help in disseminating information about my dissertation research on adolescent Muslim students living in the United States to the Muslim ummah (community) living in your area. I would be very grateful if you would pass this information along via your usual method of informing people, e.g., by e-mail, posting on bulletin boards, or announcement.

My dissertation research is entitled, "Acculturation issues of Muslim high school students in the United States." This study received (partial) funding from the Association for Spiritual, Ethical, and Religious Values in Counseling, a division of the American Counseling Association. The major research activity is for high-school-age Muslim students to complete an approximately 10-minute, online questionnaire about acculturation issues they may be facing.

As an American Muslim and a high school counselor for more than eight years, I have worked with Muslim and other bi-cultural teens who face issues associated with adaptation to mainstream American society. I am aware that parents often feel overwhelmed when faced with the deluge of cultural differences that affect their children in schools and in society. This study is intended to be a foundation of discovery for actual issues that young Muslims face growing up in America. *I am interested in learning about Muslim high school students' opinions in topics such as relationships with peers including Muslims and non-Muslims, the roles of boys and girls in family life growing up in America, how Muslims are treated in America, and how connected Muslim boys and girls feel growing up in America.*

The results from this study should be helpful to educators, parents, children, and educational professionals in ways beneficial to all. *Insha Allah* (God Willing), it also may be that this research will help alleviate some of the misconceptions that the larger society may have about Muslims living in America.

Parents of Muslim students across the United States are being sent this flyer that invites their child to participate in the online survey. Interested parents can contact me at hussain.shifa@gmail.com . I will email the parent **a standard PIN NUMBER and the URL that will allow access the online questionnaire.** *All participants receive the same standard PIN number and therefore cannot be identified by this PIN.* Use of the PIN number is part of the informed consent process. A parent indicates informed consent by providing the PIN to the student or withholding of consent by not providing it to the student. This procedure has been approved by the University of Florida Institutional Review Board (**Protocol # 2007-U-1056).**

There is no risk associated with participating in this research. The benefits include having a clearer understanding of issues involving growing up Muslim in America.

I thank you in advance for your generous participation and contribution to the literature on Muslims and their needs in America.

In the tradition of the Muslim faith,
Jazakallahu Khair,
(May God grant you good)
/s/ Shifa Podikunju Hussain

Shifa Podikunju Hussain MEd, EdS,   Larry Loesch, PhD, NCC
Doctoral Candidate   Professor, Counselor Education
University of Florida   University of Florida
shifaph@ufl.edu or 352-339-4588

APPENDIX F MUSLIM YOUTH ACCULTURATION RATING
QUESTIONNAIRE (MYARQ) PAPER VERSION

Please provide the following information about yourself.

1. I am: male ○   female ○

2. My age is: _____ .

3. My ethnicity is: Indian ○   Arab ○   Other ○

    (Please
    specify)_____ .

4. I was born in: Unites States ○   Another count ○

    (Please specify) _____ .

5. The primary language spoken in my home   English ○   Urdu ○
    is:

                                              Arabic ○   Other ○

    (Please
    specify)_____ .

6. I have lived in the United States for _____ years.

7. My father has lived in the United States for _____ years.

8. My mother has lived in the United States for _____ years.

9. I am a Muslim: By Birth ○   By Conversion ○

10. I attend: Public   Islamic   Private
                      high school ○   high school ○   high school ○

                      Other ○   (Please
                                       specify)_____ .

Please read each of the following statements carefully and then mark the response that indicates the extent to which you agree with each statement as it applies to you personally. Please be as honest as possible. Remember that your personal responses will not be shared with anyone. Use the following scale for your response to each item:

SA means STRONGLY AGREE

A means AGREE

U means UNDECIDED

D means DISAGREE

SD means STRONGLY DISAGREE

(Appendix F continues on next page)

APPENDIX F (Continued)

		SA	A	U	D	SD
1.	Muslims should marry only within their religious group.	○	○	○	○	○
2.	Muslim teenagers should behave like non-Muslim	○	○	○	○	○
3.	I should change my Muslim name so that others can say my name easily.	○	○	○	○	○
4.	I am uncomfortable socializing with non-Muslim Americans.	○	○	○	○	○
5.	Some non-Muslim Americans don't like my culture and religion.	○	○	○	○	○
6.	Muslim women should be allowed personal freedom.	○	○	○	○	○
7.	Muslim boys and girls should be allowed to go on group dates with other Muslims.	○	○	○	○	○
8.	My marriage should be arranged by my family.	○	○	○	○	○
9.	Muslim children should always obey their parents.	○	○	○	○	○
10.	I should eat *halal* Muslim/ethnic food all the time.	○	○	○	○	○
11.	Muslim women should stay home and take care of their family when they get married.	○	○	○	○	○

(Appendix F continues on next page)

APPENDIX F (Continued)

		SA	A	U	D	SD
12.	The interests of my family should come before mine.	○	○	○	○	○
13.	Muslim parents know what is best for their children.	○	○	○	○	○
14.	Muslim girls and boys are not treated the same.	○	○	○	○	○
15.	Muslim men should make all the important decisions in the family.	○	○	○	○	○
16.	Muslim women should not work outside the home.	○	○	○	○	○
17.	I should celebrate Christmas just as I celebrate Eid.	○	○	○	○	○
18.	I and/or my family have been discriminated against because we are Muslims.	○	○	○	○	○
19.	Muslims should not be allowed to practice their daily prayers in school or at work.	○	○	○	○	○
20.	My closest friends are Muslim.	○	○	○	○	○
21.	Muslim children should look after the parents in their old age.	○	○	○	○	○
22.	I should attend the Mosque and weekend religious school.	○	○	○	○	○
23.	I wish I lived in a Muslim country, not in America.	○	○	○	○	○

(Appendix F continues on next page)

APPENDIX F (Continued)

		SA	A	U	D	SD
24.	I have been teased or insulted because I am Muslim.	O	O	O	O	O
25.	I am not happy living as a Muslim in America.	O	O	O	O	O
26.	Being Muslim has had a negative impact on me and/ or my family.	O	O	O	O	O
27.	I have both Muslim and American/non-Muslim friends.	O	O	O	O	O
28.	I don't feel accepted by my non-Muslim American friends because I am Muslim.	O	O	O	O	O
29.	Muslim boys should live with their parents until they marry.	O	O	O	O	O
30.	Muslim girls should live with their parents until they marry.	O	O	O	O	O
31.	It is okay for Muslim girls and boys to talk to each other whenever they want to.	O	O	O	O	O

APPENDIX G
MYARQ ITEM FREQUENCIES,
MEANS AND STANDARD DEVIATIONS

Item	Strongly Agree # (%)	Agree # (%)	Undecided # (%)	Disagree # (%)	Strongly Disagree # (%)	M	SD
1	8(5.6)	22(15.3)	19(13.2)	47(32.6)	48(33.3)	3.73	1.23
2	1(.7)	2(1.4)	17(11.8)	44(30.6)	80(55.6)	4.09	.80
3	1(.7)	3(2.1)	6(4.2)	33(27.1)	95(66.0)	4.56	.74
4	73(50.7)	53(36.8)	7(4.9)	3(2.1)	8(5.6)	1.75	1.04
5	12(8.3)	27(18.8)	22(15.3)	71(49.3)	12(8.3)	3.31	1.12
6	71(49.7)	45(31.5)	16(11.2)	8(5.6)	3(2.1)	1.79	.99
7	15(10.5)	42(29.4)	29(20.3)	27(18.9)	30(21.0)	3.10	1.32
8	56(38.9)	31(21.5)	28(19.4)	22(15.3)	7(4.9)	2.26	1.26
9	2(1.4)	7(4.9)	10(6.9)	55(38.2)	70(48.6)	4.28	.90
10	8(5.6)	19(13.3)	17(11.9)	29(20.3)	70(49.0)	3.94	1.28
11	51(35.4)	46(31.9)	30(20.8)	12(8.3)	5(3.5)	2.13	1.10
12	3(2.1)	21(14.6)	38(26.4)	64(44.4)	18(12.5)	3.51	.96
13	0(0)	14(9.8)	28(19.6)	67(46.9)	34(23.8)	3.85	.90
14	42(29.0)	51(29.4)	17(11.9)	26(18.2)	7(4.9)	2.34	1.22
15	41(28.5)	59(41.0)	16(11.1)	19(13.2)	9(6.3)	2.28	1.19
16	84(58.7)	47(32.9)	8(5.6)	2(1.4)	2(1.4)	1.54	.79
17	5(3.5)	9(6.3)	19(13.2)	31(21.5)	80(55.6)	4.19	1.10
18	16(11.1)	49(34.0)	14(9.7)	51(35.4)	14(9.7)	2.99	1.24
19	47(32.6)	11(7.6)	13(9.0)	35(24.3)	38(26.4)	3.04	1.64
20	12(8.3)	29(20.1)	14(9.7)	43(29.9)	46(31.9)	3.57	1.34
21	0(0)	2(1.4)	4(2.8)	35(24.3)	103(71.5)	4.66	.60
22	0(0)	7(4.9)	21(14.7)	74(51.7)	41(28.7)	4.04	.80
23	37(25.7)	58(40.3)	23(16.0)	17(11.8)	9(6.3)	2.33	1.16
24	30(21.0)	38(26.6)	13(9.1)	47(32.9)	15(10.5)	2.85	1.36
25	84(58.3)	40(27.8)	14(9.7)	1(.7)	5(3.5)	1.63	.94
26	81(56.6)	46(32.2)	7(4.9)	6(4.2)	3(2.1)	1.63	.92
27	91(62.8)	46(31.9)	1(.7)	3(2.1)	3(2.1)	1.48	.80
28	58(40.3)	22(15.3)	10(6.9)	24(16.7)	30(20.8)	2.63	1.63
29	23(16.0)	42(29.2)	27(18.8)	31(21.5)	21(14.6)	2.90	1.32
30	21(14.6)	34(23.6)	21(14.6)	37(25.7)	31(21.5)	3.16	1.39
31	13(9.0)	25(17.4)	25(17.4)	47(32.6)	34(23.6)	3.44	1.27

REFERENCES

Abdo, G. (2006). *Mecca and main street: Muslim Life in America after 9/11.* New York, NY: Oxford University Press.

Abudabbeh, N. (2005). Arab families: an overview. In M. McGoldrick, J. Giordano, & N. Garcia-Preto (Eds.), *Ethnicity and family therapy* (pp. 423–436.). New York, NY: Guilford Press.

Ahmed, S. (2004). Religiosity, identity, and pro-social values and behavior: A study of Muslim youth. *Dissertation Abstracts International, 64,* 12–B.

Alghorani, M. A. (2003). Identity, acculturation, and adjustment of high school Muslim Students in Islamic schools in the U.S.A. (Doctoral dissertation, University of Texas at Austin, 2003). *Dissertation Abstracts International, 64,* 12.

Ali, S. R., Liu, W. M., & Humedian, M. (2004). Islam 101: Understanding the religion and therapy implications. *Professional Psychology: Research and Practice, 35,* 635–642.

Amer, M. M. (2005) Arab American mental health in the post-September 11 era: Acculturation, stress, and coping. *Dissertation Abstracts International, 66,* 4–B.

Association of Statisticians of American Religious Bodies. (2012). *2010 U.S. Religion Census: Religious Congregations & Membership Study.* Retrieved from http://www.rcms2010.org/

Bagby, I. (Ed.) (1994). *Muslim resource guide.* Fountain Valley, CA: Islamic Resource Institute.

Berry, J. W. (1980). Acculturation as varieties of adaptation. In A. M. Padilla (Ed.), *Acculturation: Theory, model, and some new findings* (pp. 9–26). Boulder, CO: Westview Press.

Berry, J. W. (1998). Acculturation and health: Theory and research. In S. S. Kazarian & D. R. Evans (Eds.), *Cultural clinical psychology: Theory, research and practice* (pp. 39–57). New York, NY: Oxford University Press.

Berry, J. W., Kim, U., Minde, T., & Mok, D. (1987). Comparative studies of acculturative stress. *nternational Migration Review, 21,* 491–511.

Berry, J. W., Kim, U., Power, S., Young, M., & Bujaki, M. (1989). Acculturation attitudes in plural societies. *Applied Psychology: An International Review, 38,* 185–206.

Berry, J. W., Phinney, J. S., Kwak, K., & Sam, D. L. (2006a). Introduction: Goals and research framework for studying immigrant youth. In J. W. Berry, J. S. Phinney, D. L. Sam, & P. Vedder (Eds.), *Immigrant youth in cultural transition: Acculturation, identity, and adaptation across national contexts* (pp. 1–14). Mahwah, NJ: Lawrence Erlbaum Associates.

Berry, J. W., Phinney, J. S., Sam, D. L., & Vedder, P. (2006b). *Immigrant youth in cultural transition: Acculturation, identity, and adaptation across national contexts.* Mahwah, NJ: Lawrence Erlbaum Associates.

Berry, J. W., & Sam, D. L. (1997). Acculturation and adaptation. In J. W. Berry, M. A. Segall, & C. Kagitubasi (Eds.), *Handbook of cross-cultural psychology: Social-behaviors and application* (pp. 291–326). Boston, MA: Allyn & Bacon.

Berry, J. W., Trimble, J. E., & Olmeda, E. L. (1986). Assessment of acculturation. In W. J. Lonner & J. W. Berry (Eds.), *Field methods in cross-cultural research* (pp. 291–349). Beverly Hills, CA: Sage.

Brilliant, J. J. (2000). Issues in counseling immigrant college students. *Community College Journal of Research and Practice, 24*, 577–586.

Carter, R. B. (1999). Counseling Muslim children in school settings. *Professional School Counselor, 2*, 183–189.

Creswell, J. W. (2002). *Educational research: Planning, conducting, and evaluating quantitative and qualitative research*. Upper Saddle River, NJ: Merrill Prentice Hall.

Dugsin, R. (2001). Conflict and healing in family experience of second-generation emigrants from India living in North America. *Family Process, 40*, 233–241.

El-Badry, S., & Poston D. L., Jr. (1990). Fitting in: Socio-economic attainment patterns of foreign-born Egyptians in the U.S. *Sociological Inquiry, 60*, 142–157.

El-Islam, M. F. (1983). Cultural change and intergenerational relationships in Arabian families. *International Journal of Family Psychiatry, 4*, 321–329.

El-Sayed, Y. A. (1986). The successive-unsettled transitions of migration and their impact on postpartum concerns of Arab immigrant women. *Dissertation Abstracts, 47*(06), 2370B. (AAC 8619571).

Faragallah, M. H., Schumm, W. R., & Webb, F. J. (1997). Acculturation of Arab-American immigrants: An exploratory study. *Journal of Comparative Family Studies, 28*, 182–203.

Ghuman, P. A. S. (2003). *Double loyalties: South Asian adolescents in the West*. Cardiff, England: University of Wales Press.

Hedayat-Diba, Z. (2000). Psychotherapy with Muslims. In P. S. Richards & A. E. Bergin (Eds.), *Handbook of psychotherapy and religious diversity* (pp. 289–314). Washington, DC: American Psychological Association.

Heppner, P. P., Kivlighan, D. M., & Wampold, B. E. (1992). *Research design in counseling*. Pacific Grove, CA: Brooks/Cole.

Ibrahim, F. A., & Ohnishi, H. (1997). Asian American identity development: A culture specific model for South Asian Americans. *Journal of Multicultural Counseling and Development, 25*, 34–51.

Islamic Society of North America. (n.d.). *Mission and vision*. Retrieved from http://www.isna.net/mission-and-vision.html

Kim, B. S., Brenner, B. R., Liang, C. T. H., & Asay, P. A. (2003). A qualitative study of adaptation experience of 1.5 generation Asian Americans. *Cultural Diversity and Ethnic Minority Psychology, 9*, 156–170.

Kosmin, B. A., & Lachman, S. P. (1993). *One nation under God: Religion in contemporary American society*. New York, NY: Harmony.

Lee, E. (Ed.). (1997). Working with Asian Americans: A guide for clinicians. New York, NY: Guilford Press.

Lee, R. M., Choe, J., Kim, G., & Ngo, V. (2000). Constructions of the Asian American family conflicts scale. *Journal of Counseling Psychology, 47*, 211–222.

Mansour, S. S. (2000). *The correlation between ethnic identity and self-esteem among Arab American Muslim adolescents* (Unpublished master's thesis). West Virginia University, Morgantown, Virginia.

Musleh, N. E. (1983). Effects of acculturation of the proxemic behavior of Arab-American high school students. *Dissertation Abstracts, 44*(12), 3590A. (AAC 8405998).

Myrick, R. D. (1997). *Developmental guidance and counseling: A practical approach*. Minneapolis, MN: Educational Media.

Numan, F. H. (1992). *The Muslim population in the United States: A brief statement.* Washington DC: American Muslim Council.

Penaloza, L. (1994). Altravesando Fronteras/Border Crossings: A critical ethnographic exploration of the consumer acculturation of Mexican immigrants. *Journal of Consumer Research, 21,* 32–54.

Pew Research Center. (2007). *Muslim Americans: Middle class and mostly mainstream.* Retrieved from http://pewresearch.org/pubs/483/Muslim-Americans

Pew Research Center's Forum on Religion & Public Life. (2011, January). *The future of the Global Muslim Population: Projections for 2010–2030.* Retrieved from http://www.pewforum.org/uploadedFiles/Topics/Religious_Affiliation/Muslim/FutureGlobalMuslimPopulation-WebPDF-Feb10.pdf

Phinney, J. S. (1990). Ethnic identity in adolescents and adults: Review of research. *Psychological Bulletin, 108,* 499–514.

Phinney, J. S., Berry, J. W., Sam, D. L., & Vedder, P. (2006a). Understanding immigrant youth: Conclusions and implications. In J. W. Berry, J. S. Phinney, D. L. Sam, & P. Vedder (Eds.), *Immigrant youth in cultural transition: Acculturation, identity, and adaptation across national contexts* (pp. 211–234). Mahwah, NJ: Lawrence Erlbaum Associates.

Phinney, J. S., Berry, J. W., Vedder, P., & Liebkind, K. (2006b). The Acculturation Experience: Attitudes, identities, and behaviors of immigrant youth. In J. W. Berry, J. S. Phinney, D. L. Sam, & P. Vedder (Eds.), *Immigrant youth in cultural transition: Acculturation, identity, and adaptation across national contexts* (pp. 71–116). Mahwah, NJ: Lawrence Erlbaum Associates.

Portes, A., & Rumbaut, R. (2001). *Legacies: The story of the immigrant second generation.* Berkeley, CA: University of California Press.

Project MAPS. (2001). Project MAPS: Muslims in American Public Square. *American Muslim Poll.* Retrieved from http://www.projectmaps.com/PMReport.htm

Redfield, R., Linton, R., & Herskovits, M. T. (1936). Memorandum for the study of acculturation. *American Anthropologist, 38,* 149–152.

Roysircar, G. (2003). Religious differences: Psychological and sociopolitical aspects of counseling. *International Journal for the Advancement of Counseling, 25,* 255–267.

Sam, D. L., & Berry, J. W. (1995). Acculturation stress among young immigrants in Norway. *Scandinavian Journal of Psychology, 36,* 10–24.

Shavelson, R. J. (1996). *Statistical reasoning for the social sciences* (3rd ed.). Boston, MA: Allyn and Bacon.

Shaw, A. (2000). *Kinship and continuity: Pakistani families in Britain.* Amsteldijk, The Netherlands: Harwood Academic Publishers.

Sodowsky, G. R., Kwan, K. K., & Pannu, R. (1995). Ethnic identity of Asians in the United States. In J. G. Ponterotto, J. M. Casas, L. A. Suzuki, & C. M. Alexander (Eds.), *Handbook of multicultural counseling* (pp. 155–180). Thousand Oaks, CA: Sage.

Sodowsky, G. R., Lai, E. W. M., & Plake, B. (1991). Moderating effects of sociocultural variables on acculturation attitudes of Hispanics and Asian Americans. *Journal of Counseling and Development, 70,* 194–204.

Swaiden, Z., Marshall, K. P., & Smith, J. R. (2001). *Acculturation strategies: The case of the Muslim minority in the United States.* Paper presented at the meeting of the Society for Marketing Advances, New Orleans, LA.

Szapocznik, J., & Kurtines, W. M. (1993). Family psychology and cultural diversity: Opportunities for theory, research, and applications. *American Psychologist, 48*, 400–407.

Talbani. A., & Hasanali, P. (2000). Adolescent females between tradition and modernity: Gender role socialization in South Asian immigrant culture. *Journal of Adolescence, 23*, 615–627.

Timimi, S. B. (1995). Adolescence in immigrant Arab families. *Psychotherapy: Theory, Research, Practice, Training. 32*, 141–149.

U.S. Bureau of the Census. (2003, February). The foreign-born population in the United States: March 2002. *Current Population Reports*, 20–539.

U.S. State Department. (2001). *Fact sheet: Islam in the United States.* Retrieved from http://usinfo.state.gov/usa/islam/fact2/htm

Wakil, S. P., Siddique, C. M., & Wakil, F. A. (1981). Between two cultures: A study in socialization of children of immigrants. *Journal of Marriage and the Family, 43*, 929–940.

Ying, Y. W. (1998). Educational program for families on intergenerational conflict. In E. Kramer, S. Ivey, & Y. Ying (Eds.), *Immigrant women's health: Problems and solutions* (pp. 282–294). San Francisco, CA: Jossey-Bass.

CHAPTER 4

UNDERSTANDING THE CULTURAL CAPITAL OF LEARNERS OF MUSLIM DESCENT

Mayra C. Daniel and Alexis Ball

ABSTRACT

This chapter focuses on the schooling of Muslim children in the United States. The post-9/11 era has presented numerous challenges to learners of Muslim descent. Whether their status is that of native-born citizens of the United States or they are recent immigrants, these learners confront issues related to the mismatch between the culture that their parents have inculcated in them and the norms of mainstream U.S. culture. Conflicts are deeply rooted in religious, cultural, and familial perspectives, and frequently evidenced in the learners' unsuccessful efforts to understand their teachers' expectations. This chapter is meant to introduce the reader to issues and solutions that will assure all learners of Muslim descent and their families feel a valued and integral part of the educational system. In addition, this chapter will highlight ways that teachers at kindergarten through secondary school can meet the challenge to everyone's benefit.

Growing Up Between Two Cultures: Problems and Issues of Muslim Children, pp. 89–116

While Europeans, Africans, and Asians have always lived in worlds where interpersonal interactions have been conducted in a variety of languages, citizens of the United States (U.S.) have resided in a much more sterile monolingual ambiance. It is highly likely that the privileging of the English language began when the first person of nonindigenous blood set foot in North America. The U.S. as a political entity and later country came into existence when immigrants from Europe arrived to this continent seeking either religious or political freedom. They were people who needed a new affiliation and a safe haven. The history books portray these Europeans as settlers willing to undertake any and all needed sacrifices to survive. For many, this required giving up their language of origin to communicate in English. The history books tell us that for the first immigrants, freedom of religion meant setting aside their roots. As colonization of the native peoples occurred, the greater effort was to impart, forcibly if necessary, the English language to all rather than learn mutual respect for languages and ways of being. Respect only flowed in one direction. This continued in the 20th century when those who entered the U.S. via Ellis Island were forced to Anglicize their names and expected to subordinate their cultural practices.

The reality is that immigrants never gave up their roots and ways of being even when they asked their children to speak only English. They did not do so when the U.S. consisted of 13 colonies, and they certainly are not agreeing to this in 2013. Many who long ago entered New York Harbor seemed to be born anew as U.S. citizens yet they never actually gave up their multicultural identities. In fact, a heightened sense of who they were was visible in all who contributed to forming the linguistically and culturally diverse boroughs of the Big Apple, neighborhoods such as Little Italy and Pilsen in Chicago, and Miami's Cuban community.

In the 19th and 20th centuries the idea was that the U.S. as a country become a melting pot united by one common language (Spring, 2012). Colonization meant to give birth to a nation where citizens spoke, studied through, and expressed political views solely in English. Luckily, for the strength of this nation, the U.S. never became the proverbial melting pot. First generation immigrants and subsequent generations have persisted in their efforts to represent those who came before them. They have held tightly to identities that are hybrid and defined by the multiplicity of their languages, cultures, religious practices, and personal ethics. Nevertheless, acceptance of cultural hybridity continues to be a challenge because even in this millennium many deny the existence and benefits of the country's cultural pluralism. Mandates such as the No Child Left Behind Act (United States Government, 2002), that English language learners (ELs) acquire English in less time than research suggests is possible, ignore learners' and families' cultural capital and negate the fluidity of cognitive processes across languages (Garcia, 2011). Misunderstandings may be greater for those who practice Islam because assumptions about what it means to be Muslim have been tainted by the actions of a few. Generalizations and isolationist attitudes based on fear of terrorism permeate even the most liberal academic circles.

The multiethnic linguistic landscape within the U.S. is changing the composition of the country's student populations at levels K-12. As well, it is influencing choices for instructional paradigms implemented in schools. Teachers are aware that methodologies used in schools and family outreach efforts have not been appropriate for all learners. One assumption often made is that all individuals from one part of the world hold the same viewpoints, learn the same way, practice one religion, and speak identical languages. The reality is that geographical borders within a country or continent do not mean all citizens speak the same language or hold parallel identities. In the U.S. educational system it has become clear that no single pedagogical approach works for all learners even when they hold familial ties to a single region of the world. Assumptions based on cultural practices, religions, and the languages of many immigrant groups are unreliable. For K–12 students and especially for those of Muslim backgrounds, it is vital teachers be well informed before making instructional decisions and interacting with families. Communication patterns differ across cultures and there is no room for generalizations in the Muslim world (Feghali, 1997).

The specific make-up of cultural groups within a country shapes the behaviors of its people before and after immigration. In the Muslim world there is a wide range of differences in cultural heritage. In the current millennium cultural dynamic is an influential component of how life is lived and what schooling expectations parents have for their children. Muslim majority countries are not limited to one region of the world as they extend to Europe, Asia, Africa, and the Middle East. This is why for learners from these countries as well as for immigrants to the United States, negotiations between religion and culture always pose tensions. No attitudes or situations can ever be addressed from a purely cultural or religious stance without a consideration of historical influences. In the United States, the post-9/11 era has presented numerous challenges to learners of Muslim descent. These obstacles have been mostly due to misinformation of who a practicing Muslim is, and what he/she believes.

Avoidable mismatches arise for English language learners who speak Arabic as well as for heritage language speakers and native-born U.S. citizens who practice Islam when teachers are unfamiliar with the nature and variety of religious practices, histories, languages, and cultural norms of these learners. Issues related to religious, cultural, and familial perspectives are frequently evidenced in the learners' unsuccessful efforts to understand their monolingual, non-Muslim teachers' expectations. Teachers need to investigate who their students are in order to develop an informed awareness of the cultural norms that guide their students evolving identities (Au, 2002; Skutnabb-Kangas, 1999).

Knowledge helps teachers provide learners the opportunities they need to negotiate the mismatch that arises when the customs of the home deem one type of behavior as proper and the school another. Even subtle differences contribute to challenges in communication that may impact academic success. It is essential that all teachers become aware that even learners from the same country may speak different languages, practice different religions, and hold a variety of vastly different cultural capital. Whether students are the first immigrants or are born in the U.S. and speak the family's heritage language, the languages they use to learn and the ways they use these is influenced by culture.

In this chapter we address challenges related to cultural norms and languages that may go unacknowledged yet are at the root of miscommunication in schools and communities (Andriessen, Phalet, & Lens, 2006). We focus mainly on interpretations of the *Qur'an*, Islamic values, and rules of behavior practiced by Middle Eastern Arabs. Our goal is to introduce the questioning reader to issues and solutions that will assure that all learners of Muslim descent and their families feel a valued and integral part of the U.S. educational system. In addition, the chapter will highlight ways that teachers at all levels can meet the challenge of linguistic, cultural, and religious diversity to everyone's benefit.

We are cognizant that there are many cultures in the Islamic world and this chapter will only address a few. Our description of Islamic values and rules of behavior may not be followed or practiced in these modern times by Muslims living in cultural contexts other than the Arab Middle East. For example, a doctoral student who studied with me in the United States (Mayra) over a 2-month period last winter and is a devout Indonesian Muslim, is completing her studies in a city far from her home. Each week she flies to a different island in her country and leaves her 2-year-old son with her husband and the child's maternal grandmother. She must do this in order to go where there is a university. One of the authors of this article (Alexis) is a practicing Muslim who chooses not to wear a head covering. Clearly, religious traditions are influenced by the times in which we live yet the tenets of the faith remain unchanged for those who practice Islam. As a teacher in one of my classes (Mayra) said. "I need to investigate my students' backgrounds because it is in their histories that I can learn about their present. When students feel supported, the world is theirs for the taking" (M. Pitts, personal communication, July 2012).

DEMOGRAPHICS OF MUSLIMS IN THE UNITED STATES

Data collected by the U.S. Census Bureau does not include information about religious affiliation. This means there is no accurate numerical data reported about the size of the Muslim community. The most reliable information is that based on an analysis of Homeland Security data from the Pew Forum on Religion and Culture (2011, January). Their estimates reflect a figure of 2.75 million Muslims in the country. By 2030 the Muslim population is projected to more than double, and 53% of this number is anticipated to be under age 30. School age children are expected to increase from 500,000 in 2010 to 1.8 million in 2030. Young children of less than 4 years of age currently number less than 200,000. This age group is anticipated to reach 650,000 by 2030.

Muslim immigration to the U.S. has been linked to political events and reflects immigrants' need to escape intolerable conditions. Hence, the largest increases in Muslim immigrants took place in the years between 1992 and 2010. Figures reflect a steady and sometimes staggering increase from certain countries per year. The numbers of immigrants from Bangladesh went from 3,000 to 11,000, from Somalia the change was tenfold, from 1,000–10,000, and for Pakistanis the increase was from 9,000 to 15,000. Immigrants from several other countries slightly more than doubled; Iraqis grew from 2,000 to 5,000, Moroccans from 1,000 to 4,000 and Sudanese from less than 1,000 to 2,000 (Pew Forum, 2011).

Islamophobia and Religious Freedom

Islamophobia is a term that has developed over the last several years to refer to the unfounded fear of anything Islamic or Muslim. Lean, Rehab, and Hafez (2013) define it as more than just fear causing the actions of bigots, but the action itself. In this view, the action is characterized by *misattribution* of the actions of one or very few as Islamic practices, *generalization* of an impression of an individual to the entire community, and the *reduction* of the wealth of identity held by a community to a few simplistic, erroneous bullet points, thereby erasing that identity to replace it with ones' own misheld beliefs.

While these three characteristics could theoretically be applied to any case of religious intolerance, regardless of the religion, they certainly characterize many well-known incidents involving bigotry toward Muslims. The mere mention of terms like *jihad* (a term which refers to the Islamic requirement of *service*), *Islamic fundamentalist* (a person who views religious texts in a literal way), and *Sharia law* (the system of religious rules and ways of life mandated by Islam) provoke a widely negative reaction among some who have little understanding of Islamic principles. The widespread misinformation about Muslims as well as other religious minorities and their varied practices affects and contaminates the atmosphere of our society. Limited exposure of non-Muslims and Muslims to each other has at times created mistrust and misunderstanding.

As a result of this discomfort with Islamic principles based on ignorance, ethnocentricity or religious intolerance, reactions have ranged from legal and legislative policies to heavy social pressure and criticism. The argument against these reactions rests on our country's founding principle of religious freedom. The two-pronged legal view of religious tolerance and respect for conscientious scruples includes the belief espoused by 17th century American philosopher Roger Williams that certain behaviors should be accommodated or exempted due to conscience, so for example, Menonites or Quakers were exempted from military service. The other aspect of the U.S. legal view includes the idea that no law should be persecutory, an idea supported by the writings of John Locke (Nussbaum, 2012). So, in the tradition of the American legal system, laws must always be as extensively accommodating to a person's beliefs as the nation's interests permit and the maximum liberties compatible should be afforded to all.

One of the most profound experiences in the life of a person is their experience with schooling. If this experience impedes the ability of a student to incorporate all aspects of his or her personality, life success itself will be severely affected. As Muslim students increasingly become a part of U.S. schools, it is important to understand that the risk of alienation from the school environment is high if administration, staff, and teachers, make no effort to address the biases in personnel, students and families. All students deserve access to a safe and nurturing educational environment. Comments that are critical and judgmental of a student's value system based on ignorance may prevent Muslim students from navigating internal conflicts present in multiple schema. Teachers who make efforts to understand the students' point of view and show sensitivity, will offer learners a safe-haven from the doubt about whether they are accepted socially and what compromises of identity should be made to gain that acceptance.

PREPARING INTERCULTURALLY COMPETENT TEACHERS

ELs' struggles at school are infrequently due to difficulties understanding complex ideas related to the learning in the content areas. U.S. educators are in the middle of a paradigm shift because the stark reality of children not progressing is precipitating change. Not only are the majority of teachers not trained to work with linguistically diverse learners (Reeves, 2006), they have no understanding of the cognitive advantages of growing up in multilingual environments (Bialystok, 2001; Boekmann, Aalto, Atanasoska, & Lamb, 2011). More often than not, what poses challenges for immigrants originates in mismatches between the students' and the teacher's expectations. We posit that the onus of responsibility to eliminate these mismatches rests on the teacher's shoulders and not on the students'.

It is the teacher who is in charge of assuring the classroom is a welcoming place where all learners can experience a sense of belonging. In many ways teachers host the children as they welcome them to the classroom and the school community. The classroom is a teacher's home away from home. The culturally sensitive teacher creates a learning community that is appropriately designed for the age and cultural norms of all the learners. While at first glance the task of establishing the right kind of classroom ambiance may appear easy to accomplish, this is not the case. A classroom that rocks is like a good party where everyone is engaged in conversations that enroll and enlighten. In many schools learners do not hear the music of their soul. A teacher who wishes to establish positive relationships with students must work to get to know the implicit unseen components of the learners' cultural background. In addition, the teacher has to grasp what he/she brings to the picture that may promote or discourage intercultural understanding (Sercu, 2011). Learners who sense criticism from society, or a lack of respect, will naturally feel alienated and isolated. One Muslim-American student remembers,

> By high school, I learned to be proud of my ethnic identity, but it was a different story in elementary. I felt I could not share anything about my home life at school such as food I ate, my religious practices and holidays, clothes I wore, or the language I spoke. No one would be able to relate because the other students and teachers all had the same culture/religion. Explaining these differences to my peers did not bring any appreciation but rather criticism. Teachers also never inquired to try to tie in different perspectives by asking the multi-cultural students about their culture.

It is up to teachers to make certain this does not happen.

Advocacy begins when practicing educators and/or teacher candidates explore what constitutes their classroom culture (Nieto & Bode, 2012). This must be done in a formal systematic manner that scaffolds the examination of delicate and critical issues. Once teachers become aware of the injustices that abound in schools, they work to stop these. The curricular transformations needed in schools are a vision that is formed in the minds of educators who explore, identify, and confront societal issues without flinching. Progressive educators aim to transform schools into places where the curriculum is multicultural and inclusive. They want to work in schools where cultural diversity as evidenced in language, religion, race, and ethnicity are acknowledged, openly discussed, and celebrated. Teachers whose eyes are opened create productive spaces in schools because they select curriculum that opens room for dialogue and third spaces (Bhabha, 1994).

The reality of life in schools in the U.S. is that not all teachers are prepared to plan a curriculum that is inclusive. The result is classrooms where students do not see themselves, their lives, families, and customs reflected in the books they are asked to read. As well, examples used as the means to present curricula are often woefully inadequate for the learner who sees a glass half full rather than half empty. Culturally responsive instruction is needed because it provides scaffolds to learning. If we indeed want to eliminate intolerance, we must embark all current and future teachers on a journey that opens their eyes to that which is not overtly visible. We need for them to understand the invisible colors of their diverse student populations. We must involve them in an honest examination of their level of intercultural sensitivity (Bennett, 2010).

Teacher educators in programs of teacher preparation hold the power to create the momentum needed to change schools. Social justice requires the teacher understand the specificity of context (Gay, 2010). At our university teachers who enroll in the multicultural education methods course complete a self-identity exploration. They examine who they are and reflect upon what they discovered in their examination. They consider the factors that may have contributed to the person they are and to the philosophical stances they hold as adults. The task of taking oneself apart and objectively analyzing the reasons one holds any point of view is key to deeply analyzing and understanding attitudes related to culture. After teachers do this many seem to acquire a great degree of openness while others simply allow a little light to filter through. Nevertheless, both instances lead to breakthroughs in awareness and an increased level of consciousness. At the end of the semester the teachers write a personal philosophy of multicultural education. At this point in this chapter it seems appropriate to share a few verbatim statements from philosophies written by practicing teachers (see Table 4.1). These comments serve as proof that a course focused on learning about cultures is worthwhile. We divide the comments into three categories; what teachers say they now know, what they plan to do in the future, and the ways they will change the curriculum.

Funds of Knowledge

As educators, we know that understanding and utilizing a child's funds of knowledge in the treatment of that child, the building of curriculum for that child, and the interactions with that child's parents and family are an important vehicle to student success (González, Moll, & Amanti, 2005).

Table 4.1.   Teachers' Comments

What Teachers Know	What Teachers Plan to Do	Ways Teachers Will Change the Curriculum
I have learned that cultural differences can play a role on how students and their parents view education and affect how they perform in school.	I will create an atmosphere of mutual respect where students feel at ease to share their views as well as listen to and question the views of others. It is through these experiences that students will come to appreciate and value the diversity of opinions that they will encounter throughout their lives.	It is my responsibility to instill in students a democratic sense of being, practicing the skills of questioning, dialogue, listening, the sense of the common good, a passion for public affairs in older students, the capacity to revise former thoughts or beliefs, and a belief in the moral equality and potential of all people.
Much of the history and other school topics have been told from the view of one perspective (generally the perspective of the dominant culture).	I will teach acceptance of and tolerance of all cultures, races, religions, ethnicities, and building all students' self-confidence and sense of self-worth.	Students should research and discuss current events as well as propose solutions to the world's problems.
In this class I learned that I can teach and promote multiculturalism every day with ease.	My job is to show students that we can live in cultural pluralism.	I had never considers that the materials I used may have served to reinforce stereotypes instead of transcend them.
Educators need to discourage ethnocentric thinking and create intercultural sensitivity and awareness.	Promoting social justice includes providing families with the foundational tools that can guide their children to social, emotional, and academic success.	Teachers must educate students about media bias.

When a child's background and cultural practices are intertwined with that child's religious environment, this presents the need for teachers to have an understanding of children's religious practices. Teachers who have been educated and raised in the U.S. majority Christian culture may have a more intuitive understanding of Christian student beliefs than those of religious minority students. As a result, there is a necessity for teachers to learn about and develop sensitivity to a variety of minority religious beliefs and practices. As with variant cultural practices, this can pose a challenge for teachers who are not untouched by the dominant ethno/religiocentric environment present in the United States. However, the inspiring care and love that teachers have for students makes such growth, sensitivity and open-mindedness a reality for many teachers with deeply held beliefs of their own. As mentioned elsewhere in this paper, Muslim students normally have multiple influences such as religion, cultural background, language background, ideological particularities, socioeconomic status and a particular family worldview, often stemming from the intersection of all of these elements. Any discussion of religion for a Muslim is a fine-tuned negotiation between Islam and these other aspects of their identity. The purely religious Islamic view is that religion takes precedence over culture but that is seldom the reality. For that reason, a sensitive approach is needed when considering the use of these suggestions, and validation of teacher choices should be achieved through observation of and/or discussion with the student and his or her family.

This discussion of themes and beliefs present in Islam is meant to be helpful for teachers to value and comprehend their students' religious context and can only be understood through the foundation of sensitivity discussed above. With that basis, there are some generally common themes and practices within the Islamic environment to which many Muslim children are exposed. This means that understanding those religious themes may help serve Muslim children better in schooling. Teachers may say, "But I am prohibited from using religion in my classroom." That is not what is proposed here. There are themes in religious texts dealing with science, social studies, language, art, and music that influence how Muslim students experience the classroom. Because education in the Islamic context is considered a religious obligation, the *Qur'an* (Holy Book) and Hadith (accounts of words and actions of the Prophet Mohamed) contain many references to learning, reading, writing, content area knowledge, and so forth. It is common practice to expose Muslim children to these texts at home through oral discussion and direct reading and in religious classes held outside of school time. Several types of educational references can be discussed; content area knowledge, learning strategies and disciplinary practices, attitudes about education and the education of women.

The encouragement of literacy and education for both women and men within religious texts is well-understood throughout the Muslim world. The following text is an example of this belief. "Whosoever (male or female) follows a path to seek knowledge therein, Allah will make easy for him (or her) a path to Paradise" (Hussein, 2007).

Use of content area knowledge that may be familiar to students as a result of their study of the *Qur'an*, Hadith, and other religious texts, can provide teachers with the types of themes Muslim children may already have knowledge of as a result of direct learning or household discussion. Scientific information about bees and honey (Qur'an 16:68–69), the water cycle (Qur'an 23:18, 30:24, 39:21), oceans (Qur'an 24:40) and the development of life from them (Qur'an 21:30, 24:45) tectonic plate shift (Qur'an 27:88), fetal development (Qur'an 23:12–13), astronomy (Qur'an 21:33, 36:38) and the Big Bang Theory (Qur'an 21:30), are mentioned in the *Qur'an*. The tradition of story-telling both orally and in the written word which includes (in Arabic) literary elements of poetry and prose is used extensively in the discussion and reading of religious texts (Khadra Jayyusi, 1997). The study of Islamic history and politics, specifically one of the earliest democratic systems called *Shura* council (a council of decision-makers appointed by the community) and the discussion of economic terms like interest, usury, and regulations for banking and business to address ethical business dealings, are addressed in the texts. In addition, delineation of use of images gave rise to artistic practices encompassing calligraphy and abstract forms for artistic expression and the development of new artistic media and architectural methods, especially during the period of Muslim Spain from about A.D. 800–1500 A.D. (Khadra Jayyusi, 1997), but continuing to the 21st century in various locations. Perceived limitations on music by some contributed to the creation of *Anasheeds*, a system of chants usually without musical instruments. In the present day these sometimes include drums or digital music synthesizing and other instruments. The words used in the chants refer usually to Islamic beliefs, history, and religion, as well as current events.

As a result of perceived prohibitions in Islamic texts of certain types of images or music, students in art and music classes may experience conflict with some types of content. Again, keeping in mind that students come from a variety of homes, and understanding that many Muslims enjoy art and music of all types, it is important to remember that discomfort with certain content, when it occurs, is not meant as a form of rebellion but can be a source of true conflict where the students' and families' values are being challenged. This does not mean that art and music instructors must not teach these subjects to Muslim students, or that they must change the curriculum to completely conform to their beliefs, but it does require that teachers show sensitivity and select content that is appropriate. Even for those students whose worldview does not limit participation, it is wonderful to showcase art and music from their country, culture, language or religion of origin.

There are also elements of religious practice that can are part of the funds of knowledge of Muslim students. Prayers (*Salat*), which happen at dawn (not sunrise), midday, afternoon, sunset and worldview, mark the passage of time in a unique way and may provide a heightened awareness of characteristics of certain times of day, the movement of the sun and the moon and so forth. In addition, prayers are done facing Mecca (Northeast from this location), so from a particular location *Qibla* (direction of prayer) must be determined, resulting in an awareness of direction as well. Memorization of prayers and Qur'anic verses is encouraged even in small children, so this skill may be helpful to students in learning new facts. Fasting (*Sawm*) provides an opportunity to think about nutrition and dietary needs in relation to one's physical composition and to focus on maintenance and circumstance of the needy. Because Muslims come from many different countries, it is no surprise that in the United States, mosques are used by people of diverse nationalities. Islamic thought encourages multicultural interaction, supports interracial marriage, and views all races and ethnicities as equal (Qur'an 49:13). Language learning is also encouraged (Qur'an 30:22). This in turn encourages individuals who visit those mosques to interact with people from a variety of countries, regions and language groups, allowing for contact with various cultures and ideas. While cultural groups within mosques do separate themselves to a certain extent, worship and dialogue often takes place multiculturally and multilingually, exposing Muslim children to a highly diverse environment in comparison with some of their peers. One Muslim American third grader names the languages and understands some words in them, and names countries of origin and flags. Languages such as Urdu, Indonesian, Hindi, Arabic, Berber, French, Portuguese, Spanish, Malaysian, Chinese, Korean and countries and flags such as Palestine, Israel, Saudi Arabia, Indonesia, Pakistan, India, Morocco, Algeria, Libya, Egypt, United Arab Emirates, Mexico, Puerto Rico, and Brazil among others. The student says he learned much of this information through personal contact with people from these countries.

These examples of funds of knowledge are not exhaustive or automatic, they simply provide a vehicle to discuss the wealth of information that members of this group may hold. It is up to the teacher to determine if these examples apply to individual students, or if other things not mentioned apply. Certainly, this method of looking at students' cultural capital could be used for other religious groups as well. The most important thing is to observe behavior and then consider what might be the root of it, and what information it might offer about an individual or a group (González, Moll, & Amanti, 2005).

PLURILINGUALISM AND IDENTITY

In this millennium, with the ease of global communication that current technologies provide, students live in a world where boundaries are more fluid than ever before. This fluidity makes it easier for speakers to interact using the different languages that those they love have brought into their world. The adolescent who grows up in the northern part of the urban area of Chicago Illinois may speak Arabic at the bakery, Spanish at the gas station, and English at school. This learner's three languages may be at quite disparate levels of development when linguistically examined, yet serve the purpose the speaker needs.

Language represents identity. When governments and school systems determine the languages used in schooling, what happens is that they are changing and controlling the development of the learner's identity. Students should be free to define their multicultural multilingual identities. Policy implications for schooling in the United States, a nation of people who speak numerous languages and represent myriad cultures, requires a modern day instructional paradigm that does not blindly promote an English only philosophy. For the purpose of this article, we will now define the terms plurilingual and pluricultural and discuss their significance for educational systems that seek to assure social justice and equity in schooling. It is important that educators understand what it means when a learner considers himself/herself not just monolingual and monocultural.

A plurilingual learner is an individual who understands and values all the languages in his/her repertoire and understands they each serve a different purpose. A language can hold high utility for an individual who does not speak it at a high academic level and as well be an important part of the person's identity. We believe that discourses facilitate thoughts, beliefs, values, and actions (Gee, 1990). A person's definition of the self is inextricably linked to his/her cultural capital in language and culture (Collins & Blot, 2003). A plurilingual learner is also a pluricultural being who is engaged in an ongoing interplay between the languages he/she uses. This ability is evidenced in translanguaging behaviors (Garcia, 2011). Educators who accept plurilingualism and translanguaging as a natural part of language acquisition show they value the cultures of their students and their development.

The concept of translanguaging can be used to provide an explanation of how real people use language/s to communicate and of what children do when growing up in pluricultural worlds. We want all learners to know their languages have value. To translanguage is to have fluidity in the selection of the language that one uses for a given communication. It does not mean a learner will not achieve high levels of academic language but is a process that allows a person to interact with two different people who do not have a language in common, and be able to communicate efficiently with them. Ultimately, equity in schools requires learners be given the freedom to interact in all the languages spoken by their classmates and acknowledges the right to learn in classrooms that applaud learners' cross-linguistic and cross-cultural identities.

LEARNING IN MUSLIM COUNTRIES AND
IN THE UNITED STATES

Children have their own needs at school that relate to what they were taught is and is not proper behavior at home and school. In many countries learners do not engage in small group work such as cooperative learning. In select Muslim countries students do not work in small groups that include both genders. Instruction generally follows the teacher led transmission model. Because teachers are held in such high esteem, students may not feel comfortable questioning what the teacher says. Students are taught proper behavior at school means to listen politely and accept all tasks assigned by the teacher because this demonstrates that the instructor is a knowledgeable professional. Just as in the United States, students do not call their teachers by their first name or ask personal questions.

Rote memorization is admired in many parts of the Muslim world. Perhaps it derives its high value from the Islamic practice of memorizing the *Qur'an* for the purpose of preserving it in its original form. This places a different value on memorizing (Henzell-Thomas, 2002) than what is common belief in the United States. If a teacher suspects a child is copying another student's paper, or composing answers using the exact words of the text, it will be necessary to explain expectations in the U.S. to the student before accusing the learner of being dishonest. Teachers must diplomatically discuss this challenge so that the student does not feel an internal conflict related to one of his/her most valued religious customs.

Muslim children from abroad may experience surprise and not comprehend many of the tasks they are asked to perform in schools that instruct through methodologies differing from what is commonplace in their country of origin. If reprimanded by their teachers for their reluctance to question or to express an opinion in class, learners from Muslim countries may not be able to identify why they are not pleasing their teachers. Without question, ELs from Muslim countries need to be enrolled in the type of critical pedagogy that research has demonstrated leads to higher levels of comprehension and interpretation. However, this pedagogy must be promoted cautiously to avoid confusing students who have experienced different cultural norms in schooling. Critical thinking questions may have to be scaffolded carefully so that students can gain the ability to respond. Instructional paradigms that engage learners in critical analyses of text offer avenues for learners to explore that which will later guarantee them access to the benefits of democratic world citizenship (Street, 1984, 1993). If a new student arrives, the practice of shadowing another student who is successful with the workings of the classroom for a day or two might be especially helpful for the newcomer. The teacher can prepare a checklist of items the shadowed student should be sure to point out.

Written Language

Muslim students come from countries all over the world and in some cases have a complex relationship to language. Muslim majority countries in general have a multilingual, plurilingual environment and students may operate in multiple written language systems or scripts. Foreign languages such as English, French, Spanish, Dutch, and Italian, are in use to varying degrees in these countries. Schooling in many Muslim majority countries may or may not incorporate multilingual learning, but students are often confronted with various scripts in their daily lives and throughout the process of learning to read. The process of learning to read in one writing system or another can capitalize on as well as develop vastly different cognitive skills (Fender, 2008). The Arabic language is considered very important for Muslims. Reciting verses from the *Qur'an* in Arabic is a mandatory part of the five daily prayers, even if the person reciting does not understand Arabic. It is considered highly desirable to interchange verses at a certain point in the prayer and most Muslims who pray regularly have a repertoire of memorized verses that they draw on to complete their prayers. In addition, many Muslims "read" *Qur'an* as a religious activity. In some cases, people reading the *Qur'an* are only able to decode the writing system but not understand the words they are saying. This is common in countries where Arabic is not the mainstream language, yet Muslims from many parts of the world such as Indonesia, Malaysia, Pakistan, Bangladesh, and so forth, may want to learn Arabic for religious purposes. In other cases, non-Arabic speakers are taught the written Arabic language and how to understand the meaning of the prayers as well. Another case is that Arabic native speakers come from a variety of countries and while they all understand the Arabic writing system if they are literate, the variation in dialects or *diglossia* is so pronounced at times that Arabic speakers from one region sometimes cannot understand speakers from another (Saiegh-Haddad, 2005). Because of the importance of language in religious practices, it is not uncommon for children to have exposure to the Arabic alphabet from a very early age. Some children attend weekend Arabic/Islamic school and others learn formally or informally at home. Understanding some key differences between the script used in English and the Arabic script may provide clues to reading behaviors that may confuse teachers.

Arabic and Roman Scripts

There are some key differences between Roman script (used for English), and Arabic script (used for Standard Arabic, its dialects and for Urdu, the language of Pakistan). There are some basic characteristics of Arabic script that may affect the literacy development of Arabic speakers. First of all, Arabic is read from right to left. It has no capital or lower-case letters so relationships between capital and lower-case letters should be shown to students explicitly. There is no letter "p" in the Arabic language and so Arabic speakers will often pronounce it as a "b". This should not be considered a reading error (Brisk & Harrington, 2007). Arabic is written mostly in a cursive style with some letters always being connected and others always being separate and with spaces between words as in English. There are three forms of each letter; one if it is at the beginning of a word, one if it is in the middle, and one if it is at the end. One of the most important differences is that short vowels are not written as letters. Instead, a series of accent-type (*diacritic*) marks noting the a,e,i,o,u uniquely are used above or below the letter preceding the vowel sound. For example, a word like general would be written as *g'n'r^l*. This can have a strong impact on how Arabic speakers develop spelling skills. This is the reason why special attention should be paid to vowel use with Arabic speakers. Also, most Arabic words consist of only root consonants and short vowels. Roots usually consist of three or four consonants. The Arabic root, or *masdar*, determines the core meaning of a word. For example, the sequence of the three consonants s/f/r in this order carries the meaning of the word travel. A word which includes that sequence of letters is likely to have something to do with travelling. In this example, journey-safar (n), he travels-yusafir, traveller-musafir, and embassy-sifara, all are derived from one root when the consonants conserve this order (Abu-Rabia, 1998; Abu-Rabia & Seigel, 2002). Third, fluent readers in Arabic develop automatic word recognition skills that are based on letter-sound correspondences. As a result of this type of vowel notation system, they may be more able to decipher the sentence context (e.g., structure *or syntax* and meaning *or semantics*) information necessary to achieve comprehension. Once students are more skilled, around the eighth grade, readers begin to drop vowel markings and use the root and the sentence context as a way to infer meaning. Taking this into account, there is reason to believe that Arabic readers may have a heightened ability to use context to determine meaning (Fender, 2008). For older ELs, this skill may be helpful in reading comprehension of non-native languages. On the other hand, students who come to the United States in the Middle School years, which is the period during which the vowel notations start to drop away from texts, the reading process may not be complete and this may cause a difficulty for those students to access written language unless reading is supported through this stage (Hayes-Harb, 2006; Abu-Rabia, 2002). This makes adolescence a vulnerable time for Arabic speakers because if they do not develop Arabic to a proficient level and they are just starting to learn English at that stage, it may become difficult for them to access written language at all if the educational process is interrupted before they are proficient readers of English (Abu-Rabia, 2002).

In short, there are features of the Arabic alphabet that change how Arabic speakers may approach reading development. Teachers should keep in mind that Arabic speaking students need scaffolding when it comes to vowel use and spelling and older students may benefit from activities that extend learning through the familiar activity of using context to decode meaning. Whenever possible, Arabic speaking adolescents should be supported through high school with age appropriate reading materials in Arabic. This will help them to continue developing their reading abilities to a higher level of proficiency.

LANGUAGES OF THE
MUSLIM WORLD AND CULTURAL PRACTICES

At levels K–12 in the United States, many students whose families are Muslim are bilingual but many more are plurilingual. Past colonizations have impacted the landscape of nations where the Islamic faith is practiced. In these countries the language of schooling has reflected who ran the government in different time periods. For example, in Egypt many speak French, Arabic, and/or English. Egyptians may be Muslim or Christian. Morocco's history reflects an ever-changing linguistic landscape; while some speak Standard Arabic, others converse in Berber, Moroccan Arabic, or French. Indonesians who are Muslim speak the Indonesian language and learn English as a foreign language at school. Pakistani students are likely to speak Urdu, possibly another regional language, and English to some degree. Indonesian students will usually speak Indonesian and a local or tribal language. The relationship of students to different languages as a result of colonization may also impact their level of acceptance of one language or another. Conversely, some languages may imply more prestige than others in their country of origin and so there may be less or more enthusiasm for a language based on that.

The following sections of this article offer practical suggestions that will be helpful to teachers in establishing positive relationships with students and their parents. They are not meant to serve as generalizations, but rather as starting guidelines to inform those not familiar with these populations. The most important consideration is to make no generalizations about individuals from majority Muslim countries. Offensive behavior in one country may be acceptable and not at all questionable in another. For example, Moroccans are not offended when someone sits across the table from them and shows the bottom of the shoe, yet this is a serious offense in other parts of the Arab world.

INFLUENCES OF RELIGIOUS PRACTICES ON
SCHOOLING AND LIFE

Dress is a highly visible and symbolic element of the Muslim faith. Many Muslims adhere to a strict dress code and believe it is a non-negotiable part of their daily religious activities. Others are more relaxed in their observance of this element of Islamic life. Some Muslim women wear a head covering called the *hijab* and on rare occasions a face veil called a *nikab*. Other devout Muslim women may select to not cover their hair. There is great variability. Sometimes wearing head coverings relates to the climate of the country where the person resides. For example, life in the intense heat of the Egyptian desert may be the reason why both men and women in Egypt began to cover their heads and arms at some point in history.

Some Muslim men believe they should wear a hat at all times and others believe they should not shave their beards. Women in *hijab* remove it when in settings with women or close family members who are permitted to see their hair. If schools are uncomfortable with women entering their building with a *nikab* for security reasons, they could discretely request that the woman lift her veil for another woman in private and show a form of identification.

Administrators in U.S. schools who want to implement a *hijab* color or style that is acceptable for the school dress code should only do so after consulting with families and students. It is important to respect students' rights if their choice of dress is influenced by religion and cultural norms. Dress code policies that prohibit hats could restrict the type of hat or give special permission to young men wanting to wear a religious-style hat. In the U.S. many young men wear caps and wearing these has now become a forbidden part of the school dress code in many schools. This is because of the ways gang membership has been denoted by the manner members of gangs wear their caps. Wearing caps sideways or backwards, and selecting a cap of a particular color, has been used to identify gang membership.

Daily prayers are a requirement in the Islamic faith. Many adolescents engage in prayer several times a day. Muslims are expected to pray five times a day unless they are on a long journey or in a situation that prohibits them from prayer. Women do not pray during menstruation. Especially in non-Muslim countries, decisions must be weighed often as to whether to miss a prayer for a class or for work when there is a time conflict. Some Muslims allow themselves flexibility in timing of prayer and others are careful to perform each prayer during its specified time range. For some, when faced with a situation that makes it difficult to pray, a solution is to combine prayers and/or make up prayers when it is possible to do so. Cleanliness is required for prayers unless it is not possible to make *wu'du* (the ritual washing for prayer). Children are expected to begin praying at the age of 7, but flexibility is applied until the age of 10. One issue that may come up for older students is whether to allow them time and a place for the prayer(s) that are scheduled during the school day. The prayer itself should take about 3–15 minutes including washing if necessary. There is a time range for prayer so often a student can wait for a convenient time.

During Ramadan, a religious observance that lasts approximately one month, older students will fast all day from sunrise until evening. Fasting is one of the five pillars of Islam and is obligatory for Muslims after puberty. Ramadan was the month in the Islamic calendar during which the first verses of the *Qur'an* were revealed to Mohamed. For Muslims, fasting offers an opportunity to practice restraint, good conduct and gratefulness, as well as empathize with the poor (Hassaballa & Helminski, 2006). Sometimes younger students may choose to fast with their families, although it is not considered an obligation for children. Participation in the fast binds the community. Dates are one of the most special foods for Ramadan and many Muslims use this food to break the fast. Offering or giving dates to a Muslim during Ramadan shows sensitivity and acceptance. At the end of Ramadan, once the fast ends, many Middle Eastern Muslims celebrate Eid-ul-Fitr (Eid), a very important holiday in Islam. Only in rare situations do Muslims work or go to school on this day. On Eid, a morning prayer is offered at the mosque and families spend the day visiting, eating, and participating in special activities. Children may receive gifts and/or money. The mismatch between home and school that the celebration of Eid can precipitate in Western countries relates to the fact that Eid's date is not necessarily fixed ahead of time and is instead announced the night before. Because the Islamic calendar consists of 12 months, 29 or 30 days in length, the date is approximately 11 days earlier every year. The announcement of Eid depends on the moon sighting for some, and on calculations for others. This uncertainty with the date the religious celebration falls on can confuse teachers. Students might tell the teacher they will be absent on a specific day and then the date of the celebration changes and the student is present at school. It is a good idea for parents to share information with the teachers that will answers questions that may arise before they come up.

Depending on the country of origin or other familial factors, children may be absent up to 3 days from school in celebration of Eid-ul Fitr. Eid-ul-Adha is a celebration that happens approximately 2 months after Eid-ul-Fitr and is the day when Abraham was told to spare his son. This is also the holiday when many Muslims make their pilgrimage to Mecca in Saudi Arabia (Hajj), which is an obligation for all Muslims. Hajj can only be performed during this time, otherwise it is an optional visit to Mecca. If students are going to Hajj with their families, they may be gone during the school year. It is considered very important to celebrate these religious holidays in community. Another holiday is the celebration of

Prophet Mohamed's birthday, called Al-Mawlid. While not an obligatory celebration, it is in practice a time of great celebration in some countries and/or regions. It is unlikely that students will be taken out of school in the U.S. for this third celebration but they may nevertheless hold fond memories of this day's activities. Some minority groups have other holidays that they celebrate and of course, depending on the country of origin, there may be cultural holidays that are celebrated even though they are not considered a part of Islamic worship.

Muslim students come from countries all over the world and in some cases have a complex relationship to language. Muslim majority countries in general have a multilingual, plurilingual environment and students may operate in multiple written language systems or scripts. Foreign languages such as English, French, Spanish, Dutch and Italian are in use to varying degrees in these countries. Schooling in many Muslim majority countries may or may not incorporate multilingual academic learning but students are often confronted with various scripts in their daily lives and throughout the process of learning to read. The process of learning to read in one writing system or another can capitalize on as well as develop vastly different cognitive skills (Fender, 2008).

Diet

Muslims consider pork a forbidden food except in the case of extreme hunger or malnutrition when other food is not available. The majority of Muslims do not knowingly eat pork and many avoid all products that might contain pork byproducts such as gelatins, lard and rennet (enzymes from animal intestines used to make cheese) like jello, pudding, gummy candies, marshmallows, pie crust, and cheeses. In addition, some Muslims only eat meat or animal products from animals slaughtered in a special manner. Even young Muslim children are aware that they are forbidden to eat pork. This does not mean that families who practice the Islamic faith will not attend functions where pork is served. In these situations the pork is simply not placed on one's dish. Also, even during fasting periods, Muslims will not feel offended if someone eats in front of them. All that is required is to be allowed the same religious freedom held by the non-Muslim. Parents should not hesitate to discuss dietary restrictions with their children's teachers. A conversation is just the right thing to open doors of intercultural understanding.

Appropriate Uses of the Left and Right Hand

In many Muslim countries, use of the left hand is discouraged for select activities and the left hand is considered dirty. Moroccan Muslims, for example, believe the use of the right hand relates to religious beliefs but for them the left hand does not carry the connotation of being dirty. There is a religious doctrine that when taken literally means that the devil eats with his left hand. Over time, this doctrine became a custom that is not questioned by Moroccans. Others believe it is undesirable to use the left hand for anything good and strongly consider its use for eating to be rude. As well, writing with the left hand may be allowed but is also discouraged. When teachers notice a young learner writing with the left hand, they should have a conversation with the parents to come to an agreement about what will be done at home so that all parties can work together on either right or left handed writing development. It is always appropriate for teachers to discuss with parents that being right handed or left handed is biologically determined and not a factor of environment, culture, or religion. This is a conversation that can serve to open doors of understanding of the ways the genetic make-up of our ancestors' influences that of the children born today.

Gender Roles in Muslim Cultures

It is important that Western society acknowledge the right of Muslim women to wear a *hijab* and appreciate the reasons this custom is part of the identity of many Muslims. Not all women who practice Islam wear a headscarf or *hijab*, but many young women and women do wear it to show pride in their culture and religion. The headscarf is an expression of the highly valued quality of modesty within the Islamic religion and among Muslim cultures. For some Muslim groups, use of the scarf is a personal choice and does not mean that women are uneducated, unfriendly, abused, or forced to follow the tradition by fathers or husbands. In some cases, Muslim women see their use of the scarf as a way to be appreciated for their inner beauty and intelligence rather than their physical attributes (Blake, 2009). Asking adolescent women to remove headscarves can be traumatic because of their belief that the hair and chest are private (Associated Press, 2007).

Polite Behaviors in Society

All citizens of the world are polite but they vary in the manner they demonstrate their politeness. Muslim cultures are high context cultures whose members pride themselves on great hospitality (Hall, 1981). An invitation or a visit to a North African or Arab home is usually taken very seriously by the host. A visitor will be offered food and drink and the host may feel frustrated if the visitor does not partake. It is advisable to accept at least a drink if offered in an Arab or North African home. In an Egyptian home one is most likely to be offered *karkadh'ei*, a hot tea that is red in color and also available in Mexico where it is called *flor de jamaica*. I (Mayra) remember bargaining at a jewelry store in Cairo, Egypt, at the Khan el-Khalili market while sharing *karkadh'ei* prepared with a light touch of sugar and served in a small glass. It was a ceremonial like occasion and we talked while seated in a semicircle with the store-owner. Not until we finished our beverage did we begin to discuss what we might purchase. What I brought home held a certain charm because of how we settled on price and what was explained to me about what I was buying.

If a person receives an invitation to a Muslim home and refuses it, it is customary to state the reason. If one compliments a hostess from Egypt on an item in her home, she may offer the item to her guest. The expectation could be acceptance but one can never be sure. Gift-giving in general is common in the Muslim world and when a gift is offered to a teacher, it is best to graciously accept as long as it adheres to school policy. In many homes it would be inappropriate for a teacher to be alone on a home visit with someone or a group of the opposite sex unless necessary. In many parts of the world the concept of time is flexible and although Islam strongly discourages people being late, many are comfortable being flexible with time. Muslim men may avoid eye contact with female teachers because some consider it disrespectful to look at women even when they are talking. Some Muslims may consider shaking hands to be undesirable as well. There are various reasons for this but it does not mean that the conversation is not valued or that there is an attitude that women are inferior or dirty. On the other hand, there are also Muslims that behave with fewer gender barriers and will make eye contact and shake hands freely. This will depend on the person's situation within the broader religious/cultural context. A good rule of thumb is to wait until the parent offers their hand and then shake it if offered.

Swimming Classes at School

Swimming in public may be problematic for young Muslim women living in Western countries because they believe that swimsuits show parts of the body that should always be covered except at home. Their sense of what should be private and what should be public and personal expectations do not allow them to wear what might be considered the most modest swimsuit by Western standards. Even those who do not wear a scarf may hesitate when it comes to wearing a Western style swimsuit in public and in particular, in a co-educational pool. However, there are very attractive Islamic suits for women that cover the arms, legs, and hair. They look like exercise suits that one would wear to the gymnasium in the U.S. and are made of swimsuit material. A physical education teacher can search on the internet to find a suit that is complimentary in color to the regular suits chosen for swimming class and acceptable to students who are Muslim. Teachers can make it possible for Muslim girls to participate in swimming classes if they talk with parents so their daughters have time to select and purchase swimsuits that they feel comfortable wearing.

Schools might also offer swimming classes in a women only environment before, during, or after the school day. Young men can feel extremely uncomfortable with co-educational swimming because of their belief that they have the obligation to "avert their gaze" (Qur'an 24:30) from women as a sign of respect (Mattson, 2008). Because Islam requires men to cover themselves from the navel to the knee, young Muslim men may experience discomfort if asked to wear certain swim-suit styles that are often the norm in the U.S. swim classes.

Education of Women

Our experience as educators who work with graduate students from many Muslim societies has allowed us to see that women are indeed valued and have equal access to education in many countries. Islam does not discourage the education of women. It is written in the *Qur'an* that all Muslims, male and female, have the obligation to seek knowledge (Qur'an 20:114, 35:28, 39:9). While there are Muslim groups and even governments that attempt to deny women and girls the right to an education, in Morocco, for example, King Mohamed IV passed a number of educational and family reforms in the past few years that promote women and girls' access to education. This was not difficult to implement because Muslim beliefs support equal access of boys and girls to education (Brush, Heyman, Provasniak, Fanning, Lent, & De Wilde, 2002). Similarly, in some Indonesian circles it is not unusual for a woman to reach a higher level of education than her husband. A student from Indonesia completing work towards her doctoral degree shared her perspective.

> Women are now free to pursue education as high as possible, as long as they don't forget their roles in a family as a wife and a mother. I'm lucky to have an open-minded husband who allows his wife to pursue the doctorate degree. (I. Hermagustiana, personal communication, January 25, 2013)

One of my students from Saudi Arabia shared a story about the day she arrived to the United States. Her story highlights the ways religion and human culture so delimit our interpersonal interactions within any society. She landed at O'Hare Airport in Chicago but her luggage did not arrive. She told me, "I was asking the man behind the counter for help to find my suitcases yet I could not look him in the eyes. Now I know that I must have seemed very disrespectful by U.S. standards." She further explained that, "After 2 years in the U.S. I look at everyone in the eyes regardless of their gender. I know that when I return home I will not do so."

Nevertheless, it is true that women of a low socioeconomic status (SES) living in rural areas may not experience the same support and approval to pursue an education as their upper SES counterparts living in cities and suburban areas (Sadiqi, 2003). In rural areas the expectation may be that women marry and have children if the perception is that education will not benefit the family. Families who live a long distance from an educational center may worry about their daughter's safety and propriety on the way to school, or if transportation is limited, for example the family only owns a bicycle, or motorbike, they may prefer to send sons to school.

Ways Teachers Can Reach Out to Parents

The expectations that parents and teachers have for each other can be very different across countries. It is important that teachers understand the need to reach out to parents and become familiar with what is proper behavior in their countries of origin. In the U.S. teachers' expectation of parental involvement in education for learners in elementary schools includes attending parent teacher conferences, helping with homework, and communicating through the use of a daily planner. The planner is a small book that children take back and forth from home to school that parents can use to ask questions or voice concerns without having to make a scheduled appointment with the teacher. Many times expectations are so implicit in cultural norms that they lead us to actions at an unconscious level. Teachers who want to create equitable schools will examine their assumptions for parental collaboration.

Parental participation can vary from participatory to passive depending on the origin and social class of the parent. In some contexts, it is not proper for Muslim parents to question the teacher and rare for them to visit the school, much less participate in an activity. With these prior experiences and notions, an interaction involving a conversation with a child's teacher, may be indeed intimidating. Parents will be more likely to call the school with questions or attend parent teacher conferences if the teacher explicitly reaches out and invites them to visit the school. Because teachers are held in very high esteem in Muslim societies, parents may perceive their involvement in schooling will be seen as disrespectful and do not want to demonstrate presumptuous behavior. For many, attending an open house or bringing food for a class party may be more comfortable until they have an opportunity to observe first hand what type of contributions from parents are welcome in U.S. schools.

Resolving Problems at School

Challenges at school can be viewed as a sign of misbehavior or laziness and reflect poorly on the family honor, a very important aspect of Muslim cultures. Any parent who feels confronted by a teacher wishing to discuss their child's misbehaving at school will feel uncertainty. It is necessary to be delicate when addressing negative school performance with Muslim parents. They may experience a very high level of embarrassment resulting in severe punishment being doled out at home. Children are socialized through family networks that emphasize shame over guilt (Sharabi, 1977). Hence, any action that compromises the family's honor is considered serious.

Corporal punishment in school is acceptable punishment in some cultures and one possible parent response is to physically punish students at home. Parents who were disciplined harshly as children may feel that they must discipline their children similarly. This is true across Muslim and non-Muslim cultural groups and unique to parental experiences. It is important to be cognizant that few parents, regardless of their backgrounds, use extreme forms of corporal punishment. Familial norms impact what parents do and teachers can prevent severe punishments by discussing classroom behavior management strategies with parents.

Parents who understand the reasons their child is having learning problems or recognize the child as being exceptionally bright, may arrange for private tutoring from a trusted community member. However, school-based special education supports are few and far between in Muslim countries (Project in International Reading Literacy Study, 2006). It is important to carefully explain suspected learning problems to parents. If parents do not comprehend that low achievement representing a legitimate learning problem must be solved by educational interventions, they may unknowingly crush a child's self-esteem, as well as their academic potential. It may also be appropriate to discuss what the next step will be and give parents some tools to know how to proceed to solve the problem. This will help to reduce parental anxiety about student achievement, and offer concrete alternatives to punishment as a means to support their child's success in school. Schools can schedule workshops for parents in which strategies are offered and school behavior management norms are explicitly discussed. These will give parents the needed information about what teachers expect in terms of behavior management.

CONCLUSION

The goals of this chapter are to assure Muslim parents that their children can be welcomed and succeed in U.S. schools, and to engage teachers in an exploration of the cultures of learners of Muslim descent from the Middle East. We believe that teachers who are cognizant of the reasons religion and culture impact schooling, will make the needed difference. Although this country is largely Christian, the curriculum should reflect the lives and histories of all students. Culturally responsive teachers eliminate mismatches between home and school for learners of Muslim descent when they design curricula that appropriately reflect the realities of race, ethnicity, culture, and religion.

REFERENCES

Abu-Rabia, S., & Siegel, L. (2002) Reading, syntactic, orthographic, and working memory skills of bilingual Arabic-English speaking Canadian children. *Journal of Psycholinguistic Research*, *31*, 661–678.

Abu-Rabia, S. (1998). Social and cognitive factors influencing the reading comprehension of Arab students learning Hebrew as a second language in Israel. *Journal of Research in Reading*, *21*(3), 201–212.

Andriessen, I., Phalet, A., & Lens, W. (2006) Future goal setting, task motivation and learning of minority and non-minority students in Dutch Schools. *British Journal of Educational Psychology*, *27*, 826–850.

Associated Press. (2007, June 27). California school apologizes for ordering Muslim girl to remove scarf. Retrieved from http://www.firstamendmentcenter.org/news.aspx?id=18726

Au, K. (2002). Multicultural factors and the effective instruction of students of diverse backgrounds. In A. Farstrup & S. J. Samuels (Eds.), *What research says about reading instruction. international reading*. Newark, DE: International Reading Association.

Bennett, C. (2010). *Comprehensive multicultural education: Theory and practice*. Boston, MA: Allyn & Bacon.

Bhabha, H. K. (1994). *The location of culture*. New York NY: Routledge.

Bialystok, E. (2001). *Bilingualism in development: Language, literacy, and cognition*. Cambridge, England: Cambridge University Press.

Blake, J. (2009, August 12). Muslim women uncover myths about the hijab. *CNN*. Retrieved from http://www.cnn.com/2009/US/08/12/generation.islam.hijab/index.html

Boekmann, K.-B., Aalto, A., Atanasoska,, T., & Lamb, T. (2011). *Promoting plurilingualism – majority language in multilingual settings*. Strasbourg, France: Council of Europe Publishing. Retrieved from http://www.ecml.at/tabid/277/PublicatiomID/75/Default.aspx.

Brisk, M. E., & Harrington, M.M. (2007). *Literacy and bilingualism: A handbook for all teachers* (2nd ed.). New York, NY: Routledge.

Brush, L., Heyman, C, Provasniak, S., Fanning, M., Lent, D., & De Wilde, J. (2002). *Description and analysis of the USAID Girls' Education Activity in Guatemala, Morocco and Peru*. Washington DC: American Institute for Research (ERIC Document Reproduction Service No. ED 467216)

Collins, J., & Blot, R. (2003). *Literacy and literacies: Texts, power, and identity*. London England: Cambridge University Press.

Feghali, E. (1997). Arab cultural communication patterns. *International Journal of Intercultural Relations, 21*(3), 345–378.

Fender, M. (2008). Arabic literacy development and cross-linguistic effects in subsequent L2 literacy development. In K. Koda & A. Zehler (Eds.), *Learning to read across languages* (pp. 101–124). New York, NY: Routledge.

Garcia, O. (2011). From language garden to sustainable languaging: Bilingual education in a global world. *NABE Newsletter. 34*(1), 5–9.

Gay, G. (2010). *Culturally responsive teaching: Theory, research, and practice*. New York, NY: Teachers College Press.

Gee, J. (1990). *Social linguistics and literacies: Ideologies in discourses*. New York, NY: Falmer Press.

González, N., Moll, L., & Amanti, C. (Eds.). (2005). *Funds of knowledge for teaching in Latino households*. Mahwah, NJ: Lawrence Erlbaum Associates.

Hall, E. (1981). *Beyond culture*. New York, NY: Anchor Books.

Hassabalah, H., & Helminski, K. E. (2006). *The beliefnet guide to Islam*. New York, NY: Three Leaves Press.

Hayes-Harth, W. (2006). Native speakers of Arabic and ESL texts: Evidence for the transfer of written word identification processes. *Tesol Quarterly, 40*(2), 321–339.

Henzell-Thomas, J. (2002, July). *Excellence in Islamic education: Key issues for the present time*. Bath, England: The Book Foundation. Retrieved from http://thebook.org/tep-articles/excellence.shtml

Hussein, A., (with Imam Muslim Ibn al-Hajj). (2007). English translation of Sahih Muslim (Vol. 7) (Nasiruddin Al-Khattab, Trans.). Riyadh, Saudi Arabia: Darussalam.

Khadra Jayyusi, S. (1997). *The legacy of Muslim Spain*. Leiden, The Netherlands: E.J. Brill.

Lean, N. R., & Hafez, F. (2013, February 23). *Nature, origin and the manufacturing of Islamophobia*. Paper presented at the 2013 Symposium on Facing Religious Intolerance: Islamophobia in the 20th Century, at the American Islamic College, Chicago, IL.

Mattson, I. (2008). Respecting the Qur'an. Retrieved from http://www.isna.net/articles/News/RESPECTING-THE-QURAN.aspx

Nieto, S., & Bode, P. (2012). *Affirming diversity: The sociopolitical context of multicultural education*. Boston, MA: Allyn & Bacon.

Nussbaum, M. C. (2012). *The new religious intolerance: Overcoming the politics of fear in an anxious age*. Cambridge, MA: Harvard University Press.

Pew Forum on Religion and Public Life. (2011, January). *The future of the global Muslim population: Projections from 2010–2013*. Washington, DC: The Pew Forum.

Project in International Reading Literacy Study. (2006). National Center for Educational Statistics. Retrieved from http://pirls.bc.edu/PDF/PIRLS2006_international_report.pdf

Reeves, J. R. (2006). Secondary teachers attitudes toward including English-language learners in mainstream classrooms. *Journal of Educational Research, 99*(3), 131–142.

Sadiqi, F. (2003). *Women, gender, and language in Morocco.* Boston, MA: E. J. Brill.

Saiegh-Haddad, E. (2005). Correlates of reading fluency in Arabic: Diglossic and orthographic factors. *Reading and Writing: An Interdisciplinary Journal, 18,* 559–582.

Skutnabb-Kangas, T. (1999) Education of minorities. In J. A. Fishman (Ed.), *Handbook of Language and Ethnic Identity.* New York, NY & Oxford, England: Oxford University Press.

Sercu, L. (2011). The acquisition of intercultural competence: Does language education help or hinder? In G. Zarate, D. Levy, & C. Kramsch (Eds.), *Handbook of multilingualism and multiculturalism* (pp. 45–50). Paris, France: Editions des Archives Contemporaines.

Sharabi, H. (1977). Impact of class and culture on social behavior: The feudal bourgeois family in Arab society. In L. C Brown & N. Itzhowitz (Eds.), *Psychological dimensions of Near-Eastern studies.* (pp. 240–256). Princeton, NJ: The Darwin Press.

Spring, J. (2012). *Deculturalization and the struggle for equality: A brief history of the education of dominated cultures in the United States.* New York, NY: McGraw-Hill.

Street, B. (1993). *Cross cultural approaches to literacy.* Cambridge, England: Cambridge University Press.

Street, B. (1984). *Literacy in theory and practice.* Cambridge, England: Cambridge University Press.

United States Government. (2002). *Public Law 107–110, 107th Congress, 115 Stat.* 1425–2094. Retrieved from http://www2.ed.gov/nclb/landing.jhtml

PART III

ISSUES RELATED TO IDENTITY FORMATION OF MUSLIM CHILDREN

CHAPTER 5

AMERICAN MUSLIM IDENTITY

NEGOTIATING THE *UMMAH* AND THE AMERICAN PUBLIC SCHOOL SYSTEM

Lesliee Antonette and Lara Tahoun

ABSTRACT

This chapter considers the ways in which the sociocultural identities of Muslim children (those who are or whose families are practitioners of the Islamic faith) are shaped by the tension created between the *Ummah* (sociocultural, religious communities) in which their families participate and the cultural expectations of the American Public School System (APSS). This work considers the use of the phrase "American Muslim," and the problematic definition of chronological generations of American Muslims as these issues relate to identity development in contemporary Muslim children who are participating in the APSS. American Muslims have been represented as perpetual immigrants, with no historical roots in the United States (U.S.). This understanding of American Muslim identity feeds myriad forms of xenophobia expressed in times of national (American) crisis. A clear definition of a Muslim immigrant generation, and first and second generations of American born Muslims clarifies the historic and generational presence of Muslims in America. This

Growing Up Between Two Cultures: Problems and Issues of Muslim Children, pp. 119–143
Copyright © 2014 by Information Age Publishing
All rights of reproduction in any form reserved.

clarification allows for the use of narratives written by and about "first" gen-eration American Muslims in the APSS curriculum (the concept of including fiction and nonfiction texts that deal with current issues related to being Muslim in America is just beginning). These narratives provide American Muslim children currently participating in the APSS a description of the marginalization they often "feel" but cannot clearly identify. The practice of marginalization, especially in times of domestic peace, is subtle. When America is in crisis, however, marginalization often becomes outright bigotry and discrimination. This is when the presence of the *Ummah* is most apparent, although it is always present and working in the lives of American Muslims. Reading texts written by and about Muslims who as children participated in the APSS, in times of peace and military conflict, in a critical multicultural classroom allows American Muslim students, and their non-Muslim counter-parts to recognize how both the *Ummah* and the traditions of the APSS exist in a state of constant conflict. This conflict need not be resolved but it does need to be managed This chapter is viewed as a beginning of the negotiations between the *Ummah* and the APSS, so both can provide the support needed by the children they share.

CULTURAL AND ETHNIC DIVERSITY IN MUSLIM COMMUNITIES

Writing about American Muslims imparts a series of issues that must be addressed, the least of which is the vast diversity within a category that is only now taking shape in American academic discourse. While the 2010 census did not collect data on religious affiliation, the Council on Foreign Relations estimates that the Muslim population in the U.S. could be as high as 2% of the total population, between 2 and 7 million individuals. The majority of Muslims in the U.S. identify themselves as Sunni, about 10% identify themselves as Shia (Shiite) and a small percentage identify as Druze or Sufi (Johnson, 2011, Muslims). In addition, "20% of Muslims in America are native-born American blacks, most of whom are converts" (Barrett, 2007, p. 6).

The gap in numbers could be attributed to the way in which Muslim identity is understood as one who practices a cultural lifestyle *and/or* the practice of Islamic religion as codified in the *Qur'an* (the Holy book of Islam). The diversity among American Muslims may seem to present a staggering number of differences; however, one only need consider the number of Catholic and Protestant subgroups within those two major religious groups. The difference is not in the number of sects, denominations or interpretations affiliated with any one religion, it is in the ways in which individuals define themselves in relation to religious or cultural organizations.

MARGINALIZED MUSLIM IDENTITY IN THE APSS

The APSS has integrated multicultural curricula in uneven and disparate ways. The ways in which the word "multicultural" is understood and taught in educator preparation programs in the United States can widely vary. The result is that the majority of contemporary American school-aged children have received a traditional Western-centric education. For those students who belong to underrepresented ethnic groups this means that cultural education is, often, provided at home or institutions that serve close-knit ethnic communities. Students and teachers who belong to an ethnic group that is recognized as representative of the dominant culture remain ignorant of the significance and value of the cultural diversity surrounding them. This often leads to acts of subtle prejudice and hostility in or even violent ways when faced with the need to negotiate cultural difference. One need only think of the days following 9/11 to verify the logic of this statement (Antonette, 2003).

Currently, there is a significant xenophobic response to Muslims in America. The Internet is filled with articles and blogs critiquing APSS inclusivity of Islamic education or even the teaching of the most basic principles of Muslim culture. In the article "Islam in America's Public Schools: Education or Indoctrination?" Stillwell (2008) relates the story of a Houston, Texas APSS Middle school where a Principal required all students to attend a presentation on Islamic awareness. This was done in response to a physical assault on a Muslim student that resulted in the hospitalization of that student. Reaction to the Principal's decision was immediate and delivered with intense pressure from irate parents, Christian religious leaders and radio talk show hosts who characterized the presentation as "Islamic indoctrination" (Islam). This kind of response on the part of non-Muslim Americans who support, for example, beginning every class in the APSS with the Pledge of Allegiance, which places every student "under God" illustrates the denial of the imbrication of a specific religious belief system that stands as the foundation of the APSS. This presence in all of its subtle guises (interrupting class to "God Bless" someone who just sneezed, textbooks that favor a Western European history, and religious holidays that allow "time off" from school, for example).

As we write this chapter the country is dealing with the aftermath of the explosions at the Boston Marathon (April 15, 2013). Unfortunately, the suspects in this case are Muslim immigrants from Russia. The alleged actions of these individuals raise the level of an already too present xenophobia that supports anti-Muslim sentiment. It justifies, in the minds of some mainstream Americans, the prejudice and discrimination that may be exercised upon American Muslim children in the APSS. American Muslim students are faced with the untenable choice of either hiding their socioreligious identity or struggling with the expectations of teachers and classmates to serve as the representative of all forms of Islamic practice. It is this kind of pressure, a subtle prejudice, that American Muslim children "feel" everyday in the APSS. All too often they receive no validation of that feeling while at school. The Ummah in each Muslim community will respond differently, so some children may have that feeling validated at home while others may not (Haddad, Senzai, & Smith, 2009).

Acts of subtle prejudice shift to physical and emotional violence following an event such as 9/11 or the Boston marathon explosions. If the APSS had curriculum in place that encouraged teachers to provide accurate information about Muslim culture the curriculum could support conversations in the classroom that would inform students and not frighten them. All students in the APSS would know that the larger Islamic *Ummah* does not condone terrorist action. These conversations would protect American Muslim students because all American students could be expected to respond to these events with knowledge and understanding, rather than with fear and violence. If the APSS institutionalized the use of narratives written by first generation American Muslim writers then teachers would have grade level appropriate materials that could provide context for conversations about larger sociocultural events. In so doing, the APSS might contribute to an American culture that would include American Muslim children (Antonette, 1998).

While the word "multicultural" has certainly been circulated much more frequently in educational discourse since 9/11, there remains the problem of a school system that is very slow and generally resistant to change. The ways in which the APSS has, or more pointedly, has not employed a universally understood multicultural curriculum, or encouraged the development of multicultural pedagogy complicates the already complex process of assimilation experienced by Muslims in America (Antonette, 2003).

The development of an American Muslim identity has occurred in the Muslim population more slowly than it has in other immigrant ethnic groups. Part of the issue is the strong presence of the *Ummah*. One of its roles is to serve as a constant reminder of the duties of Muslim life. Assimilation is also slowed by physical appearance. Members of underrepresented ethnic groups whose *appearance* does not *match* the stereotypic image of "an American" tend to assimilate more slowly into the dominant culture. Another contributing factor is the way in which generations of Muslim presence in America has not followed the typical chronological progression of other underrepresented ethnic identities in the United States (McGoldrick, Giordan, & Garcia-Preto, 2005).

Patricia Smith (2011) discusses the experiences of a 17-year-old high school student, Sana Haq, who lives in Norwood, New Jersey, and whose religious practice would be considered "devout" by non-Muslim standards.

Haq "prays five times a day, as Islam requires [and] wears only modest clothing" (Islam). When asked, she, described herself as not "American, not Pakistani, not a teenager" but as a Muslim (Islam). While not true of all Muslims, Sana Haq's Pakistani identity and the physical features that accompany that identity do not correspond to the stereotypic image of an "American." Her choice of modest clothing, also sets her apart, visually, from many of her contemporaries. Her self-identification as Muslim and "not American" is also a factor in the ways in which this first generation American Muslim will assimilate into American culture. Her choice of privileging her Muslim identity over her American identity is supported by the large urban *Ummah* in which Sana Haq's family participates. There is strength in numbers. More to the point, Sana Haq's proclamation of her Muslim identity is unique to and typical of a first generation American Muslim. Her choice, as well as, her physical appearance will be met with social, political, and religious backlash in the APSS. Sana Haq seems to be unaware of this reality. This could be the result of the power of her *Ummah* or it could be the result of what appears to be her generation's disregard of the assimilatory power of the APSS. This gap between recognition and reality is the single most problematic issue experienced by contemporary American Muslim students in the APSS.

GENERATIONAL AMERICAN MUSLIM CULTURAL IDENTITY

After careful consideration of cross-disciplinary research related to Muslim identity and culture in the U.S. we have decided to use the phrase "American Muslim." The overriding argument against this phrasing is that placing the noun "American" before the noun "Muslim" privileges secular or national identity over religious or cultural identity that involves complete submission to the Divine. This is problematic because Muslim life is commonly understood, in an ideal sense, as one of being in constant submission to the divine language, that is, the *Qur'an*. It is argued that it is for this reason that the use of the signifier, "Muslim" should take linguistic precedence over any other socio-politico-cultural identity one may have. We honor that line of thinking. However, we believe that, ironically, the use of the rules of American English grammar actually allow for a privileging of Muslim identity.

According to the rules of grammar in American English, "nouns, when working as adjectives, always come first or before the noun it is describing" (Galloway, 2011, Muslim). When the word Muslim is placed before the word American, with or without a hyphen, it serves as an adjective that modifies the noun, American. American, then, becomes an identity, that can be modified by any other identity. The use of the phrase "American

Muslim" puts American identity in the position of modifying Muslim identity, according to the rules of American English Grammar. Muslim identity, then, is the primary and immutable identity. It is modified but not effaced by American identity. Privileging Muslim identity, in this way linguistically, contributes to the building of a strong community presence that supports religious practice and honors American national identity.

Curtis (2010) writes that there have been "Muslim Americans" in the APSS since the beginning of the 20th century. He reports that it did not take long for this early generation of Muslims to realize the disintegration of Muslim identity that occurred in their children but some, as in many other underrepresented groups, felt that was a positive change. *The Encyclopedia of Muslim Americans* provides a rich and detailed timeline of Muslim presence in what is currently identified as the United States. This history begins with Muslims enslaved and brought to the U.S. as part of the slave trade in the 15th through 19th centuries. In the discourse related to generational Muslim identity in the United States, this group is rarely considered and when it is, it is not considered as an immigrant generation or a "first" generation.

The *early* wave of modern Muslim immigration to the U.S. that occurred at the end of the 19th century and the beginning of the 20th century, is sometimes considered a "first" generation. This group emigrated primarily from the Lebo-Syrian region and was largely unschooled and illiterate.[1] They brought with them a first-hand experience of war, poverty and the forced assimilation of the religious beliefs of the Ottoman Caliphate. For this immigrant group there was no doubt that a safe life in the U.S. could be had through public assimilation. Their offspring who can identified as "first" generation American-born Muslims, also considered assimilation to be a positive change in the lives of their children. However, their experiences in the APSS provided them with a much different assimilation process than their parents had (Curtis, 2010, p. xxiv).

The *middle* wave of modern Muslim immigration to the U.S. occurred in the mid-20th century. Following the logic used to define the relationship between the early wave of modern Muslim immigrants and their American born children, it might be tempting to name this middle wave of immigrants as a "first" generation, and a majority of the discourse actually does do so. The early wave and the middle wave of Muslim immigrants in the U.S. have both been identified in the discourse as "first" generations. This is problematic because, even though separated by half a century, they have more in common with one another than either immigrant group has in common with their children: the "first" generations of American Muslims. One important difference between immigrant generations seems to be their understanding of and relationship with the Islamic *Ummah*. The difference between immigrant generations and their American born offspring is their understanding of and relationship with the APSS.

The second modern wave or the "middle" wave of Muslim immigrants who came into the U.S. to escape the tumultuous political environments that resulted from conflict within the Arab League of Nations, the Israeli occupation of Palestine, Egypt, and Lebanon, the Iranian revolution, the development of Pakistan and the U.S. sanctioned Afghan-Russian war. Like the early middle wave of Muslim immigrants, the modern middle wave of Muslim immigrants were aware of governments that seized property and arbitrarily imprisoned its citizens. Together, these two middle immigrant generations built a functional American *Ummah* on the foundations laid by the early modern immigrant generations who built small enclave communities that banded together for comfort and support through the practice of Islam. The modern *middle* wave of Muslim immigrants were more ethnically diverse, tended to be better educated, had a stronger command of the English language, and was more politicized due to the circumstances under which they had emigrated. They tended to politicize the small communities built by the early modern generations. The confidence with which the middle wave of Muslim immigrants approached the development of the American *Ummah* was a double-edged sword because it allowed them to raise a second generation of American Muslims who believed in their inherent right to a place in American culture with all the rights and protections afforded an American citizen This should not have been a problem, however, the time in which the later middle generation immigrated was a tumultuous time in America's cultural history (Curtis, 2010, p. xxiv).

Curtis (2010) captures the problematic identification of chronological generations of Muslims in America when he writes that non-Muslim Americans often consider all Muslims to be somehow "new, as foreign, "fresh of the boat" [FOB] (p. xv). However, he adds, "many first-generation Muslim Americans often talk about fellow Muslim Americans in the same way" (p. xv). Curtis does not clarify the relationship between FOB, Muslim immigrants, and "first" generation American Muslims: This allows for the identification of at least two generations of Muslim presence in the United States: An *immigrant* generation and a "first" generation.

Unlike the ways in which many other immigrant groups are identified by chronological generations, generations of American Muslims are categorized in ways that give the impression that this ethnic group has made no movement forward. They are frozen forever in the minds of Americans both native born and naturalized as the FOB and "first" generation. Counting an immigrant generation and a "first" generation of American born Muslim allows for a shift in the perception of American Muslims as not having earned a place in American history and culture.

The chronology provided by Curtis and the suggestions for defining generations provided by the Pew Foundation allows for the probability that there is actually an immigrant generation whose experiences are quite different from their "first" American born generation of children at a, "similar stage of life" (Mapping, 2009). Peek (2005) defines adult immigrants as a "first" generation and a 1.5 generation as the children that emigrated with their parents "before reaching adulthood" (p. 222, fn. 6). She argues that the experiences of the 1.5 generation share more in common with those of the "second" generation. When the immigrant generation is counted as just that—an immigrant generation—then the generation of American born children they produce can be defined as the "first" generation. This provides a generational momentum in the chronology of Muslim presence in America, and it allows for an understanding of the role the APSS plays in the development of American Muslim identity. The immigrant generation did not experience the APSS. Their children, both "first" generation and the 1.5 generation, identified by Peek, had to negotiate both the developing *Ummah*, built by their immigrant generation parents and the APSS they were mandated by American law to attend.

The children born in the United States, to Muslim immigrants of the middle and early modern periods must be counted as the first generation of American Muslims. From this point forward the word "first" when prefacing the word "generation" will not be placed in quotation marks. From this point forward we refer to the first generation of American Muslims as defined above. The experiences of this first generation and those of the 1.5 generation are quite similar in that they were aware of the presence of an Islamic *Ummah* that their immigrant parents had built over the years. The role of the *Ummah* for the immigrant generation Muslim was to solve social, cultural, and religious problems. It offered the immigrant generation unity, protection, and clear models of acceptable Islamic behavior. As some first/1.5 generation American Muslims continued their practice of Islam as a lifestyle that casually observed the Five Pillars of the religion of Islam, the *Ummah* was a connection to a cultural past that served as a reminder of their hybrid identity. For those who embraced Islam as a lifestyle and a religious practice, it provided a community of believers.

First/1.5 generation Muslim children were forced to negotiate a hybrid identity. They could not move past what Homi Bhabha refers to as "narratives of originary and initial subjectivities" (Bhabha, 1994 as cited in Antonette, 1998, p. 47). This generation was truly caught between the home cultures of their immigrant parents and the culture of the APSS, which insisted on their choosing one identity over another. To understand the issues faced by contemporary American Muslim children in the APSS one must have a clear understanding of the generational chronology of Muslim presence in the United States.

CONSTRUCTING AMERICAN MUSLIM IDENTITY

The study of American Muslim culture is currently considered a subtopic of Arab-American studies. Salaita (2011) explains that "Arab American studies ... in many ways ... [is] an emerging subject" (p. 1). This, in and of itself raises the problem of conflating Muslim identity with Arab cultural or national identity and could be used to reinforce the stereotype that all Muslims are Arab. Shaheen (2009) explains, the image of the Arab has, since Hollywood first made movies, been negative. This very long history of representing people of cultural or national Arab identity has strongly reinforced stereotypes in the minds of mainstream Americans. Further, by the close association made by dominant culture Americans between Arab and Muslim, those who live a Muslim lifestyle and practice the Islamic faith, in the U.S. are often misidentified as "Arab" (p. 19).

Salaita (2011) writes that much like the "study of Arab American literature, you find something diverse and heterogeneous" in the study of American Muslim literatures that Western trained academics build into categories that attempt to contain all of that diversity and heterogeneity (pp. 3–4). Further, he argues that Arab American studies is a fundamentally American area of study. So too, is American Muslim studies. American Muslim identity is an American identity. Muslims in America are no less American than say, the Amish in America, even though their cultural values and religious beliefs call upon them to set themselves apart from the dominant American values and beliefs (p. 6).

Constructing any category of human identity is a political process that allows academics to gain mastery over something called "Muslim Studies," for example. Salaita (2011) warns that these categories must be constructed in a way that allow for the broadest possible terms. He states, "Iranians, Afghans, Turks, and Pakistanis ... are predominantly Muslim, a commonality they share with Arabs" yet we must remember that each of those national identities is "culturally and geographically distinct" (pp. 7, 9). It is this precise cultural distinction that we do not want to efface in the process of constructing the category of American Muslim identity. However, in order to construct an American Muslim category we must make the religious observance and practices that comprise a Muslim identity our primary focus. National and/or cultural heritage for our purposes are secondary.

THE *UMMAH* AND THE APSS

Because of their experiences in American public schools or because of the presence of the *Ummah*, first/1.5 generation American Muslims understood the need for an open, nonjudgmental and ongoing dialogue between home life and public school life. This process was not made easy by the APSS or the *Ummah*. Curtis (2010) explains that "Muslim American" students hoping to participate in American school systems consistently find, over time, that the ability to maintain a Muslim identity while at school has proven to be difficult. The level of difficulty with which these efforts have been met are supported by the growing trend of Muslim Americans who either home school or send their children to Islamic schools that are more in line with their religious practices (pp. 165–166).

In addition to the assimilatory nature of the organizational structure of the American public school system, generations of "color-blind" pedagogy has served to marginalize all but mainstream American student identities. The philosophy that all teachers must treat all students alike defies logic. It is a simple philosophy that promotes the appearance of equality but functions as a mechanism of coerced assimilation, for both student and teacher. Teacher training programs that practice color-blind pedagogy prepares teachers to work in lock step with one another. Students who do not meet the qualifications of a mainstream student have important parts of their personal identities ignored or shamed into silence (Antonette, 1998, 2003; Banks, 2001; Smith, 2011). Paolo Friere argues that,

> Education is by nature social, historical, and political.... The idea of an identical and neutral role for all teachers could only be accepted by someone who was either very naive or very clever. Such a person might affirm the neutrality of education, thinking of school as merely a kind of parenthesis whose essential structure was immune to the influences of social class, of gender, or of race. (Friere, as cited in Shor, 1987, p. 211)

A recent example demonstrates the point. A student teacher fulfilling her field experience requirement for her secondary education program at a Pennsylvania state college reported observing what she *felt* was a disturbing exchange between a teacher and a student, in a middle school classroom. The student teacher, a first generation *muhajabah* (a Muslim woman who covers her hair with a scarf), explained that while she was assisting a group of students at a work station, the sponsoring teacher came up to an Anglo American female student seated at that workstation and began stroking her long blonde hair. As she did so, she looked around the table at the other students, two Latina students, one White male student and the student teacher, and repeated, a number of times, "I love your hair, your hair is so beautiful, I wish I had your hair." A generous explanation of this scene might be that the teacher was expressing a personal preference and felt the need to compliment the student whose hair she was stroking. However, the level of discomfort expressed later, to the student teacher, by the two Hispanic female students, and also reported by the student teacher, to her supervisor, suggests that some other dynamic was at work.

It is difficult to avoid the possibility that the sponsoring teacher was communicating a cultural bias. Her, not so subtle, preference for the blonder, straight-haired student, and the comments made to the group, as a whole, suggest that this could have been a signal to her students that she acknowledged the difference between the student whose hair she was stroking and the *muhajabah* student teacher, whose hair could not be touched or admired. This serves both prongs of the color-blind program. The sponsoring teacher made the student teacher aware of her difference from the sponsoring teacher, which is not allowed in the color-blind system; and, she communicated to the students that because of the difference between the sponsoring teacher and the student teacher that only one of them could be "The Teacher." This scenario also suggests a not so subtle prejudice the teacher may hold against the Latina students, whose hair was visible but not admired.

When considering that "at the level of school and classroom, the context of learning is reflected in students' perception of classroom environment, the nature of the learning task, assessment methods, attitudes and expectations of peers and teachers, students' interactions with their peers and teachers" (Salili, Chiu, & Hong, 2001, p. 1), the interaction between teacher and blonde student could be clearly perceived by the other students at the table as a negation of their value. The interaction between teacher and other students (she addressed them visually as she spoke), the interaction between the teacher and student teacher (at whom she did not look), and the interaction between the Hispanic female students and the student teacher, who all looked at each other, and later expressed their "confusion" to one another signifies that an intense communication had occurred and it seemed, to the student teacher and her supervisor, that it clearly signaled the preferences of the sponsoring teacher. The message, it seems, is that long, straight blonde hair is what the teacher values. The inference that could be made by the students in the room who do not have long blonde hair is that s/he is not valued by the teacher. When considered in the specific light of APSS culture, one might conclude that having hair that can be stroked, no matter what color or length, is preferable to hair that cannot be visually admired. The cultural value system of the school is reified through the juxtaposition of this particular sponsoring teacher's actions and the presence of the *muhajabah* student teacher.

After processing the scenario with her supervisor, the student teacher reached the conclusion that "that teacher has a problem." This is not a typical response. This young, well-educated, *muhajabah* did not "take the hint." Read through the coercive function of the color-blind practice, the younger teacher should have questioned herself. She should have been wracked by doubts of her ability or her "fitness" to teach. The assimilatory practice of the sponsoring teacher "should" have shaken her to her core until she decided that she would conform and thereby be accepted and respected. However, she had a strong connection to her *Ummah* that allowed her to decide to wear the veil in the first place, and to continue to wear it in the face of the marginalization she would surely face.

The concept of the Islamic *Ummah* is an ancient one; however, it continues to shift to meet the needs of every era since the time of the Prophet Muhammad, *peace be upon him (PBUH)*. Often translated as "Muslim Community" the term *Ummah* designates a fundamental concept in Islam (Esposito, 1995, vol. 4, p. 267). The history of the "Constitution of Medina" is the document that codified the presence and role of the *Ummah* historically. It provides a strong parallel to the history of contemporary Muslim emigration.[2] During his lifetime, the Prophet Mohammed, *PBUH*, defined the *Ummah* as those related to him by lineage. However, the "Constitution of Medina" was later used to define the Islamic *Ummah* as an entity that supports social, political, and religious life under Islam (Uri, 1985, pp. 5-12). The Islamic *Ummah* in its traditional and purest form is a global community of Muslims, a brother/sisterhood of the shared belief in the *Qur'anic* revelation through Allah's messenger, Mohammad, *PBUH*, that transcends race, nationality and political affiliations. The *Ummah el Islamayya* is just now beginning to recognize the new American *Ummah* that appears to be more lenient in its acceptance of Western practices (Murad, 2001; Younis, 2012).

The student teacher and the student, Sana Haq, are first generation American Muslims as defined above. They both exhibit a strong and public display of their Muslim identity. They appear to recognize no danger of marginalization or physical threat related to their very public, visual difference from mainstream Americans (Anglo). This can be related to the quality of their relationship to their *Ummah* and the courage of their conviction. They are to be admired, but as we have seen in the situation of the student teacher, the representative of the dominant culture does not respond with admiration. What can be inferred by this incident is that this student teacher will find it difficult to find work in an American public school, and it is likely that she will be marginalized by her peers, if she does find work in an American public school. The subtle marginalization demonstrated in the situation described by the student teacher was something she "felt." Second generation Muslim students appear not to notice or perhaps they just ignore the subtle racisms they encounter. First generation Muslim students recognized it but without the presence of a supportive community they could easily blame themselves as lacking in some way.

NONCRITICAL AMERICAN MULTICULTURALISM AND THE APSS

As of this writing (2013) American public schools have failed to provide positive representations of Muslim identity in most classrooms. What little information students might be given seems to be confined to history lessons that discuss waves of immigrants or world religions. This is a technique used in American schools to coerce assimilation through the use of educational materials. In the APSS, faculty and administrators are presented with many options in educational materials, yet, what continues to serve as history, social studies, and English language arts texts in many American K–12 schools provide limited coverage of "minority" identities and focus primarily on the immigrant experiences of underrepresented cultural groups. It is only after a cultural group gains the political power to demand more than a paragraph of representation that they are provided a "positive history." This is a history that illustrates the difficulty encountered by immigrant generations but also includes significant contributions made by members of those groups, not only in the United States, but world-wide. When only a "negative" history is provided it effectively (subtly) teaches students who identify with the cultural group portrayed, in this case Muslims, that the fact they made it to America is a phenomenal accomplishment made by their predecessors and that nothing more could or should be expected of them (Antonette, 2003, p. 34).

Traditional APSS multicultural curriculum is based on "Food and Fun" fairs. They rarely offer students the opportunity to critically engage in the experience; to process differences between and among themselves in a structured and safe classroom; or to bring the experiences home, so they can be discussed within the home, with family and informed by family practices and beliefs. Another problem with the "Food and Fun" fair is that along with approved school holidays they tend to relate to some cultural/religious groups but not to others. This provides the *illusion* of privileging a multicultural student body. However, the absence of Muslim "Food and Fun" fairs, and the lack of observance of Muslim holidays, in most but not all American public schools, can be quite confusing for a Muslim student.

The use of narratives written by first/1.5 generation American Muslim illustrates "positive" history through the presentation of their parents' immigrant experiences, as they perceived them; but, more importantly, they display the radical pattern of critical thinking that was required to negotiate home cultures deeply steeped in the Islamic *Ummah* or homes in which the American *Ummah* was still a distant but attainable possibility, *and* build a public identity that did not betray home life but provided anonymity and some level of protection from non-Muslim students in the APSS. Still, young women who choose to don the veil and the young men who choose to grow a short beard in postpuberty are not acknowledged by mainstream society as being participants of it. Their road seems to be longer and much more difficult, if not dangerous, than those Muslims that shed external representations of Islamic identity.

Teaching literature called "multicultural" is difficult. The term, multicultural, when used to describe literature or books, has longed been understood by librarians as those works written by or about human beings that are "O"ther than those of the dominant culture (Said, 1979). For many years this was understood by Education and English faculty as global/national identities that were not American. However, in America, it is crucial that multicultural texts be understood as those written by and about ethnic identities that are not considered to be representative of the dominant Anglo American culture. Reading " multicultural" as both representative of domestic ethnic difference and global/national difference allows domestic ethnic identity to be understood as, "somehow not quite American" (Antonette, 2003, p. 29). This distinction is important to understand because it contributes to the dearth of multicultural curriculum in American schools.

As an institution of assimilation, the function of the APSS is to focus on the monocultural aspects of U.S. history, culture and values. As Heble and Mehta (2013) argue the "inclusion of cultural and contextual approaches to the study of literature has long been accepted as imperative in the literature classroom" (p. 86). In teacher training programs it is crucial that training in the teaching of "diverse worldviews" is provided along with opportunities that allow student teachers to exercise their abilities to approach both text and student with a "critical understanding of communities" (p. 86).

When multicultural literature is taught without an accurate "culture and context" approach it invites the epidemic spread of negative stereotypes. The American Muslim community has enough of that already. This is one reason why narratives written by first generation American Muslims can be effective. They provide the cultural context needed for a critical consideration of cultural difference. It then requires the teacher to make sure s/he understands the non-English language that may be used, the basic characteristics of the nation/state, home culture represented, and the Five Pillars of Islam. This list is not exhaustive and it is not meant to trivialize the writing or the content of the work. However, a lesson in teaching multicultural literature will have to wait. The point is that texts written by and about first/1.5 generation American Muslims seem to carry both the *Ummah* and the APSS in ways that allow American Muslim and non-Muslim readers to engage cultural identity at the level of interpersonal relationships. Readers and educators can begin to consider what is cultural and what is personal between the characters. This sets the stage for both the educator and the students to have access to this historically vilified and "foreign" group in a nonconfrontational format that cannot be confused with or read as Islamic indoctrination.

This chapter will end by using short excerpts from 1.5 generation, Syrian, American Muslim, Mohja Kahf's (2006) novel, *The Girl in the Tangerine Scarf* and first-generation, Lebanese, American, Muslim, Alia Yunis' (2009) novel, *The Night Counter.* Both texts are appropriate for grades 10-12, but some chapters of each could be used effectively in grades 4-9. Both texts provide "positive" histories. Both texts could be used to carry on an open dialogue between home and classroom. Both texts demonstrate the ways in which first generation American Muslims struggle to produce a hybrid identity and the ways in which some second generation American Muslims avoided that negotiation. Because they are works of fiction, they allow students and teacher to maintain the critical distance from the text that allows for critical thinking about the text.

In Mohja Kahf's (2006) novel, *The Girl in the Tangerine Scarf*, the main character, Khadra describes some of the experiences of the 1.5 generation Muslim American. Khadra's family came to the U.S. from Syria in the middle of the 20th century, part of the modern middle wave of Muslim immigration. The family joins an Islamic community when Khadra's father, Wajdy, accepts a position at the *Da'wah* Center (Outreach Center) just outside of Indianapolis, Indiana.[3] There, he commits his life and the lives of his family members to building Muslim communities in the U.S. where "practicing Islam is hard" (p. 14). These difficulties are defined as the inability to safely practice all five pillars of Islam: belief in one God who revealed his message to His Prophet Muhammad (*PBUH*), daily prayer, charity work, fasting during the holy month of Ramadan, Hajj-pilgrimage to Mecca a Holy city in Saudi Arabia, as well as, many of the cultural aspects of a Muslim lifestyle: the eating of *Halal* (religiously prescribed foods), and dressing modestly for both genders, which includes wearing *Hijab*, (head scarf) for women, and other religious and cultural observations. The APSS, as described by Kahf was a mine-field fraught with overt bigotry, as well as, unintentional practices that were just as damaging. Kahf (2006) writes that

> one day Mrs. Brown poured Candy Corn into a little flowered plastic cup on Khadra's desk. Khadra said, "I can't eat this, her round baby-fat face grave. Why not sweetie? Mrs. Brown said, bending low so her white face was next to Khadra's. There's a pig in it! Mrs. Brown laughed a pretty laugh and said, no, there isn't a pig in it, dear. (p. 13)

Even by today's standards, to a non-Muslim, eating the candy corn may seem innocuous or even trivial. However, in Khadra's devout household eating pork or anything with pork products in it is considered to be *haram* (sinful) even when consumed accidentally. Young Khadra believed in Mrs. Brown's authority to not only educate but to protect her students. Even though Khadra had been taught at home that the gelatin in most American candy is made from rendered animal parts such as tendons, ligaments and soft tissue, she believed that Mrs. Brown was right and that candy corn must be an exception to what she had been taught at home.

At the end of the day, on the school bus ride home, Khadra shared with her brother, Eyad, what had happened, and denies to him that she actually ate the candy. Eyad confirms that "candy corn has pig in it" (p. 13). At the age of 5, Khadra confessed to herself that she did eat the candy and realized that she "was tainted forever" (p. 13). While this is not true in the Islamic religion, her family had not prepared Khadra for the negotiation of the unintentional acts that can occur outside of the *Ummah*. Therefore, she felt tainted at this young age. Had Mrs. Brown not so quickly dismissed Khadra's concern she could have quite easily confirmed that candy corn does use gelatin and that gelatin in the 1970s was primarily made from pork parts. Had she taken just 5 minutes to ask a colleague or to even question Khadra's logic, the trauma that Khadra experienced might have been averted. Khadra would not have felt tainted. She would have felt safe in the care of Mrs. Brown and she would have recognized Mrs. Brown as a teacher who cared about the values that Khadra held dear. If Mrs. Brown had practiced a multicultural pedagogy she would have stopped to consider that there may be ways to understand Candy Corn that were different from her own understanding. Instead, the moment Khadra discovered that the American candy was made from pork, a fissure in the trust that existed between the student and teacher developed and would only widen over time. This is the danger of "color blind" pedagogy. It created tension between the culture of the school, as represented by Mrs. Brown and the culture of Khadra's *Ummah*.

Later, in middle school Khadra is taunted by a few of the local boys who tear her *Hijab* (headscarf). Having "come of age" Khadra is delighted to wear *Hijab* because that is the accepted practice in her *Ummah*. Her mother wears *Hijab*. All the women she admires in the *Ummah* wear *Hijab*. It is the expectation within the *Ummah*, and Khadra looks forward to meeting that expectation. As Khadra tries to repair her torn *Hijab*, she knew, "Mama was going to freak out, "Where is your scarf? Why did you take it off? Her father would say gravely, "But, why were you talking to a boy anyway? 'They didn't get it'" (p. 125). Regardless of the abuses that Khadra faced on a day to day basis because of her religion, her struggles were viewed as insignificant in the light of how the Prophet Muhammad (*PBUH*) and his followers suffered for their Islam. Because Khadra had reached the age of physical maturity, she was believed to be capable of the task of protecting her modesty.

Khadra's parents never approached the school or the teacher to ask how their daughter could have experienced this kind of assault on her modesty. No one from the school contacted Khadra's home to assure them that the school did not condone such behavior. In fact, "Mr. Eggleston came out of his room down the hall … shook his head, gave her a look of mild disapproval, and went back inside" (p. 125). It must be noted that the Islamic *Ummah* of Khadra's community also included at least one family of American National Muslims who could have informed Khadra's parents of the difficulty that Khadra would encounter when she went to school wearing the *Hijab*. Had this happened, perhaps, her loving and caring immigrant generation parents, Ebtehaj, her mother, and, Wajdy, her father, would have approached the school; however, those members of the *Ummah* who knew APSS culture did not provide the necessary information and their silence, unfortunately, made them complicit in the *Ummah*'s failure to support Khadra in her religious practice.

Khadra also describes an educational system bereft of any kind of appreciation of nondominant cultural values. Whenever Khadra wrote an essay that in some way did not directly reflect back the teacher's own perspective, Khadra would receive a poor grade. If she mimicked the teacher; she received a good grade (p. 120). Khadra notes, "if the schoolbooks didn't say so, Islamic civilization was responsible for most of the good scientific inventions in the world, up until the last hundred years or so" (p. 123). The schoolbooks did not mention that.

First generation American Muslim narratives, like American, Syrian, Muslim, Mohja Kahf's (2006) novel, *The Girl in the Tangerine Scarf*, are essential to the education of contemporary American Muslim students because these works provide a clear picture of the sociopolitical dynamics necessary to negotiate both the public and private spheres of their lives. Kahf's novel in particular illustrates Islamic practice and Muslim home life in ways that would benefit both Muslim and non-Muslim students. It provides detailed description of the prejudice and bigotry that many American Muslim students feel but cannot quite articulate, such as that reported by the student teacher mentioned above. It also provides clear cultural information for those non-Muslim readers who would like to avoid offending their Muslim schoolmates, and it demystifies Islam.

First/1.5 generation children, as represented in Kahf's novel, had no choice but to consider their religious identities on a daily basis. They were painfully aware of the pressure to assimilate, which was not an option condoned by Khadra's *Ummah*. Kahf writes, "maybe we don't belong here, Khadra thought, standing next to Hanifa in the crowd at Zuhura's graveside. Maybe she belonged in a place where she would not get shoved and called 'raghead'" (p. 97). Khadra's well-meaning, immigrant generation parents were not equipped to address or, in many cases understand, the inequities their first generation children experienced in the APSS.

Gloria Anzaldua (1987), in her groundbreaking work on Chicana identity, talks about hybrid identity as the painful results of "cultural collision" (p. 102). Immigrant generations experience many cultural collisions, not the least of which is the loss of "home." Rarely does the immigrant generation stop using the "home" language. But, almost the exact opposite happens in the first/1.5 generation. For this generation the collision begins when they enter the APSS. (Brown, 1970; Rodriguez, 1983; Shen, 1994).

Alia Yunis' (2009) novel, *The Night Counter*, provides a multigenerational illustration of the function of the *Ummah* for the Muslim immigrant generation, first/1.5, and second generation American Muslims. The story follows the Lebanese, American Muslim, Abdullah family late of Dearborn, Michigan whose members are now spread around the United States. The matriarch, Fatima, counts down to what she believes to be her last 1,000 nights left to live. She does this in Santa Monica, California while staying with her second generation Grandson, Amir, an actor who finds no difficulty in taking parts that require him to portray stereotypic Muslim characters who are always dressed with guns or bombs. He is unaware of his grandmother's plan to die in his arms as soon as she sees him married, "*Inshallah*." Fatima repeats this term "God Willing" 51 times throughout the novel.

Fatima immigrated to the U.S. as a young bride and she held onto her Lebanese Islamic identity. While she may be an American citizen, she is first and foremost an Arab Muslim. Fatima's first husband, Marwan, died just after Fatima became pregnant with their first child. A family friend, Ibrahim, also Lebanese Muslim, married Fatima and together they raised 10 children in one of the largest Muslim cities in the United States, Dearborn, Michigan.[4] Fatima does not subscribe to the traditional practice of veiling, but it is obvious that she tries hard to be a devout and pious woman. Her constant *dhikr* (the remembrance of Allah, *Sobhana wa taalah*, meaning there is no power higher than God; often found in Islamic text written in English as SWT), is an extremely important aspect of Islamic identity and follows, in importance, only the practice of the five Islamic pillars.

Fatima's eldest daughter, first generation, Laila, who never leaves Dearborn, "remember[s] that when she was a girl, it was very rare to see a head scarf, let alone an abiya [a dress usually worn in the house in certain Muslim cultures], in Dearborn [Michigan]. The Arabs of her childhood had been blenders; they just mixed into the rest of the country" (Yunis, 2009). p. 93). Laila, whose mother, Fatima was a part of the early modern immigrant generation, views, not only her mother, but herself as a "Blender." She marries a Muslim immigrant, Ghazi, however, unlike their Muslim immigrant friends, they do not speak Arabic in their home. Laila lives her entire life in the largest, most thriving Islamic *Ummah* in the United States.

When Laila is diagnosed with cancer, she responds in a typical American way. She becomes angry with God. As a result of this feeling of emotional distance from the *Ummah*, even though many members of the *Ummah* did rally around her, she does something that her Muslim immigrant genera- tion mother would never dream of doing. Laila purchases pork, which is *Haram*. She cooks the meat and serves it to her husband and their guests, who unaware, begin to eat the pork until her stepfather, Ibrahim, suspects what she has done and insists that everyone at the table stop eating the "non-*Halal*" meat but only eat Laila's "speciality" the grape leaves. Ibrahim is mortified at what Laila has done and understands that she would be forever shunned by the *Ummah* should anyone ever learn what she did. "Many hours later ... Laila got up ... and pulled Ghazi's prayer rug out of the linen closet. She faced the direction in which Ghazi said Mecca lay. Then she did the only thing she knew to be true and right" she prayed (Yunis, 2009, p. 115). Laila's strong connection to the *Ummah* allows her to recognize that what she has done is wrong. However, her actions can be read as the cultural collision that forms Laila's hybrid identity. Laila par- ticipated in the APSS, she was familiar with the dominant culture's practice of eating pork, and she also knew it was not an acceptable practice in her Muslim community. Her hybrid identity allows her to participate in the cooking and serving of the pork as a way of expressing her anger at God and her husband who sought comfort in his own practice of Islam.

Fatima's third daughter, first generation American Muslim, Randa, has been chipping away at her cultural and religious identities since prepubes- cence. Fatima remembers that "Randa was the child from whom Ibrahim and I went from being called Mama and Baba to Mom and Dad. Randa made all the kids follow her, except Laila who was already *too* used to Mama and Baba" (Yunis, 2009, p. 194). This is the beginning of Fatima's recount- ing all the ways in which they lost their daughter to the American way of life, such as getting a hula hoop, dressing sexy, going off to an away camp with her American friends, and finally striving to save up for a cheerleader uniforms. Fatima and Ibrahim are complicit in the continuation of these behaviors when they only scold Randa by saying, "*aabe* [shame]" rather than *Haram* [sin] (Yunis, 2009, p. 51). In this way they contribute to the tension between the identity Randa is trying to build in school and the *Ummah* of their community. In their attempt to exercise Islamic practice allowed for by the American *Ummah*, they sent mixed messages about their own values and beliefs and the expectations they had for their childrens' practice of Islam, which allowed Randa to move away from her Muslim identity almost completely.

When we finally meet Randa, or "Randy" she describes the lengths to which she went to finalize her transformation into an American woman and yet she cannot help but acknowledge her hybridity. She says, she was very glad that Bud [Bishar Bitar, her husband] was almost pale, not dark like Laila's and Nadia's husbands; didn't have an accent; and had a last name that could pass as anything, even Jewish. Just to make sure they weren't mistaken for Arab or Jewish in Texas, Randy got a nose job to get rid of the bump she'd inherited from Fatima. Then she had given all her girls solid American names: Loretta, June, and Dina. She had named her youngest daughter after Dina Merrill … she didn't discover until years later that Dina was a far more common name in the Middle East than in the States. (Yunis, 2009, pp. 161–162)

It is not an uncommon thing for many first/1.5 generation American Muslims to move away from both their religious and ethnic identities to some degree in order to incorporate parts of the dominant culture into their identities. However, Randy's actions are extreme in nature. Her attempts to distance herself from the *Ummah* are demonstrated in the character of her daughter, second generation American Muslim, Dina.

As a child growing up with parents who tried to ignore their own hybridity and as a student in the APSS, Dina had no experience with Muslim culture or Islamic practice. Dina was head cheerleader in her high school and she dated an "All-American" local football hero, she "did not have the bumpy nose, but she had the vibrantly lush hair Fatima had … although Dina's was perfectly blond" (Yunis, 2009, p. 154). Dina knows her immigrant grandparents are Lebanese Muslims. She understands that this cultural heritage is part of who her parents are but she seems absolutely gobsmacked when she meets American, Palestinian, Jamal Masri, who, for the first time in Dina's life, refers to her as anything other than American. Jamal tells Dina that "Bitar is a pretty well-known Palestinian family name" (Yunis, 2009, p. 159). Knowing this did not comfort Dina. "It made her uncomfortable" (Yunis, 2009, p. 159). Dina could not conceive of herself as Muslim or Arab. Indeed, the only time she even thought about Arabs, "which she rarely did" was when she was "watching the latest terror alert on Fox News" (Yunis, 2009, p. 159). Dina's All-American girl identity is not an act. Her parents hybridity and the way they responded to it, by distancing themselves and their children from the *Ummah* put Dina in the position of believing that she had no need to negotiate her cultural and national identities.

Dina decides to join Jamal as a relief worker in a Palestinian refugee camp in Lebanon over her summer break not because she feels any connection to the Arab identity but because she is attracted to Jamal. After a few days in the camp, Dina is given a small group of children to whom she is to teach English. She uses all her best American cheerleader skills to excite the students who, with just as much enthusiasm, repeat the words they have just learned for a visiting reporter. The kids fell into squad formation. 'Eyes, ears, nose, and toes', they chanted for the camera using hand drills to point out the eyes, ears, nose and toes on the kid next to them. (Yunis, 2009, p. 180)

Dina utilizes the only method of teaching she understands, empty rote memorization with fun exercises.

After a few weeks in the camp Dina goes with Allison, one of the camp workers, to visit families in the local town. In the home of a very poor seamstress, Allison introduces Dina to Sarah. By way of introduction, Sarah brings out a "yellowed envelope" and hands it to Dina. Allison explains that this is the deed to a home in Palestine that Sarah's family owns but in which they are not able to live. Sarah hands Dina the envelope and Allison says, "They like to show these to foreigners because they think no one believes their story. Pretend to read it, why don't you" (Yunis, 2009, p. 182). Dina looked at the document and treated it with a level of respect that equaled the pride Sarah had for it.

> "I am sorry," Dina said. She couldn't think of what to add to that.
> "No, no be sorry," Sarah answered. "I go back one day, inshallah."
> "Inshallah." Dina nodded. Having no other viable answer, she had spoken her first Arabic word. (Yunis, 2009, p. 182)

The utterance of that one Arabic word (her grandmother's constant *dhikr*) is the beginning Dina's cultural collision. In going to Lebanon, Dina finds her cultural heritage and begins to learn how it has shaped her family and her life, and she begins to feel the presence of the *Ummah*. As a second generation American Muslim, Dina never had to negotiate hybridity the way that 1.5 generation Khadra did, or even her own, first generation, mother, sister, Randy, and Aunt Laila. If Dina had been introduced to first/1.5 generation Muslim American writing, she might have recognized some shadow of her heritage that might have enticed her to investigate it. It isn't that she disavows her Muslim heritage. She is ignorant of it.

The teaching of first/1.5 generation American Muslim writings, especially the works of poetry and fiction can provide nonthreatening introductions to Muslim culture for both Muslim and non-Muslim alike. Marcia Hermansen (2009) writes:

> despite the multiplicity of cultural expressions surrounding Islam, in all Muslim societies the family plays an important role during childhood, youth, and, in fact, throughout the person's entire life.... This is contrasted with America, a culture where separation from family is usually seen as a necessary part of development. (p. 96)

Hermansen articulates the "cultural difference" that Bhabha explains is the most important part of the process of constructing identity. One must move beyond the original identity, in Dina's case the identity of her mother and grandmother. However, in order to move beyond that identity, one must first become aware of it. While the struggle for personal identity and the tensions experienced may differ from one generation to the next, the power of the *Ummah* at family, cultural and political levels provide an unchanging and omnipresent source of Muslim identity against which hybrid or hyphenated identities can be shaped.

The use of work written by first/1.5 generation American Muslims is not to be used as a model for writing instruction or a strategy to negotiate hybrid identity but as a lesson in the ways in which these particular generations of American Muslims frequently experienced alienation from their home culture and marginalization from their school culture. Second generation, Dina appears to be immune to the need to negotiate an identity. Understanding the history that affords her the illusion of a nonproblematic identity could allow her the skills she needs to negotiate the institutions of American culture that are meant to assimilate her and efface her Muslim identity. The work of first/1.5 generation American Muslims illustrate these experiences and they can also provide a foundation upon which new responses to ruptures in America's social fabric can be learned by both Muslim and non-Muslim Americans.

Negotiating American Muslim identity as the *Ummah* shifts from an Islamic focus constructed by the immigrant generation to the American *Ummah* constructed by first generation American Muslims, while negotiating the culture of the APSS is ongoing and complex. Because we are dealing with American Muslim identity, this process is not only difficult for the American Muslim student but also for the non-Muslim students and teachers who do not understand the complexity of the process. In addition, the ethnic diversity within the category of Muslim American identity is far more complex than the discourse in Muslim Studies has been able to suggest, as yet. In light of American xenophobia this field of work needs to occur quickly. Further, the APSS and the American *Ummah* need to collaborate on the development of curriculum that supports students as they negotiate their American Muslim identities within both the *Ummah* and the APSS. The use of narratives written by and about first and second generation American Muslims would be a useful place to begin that work.

NOTES

1. The first modern wave of Muslim immigrants into the U.S. escaped the tyranny of the Ottoman Caliphate. This wave of immigration also included the

members of the Pen League and other Christian intellectuals (Curtis, 2010, p. xxiv).

2. The "Constitution of Medina" defined the relationship between Muslims and Jews who lived in and around Medina (now a part of Saudi Arabia). It was written and codified sometime between C.E. 62 and 67. This document also defined the presence and the role of the Islamic *Ummah*. The document is quite controversial in that it seems to name those who are *of* the *Ummah* and those who are not. To this day the *Ummah* of each community constructs the expectations for proper Islamic practice and appropriate Muslim behavior in ways unique to its community. This in no way lessens the power of the *Ummah* over the members of the community (Uri, 1985, pp. 5, 12).

3. In Kahf's novel the word *da'wah* refers to "the dimensions of religious outreach or mission activity in the modern Islamic world" (Esposito, 1995, Vol. 1, p. 343).

4. Established in 1963, the Islamic Center has been serving the needs of Muslims in the greater Detroit area of which Dearborn is a part, as well as, throughout the United States. For more information go to: http://www.icofa.com/index.php/about-us/history-of-islamic-center (History of the Islamic Center, n.d.).

REFERENCES

Antonette, L. (1998). *The rhetoric of diversity and the traditions of American literary study: Critical multiculturalism in English. Critical studies in education and culture series.* Westport, Connecticut: Greenwood Publishing Group.

Antonette, L. (2003). Liberal and conservative multiculturalism after September 11. *MultiCultural Review, 12*(2), 29–35.

Anzaldua, G. (1987). *Borderlands, La Frontera: The New Mestiza.* San Francisco, CA: Aunt Lute.

Banks, J. A. (2001). Citizenship education and diversity implications for teacher-education. *Journal of Teacher Education, 52*(1), 5–16.

Barrett, P. (2007). *American Islam: The struggle for the soul of a religion.* New York, NY: Farrar, Strauss and Giroux.

Bhabha, H. K. (1994). *The location of culture.* New York, NY: Routledge.

Brown, D. (1970). *Bury my heart at Wounded Knee: An Indian History of the American West.* New York, NY: Henry Holt.

Curtis, E. (2010). *Encyclopedia of Muslim-American History.* New York, NY: Facts on File.

Esposito, J. (Ed.). (1995). *The Oxford Encyclopedia of the Modern Islamic World* (Vol 1). New York, NY: Oxford University Press.

Esposito, J. (Ed.). (1995). *The Oxford Encyclopedia of the Modern Islamic World* (Vol 4). New York, NY: Oxford University Press.

Galloway, L. (2011). Muslim-American or American Muslims: Here is why it Matters.*Muslim Matters.org,* 1/7/13. Retrieved from http://muslimmatters.org/2011/04/19/muslim-american-or-american-muslims-here-is-why-it-matters

Global Religious Landscape. (2012). The Forum on Religious and Public Life. *Pew Research Center.* Retrieved from http://www.pewforum.org/future-of-the-global-muslim-population-regional-americas.aspx

Haddad, Y., Senzai, F., & Smith, J. I. (Eds.). (2009). *Educating the Muslims of America.* New York, NY: Oxford University Press.

Heble, A., & Mehta, S. R. (2013). A tale of two cultures: The Omani–Indian encounter in the literature classroom. *Arts and Humanities in Higher Education.* Published online before print. Retrieved from http://ahh.sagepub.com/content/early/2013/01/07/1474022212469787.full.pdf+html

Hermansen, M. (2009). South Asian Muslim American girl power: Structures and symbols of control and self expression. *Journal of International Women's Studies 11*(1), 86–105.

History of the Islamic Center. *The Islamic Center of America.* (n.d.). Retrieved 2/26/13 from, http://www.icofa.com/index.php/about-us/history-of-islamic-center

Johnson, T. (2011). Muslims in the United States. *Council on Foreign Relations.* Retrieved from http://www.cfr.org/united-states/muslims-united-states/p25927

Kahf, M. (2006). *The Girl in the Tangerine Scarf.* New York, NY: Carroll and Graf.

Mapping the Global Muslim Population: A Report on the Size and Distribution of the World's Muslim Population. (2009). *The Pew Forum on Religion & Public Life.* Retrieved from http://www.pewforum.org/Muslim/Mapping-the-Global-Muslim-Population(7).aspx

McGoldrick, M., Giordan, J., & Garcia-Preto, N. (2005). *Ethnicity and family therapy,* (3rd ed.) New York, NY: The Guilford Press.

Murad, A. (2001). *Reliance on Allah: The cure for an Umma in crisis* (DVD Video Lecture). Miami, FL: MeccaCentric Da'wah Group.

Peek, L. (2005). Becoming Muslim: The development of a religious identity. *Sociology of Religion, 66*(3), 215–242.

Rodriguez, R. (1983). Hunger of memory: *The Education of Richard Rodriguez.* New York, NY: Random House.

Said, E. (1979). *Orientalism.* New York, NY: Vintage Books.

Salaita, S. (2011). *Modern Arab American fiction: A reader's guide.* Syracuse, NY: Syracuse University Press.

Salili, F., Chiu, C. Y., & Hong, Y. Y. (Eds.). (2001). The culture and context of learning. In *Student motivations: The culture and context of learning.* New York, NY: Kluwer.

Shaheen, J. (2001). *Reel bad Arabs: How hollywood villifies a people.* New York, NY: Olive Branch Press.

Shen, F. (1994). The classroom and the wider culture: Identity as a key to learning english composition. In S. Maasik & J. Solomon (Eds.), *Signs of Life in the USA: Readings on Popular Culture for Writers.* Boston, MA: Bedford Books of St. Martin's Press.

Shor, I., & Friere, P. (1987). *A pedagogy for liberation: Dialogues on transforming education.* South Hadley, MA: Bergin & Garvey.

Smith, P. (May 9, 2011). Islam in America. *The New York Times Upfront Newsmagazine for Teens,* Retrieved from http://teacher.scholastic.com/scholasticnews/indepth/upfront/features/index.asp?article=f0109a

Stillwell, C. (2008, June 11). Islam in America's public schools: Education or indoctrination? *San Francisco Chronicle*. Retrieved from http://www.sfgate.com/politics/article/Islam-in-America-s-public-schools-Education-or-2482820.php

Uri, R. (1985). The "Constitution of Medina": Some notes. *Studia Islamica, 62*, 5–23.

Yunis, A. (2009). *The night counter*. New York, NY: Three Rivers Press.

Younis, A. (2012, February). Is there space for American Muslims in the Ummah? *Huffington Post*. Retrieved from http://www.huffingtonpost.com/ahmed-younis/is-there-space-for-meric_b_1179739.html

THE PERSONAL ASPIRATIONS AND CHERISHED IDEALS OF MUSLIM ADOLESCENTS LIVING IN NORWAY AND SINGAPORE

Deborah A. Stiles and Osman Özturgut

ABSTRACT

Norway and Singapore are two countries where both ethnic majority and ethnic minority adolescents endorse prosocial behavior, civic harmony, and religious tolerance. In this multimethod study, 332 Muslim and 432 non-Muslim young adolescents (mean age = 13.7) described the ideal man and woman by rating the importance of 10 qualities and drawing pictures of the ideal man or ideal woman. Two hundred sixty-eight of these participants also listed their future occupational possibilities. It was hypothesized that most participants would express prosocial values. Additionally, it was hypothesized that Muslim adolescents would demonstrate higher aspirations and occupational ambitions than non-Muslim adolescents and that minority Muslim adolescents would be likely to adopt some values of the majority culture in

Growing Up Between Two Cultures: Problems and Issues of Muslim Children, pp. 145–163

which they lived. Adolescents from Norway and Singapore drew many pictures of the ideal person helping others. Muslim and non-Muslim adolescents valued kindness, honesty, and liking children but differed in how important they thought these qualities were for the ideal ($ps < .05$). Muslim adolescents expressed higher career aspirations than non-Muslims ($p < .01$). Muslim Singaporeans seemed to incorporate aspects of latest fashions and brand names into their identity constructs more often than did Muslim Norwegians, whereas Muslim Norwegians incorporated nature, the outdoors and sports more often than did Muslim Singaporeans. In summary, regardless of their religious and ethnic backgrounds, the Norwegian and Singaporean youth in this study espouse prosocial values and show positive identity development, ideals and aspirations. However, the Muslim adolescent participants in this study came from especially supportive environments in Norway and Singapore and may not be representative of the Muslim youth in those countries.

When Muslim adolescents grow up in countries where they are ethnic and religious minorities, they are presented with several social, emotional and educational issues and challenges they must face in order to live successfully in two very different cultures. Muslim youth living in the West experience stereotyping and discrimination, sometimes to an extreme degree. In a multimethod study of 70 Muslim American adolescents Sirin and Fine (2007) found that 84.3% of the adolescents reported discrimination in the past year because of their religion or ethnicity; they also found that the perception of discrimination increased with age. In the Netherlands, Van Geel and Vedder (2010) studied 255 Muslim adolescents using written questionnaires and in the introduction of their article they reported that about half of native-born Dutch adolescents express negative feelings towards Muslims and that Muslim youth living in the Netherlands experience economic discrimination and a lack of opportunity for advancement. In a large-scale study of 5,366 immigrant youth living in 13 Western societies Berry, Phinney, Sam, and Vedder (2006) gathered data using a structured written questionnaire comprised of several scales. Berry et al. found that Muslim youth were the religious group most likely to adopt a strong ethnic orientation. They found that perceived discrimination had negative effects on adolescents' sense of well being and psychological and sociocultural adaptation.

Incidents of reported discrimination have been rare in the countries of Norway and Singapore where both ethnic majority and ethnic minority adolescents endorse prosocial behavior and civic harmony and there is relatively less tension and more acceptance of religious differences (Chang, Gopinathan & Kam, 1999; Chong & Yip, 2003; Leirvik, 2003). In *The Thoughts of Youth: Adolescents: An International Perspective on Adolescents' Ideal Persons*, Gibbons and Stiles (2004) found that valuing of kindness, honesty, altruism, and concern for children were especially high in Norway and Singapore when compared to the other countries studied. The social environments, government policies, and national values of these two countries promote understanding, tolerance, and the welfare of all citizens; overall these are good environments for young people as they are growing up.

Most psychologists agree that the central task of adolescence is identity formation and "bicultural development is one natural pathway for immigrant children and other children growing up in a multicultural context" (Sam & Oppendal, 2002, p. 25). Norway and Singapore, two countries that promote peace and understanding, may foster healthy bicultural identity development of their adolescent minorities.

Norway has a population of about 4.7 million, a GDP per capita of $53,400, and is ranked first among 187 countries on the Human Development Index rank as reported by the United Nations Development Program (UNDP). Norway is the sponsor of the Nobel Peace Prize and a world leader in the proportion of GNP provided in aid to the world's poorest countries. In Norway freedom of religion is guaranteed. The majority of Norwegians are of Christian heritage; Islam is the largest of the non-Christian religions. Tolerance, honesty, human kindness, independence, and equality (especially as it relates to gender-roles) are important Norwegian ideals.

Singapore has a population of about 5.35 million, a GDP per capita of $59,700, and is ranked 26th of 187 countries on a Human Development Index.

> Singaporeans consider their nation to be unique among modern societies because they hold to traditional Asian values while also prizing modern ideas and progress.... [In Singapore] there is an extremely strong emphasis on racial harmony and relevant historical events. As the tiny city-state is a multiracial [sic] society, materials that may breed ill-will among its population or cause religious disharmony are not tolerated, even on the Internet. (ProQuest Information and Learning, 2005, p. 1)

Singapore's three major ethnic groups are Chinese, Malay, and Indian. Ethnic Chinese in Singapore are Buddhists, Taoists, Confucianists, and Christians. Ethnic Malays are almost entirely Muslims; Malays include peoples originating in Malaysia and Indonesia. Ethnic Indians are mostly Hindu. Whatever their ethnic group, the values of Singaporeans are referred to as Asian values; Singaporeans value discipline, self-control, education, honesty, interdependence, harmony, conformity, and humility.

In Norway and Singapore, Muslims belong to religious and ethnic minority groups and although they enjoy many advantages living in these countries, they are less privileged than members of the majority groups. For example, the labor immigrants are able to find affordable housing in

Grønland, Central-Eastern Oslo, which is among the most deprived areas of the city (Bangstad, 2011). Most Muslims in Norway came there as part of the labor migration of the 1970s (first Pakistani, Turkish, and Moroccan labor migrants arrived in Norway in the late 1960s), to join relatives in Norway, or as refugee and asylum seekers when Norway officially stopped labor migration in 1975.

Norway is a wealthy country that is committed to social equality, but Muslims in Norway tend to live in more modest housing, have lower levels of school achievement, and higher unemployment rates than Norwegians of Nordic origin. The majority of Muslims in Singapore did not come to Singapore as immigrants, but they have lived there since the nation gained independence in 1965. On average, Muslims in Singapore have lower incomes and lower levels of school achievement.

Purpose of the Study

The intent of this study was to better understand the personal aspirations and ideals of ethnic majority adolescents and ethnic minority adolescents (of Islamic heritage) living in Norway and Singapore through examining their future goals and ideas about the ideal man and woman. In this multi-method study 332 Muslim and 432 non-Muslim adolescents described the ideal person and drew a picture of the ideal man or ideal woman engaged in an activity. An additional 268 of these adolescents identified their choices for future occupations. It was hypothesized that prosocial values would be espoused by the majority of adolescents and that Muslim adolescents would have higher aspirations and more concern about future employment possibilities than non-Muslims. It was further hypothesized that the minority Muslim adolescents would embrace certain values held by the majority in their respective host countries: nature, sports and gender-role equality in Norway and traditional gender-roles, an intense work ethic, and pursuit of material well-being in Singapore.

METHOD

Participants

This study of 764 youth involved a total of 366 girls (11–17 years, mean age = 13.71) and 398 boys (11–17 years, mean age = 13.65) in Norway and Singapore. The study in Norway involved 165 adolescent children of Islamic heritage and 247 children of Christian heritage; in Singapore the study involved 167 adolescent children of Islamic heritage, and 185 whose heritages were in the Chinese values of Buddhist, Taoist, and Confucianist traditions. Participation was anonymous and voluntary; .9% omitted their ages and 34.3% omitted their fathers' occupations.

Participants in Norway were recruited from three Oslo area public schools that had large numbers of immigrant and refugee students. Most Muslim students had parents from Pakistan, Turkey, Morocco, Iran, Iraq, and Somalia. Bratt (2002) found that Muslim immigrant groups with different ethnic backgrounds in Norway appear to hold a common in-group identity. Although the participants attended the same schools and were living in the same communities, the Nordic Norwegians had more fathers with higher occupational status than the Muslim immigrant groups did. Of those students listing fathers' occupations, a larger proportion of non-Muslim students (50%) than Muslim students (32.3%) had professional fathers ($p < .05$).

Participants in Singapore were recruited from Muslim and Chinese cultural/religious centers and five government schools. In Singapore, adolescents understood the term race to refer to culture, religion, and ethnicity. Muslim students in Singapore most often described their "race" as Malay (94%), but also as Javanese, Boyanese, and Islam. Of those students listing fathers' occupations, 33% of Muslim students and 40% of non-Muslim students had fathers who had professional occupations.

It should be noted that the Muslim youth participating in this research study came from especially supportive youth environments. In Norway the teachers who chose to let their students take part in the research study, were the teachers who had created welcoming, open, supportive classroom environments for their students (Stiles & Ericksen, 2003). In Singapore the Islamic religious and cultural leaders who approved the research study, were adults who had created welcoming, nurturing organizations specifically designed for Muslim youth.

Materials

Participants rated (on a scale of 1 to 7, with 7 indicating very important) the importance of 10 qualities of the ideal man or woman and drew a picture of the ideal engaged in an activity. Two hundred sixty-eight of these same adolescents also listed their future occupational possibilities. Participants in Singapore completed questionnaires in English, the language of instruction in schools there. Participants in Norway completed questionnaires in Norwegian; these were translated into English and back-translated into Norwegian for verification.

Procedure

Multivariate ANOVA's were used to study ratings of the 10 qualities of the ideal; chi square tests were used to study drawings of the ideal man or woman. Drawings were scored on 25 categories; 13 categories relevant to the study were analyzed statistically. Inter rater reliability on the drawings has ranged from to .67 to 1.00 (Stiles & Gibbons, 2001). For Muslim and non-Muslim adolescents living in Norway and Singapore, the two most popular future occupations were identified and ANOVA's were used to study the number of professions being considered as possibilities.

Limitations

The multimethod approach is a strength of this study; a possible weakness is that all of the instruments used in this study were self-report measures. This study included three self-report measures—a questionnaire on the ideal person, a listing of occupational possibilities, and a drawing of the ideal person. The questionnaire on the ideal person was limited to 10 predetermined choices, which may or may not have been the most relevant and meaningful for youth from Singapore and Norway. The drawing of the ideal person was open-ended and allowed for individual and cultural interpretations; yet, drawings are not easily subjected to statistical analyses. The listing of occupational possibilities was an open-ended survey, but students with writing difficulties may have found the listing to be challenging. Due to the smaller sample size in the investigation of the listing of occupational possibilities, findings pertaining to future work should be interpreted cautiously.

The findings from all the three self-reporting instruments used in this study should be interpreted cautiously. The use of any self-reporting instrument has to account for the probability that respondents might provide responses that reflect either social acceptability or adolescent rebellion. The incidence of socially desirable responses might be higher in Singapore than Norway, thus comparing data between these two countries might not produce valid and reliable results.

The Muslim adolescent participants in this study may not be typical. They were all volunteers who consented to take part and obtained consent from their parents. The participating schools and organizations in this study were the ones that chose to take part; some schools and organizations declined. The adults from the participating organizations demonstrated that they care about the social, emotional and educational well being of the youth they serve. The individual educators were eager to let their students be involved. Consequently, the youth came from especially supportive environments in Norway and Singapore; the participants in this study may not be representative of the Muslim youth in those countries.

Also, the data were collected before the recent shootings in Norway in July of 2011 (see Galpin, 2011), since then relationships between Muslim and non-Muslims in Norway may have become even more complicated.

RESULTS

Ratings of Ideal

Table 6.1 presents the means and standard deviations for each of the 10 qualities of the ideal person. There were no significant interactions between religious heritage and residence. Muslim and non-Muslim adolescents differed in how important they thought it was for the ideal man and woman to like kids, to have average height and weight, to be very intelligent, to have a lot of money, to be kind and honest, to have good looks and to have a good job, F s (1, 742) = 4.26, 10.32, 38.93, 23.66, 8.63, 7.78, and 14.23, respectively, $ps < .05$. Norwegian and Singaporean adolescents differed in how important they thought it was for the ideal man and woman to like kids, to have a lot of money, to be sexy, and to have a good job, F s (1, 742) = 5.21, 4.16, 25.58, and 4.03, respectively, $ps < .05$.

Table 6.1.   Means and Standard Deviations of Ratings of Importance of 10 Qualities of the Ideal Person

	Muslims	Non-Muslims	Norwegians	Singaporeans
Kind and honest	6.47 (1.18)	6.70 (.76)	6.66 (91)	6.54 (1.04)
Likes kids	5.92 (1.41)	5.70 (1.30)	5.89 (1.29)	5.69 (1.44)
Good job	5.83 (1.41)	5.34 (1.41)	5.42 (1.41)	5.73 (1.41)
Very intelligent	5.49 (1.43)	4.80 (1.47)	5.01 (1.47)	5.23 (1.51)
Fun	5.44 (1.54)	5.43 (1.30)	5.44 (1.33)	5.42 (1.50)
Good looks	5.13 (1.77)	4.77 (1.69)	4.97 (1.76)	4.87 (1.71)
Average ht. wt.	5.02 (1.68)	4.58 (1.77)	4.69 (1.74)	4.88 (1.74)
Lot of money	4.21 (1.89)	3.51 (1.74)	3.67 (1.93)	4.01 (1.70)
Popular	3.74 (1.90)	3.52 (1.77)	3.58 (1.84)	3.66 (1.81)
Sexy	3.71 (2.23)	3.78 (2.03)	4.11 (2.13)	3.30 (2.13)

In *The Thoughts of Youth: Adolescents: An international Perspective on Adolescents' Ideal Persons*, Gibbons and Stiles (2004) created profiles of responses to the 10 qualities of the ideal comparing the answers of youth from collectivist countries with youth from individualist countries. The ranking profile of youth from collectivist counties was compared with the ranking profile by Muslim youth living in Singapore and Norway. Their responses were highly correlated, $p(8) = 0.95$, $P = 0.00002$.

Drawings of Ideal

Table 6.2 presents the percentage of drawings featuring each of certain qualities of the ideal person. Muslim adolescents drew significantly more pictures than non-Muslim adolescents of the ideal man and woman with religious themes, traditional gender roles, and studying or thinking. They drew significantly fewer pictures in which the ideal person was depicted with a sexual emphasis or as smoking, drinking or using drugs.

In addition to comparing the drawings Muslims and non-Muslims and Norwegians and Singaporeans on 13 categories, specific comparisons were made on six categories between Muslim adolescents living in Norway and Muslim adolescents living in Singapore. Significantly more Muslim adolescents in Norway (23.8%) than Muslim adolescents in Singapore (7.1%) drew pictures of sports, $p < .001$, significantly more Muslim adolescents in Norway (23.8%) than Singapore (8.2%) drew pictures of nature and the outdoors, $p < .01$, and significantly more Muslim adolescents in Norway (10.1%) than Muslim adolescents in Singapore (.6%) drew pictures of showing the ideal with a sexual emphasis, $p < .001$. Significantly more Muslim adolescents in Singapore (18.1%) than Norway (6.1%) drew pictures of the ideal with brand names or insignia. Although Muslim adolescents did not differ with respect to gender-roles, significantly more non-Muslims in Norway than non-Muslims in Singapore drew the ideal in traditional roles ($p < .01$) and significantly more non-Muslims in Norway than non-Muslims in Singapore drew the ideal in nontraditional roles ($p < .001$). Examples of nontraditional gender roles were the ideal man doing housework and the ideal woman repairing machines.

Occupational Aspirations

The most popular occupational possibilities listed by Nordic Norwegians were police officer and professional athlete; the most popular occupational possibilities listed by Muslim adolescents in Norway, by Muslim adolescents in Singapore, and by Chinese adolescents in Singapore were medical doctor and business person/manager. Muslim and non-Muslim adolescents and Norwegian and Singaporean adolescents differed in how often they selected professional occupations as possibilities F s $(1, 267) = 9.93, 18.30$, respectively, $ps < .01$. Compared with the mean number of professions listed by non-Muslim adolescents, the mean

Table 6.2. Percentages of Drawings Displaying Certain Qualities of the Ideal Person

	Muslims	Non-Muslims	Norwegians	Singaporeans
Helping, caring for others, nurturing	29.4	26.5	29.3	26.3
Smoking, drinking, drugs	.3	2.8*	2.9	.3**
Sexual emphasis	5.7	12.5**	16.0	2.3***
Religious themes	6.4	1.1***	1.7	5.5**
Nature, outdoors	13.5	27.1***	33.3	12.3***
Sports	12.7	18.6	30.2	7.3***
Nontraditional gender-roles	11.7	13.8	17.7	7.1***
Traditional gender-roles	30.4	24.3*	30.4	23.3*
Working in a paid job	31.9	29.5	32.9	29.7
Achievement and success	14.1	13.7	13.0	14.8
Studying, thinking	21.2	13.8*	19.4	17
Brand names or insignia	12.8	9.0	14.8	7.0**
Money, wealth	9.4	7.0	6.1	10.3*

Note: * indicates significant difference at $*p < .05$. $**p < .01$. $***p < .001$.

number of professions listed by Muslims was higher ($M = 3.06$, SD $= 3.14$, $M = 1.86$, $SD = 2.27$, respectively); compared with the mean number of professions listed by Norwegian adolescents, the mean number of professions listed by Singaporeans was also higher ($M = 3.26$, $SD = 3.20$, $M = 1.57$, $SD = 1.28$, respectively). Fathers' occupational status did *not* significantly affect the number of professional occupations chosen ($p < .08$). Unfortunately, there was a small sample listing future occupations and information on fathers' occupations was often missing. Also missing was information about educational track for most Norwegians. In Singapore where 199 students reported their educational track, students in the highest and elite educational track listed significantly more professional occupations ($M = 4.31$, $SD = 3.77$) than students in moderately advanced track ($M = 3.14$, $SD = 2.80$) and students in the general academic track ($M = 2.35$, $SD = 2.71$), $F(2, 198) = 6.91$, $p < .01$.

DISCUSSION

Prosocial Values

This sample of adolescents expressed prosocial values. Adolescents from both countries and from both Muslim and non-Muslim heritages assigned their highest ratings to the importance of the ideal person being kind and honest. More than 25% of these adolescents (from both countries and religious heritages) illustrated the ideal person helping, caring for, and nurturing other people. Figure 6.1 shows the ideas of a 15-year-old Javanese girl from Singapore who drew this picture of the ideal man with a heart of gold who is always giving a helping hand; the ideal man likes helping others and in this case, he is helping an old woman.

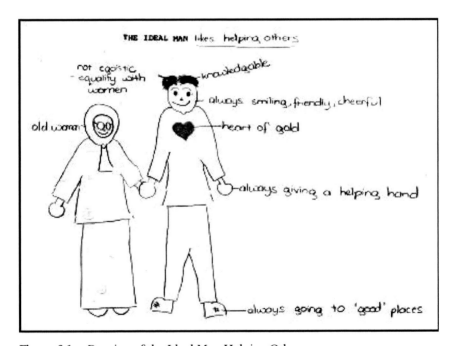

Figure 6.1.   Drawing of the Ideal Man Helping Others.

The drawings in Figure 6.2 also illustrate helping other people. A 13-year-old boy of Pakistani heritage living in Norway made the drawing on the left, which shows a father caring for his son. A 12-year-old boy of Pakistani heritage created the drawing on the right shows the ideal man being most kind and helpful and providing directions to a "dear lady" in Oslo.

Figure 6.2.   Drawings of the Ideal Man Helping His Son and the Ideal Man Helping with Direction.

The drawing on the left of Figure 6.4 also illustrates helping other people; in this drawing a 16-year-old girl of Pakistani heritage living in Norway drew the ideal woman as a lawyer defending her client. Many ideal person drawings by Muslim adolescents living in Norway and Singapore illustrated prosocial behaviors such as helping others, caring for children, being kind, practicing religious beliefs, showing religious tolerance, and refusing to smoke, drink alcohol, or take drugs (see Figure 6.3).

A 13-year-old Boyanese girl from Singapore made the ideal man drawing on the left side of Figure 6.3. She writes "no smoking, no drinking." Only one Muslim adolescent from Singapore drew the ideal smoking and *no* Muslim adolescents from Norway drew the ideal smoking, drinking or taking drugs. The rejection of illicit substances by adolescent Muslims in both Norway and Singapore is significant, $p < .05$ (see Table 6.2).

In this study, religious practices and beliefs were not studied directly, but their importance can be inferred from the themes in the drawings and questionnaires. The majority of Muslims in Norway migrated from Pakistan, Turkey, Morocco, Iran and Iraq. They generally follow the Arab/Middle Eastern interpretation of Koran wherever they live. They learn to recite Koran beginning from the young ages and follow the codes of behavior based on that interpretation. Four Muslim adolescents in Norway drew the ideal person praying or studying the Koran. We believe that the Singaporean Muslim adolescents in this study were similarly religious. Most (94%) of the Muslim adolescent participants in Singapore were of Malay heritage, a few had Indonesian heritage. In a study of religion, language, and youth in Singapore, Vaish (2008) found that all of the 206 Malay youth studied reported that their religion was Islam. Vaish also found that the Malay youth reported that they pray silently in their mother tongue, but, when asked to give an example of a prayer, they most often provided a prayer in Arabic. Fifteen Muslim adolescents in Singapore drew the ideal person praying, studying the Koran, or going to a mosque. (The difference between the proportions of religious themes drawn by Muslim youth in Norway compared with Singapore was not statistically significant). On the right side of Figure 6.3 sixteen-year-old Muslim boy from Singapore drew the ideal man . In his drawing the ideal man is "going to Mosque for weekly Friday prayer." Significantly more Muslim than non-Muslim adolescents drew religious themes in the ideal person drawings, $p < .001$ (see Table 6.2).

Figure 6.3.   Drawing illustrating proper conduct and religious observance.

Another characteristic of the responses of the Muslim adolescent participants is that their "profile" is much more typical of youth from collectivist countries than youth from individualist countries. This is true for Muslim adolescents from both Singapore and Norway. In general, the Muslim youth do not endorse the individualistic life—enjoying, exciting, hedonistic – in the ideal surveys or drawings (see Table 6.2 and Figures 6.1, 6.2, and 6.3). The Muslim adolescents give significantly higher ratings than non-Muslims to the importance of being very intelligent and have a good job and they rarely draw the ideal with a sexual emphasis or using drugs or alcohol.

High Occupational Aspirations

Higher aspirations were held by Muslim adolescents compared with non-Muslims. This sentiment is evident in Muslim adolescents' relatively stronger endorsement of the importance of having a good job, being very intelligent, and having a lot of money, and in the significantly greater number of professional occupations listed. Muslim adolescents also drew significantly more pictures than non-Muslim adolescents of the ideal person studying or thinking.

Singaporeans compared with Norwegians also gave stronger endorsements to the importance of having a good job, and having a lot of money and they listed a significantly greater number of professional occupations. Singapore is a meritocracy and in Singapore occupational aspirations were significantly related to adolescents' educational track.

So, why do Muslim adolescents compared with non-Muslims adolescents in their respective countries hold higher occupational aspirations and place greater emphases on intelligence and studying? It may be that they perceive education and professional training as the best way to improve their economic condition and serve their families and communities. Given that the parents of the youth emigrated from developing nations, further education is seen as the way for them to have a comfortable future and the privileges (that are only afforded by the educated people), while also providing them with the opportunities to support their parents in the future. Previous research has found that new immigrant and minority group youth may have higher achievement motivation than their majority group peers (Stiles, Gibbons, Lie, Sand & Krull, 1998; Suárez-Orozco & Suárez-Orozco, 1995). Receiving a further education will not only help them accumulate financial capital but will further help them accumulate social and cultural capital. For example, social capital is operated not only to the deployment of economic capital but also to secure resources for achieving advantages in the privileged educational pathways and market for their families (Archer & Francis, 2006).

Evidence of Successful Psychological Adaptation

Some authors have noted better psychological adjustment of ethnic minority Muslim adolescents than their peers. For example, Van Geel and Vedder (2010) explained that Muslim adolescents had a higher self-esteem and fewer psychological problems than the adolescents of Dutch heritage living in the Netherlands. In their study of 13 societies Berry et al. (2006) found that Muslim adolescents had the most positive psychological adaptation when compared with youth in the religious categories of Eastern,

Judeo-Christian, and no religion. In our study, the questionnaires and drawings by both Muslims and non-Muslims living in Norway and Singapore provided ample evidence of well-being and prosocial values.

A few differences emerged. Muslim adolescents drew more religious themes and fewer pictures of smoking, drinking, or taking drugs (see Figure 6.3). They were also less likely to draw the ideal person with a sexual emphasis. About 18% of adolescents, almost always boys, draw the ideal woman (not the ideal man) in a highly sexualized and sometimes lewd way.

Sirin and Fine (2007) titled their multimethod study, "Hyphenated Selves: Muslim American Youth Negotiating Identities on the Fault Lines of Global Conflict." They described interviews and drawings by Muslim boys showing, "hyphenated selves ... splintered with the weight of the world; split open with the searing knife of global conflict" (p. 157). We also collected drawings, but did not notice illustrations of a "split" or "splintered" selves, but we did see drawings that suggested bicultural selves. Chen, Benet-Martinez, and Bond (2008) explain that immigrants high on bicultural identity integration demonstrate better psychological adjustment with regards to increased self-esteem and self efficacy than those that are low on bicultural identity integration.

Evidence of Bicultural Identity Formation

It was hypothesized that the minority Muslim adolescents would embrace certain values held by the majority in their respective host countries. Results concerning this hypothesis were complex and somewhat unexpected. Singapore is a more conservative country than Norway and gender-role equality is a cherished ideal in Norway therefore it was expected that Muslim adolescents in Singapore would be more conservative and Muslim adolescents in Norway would be more nontraditional. But it was *not* the case that Muslim adolescents in Norway compared with Muslim adolescents in Singapore differed significantly in how often they drew the ideal in either traditional or nontraditional gender roles. Although Muslims drew more traditional gender-roles than non-Muslims, Norwegians *not* Singaporeans illustrated more traditional gender-roles. In egalitarian Norway, many Muslims and non-Muslims drew the ideal women caring for children and the ideal man participating in "male" sports (see Figure 6.4 right side). As a result, the proportions of traditional gender-roles drawn by Muslims from Norway and Singapore were similar (32% and 29%) and the proportions of traditional gender-roles drawn by non-Muslims from Norway and Singapore were significantly different (29% and 18%, p <.01). Another unexpected outcome concerned nontraditional gender roles; 12% of Muslims in Singapore and 12% of Muslims in Norway drew nontraditional gender-roles (see Figure 6.4 left side). Nordic Norwegians drew many traditional *and* nontraditional gender-roles. Nontraditional gender-roles drawn by non-Muslims from Norway and Singapore were significantly different (30% and 2%, p <.001)

Figure 6.4.   Drawings illustrating nontraditional and traditional gender roles.

As Muslim adolescents are growing up and constructing their identities in Norway and Singapore, they select which aspects of their cultures to embrace. As Nagel (1994) points out that

> culture is not a shopping cart that comes to us already loaded with a set of historical, cultural goods. Rather we construct culture by picking and choosing items from shelves of the past and the present.... In other words, cultures change: They are borrowed, blended, rediscovered, and reinterpreted. (p. 162)

Becker (1997) argued that the immigrant children growing up in the societies would eventually learn to code-switch, adapting their thinking to the host nation, while maintaining their identity when involved with the people from their home nations. In this case, they use code-switching as an identity marker of membership.

It appears that within the nontraditional, egalitarian Norwegian society, Muslim and non-Muslim adolescents have embraced both traditional and nontraditional gender-roles; in the more traditionally-minded country of Singapore, Muslim (but not non-Muslim) adolescents have embraced both traditional and nontraditional gender-roles. This is an example to how Muslim immigrant children adapt their thinking to also embracing nontraditional gender roles even though they come from a cultural background that does not value gender egalitarianism but values males over females, especially in social contexts. That is, Muslim youth are comfortable with their multiple bicultural identities and are able to negotiate between the more conservative world of their parents and the secular world outside their homes.

Examples of nontraditional and traditional gender-roles can be seen in Figure 4 which shows two drawings by adolescents of Pakistani heritage living in Norway. The drawing on the left shows a girl's drawing of the ideal woman in a professional job and the drawing on the right shows a 13-year-old boy's drawing of the ideal person participating in sports.

These drawings are characteristic of the drawings from Norway in that they illustrate a nontraditional gender role, helping others, a traditional gender-role activity, sports, and the outdoors. Figure 6.1, a drawing by a Muslim girl from Singapore, is also interesting because it depicts both traditional Asian values and modern ideas in Singapore. According to this adolescent girl, the ideal man values service and shows respect for his elders; the ideal man helps an older person and enjoys serving others. He also believes in gender equality and seems to enjoy modern symbols of status as indicated by his brand name shoes that take him to "good" places.

Singapore is world famous for shopping; the Orchard Road area in Singapore is internationally known. In *The Thoughts of Youth: Adolescents: An international perspective on adolescents' ideal persons*, Gibbons and Stiles (2004) found that only adolescents from Singapore and the U.S. included shopping in their descriptions of their favorite free time activities. Therefore, it is not surprising that Muslim adolescents in Singapore showed a greater inclination to draw the ideal wearing brand names or insignia than Muslim adolescents from Norway.

Muslim adolescents living in Norway more often drew pictures of nature and sports than Muslim adolescents living in Singapore; like other Norwegians they showed that they cherish the outdoors. The greater valuing of sports and the outdoors by Norwegian Muslims than Singaporean Muslims may be examples of how Muslim adolescents in Norway are bicultural and are adapting to the norms of their country. Or, because the forefathers of most Muslims in Norway originally came from rural areas, enjoying nature and the outdoors may have special appeal for them. Agricultural societies, where the immigrants first came from, depended on nature and living in harmony with nature. That is, the shared cultural knowledge of the youth might as well be related to their parents' upbringing and the value systems this upbringing brings with it (Wyer, Chiu, & Hong, 2009).

This present study found evidence for an adolescent identity formation process that includes cultures being "borrowed, blended, rediscovered, and reinterpreted." In both countries adolescents cherish prosocial values. The Muslim Singaporeans appear to be most attuned to the prestige associated with brand names and insignia and the most closely identified with religion. In Norway the Muslim adolescents are in favor of traditional gender-roles, nontraditional gender-roles, nature, the outdoors, and sports. These adolescents are well-integrated in the societies they live in and are able to adopt both cultural values effectively. They are able to understand the nuances of both cultures they grow up with and are able to borrow and blend appropriately.

The adolescents' views on occupational aspirations suggest that Muslim youth in Norway and Singapore will become well adjusted, successful individuals, eager to contribute to the society in which they live. The occupational aspirations are a little more difficult to interpret due to missing information; yet this appears to be a promising direction for future research. Larger sample sizes in both countries might reveal more significant relationships between fathers' occupations and professional aspirations in Norway and educational track and professional aspirations in Singapore.

A strength of this study of the personal aspirations and cherished ideals of Muslim adolescents living in Norway and Singapore is that multiple methods were used to gather an understanding of the youth. Utilization of this methodology provided the researchers with additional perspectives and insights that are beyond the scope of any single method. Although each method provided different insights, an overall picture emerges of ethnic and religious minority Muslim youth embracing prosocial values, adapting successfully, and preparing for responsible and productive adult lives.

ACKNOWLEDGMENTS

This research was supported in part by the following awards to the first author: Fulbright Award for research in Norway, a Messing Award for research in Singapore, and a Webster University Faculty Research Award for studies in Norway.

REFERENCES

Archer, L., & Francis, B. (2006). Challenging classes? Exploring the role of social class within the identities and achievement of British Chinese pupils. *Sociology*, *40*(29), 29–49.

Bangstad, S. (2011). The morality police are coming! Muslims in Norway's media discourses. *Anthropology Today, (27)*5, 3–7.

Becker, K. R. (1997). Spanish/English bilingual codeswitching: A syncretic model. *Bilingual Review, 22*(1), 1–37.

Berry, J. W., Phinney, J. S., Sam, D., & Vedder, P. ((2006). Immigrant youth: Acculturation, identity and adaptation. *Applied Psychology: An International Review 55*(3), 303–332.

Bratt, C. (2002). Contact and attitudes between ethnic groups: A survey-based study of adolescents in Norway. *Acta Sociologica, 45*, 107–126.

Chang, A. S. C., Gopinathan, S., & Kam, H. W. (1999). *Growing up in Singapore: Research Perspectives on Adolescence.* Singapore: Prentice-Hall.

Chen, S., X., Benet-Martínez, V., & Bond, M. H. (2008). Bicultural identity, bilingualism, and psychological adjustment in multicultural societies: Immigration-based and globalization-based acculturation. *Journal of Personality, 67*, 803–837.

Chong, H. K., & Yip, J. (2003). *The state of youth in Singapore.* Singapore: National Youth Council.

Galpin, R. (2011). *BBC News: Norway's Muslim immigrants ponder future.* Retrieved from http://www.bbc.co.uk/news/world-europe-14316670

Gibbons, J. L., & Stiles, D. A. (2004). *The thoughts of youth: An international perspective on adolescents' ideal persons.* Greenwich, CT: Information Age Publishing.

Leirvik, O. (2003). Islam and Christian-Muslim relations in Norway: Popular realities, political and religious responses, interfaith cooperation. *Islamochristiana, 29*, 121–140.

Nagel, J. (1994). Constructing ethnicity: Creating and recreating ethnic identity and culture. (Special Issue on Immigration, Race, and Ethnicity in America) *Social Problems, 41*, 152–177.

ProQuest Information and Learning. (2005). Republic of Singapore. *CultureGrams-World Edition.* Retrieved from http://onlineedition.culturegrams.com.library3.webster.edu/secure/world/world_country.php?contid=3&wmn=Asia&cid=143&cn=Singapore

Sam, D. L., & Oppedal, B. (2002). *Acculturation as a developmental pathway.* In W. J. Lonner, D. L. Dinnel, S. A. Hayes, & D. N. Sattler (Eds.), *Online readings in psychology and culture* (Unit 8 Chapter 6). Retrieved from Center for Cross-Cultural Research, Western Washington University, Bellingham, Washington.

Sirin, S., & Fine, M. (2007). Hyphenated selves: Muslim American youth negotiating identities on the fault lines of global conflict. *Applied Developmental Science. 11*(3), 151–163.

Stiles, D. A., & Ericksen, T. H. (2003). Psychosocial aspects of migration in Norway. In L. L. Adler & U. P. Gielen (Eds.), *Migration: Immigration and emigration in international perspective* (pp. 207–221). Westport, CT: Greenwood Publishing.

Stiles, D. A., & Gibbons, J. L. (2001). *Manual for Evaluating Individual and Social Values Expressed in International Adolescents' Drawings of the Ideal Woman and Man.* Jamaica, NY: World Cultures.

Stiles, D. A., Gibbons, J. L., Lie, S., Sand, T., & Krull, J. (1998). Now I am living in Norway: Immigrant girls describe themselves. *Cross-Cultural Research: The Journal of Comparative Social Science, 32*, 279–298.

Suárez-Orozco, C., & Suárez-Orozco, M. M. (1995). *Transformations: Immigration, Family Life, and Achievement Motivation among Latino Adolescents*. Stanford, CA: Stanford University Press.

Vaish, V. (2008). Mother tongues, English, and religion in Singapore. *World Englishes, 27*, 450–464.

van Geel, M., & Vedder, P. (2010). The adaptation of non-Western and Muslim immigrant adolescents in the Netherlands: An immigrant paradox? *Scandinavian Journal of Psychology, 51*, 398–402.

Wyer, R. S., Chiu, C., & Hong, Y. (2009). *Understanding Culture: Theory, Research, and Application*. New York, NY: Psychology Press, Taylor & Francis Group.

CHAPTER 7

TRYING TO FIT IN

Ismaili Youth Identity In
Post-9/11 Canada

Hafiz Printer

ABSTRACT

There is very little written on the experience of second generation Ismaili
youth growing up in Canada. This chapter looks to explore the available
research on Ismaili youth to better understand how they view their religious
and ethnic identity. The focus of the chapter is to explore whether Ismaili
youth in Canada consider themselves to be Muslim. The results were mixed,
with those facing discrimination preferring to avoid calling themselves
Muslim, while youth who were not questioned about their religion remaining
content holding onto the label. The youth that felt comfortable stating they
are Muslim did, however, feel uncomfortable with their South Asian ethnicity
as a result of negative stereotypes they face. This implies that Ismaili youth, in
their attempt to fit into Canadian society, distance themselves from identities
which result in discrimination and stereotyping. Though the Ismaili youth
believe Canadian society is pluralistic and multicultural, the selective application of these concepts points to a large difference between theory and practice.

Growing Up Between Two Cultures: Problems and Issues of Muslim Children, pp. 165–184
Copyright © 2014 by Information Age Publishing
165

It had been some time since the event occurred, though it was still fresh in everyone's minds. As the time grew from days into weeks and weeks into months, so too grew the questions and the spotlight. I was never one to prefer the spotlight and so when it was cast upon me, or so I felt, I was understandably bewildered. It was the first time I had been asked about this particular aspect of myself. The response came easily enough to me; "We're not like those *other* Muslims" or sometimes "I'm Ismaili, I'm not Muslim." I knew I was Muslim, but I also knew I was very different from the "Muslim" that was being depicted in the media after the attacks of September 11, 2001, and embedded in the collective consciousness of the West. With those few words I was now exempt from answering further questions about Islam and what was being associated with it. In their eyes I was not a Muslim and so was released from judgement. I no longer had to answer questions, which I was fine with since I did not have the answer to their questions to begin with.

At the time, I felt no qualms about my response. However, this stayed with me as, nearly a decade later I completed a Masters in Muslim Societies and Civilizations. Now, working as a religious education teacher within the Ismaili-Muslim community, I find myself wondering if these issues still continue to afflict Ismaili youth in Canada. On the surface it may seem as though Ismaili youth prefer to distance themselves from the label "Muslim" because of the negative baggage that may come along with it, yet in reality the issue is much more complex. This chapter will explore the current research on Ismaili Canadian youth, to better understand the issue. As Peeks (2005) points out, "little is known regarding the identity formation process of Muslim-Americans, particularly for the second generation" (p. 220). Though there is growing diversity amongst the Ismaili population in Canada, the majority of research that has been conducted has been focused on second generation Canadian-Ismaili youth of South Asian background whose parents immigrated to Canada in the 1970s after spending a generation or two in East Africa. As this chapter is based on the current literature, it too shall focus on this particular segment of the Ismaili community in Canada.

WHO ARE ISMAILIS?

The Muslim community is comprised of a diverse number of interpretations and traditions "that reflect a rich intellectual, spiritual, and institutional pluralism" (Nanji & Daftary, 2006). At the death of the Prophet Muhammad in the seventh century, the Muslim community or *Ummah*, developed various understandings of how to continue to live by the message brought by the Prophet. These understandings coalesced into the two major branches of Islam we see today, the Sunni and Shi'a. The Sunnis are the larger of the two, comprising nearly three quarters of the *Ummah* while the Shi'a comprise the remaining. Other small groups, such as the Sufis, do also exist. The Sunni interpretation believes that Prophet Muhammad was the final messenger of God, and the role of a spiritual guide in human form had been ceased after him. They rely on the revelations of the Quran, the sayings of the Prophet or *hadith* and the actions and stories of the Prophet or *Sunna*, from which the group also receives their namesake. Within the Shi'a interpretation, it is believed that the Prophet had designated his cousin and son-in-law, Ali, as his successor to guide the *Ummah* on spiritual and moral matters. The term Shi'a translates to something between partisan and adherent, and refers to those Muslims that accepted Ali as the holder of authority in the Muslim community. Shi'as believe that Ali inherited the spiritual knowledge, *nass*, of the Prophet and that this knowledge is passed down through the hereditary lineage of Ali and the Prophet's daughter Fatima. This institution is known as *Imamat*. The notion of an *Imam*, also exists within in Sunni Islam but in a very different sense than in Shi'a Islam. It is important to distinguish the difference between the meaning for Sunnis and Shi'a. Within Shi'a Islam there can only be one Imam, a direct descendant from the Prophet who also acts as a spiritual guide; whereas for Sunnis, an Imam is a person who leads the formal prayers and so there can be many Imams.

Within Shi'a Islam, as with any other Muslim group, there is a great deal of diversity. The Shi'a are divided into a number of various sects based on divisions that arose about who was believed to be the rightful Imam. The *Ithna Asharis* or, as they are more commonly known, the Twelvers, comprise the largest sect in Shi'ism. The Ismailis are the next largest branch within Shi'i Islam, and are further divided into two groups, the Mustali Ismailis and the Nizari Ismailis. It is important to note then, that the Ismaili community, or *jamat,* is a minority within a minority in Islam. This chapter will focus on the Nizari Ismailis, who I will just refer to simply as Ismaili in what is to come below, hoping the reader will keep in mind that it is the Nizari branch which is being discussed. The Ismailis, "give allegiance to the H. H. Aga Khan IV, Shah Karim, the 29th Imam, whom they believe to be the successor and direct descendant of the Prophet and Ali" (Nanji, 1983, p. 150). The Imam provides the Ismaili community with spiritual and worldly guidance for the current times. As a result of having a living guide Ismaili practices tend to differ from those of the Sunni branch of interpretation and even other Shi'a branches.

This Ismaili community does, however, have much in common with the larger Muslim *Ummah*. They acknowledge that there is no god but God and that Muhammad is his messenger, the *shahada*; they follow the teachings of the Quran and recite their prayers in Arabic. "They also follow the five pillars of Islam, which include the *shahada* (mentioned above), *salat* (prayer), *zakat* (alms-giving), *sawm* (fasting) and *hajj* (pilgrimage)" (Husain, 2012, p. 10). The form in which some of these pillars are expressed, however, may differ. For instance Ismailis pray three times a day during the morning and evening times whereas generally Sunnis will pray five times throughout the day. It is however, due to these differences in practice that Ismaili youth face difficulties, from both within the greater *Ummah* as well as without.

I'M ISMAILI I'M NOT MUSLIM

In the fall of 2011 there was some contention over the leading of Friday prayers by a Sunni Imam in a Toronto middle school. Aside from the inevitable argument to keep religion out of schools, another tension resulted from this incident. These Friday prayers placed the Ismaili-Muslim students at the school in a peculiar position. Their non-Muslim schoolmates noticed the Ismaili students did not go to the cafeteria to observe the prayers with the other Muslims students. This resulted in questions of why they had not gone. When those students who had attended the prayers returned, they would also question the Ismaili students about why they had not attended prayer, with some even commenting that it was because the Ismaili students must not really be Muslim. This experience was relayed to me by several of my Ismaili students who attend the school, and whom I see during our weekend religion education classes, which are ironically held in the same school.

The above example speaks to a series of issues that Ismaili youth face in Canada. These include the ways in which they are viewed within but also outside of the Muslim *Ummah*, as well as their ability (or lack thereof) to articulate their religious identity. Ismailis have long been told that they are not Muslim enough (Malak, 2008). Within Canada, Ismailis have had to struggle to be considered truly Muslim. This reality was made clear in a *Globe and Mail* article by Tarek Fatah (2004) where he wrote:

> In the weeks leading up to the [2004 federal] election many Muslim organizations published a list of Muslim candidates running for Parliament. Conspicuous by their absence on these lists were the names of Liberal Yasmin Ratansi and sitting Conservative MP Rahim Jaffer. They were ignored because they belonged to the Ismaili sect of Islam and thus are no considered worthy of the label Muslim.

The exclusion of Ismailis from the candidate list reflect the sentiment in the comments made by some of the middle school students. It is as though there are degrees of "Muslim-ness" that range from the authentic to the inauthentic. It is at the inauthentic end of the spectrum, where Ismailis seem to have been relegated. This spectrum of "Muslim-ness" only serves to essentalize what it means to be a Muslim, so that those who do not follow a certain set of generally accepted practices, such as fasting and praying certain times, are considered to be less Muslim or not Muslim at all. This homogenizing of what constitutes a Muslim is dangerous. "If being a Muslim is treated merely as an all or nothing adherence to a specific set of practices, this would dramatically reduce both the ideological import of Islam as a culture and an ethical philosophy, and the number of people who are Muslim" (Mehdi, 2008, p. 21). Nonetheless, it is as a result of such views that the Ismaili-Muslim youth find themselves being disregarded as true Muslims. What is seen here then is not the labelling of identity, which is usually the culprit in muddying the waters of identity politics but rather an erasure of identity altogether.

Ismaili youth are faced with being told that they are not real Muslim, but they may themselves feel this way as a result of their own lived experience, of feeling disconnected from the larger *Ummah*. Muhammedi (2010) in his study, found that Ismaili youth in Vancouver feel comfortable identifying themselves as Ismailis but hesitant in identifying as Muslim. Instead what he, and others (Ali, 2008; Husain, 2012; Zaver, 2010), found was that there was indeed a divide between Ismaili youth and their connection with the *Ummah*. One of the youth in Muhammedi's study explained, "I don't think we are Muslim because we don't fit in with the rest of them ... they all know Arabic, and do Muslim things that we don't" (Muhammedi, 2010, p. 34) Another student in the study expanded on this point stating, "it feels like our religion is totally different ... but it also feels like we are totally different" (Muhammedi, 2010, p. 34). It seems that Ismaili youth have a difficult time placing themselves within the larger *Ummah* because they cannot relate to the language and practices of the majority group. A lack of understanding of, and adherence to what is seen as the dominant group's membership criteria results in a pervading feeling that Ismaili youth do not belong, that they are "different" and that they do not "fit in." (Muhammedi, 2010, p. 34). Generally Ismaili youth seem to be lacking the framework to enter into the larger conversation of what it means to be Muslim. They are searching for a way to enter into this dialogue and to express that they are comfortable being Muslims, though they have a particular belief system and different forms of practice.

It is ironic that, though they may not be seen as Muslim within the Muslim community, Ismaili youth are often relegated under the Muslim umbrella by non-Muslims, many of whom still tend to view Islam as a monolith. As Ali (2008) explains, "this puts Ismailis between the proverbial rock and a hard place. Outside of the *Ummah*, they are part of the monolithic Muslim identity, yet inside they are often excluded" (p. 103). As a result of this, Ismaili youth find themselves being placed between two very different camps without a sense of belonging in either. Thus, Ismaili youth are faced with series of decisions about how they would like to be portrayed. Should they continue to claim they are Muslim though they are told that they are not by the larger Muslim community? If so they must find a way to explain to others how they are Muslim despite not feeling connection with their Muslim peers. It is a very delicate balancing act. More often than not they choose to place themselves outside of the Muslim *Ummah*, and thus the monolith. This is a solution that some Ismaili youth tend to arrive at. Although choosing to disassociate seems to clear up the tension and anxiety that Ismaili youth may feel while speaking with others, by removing themselves from the conversation around "Muslim-ness" they no longer have a voice within it. Part of this may be as a response to the rejection they feel being designated as not Muslim enough. In this sense it is a coping mechanism, I do not want to be a member of a group that does not want me, and thus a duel rejection of Muslim identity occurs—Ismaili youth are not recognized by the *Ummah* and so Ismaili youth do not want to recognize the *Ummah* in turn, leading to self-made claims that they are not Muslim.

Whatever the identity conflict may be, Ismailis are Muslim. It would be an absurdity to claim to be the former and not the latter. Students are fully aware of this, they know that they are Muslim, but yet do not wish to publicly acknowledge it. The root of this goes beyond being rejected by the *Ummah*. Generally, Ismaili youth are unable to accurately articulate how they belong to the Muslim *Ummah* when questioned by Muslims and non-Muslims alike (Printer, 2011; Zaver, 2010). Instead some choose to place themselves outside of the *Ummah* identifying themselves not by what they are but by what they are not—I am Ismaili, I'm not Muslim. It is easier to state that you are not something than to explain how you are. In one fell swoop Ismaili youth are exempt from having to answer the questions posed to them that they feel uncomfortable trying to answer because they do not have the language in which to answer. This removal from the conversation was addressed above, as was the idea of an erasure of identity; however in this instance the erasure comes from the Ismaili youth themselves as they claim to not be Muslim, not from Muslim peers. These Ismaili youth are unable to articulate how the Ismaili interpretation fits within the larger *Ummah* or explain that the legitimization of their interpretation does not negate other interpretations that exist. This is in part due to having to work within a framework that claims their understanding is not legitimate, that they are not Muslim enough, as well as Ismaili youth having a difficult time explaining their Ismaili identity and how they fit within the *Ummah*.

Disassociating oneself from being identified as Muslim may also be pragmatic. The word "Muslim" has developed a great deal of negative baggage over the past several decades. As Siddiqui (2008) notes, "Canada has not been immune from post-9/11 Islamophobia and the politics of fear"

(p. 1). Ismaili students are aptly aware of the negative stereotypes associated with the label "Muslim." Printer (2011) found that when asked what words come to mind when they hear the term "Muslim," youth would respond with "terrorist," and "bomb," though students admitted that they are aware that these are stereotypes. Ross-Sheriff and Nanji (1991) received similar responses from Ismaili youth over two decades earlier, implying that this is not a new trend, nor solely a result of the September 11 attack, though the event exacerbated these tensions. Negative assumptions about Muslim have not emerged out of thin air; rather they may be a reflection of popular opinion of Muslims within Canada. As Ross-Sheriff and Nanji explain,

> The most serious cultural conflicts experienced by Ismaili youth arise from the negative attitudes towards Muslims in the larger North American society that have become especially prevalent in recent times.... As a result some of these [Ismaili] adolescents sometimes felt hesitant to be identified as Muslim. (p. 107)

Facing discrimination, and feeling uncomfortable or unable to explain that within Islam there is a rich variety of understandings, practices and tradition, the Ismaili tradition being one, students prefer to distance themselves. One student in Muhammedi's (2010) study explained, "There are so many examples of racism towards Muslims at my school and that is why I make sure people know I am a different kind of Muslim, a peaceful one" (p. 34). This distinction between "good" and "bad" Muslims has played out within the media. Whereas the image of "Muslim" has been vilified, "Ismaili" has been "depicted positively as welcome contributors to the country... [and] generally at ease with Western norms" (Karim, 2011, p. 266). Media coverage around the community tends to focus on the positive contributions that they bring to Canadian society. The annual World Partnership Walk which raises money for international development, the funding for the Center of Pluralism in Ottawa by the Ismaili Imam and the construction of an Ismaili Center in Toronto have all received extensive media coverage. The Ismaili Center in Toronto has recently been touted in a *Toronto Star* article by Hume (2013) titled, "Ten Things Toronto Can Look Forward to in 2013" which stated:

> Occupying a large suburban site at Eglinton Ave. E. and Wynford Dr., the Aga Khan Museum and Ismaili Centre will transform this part of Toronto. Already the magnificent complex is turning heads—or now, mostly those watching as they drive by on the northbound DVP. When complete, its effect will be felt across the city. The architects—including Fumihiko Maki and Charles Correa—have created a place of surpassing beauty. As an act of faith in Toronto, a gift to the city, the centre is unparalleled.

Ismaili youth feel a sense of pride in seeing their community portrayed in such a light. They are also fully aware of this incongruence between the depiction of Ismailis and that of Muslims and use this to their advantage. One Ismaili youth explained,

> Muslims, not Ismailis, are in the news every night and my friends always make jokes about how I am a terrorist.... Even my teacher at school sometimes asks me stuff about being a Muslim and the connections with violence. I don't have an answer for her, I simply just say I am Ismaili, it is different. (Muhammedi, 2010, p. 37)

This repositioning allows the student to remove themselves from the stigmatism, questions and spotlight associated with being Muslim and one can see why this would be an appealing alternative. However, this redefining of boundaries clearly delineates Ismaili and Muslim placing them at odds with one another. It is here once again, that "othering" begins to take root —"I'm Ismaili, we're not like those other Muslims" or "I'm a different kind of Muslim, a peaceful one." From here it is only a small step from complete disavowment, "I am Ismaili, I'm not Muslim."

I AM PROUD TO BE MUSLIM, AND AFRICAN

Though, as discussed above, some Ismaili youth disassociate from being Muslim, it is also true that many Ismaili youth are comfortable stating they are Muslim and actually prefer to refer to themselves as Muslim over Ismaili (Husain, 2012; Printer, 2011). When Printer (2011) asked a group of Ismaili youth how they would articulate their religious identity in public, nearly all responded with "Muslim," with only one responding with just "Ismaili." One of the youth explained the reason: "Ismailis are a small group of Islam, most people do not know what it is," while another youth added that, "I would generally refer to being a Muslim since it would be easier for the person to understand" (p. 81). Many of the youth shared this sentiment. They also shared that they felt pride in being Muslim. The comfort that students felt in proclaiming themselves as Muslim in Canada can in part be contributed to several factors. The West has largely educated itself about Islam following the September 11 attacks. In the 10 years since the attacks global and national tensions have subsided, especially in Canada. Those taking part in many of the recent studies on Ismaili youth in Canada were infants at the time of the attack and did not have to face the brunt of the negative reactions, which have since receded. Furthermore, the impact on the national psyche was not as salient in Canada as it was on the United States. It seems the old adage "time heals all wounds" holds some weight in this instance. As a result, Ismaili youth feel comfortable presenting their religious identity as Muslim in the public sphere.

This proclaimed identity may, however, be the result of convenience rather than a genuine connection with being Muslim. The students' comments in the previous paragraph point to a reluctance to explain being an Ismaili-Muslim, preferring instead to use the general classification of Muslim. Printer (2011) and Zaver (2010) found that Ismaili youth felt uncomfortable and ill at ease when asked to articulate what it means to be an Ismaili. Ismaili youth in Zaver's study stated, "I wouldn't feel very confident because I don't or wouldn't really know how to explain it" and "I feel kind of comfortable but not really, depends on who I'm talking too (sic) and what they ask for. Usually I wouldn't really know what to say" (p. 62). Similar thoughts were echoed by students in Printer: "If you say that you are Muslim … most of the time they just won't say anything, but if you say that you are Ismaili and they don't know what it is, automatically they are going to be curious and ask more," with another youth adding, "That's just unnecessary conversation … I just say I'm Muslims, I don't mention that I'm Ismaili at all" (p. 80). The label Muslim involves less explanation than Ismaili. By stating that they are Muslim it is no longer necessary to have to explain themselves. The word Muslim is already known in popular discourse whereas Ismaili may not be. As mentioned earlier, Ismaili youth find it difficult explaining their Ismaili identity to others (Husain, 2012; Muhammedi, 2010; Printer, 2011; Zaver, 2010). As Ali (2008) so poignantly articulates, "Specificity demands effort and education" (p. 100). To explain what it means to be Ismaili places a great demand on an Ismaili youth to exert a considerable effort as well as have a certain degree of understanding. Besides, for many of the Ismaili youth interviewed it was a moot point. Their whole lives they have been told that they are Ismaili-*Muslims*. They do not have a problem calling themselves Muslim because as Ismailis they have grown up as Muslims.

Living in Canada was also a factor listed by students to explain their ease in stating they are Muslim. Many students explained that Canada is a multicultural country that is accepting of difference and thus they see no issue in saying they are Muslim when asked about their religion. There is a caveat however; students generally admitted that they are very rarely, if ever, asked about their religion. When questioned about this one youth exclaimed, "this never even comes up," to which another youth expanded, "If it happens it's really rare and it'll be really general so, it's like it doesn't even matter" (Printer 2011, p. 81). In contrast to Ismaili youth who are being questioned about their religion, these youth do not have to face the same kind of scrutiny. As a result they have not had to think very deeply about how they articulate and project their religious identity in the public sphere. They need only to state that they are Muslim on the rare occasion that they are asked and this is generally accepted. Things were not so simple for the Ismaili youth who have to explain their religious identity. However, it should be noted, religion just does not come up as a point of conversation in these youths daily lives, after all why would it? In my adolescent years before September 11 I can only recount a handful of times I was asked about my religion, and as these youth do now, I was able to get by just saying Muslim. Since these Ismaili youth are not questioned about their religious identity, or at least not questioned deeply, they do not feel the anxiety and tension surrounding the use of the term Muslim. Most youth will not engage in these kinds of conversations and dialogues until they have reached university, which is still several years away (Hussain, 2008). In the interim, Ismaili youth will develop emotionally and intellectually allowing for greater maturity when they do begin these conversations.

The Ismaili youth who feel able to identify as Muslim do so partly because they only ever come into contact with a few Muslims of different interpretations. Hence, these Ismaili youth are not likely to find themselves in many situations having to differentiate between their interpretation of Islam and another. Generally for these youth in Canada their Ismaili Identity is hidden. Sirin and Fine (2008) share an anecdote of a conversation between two middle school students:

"You don't look Muslim."
"How do you look Muslim? It's a religion."

Though the second student makes an excellent point, one can indeed look as though they belong to a particular religion. Identity markers help others identify and categorize a person into a particular religious identity. An example of such a marker could be the wearing a cross which could be used to identify someone as Christians. For Muslims, there are stereotypical and iconic images that come to mind, such as the hijab or other forms of clothing that are considered Muslim. Ismaili youth do not fit within this image. They dress in Western clothing, they do not stop for midday prayer, they do not stand out as "Muslim" and so are not questioned about being Muslim. A Canadian Ismaili youth would have to proclaim that they are Muslim for others to know, you would not be able to tell simply by looking at them.

However Ismaili youth are sometimes identified as South Asian by their physical features. "Their skin tone and features allow others at a glance to identify them as South Asian, in a way they could not for Muslim. For this reason, they must deal with more issues about their ethnicity than they would for their religion" (Printer, 2011, p. 40). What is interesting to note is that these Ismaili youth tend to distance themselves from their South Asian identity, despite Canada being multicultural and accepting as some students stated earlier. The difference here, though, is that they are being questioned about and being treated differently because of their ethnicity. As a result, these Ismaili youth mirror the response of the Ismaili youth questioned about their Muslim identity—they disassociate. This disassociation implies that it is not Muslim-ness or South Asian-ness that students prefer to avoid, but rather a perceived "otherness," regardless of what form this may take, be it religious or ethnic.

When asked about their background many Canadian Ismaili youth prefer to identify themselves as African as opposed to South Asian. This may be because their parents are from East Africa and so they see themselves as African as well. It may be that Ismaili youth find "South Asian" too foreign and distant for them making it difficult to feel a connection. Ali (2008), writing about her experience growing up as an Ismaili in Canada illuminates this point by stating, "It never occurred to me to say "Indian" —India after all was a country that belonged to my grandparents not me" (p. 99). I never considered myself to be South Asian as I was growing up either. I did not speak any of the languages, dress in Indian garb or do any of the things that, in my mind, I associated with being Indian. I much preferred to think of myself as African-Canadian, like many of the youth that I interviewed. Ismaili youth can feel a connection with Africa through their parents' stories and experiences. Ismaili youth associate what takes place in the home as being African, even if it is in fact South Asian or an Indo-African fusion. In a typical Canadian Ismaili home, English is generally the main language spoken but one can still find sprinklings of Swahili along with Urdu, Kutchi or Gujarati. Distinguishing between these various languages is another thing. Ismaili youth may mistake this patchwork of languages as a single language, an African one since they know their parents are from Africa.

While working with street youth in Kolkata, I witnessed an incident of one youth hitting another. Thinking I had told the culprit to stop in their own language (for at this point I had realized the patchwork also included South Asian dialects), I was met only with blank stares and finally a response of, "Sir YOU have to speak English, we don't understand you." As it turns out I had told them to stop hitting each other in Swahili. Humorous (and embarrassing) as this story may be, it illustrates the point that one language can easily be misconstrued as another in the minds of an Ismaili youth, but also that this African aspect of Ismaili youth identity takes a very real form in the use of Swahili at home.

"That students view themselves as African is as valid, if not more so than being South Asian because they can connect with it, identify with it and to some degree understand it" (Printer, 2011, p. 57). Therefore, when students are asked about their background they feel no misgivings about stating they are African instead of South Asian. This can also be seen as a re-appropriation of identity—they are *choosing* to be African instead of *being told* that they are South Asian. Oftentimes this seems to work. As Ali (2008) recants in her own experience, "brown equated to black and so they applied their stereotypes of black people on me" (p. 100). Since Brown equated to Black and Black people are from Africa there was no issue in seeing her as African. But what happens when Brown does not equate to Black? Printer (2011) found that Ismaili youth tended to be questioned by their peers when claiming to be African. They would be asked if they are African why are they not Black? "When asked how that is possible, they can quickly point to the link in the chain that is not so far away" (Printer, 2011, p. 56). When questioned about their identity they have an answer readily at hand—"My parents are from Africa so I am African." This easy answer is somewhat problematic as it is a superficial statement that students find difficult to explain when probed further. As Baldwin (1991) explains, "An invented past can never be used; it cracks and crumbles under the pressures of life like clay in a season of drought" (p. 81). Though this may not be an invented past, it may be a one-dimensional one, leaving students with a feeble rebuttal.

Aside from feeling a connection with their parents past, why would some Ismaili youth in Canada prefer to be seen as African instead of South Asian? It seems that a large reason for dismissing their South Asian identity is to avoid the negative stereotypes associated with it. This is interesting, as this was also the reason some Ismaili youth preferred to distance themselves from the label Muslim. Kanji (2010), looking at issues faced by Ismaili youth in Canada found that, "students of South Asian background are alienated due to their complexion (brown in color), their ethnicity and their label as an immigrant or minority group" (p. 10). Raby (2004) and Patel and Crocco (2003) had similar findings, noting that South Asian students are the focus of racist comments and humour. Ismaili youth are fully aware of such behavior, having faced comments made to them based on their skin colour such as, "go drive a taxi" and "go eat curry" (Printer, 2011, p. 56). When Ismaili youth are made to feel "their culture ... and identity are unacceptable, the impact on [their] sense of security and self-esteem will be clearly negative" (Schumann, 2011, p. 11).

What is interesting is that Ismaili youth themselves, have adopted and use negative stereotypes about South Asians. Having grown up in Canada, these youth have also grown up imbibing stereotypes about South Asians and the language of the "other." It is not unheard of to hear an Ismaili youth born in Canada use the term Paki in a derogatory way. Many of the students that I spoke with have also developed a language around the word "Brown," using it to poke fun at Brown people, Brown music, Brown food. Though they know that they themselves are Brown, they use the word with an apparent hint of disdain. The use of the word Brown also alludes to simplistic characterizations into Brown, White, Black, and so forth, where

Brown is clearly placed on one of the lowest rungs of the hierarchy. The term Brown is also used to denote difference between "normal" clothes and "Brown" clothes. Here again we see an essentialization of an entire group of diverse peoples into a singular term. Beharry and Crozier (2008) in their study noticed intraethnic discrimination and stereotyping among second generation South Asian girls in Canada. This implies that the breadth of the issue of negative associations towards "brown" extend beyond just Ismaili youth.

With such negative associations it is not surprising that Ismaili youth tend to supress their "Brown-ness" in an attempt to blend in. One way in which they do this is through dress. Peeks (2005) posits that, "dress … serve(s) as [an] important marker that help promotes individual self-awareness and preserve group cohesion, as ethnic … heritage is displayed and thus maintained" (p. 219). The Ismaili youth in Printer's (2011) study tended to feel uncomfortable wearing "cultural clothing" out in public, or even being seen with those who were wearing cultural clothing. One youth explained that even if he was out with family he would distance himself from them if they were dressed in cultural clothing (Printer, 2011). When the girls were asked about wearing cultural clothing in public one replied that she would, "go home and change" while another stated, "I probably wouldn't want to go somewhere, where there are people from school or something because it's different" (p. 82). When asked why this was, since the students had previously claimed they felt accepted into Canada's multi-cultural society, one of the girls explained, "For me it's like, I wouldn't want to just draw attention. I mean like even if you see someone in a kimono in a restaurant, it's kind of weird too. I just wouldn't want, in general I wouldn't want to draw attention to myself" (Printer, 2011, p. 82). The sentiment that clearly came across in the discussion with these Ismaili youth was that wearing cultural clothing made them feel as though they stood out which led to a feeling of embarrassment. As one of them explained, "it's not normal Canadian clothing," which begs the question of what counts as normal Canadian clothing? If South Asian clothing does not count then this aspect of South Asian identity is at odds with Canadian identity. Students have understood Canadian to be multicultural and accepting, but by placing South Asian cultural clothing outside of "Canadian" it no longer needs to be accepted as part of the multicultural argument that students used to justify feeling accepted as Muslim, though not South Asian. That wearing of a kimono in the public sphere is also considered abnormal by Ismaili youths only shows that their understanding of multiculturalism is in itself limited. Ismaili youth want to fit into their Canadian society and thus do not want to stand out by looking "different." There is an old Japanese proverb that states, "The nail that sticks out gets hammered down."

In wanting to fit in Ismaili youth reject the identity that makes them stick out, be that "Muslim," South Asian, or "Brown."

BEING CANADIAN

What does it mean to be Canadian? The Canadian Broadcasting Corporation posed this question to Canadian public in the 1960s in an effort to understand how Canadians view themselves. The winning response was "As Canadian as possible under the circumstances" (Sumara, Davis, & Linda 2001, p. 144). The fact that this was the winning response indicates just how difficult it is to explain what it means to be Canadian because there is no standard answer to the question. This is because, as Sumara et al. (2001) explain, "Canada … develop(ed) a system of governance that embraced the notion that identities, individual and collective, were not pre-given or discovered but where continually invented, including the invention of a national character" (p. 154). What it means to be Canadian is difficult to understand, as it is not just one thing but many. As with any identity it is fluid, not rigid and so cannot be pinned down. However, what does it mean to be Canadian must be asked to understand how Ismaili youth view their various multiple identities in relation to living in Canada.

When Ismaili-Muslim youth were asked what they think it means to be Canadian, Muhammedi (2010) found that students felt Canadian meant having a sense of pride in being Canadian as well as being accepting of others and "multicultural." Printer (2011) found similar results with Ismaili youth also bringing up "practicing Canadian and [their] own culture." This finding make sense since Canada prides itself on being the only nation to have an official multicultural policy and law (Karim, 2005). When a group of Ismaili youth were asked to define multiculturalism, one student's definition simply stated: "CANADA"(Printer, 2011, p. 80). The majority of responses from the remainder of the youth pointed to pluralism. The problem is that terms such as pluralism and multiculturalism are difficult words to understand and define, much like the term Canadian. These words have, however, become the buzz words which are tossed around popular discourse and taken up by students. Ismaili youth, and one would assume most Canadian youth, have only a very superficial understanding of terms such as pluralism and multiculturalism, often using one to define the other in what becomes somewhat of a cyclical endeavour. If Ismaili youth root their identity in being Canadian, which in turn influences their other identities, it becomes very problematic as these youth are working within a framework of clichés. Terms such as multiculturalism and pluralism need to be explored within the context of the students lived realities to see whether or not they really do fit within this context.

What then is the reality of multiculturalism in the lives of Ismaili youth? Ismailis in Canada have adjusted to their surroundings quickly and have become accepted as part of Canadian society. The ease with which this has taken place is the result of first generation Canadian Ismailis having been exposed to Western culture prior to their move to Canada. As Nanji (1983) explains,

> For them the transition to North American living did not represent a major adjustment. In modes of dress, language, and to a certain extent lifestyle, African Ismailis and in particular the younger generation were already pre-pared to face life in new lands. (p. 159)

What is accepted, then, is Canadian culture and those things that are considered acceptable within that culture. For instance, Ismaili youth stated they would feel comfortable speaking in another language or eating Indian food in public. The reason being that both of these are accepted in Canadian society; Canada already being a bilingual nation and Indian food finding a niche in Canadian society decades ago. Wearing cultural South Asian clothing in public however is not acceptable unless it is within the confines of an ethnic enclave such as "Little India." In this we see an internalized acceptance of what is considered acceptable and not acceptable within Canadian society.

The idea of multiculturalism is not only to embrace the differences found in society but also to embrace the different components of one's own identity. However, in order to be able to embrace, one first needs to be able to understand, only once something is understood can it be explained. Ismaili youth are constantly finding themselves navigating between various worlds at an age when they are trying to understand, for themselves, their culture and identity. This is a difficult task indeed, and would explain the struggle Ismaili youth face when trying to articulate their various identities, especially their religious and ethnic identity. It is true these youth can accept an identity even if their understanding of it is a superficial one, granted that they are not pushed to explain it beyond surface level. If, however, Ismaili youth are asked to explain an identity that they only have a superficial understanding of, they then disassociate with that identity to avoid both internal and external conflict. When Ismaili youth are not questioned about an aspect of their identity they do not necessarily need to fully understand that identity because there is no need to. This was the case with the youth who felt comfortable stating they were Muslims, since they were rarely, if ever, asked about their religion. This becomes problematic once Ismaili youth are asked to explain their Muslim identity. At this point, they would have to explain something they may not necessarily understand themselves, or at least at a level where they could feel comfortable explaining it to others. This then, gives rise to claims from some Ismailis that Ismailis are not like those *other* Muslims, or that Ismailis are not Muslims at all.

Ismaili youth feel more confident identifying as Canadian than they do as Muslim. The reason for this is that Ismailis feel that Ismaili values are compatible with Canadian values.

> Sociological research has shown that young Ismailis in British Columbia generally approach Canadian and Ismaili values without dissonance. Canadian multiculturalism has played a critical role in the establishment of the Ismaili community in Calgary. This appears to be quite representative of the *jamat* in the rest of the country. (Karim, 2000, p. 266)

An Ismaili youth in Muhammedi's (2010) study presented this viewpoint, "I think it is very possible to be Canadian and Ismaili at the same time, they both have the same values" (p. 38). When speaking of what those values might be, another youth elaborated saying, "There are many shared values that Ismailis and Canadians have, all of them really. We believe in respecting people, taking care of the elderly, being honest … and those are all part of being a good Canadian citizen!" (Muhammedi, 2010, p. 39). What the Ismaili youth failed to recognize though, is that these are the same values upheld by all Muslims, not just Ismailis. Many of these values are exemplified in the founding Prophet of Islam. His Highness the Aga Khan, spiritual leader for the Ismaili community, expressed these values when speaking of the Prophet at the International Seerat Conference (1976):

> The Holy Prophet's life gives us every fundamental guideline that we require to resolve the problem as successfully as our human minds and intellects can visualise. His example of integrity, loyalty, honesty, generosity both of means and of time; his solicitude for the poor, the weak and the sick; his steadfastness in friendship; his humility in success; his magnanimity in victory; his simplicity; his wisdom in conceiving new solutions for problems which could not be solved by traditional methods, without affecting the fundamental concepts of Islam—surely all of these are foundations which, correctly understood and sincerely interpreted, enable us to conceive what should be a truly modern and dynamic Islamic Society in the years ahead. (para. 15)

However, Ismaili youth who have placed themselves outside of the larger Muslim *Ummah*, may view Muslims within the confines of a rigid dogmatism that they do not see aligning with their own or Canadian values. This is unfortunate because, as Siddiqui (2008) points out, Canadian Muslims "share the same sense of belonging and hold the same values, hopes and fears as their fellow-citizens" (p. 13). This is not to say that all Canadian values are essentially Muslim or Ismaili values. It is true that Ismailis do share many Canadian values, which would explain why Ismaili youth feel comfortable in Canada, but certain values around social habits such as drinking, which is a large part of Canadian culture, do not align with Ismaili or Muslim values.

LEFT AT THAT?

Though some Ismaili youth have voiced their inability to connect with the larger *Ummah,* this does not mean that they do not want to understand it. Zaver (2010) found that when Ismaili youth are provided with a safe space in which to ask questions they are very much interested learning more about different interpretations of the faith. When this space was provided Ismaili youth posed questions not about Ismaili specific practices but rather about practices that are seen to belong to the larger Muslim *Ummah.* A whole conversation was framed around *What is Halal? What makes something Halal? How does one keep Halal?* with an understanding of these questions being co-constructed amongst the students. Through this conversation the youth attempted to negotiate and understand the language behind what it means to be Halal, which essentially is the language behind what it means to be Muslim. The conversation transitioned into how the youth found it difficult to engage in Muslim practices, specifically how it is difficult to keep Halal in Canada, naming fast food restaurants such as McDonald's as an example. Clearly, sometime during their lives they have been told that eating at McDonald's is not Halal, or possibly even told they do not keep Halal because they do eat at McDonald's. They wanted to know more about that concept because they did not know how to explain it. There does seem to be an urge to be able to understand such concepts, which would explain why the students raised the issue when given space in which to do so.

Within the conversation, the Ismaili youth brought up explanations they had received previously by parents, other family members or friends about the restriction around pork. This was mainly "pigs are dirty animals." However, the Ismaili youth did not feel satisfied with this answer, feeling it was not good enough. It is interesting to note that Ismaili youth are not satisfied with receiving vague or surface level answers about practices within Islam, which mirrors how society responds when students give vague and surface level answers to questions about their religion. Since Ismaili youth were not satisfied with the vague answers they received, there was a yearning to keep asking questions until they received satisfactory answers. It stands to chance then that this is what will take place in society in general, when Ismaili youth are asked questions about their religion. However, if Ismaili youth have an impoverished understanding of their religion they become stuck when questions are posed beyond the surface level.

The dialogue that Ismaili youth are currently using is a language around "Muslim-ness," which relegates some Muslim as the "other." The problem stems from Ismaili youth receiving information, such as the one regarding pork, that do not allow them to undo or dissolve this otherness concept. It does not give them the language used by the norm, the dominant society around them which would help them explain certain aspects of what it means to be a Muslim without creating a division. For instance, saying that pork is dirty still promotes an otherness because it does not fit within the language of the dominant Canadian society. If society at large is eating pork and saying that it is rational to eat pork, Ismaili youth saying that pork comes from a dirty animal does not help dissolve their otherness, if anything it widens the divide. This lack of articulation may be another reason Ismailis push aside their "Muslim-ness" in Canadian society. By choosing to do something different, such as keeping halal, one begins to stand out from society. Ismaili youth have already shared that they feel uncomfortable about standing out in society and so they disassociate instead. This is not to say that Ismailis do not adhere to religious dietary restrictions, they do but it becomes a point of contention.

Canadian society is the dominant society in which Ismaili youth live, and in their attempt to fit into their society, they tend to push aside aspects of their other identities which they feel others them. This is odd since the ideal that Canada promotes is not one where everyone must do the majority opinion. Canada is recognized for being a pluralistic society. But what does it mean to be pluralistic? A claimed pluralism and a lived pluralism are two very different things; a lived pluralism is much more complicated. Differences are not always embraced, many times it is isolated, and therefore a disassociation from an identity takes place and one begins to deny this difference. In several studies on Ismaili youth (Muhammedi, 2010; Printer, 2011; Zaver, 2010) it has been seen that Ismaili youth tend to be doing this to themselves, in regards to distancing themselves from "Muslim-ness" or "Brown-ness." This is partially due to the baggage that is associated with being labelled as a particular religious or ethnic group. Pluralism is not just being informed of other cultures but also embracing other cultures. Islam is the second largest religion in the world, while South Asians are the largest visible minority group within Canada (Statistics Canada, 2006). Is our society informed enough about each of these groups to accept them? Are our South Asian Ismaili-Muslim youth informed enough about these identities to feel comfortable in these roles? At this point I do not have a definite "yes" to either question. It is because of this that it is important for space to be created to ask questions and to build knowledge so that youth can have a better understanding of what it means to be a Canadian Ismaili Muslim.

REFERENCES

Ali, A. (2008). A case of mistaken identity: Inside and outside the muslim *Ummah*. In N. Bakht (Ed.), *Belonging and banishment: Being Muslim in Canada* (pp. 99–104). Toronto: Couch House Printing.

Baldwin, J. (1991). *The fire next time*. New York, NY: Vintage International.

Beharry, P., & Crozier, S. (2008). Using phenomenology to understand experiences of racism for second-generation South Asian women. *Canadian Journal of Counselling, 42*(4), 262–277.

Fatah, T. (2004, July 23). Yasmin Ratansi, Canada's First Woman Muslim MP. The Globe and Mail. Retrieved from http://www.theglobeandmail.com/servlet/story/RTGAM.20040723.wcomment0723/BNStory/Front/

His Highness the Aga Khan. (1976, March 12). Presidential Address at the International Seerat Conference Karachi, Pakistan. Retrieved from http://www.iis.ac.uk/view_article.asp?ContentID=101444

Husain, N. (2012). *Teaching Muslim societies and civilizations: The assessment of Muslim identity* (MA Report). London, England: IOE.

Hussain, A. (2008). The Diaspora in the West. In A. Rippin (Ed.), *The Islamic World*. (pp. 131–41). London, England: Routledge.

Hume, C. (2013, January 1). Ten Things Toronto Can Look Forward to in 2013. *The Toronto Star.* Retrieved from http://www.thestar.com/news/gta/2013/01/01/hume_ten_things_toronto_can_look forward_to_in_2013.html

Kanji, S., (2010). *The ethics and development curriculum: Addressing challenges facing Canadian Ismaili students* (MA Report). London, England: IOE.

Karim, K. H. (2011). At the interstices of tradition modernity and postmodernity: Ismaili engagements with contemporary Canadian society. In F. Daftary (Ed.), *A modern history of the Ismailis: Continuity and change in a Muslim Community* (pp. 265–296). London, England: I.B.Tauris Publishers.

Karim, K.H. (2000). The quest for excellence: Towards a cultural renaissance? *The Ismaili United Kingdom, 20*, 1–7. Retrieved from, http://www.iis.ac.uk/SiteAssets/pdf/quest_for_excellence.pdf

Karim, K. H. (2005). The elusiveness of full citizenship: Accounting for cultural capital, cultural competencies, and cultural pluralism. In C. Andrew, M. Gattinger, M. S. Jeannotte, & W. Staw (Eds.), *Accouting for culture: Thinking through cultural citzenship* (pp. 146–158). Ottawa, Ontario: University of Ottawa Press.

Malak, A. (2008). Towards a dialogical discourse for Canadian Muslims. In N. Bakht (Ed.), *Belonging and banishment: Being Muslim in Canada* (pp. 74–84). Toronto: Couch House Printing.

Mehdi, S. M. (2008). Bearing the name of the prophet. In N. Bakht (Ed.), *Belonging and banishment: Being Muslim in Canada* (pp. 17–25). Toronto: Couch House Printing.

Muhammedi, R. (2010). *Canadian Ismaili Muslim Youth: Issues of Identity and Value Association*. (MA Report). London, England: IOE.

Nanji, A. (1983). The Nizari Ismaili Muslim community in North America: Background and development. In E. H. Waugh, B. Abu-Laban, & R. B. Qureshi (Eds.), *The Muslim Community in North America* (pp. 149–164). Edmonton: The University of Alberta Press.

Nanji, A., & Daftary, F. (2006). What is Shi'a Islam?" In V. J. Cornell (Ed.), *Voices of Islam: Voices of traditions* (Vol 1, pp. 217–244). Westport, CT. Praeger.

Patel, V., & Crocco, M. S. (2003). Teaching about South Asian women: Getting beyond stereotypes. *Social Education, 67*(1), 22–26.

Peeks, L. (2005). Becoming Muslim: The development of a religious identity. *Sociology of Religion, 66*(3), 215–242.

Printer, H. (2011). *Navigating through multiple identities: A Canadian Ismaili youth perspective*. (MA dissertation). London, England: IOE.

Raby, R. (2004). There's no racism at my school, it's just joking around: Ramifications for anti-racist education. *Race, Ethnicity and Education, 7*(4), 367–383.

Ross-Sheriff, F., & Nanji, A. (1991). Islamic identity, family and community: The case of the Nizari Ismaili Muslims. In E. H. Waugh, S. McIrvin Abu-Laban, & R. Burckhardt Qureshi (Eds.), *Muslim families in North America* (pp. 101–117). Edmonton: The University of Alberta Press.

Schumann, S. (2011). *Hybrid identity formation of migrants: A case study of ethnic Turks in Germany—Seminar Paper*. Norderstedt, Germany: GRIN Verlag.

Siddiqui, H. (2008). Muslims and the rule of law. In N. Bakht (Ed.), *Belonging and banishment: Being Muslim in Canada* (pp. 1–16) Toronto: Couch House Printing.

Sirin, S. & Fine, M. (2008). *Muslim American Youth: Understanding Hyphenated Identities through Multiple Methods*. New York. New York University Press.

Statistics Canada. (2006). 2006 Census: Ethnic origin, visible minorities, place of work and mode of transportation. Retrieved from http://www.statcan.gc.ca/daily-quotidien/080402/dq080402a-eng.htm

Sumara, D., Davis, B., & Linda, L. (2001). Canadian identity and curriculum theory: An ecological, postmodern perspective. *Canadian Journal of Education, 26*(2), 144–163.

Zaver, A. (2010). *Recreating a third space in the RE classroom: Using dialogue to understand faith*. (Mteach dissertation). London, England: IOE.

PART IV

THE ROLE OF GENDER IN ACCULTURATION AND IDENTITY FORMATION

CHAPTER 8

DISCOURSE ON EQUITY AND SOCIAL JUSTICE IN A MUSLIM HIGH SCHOOL IN ISRAEL

A Case Study

Khalid Arar

ABSTRACT

Few studies have investigated equity and social justice discourse in educational institutions in developing societies; such studies are especially sparse in Arab society in Israel. The present study aimed to clarify the construction of discourse concerning equity and social justice in an Arab high school in Israel, pointing up the gendering of certain activities and identifying differences in the perceptions of male and female staff and students regarding educational experiences at school (if they existed); and whether the school promotes debate and socialization for equality between the sexes? An ethnographic case study was conducted in an Arab Muslim senior-high school in Israel. Observations, personal interviews and a focus group were employed to glean the perceptions of teachers (including the principal) and students concerning (1) the way that the school constructs discourse concerning equity

Growing Up Between Two Cultures: Problems and Issues of Muslim Children, pp. 187–206
Copyright © 2014 by Information Age Publishing
187

and social justice especially in respect to gender, (2) the students' learning contents and (3) the construction of Muslim male and female teachers' behaviors in their natural environmental reality. Findings provide insights concerning the Arab Muslim high school in Israel, indicating that although official rhetoric supports an equitable society within the school the influence of the traditional environment supports a covert inequitable culture. It is concluded that there is a need for empathetic educators-students dialog, a need to listen to the voice of the younger generation, and to address the challenge of Muslim Arab society's norms in order to promote more egalitarian perceptions and practices.

INTRODUCTION

Copious studies have related to discourse concerning equity and social justice in schools (Francis, 2010; Fuller, 2011; Grogan & Shakeshaft, 2011; Lindsey, Lindsey, & Terrell, 2011; Renold & Allan, 2006; Smith, 2012), this is complemented by increasing research on gender and social justice in education in developing societies. However there is still little theoretical conceptualization of empirical data concerning equity promotion in Arab Muslim high schools, especially in Arab Muslim high schools situated in a multicultural reality such as exists in Israel.

Contemporary discourse on gender is mainly drawn from post-constructivist theories, assuming that gender is a fluid social construct, and calling for a more realistic gendering, not based on physical sex-related perceptions (Connell, 2005). For example: "*social learning theories investigate the binary construction of gender in society's institutions and representatives,*" pointing out how distinguishing *binaries* such as male activity/female passivity have worked to consolidate gender characteristics and categorization (Francis, 2010, p. 477). In the context of schools, it may be possible to overcome such binary construction, at the levels of the school, classroom and learning program, yet, definitions of masculinity and femininity are still determined by various social, cultural, status and ethnic norms (Grogan & Shakeshaft, 2011). More fluid definitions are not given much weight in schools, and learning contents consistently perpetuate 'infected' processes that preserve traditional definitions of male and female functions and abilities (Francis, 2010).

It is unclear how these processes are reflected in the Arab-Muslim high school in Israel, situated in an indigenous minority society, which seems to be undergoing gradual transition from a traditional Arab Muslim culture to modern values and norms (Arar & Shapira, 2012). One indication of this transition is the increased inclusion of girls in Muslim schools. Improved academic successes in the Arab education system at the end of the 20th century were largely the result of increased regular attendance of girls in high school, whose matriculation exam achievements exceeded those of boys. The lack of research and theory concerning gender, social justice and equity in this context motivated the present study.

Equity and Social Justice in Education

In recent years, educational research has become increasingly interested in equity and social justice, reflecting the aspiration that "all children can learn" that underlies so many schools' mission and vision statements (Lindsey et al., 2011, p. 25). These terms and phrases seem to be largely rhetoric and it is difficult to see their implementation in schools' policy and practice (Blankstein & Houston, 2011). The report to the Equalities Review published in 2007 (University of London, 2007) told us a great deal about fairness and equity, defining an equal society as one that:

> Protects and promotes equal, real freedom and substantive opportunity to live in the ways people value and would choose, so that everyone can flourish. An equal society recognizes people's different needs, situations and goals and removes the barriers that limit what people can do and can be. (p. 6)

Equality it seems also includes the right to be different. While equity is a difficult term to define and measure, it can mean different things to different people, equity might be fairness in treating everyone equally (equality of opportunity), or might be treating people differently so that certain outcomes can become more equal, and therefore, more fair (equality of outcome) (Smith, 2012, p. 3).

In the context of education, Rahima Wade (2007) argued that:

> Starting in the kindergarten we must educate youth to care about humanity and to begin to understand the immensity of the challenges that will face them as adults. We must embark upon teaching them the skills and knowledge that will ultimately enable them not only to live productive and empowered lives but also to work alongside like-minded others for the betterment of those who suffer from oppression and other inequalities. (pp. 1–2)

Chapman and West-Burnham (2010) take this a step further, explaining what is meant by "betterment", so that a socially just society is seen as one that achieves "well- being" for all its citizens:

> In very practical terms a society committed to social justice would ensure that every child grows up experiencing optimum levels of well-being … a socially just society ensures that every child, irrespective of his ethnicity, social background, parentage, post code or any variable, has an entitlement

in terms of equality and equity to the benefits of growing up in a modern, democratic and affluent society (pp. 29–30).

However, Garratt and Forrester (2012) noted that social justice in education: "necessitates that access to same quality of educational processes should be *equitable*, even if there are unequal outcomes as a consequence" (p. 43). Contrastingly, Sapon-Shevin (2010) argued that:

> our goal cannot be to mirror the injustice and inequities of the broader society (and world) but rather, to provide students with the skills, attitudes and confidence they need in order to actively transform the world. My operational definition of social justice is "doing what is right for our students in an equitable manner."

In her review of the literature on social justice, North (2008) analyzed the tensions and contradictions that arise between competing models of social justice, especially "recognition" and "redistribution" She indicates that cultural groups compete for respect and dignity in order to gain "recognition", while underprivileged socioeconomic classes vie for equitable sharing of wealth and power by "redistribution." As in the larger society, both these processes are played out in schools. If recognition and redistribution are attained, our schools can become sites of justice, inclusion, and caring in which students see and experience new ways of interacting with their peers and increasingly broader communities (Sapon-Shevin, 2011). To implement such a vision, school leadership needs to actively promote social justice. Identifying the core requirements for school leadership for social justice, Theoharis (2009) asserted that school leaders must (1) acquire a broad, reconceptualized consciousness/knowledge/ skill base; (2) possess core leadership traits; (3) advance inclusion, access and opportunity for all; (4) improve the core learning context, both the teaching and curriculum; (5) create a climate of belonging; (6) raise student achievement; and (7) sustain oneself professionally and personally. However, Fuller (2011) indicated that society genders certain roles and activities, indicating who should perform them, rather than how they should be performed. Thus certain roles are identified as either "feminine" or "masculine" and these gender expectations continue to influence the acceptance and functioning of men and women in these professions, including school principals.

Since gender is a "structuring code as well as cultural expression" (Hey & Bradford, 2004, p. 68), social gendering, shaped by factors such as culture, religion, ideology and the socioeconomic system, significantly influences the substance and practice of organizational roles. Theories that see justice as harmony and those that see justice as equity both advocate treating people differently; however, according to Smith (2012) aiming for justice as harmony may produce different (and possibly unequal) outcomes;

this may mean that the hard working students and oppressed girls actually deserve more work and attention from their teacher (Smith, 2012).

Structure and learning contents also reflect the state of equity in a school. History testifies that at least since the 1950s, the structure and learning contents of educational organizations faithfully represented a primarily gendered discourse. In order to locate femininity in school discourse, Francis (2010) and also Fuller (2011) argue that poststructuralist feminist theories should be used as a lens to clarify the masculine privilege that has dominated educational institutions. These theories indicate that the school as an organization is enchained within a largely gendered discourse and practice, especially when femininity is structured in terms of the control of the masculine other (Arar & Oplatka, 2012).

The Research Context: Arab society in Israel

Arab society in Israel is very heterogeneous encompassing a variety of cultures, religions, ideologies, statuses and geographical regions (Khamaise, 2009). Each constituent sector is influenced by internal processes of modernization and external processes engendered by contact with Jewish society. The total Arab minority constitutes 20% of Israel's general population. Within this population, in 2009, 82.1% were Muslims, 9.4% Christians and 8.5% Druze (Central Bureau of Statistics, 2009, Table 2.1). Although Arabs live in separate towns and villages they are in constant contact with the Jewish population through their work, trade and higher education (Arar & Shapira, 2012).

Some scholars view Arab Muslim society in Israel as a society in transition from traditional norms and values to modernity (Arar & Shapira, 2012). Arab identity in Israel is usually described in terms of the tension between traditional and modern values, often ignoring the dimension of structural subjugation that the Arabs, minority citizens of the state endure (Arar & Mustafa, 2011). The centralized education system aims to control, supervise, unify and critique activity in school, maintaining a lack of equal educational opportunities for the Arab minority, through a "concentration of disadvantage" (Mazawi, 1999). Arab and Jewish education are separated and not equal either in means or outputs (Golan-Agnon, 2006).

The implementation of the Compulsory Education Act in the Arab education system led to an increase in girls' school attendance and the reduction of school dropout, especially in junior-high and senior-high schools. The proportion of girls is higher than the proportion of boys in both high schools and higher education institutes where they constitute 64.7% of all Arab students (Arar & Mustafa, 2011).

Gender power and status differences in Arab-Muslim society restrict women's potential for active participation in all life domains (Arar & Mustafa, 2011). Since patriarchal society expects women to remain at home, fulfilling their traditional roles as homemakers and mothers, the regular attendance of girls in Arab high schools is not self-evident and can be seen as an indicator of change in Arab society (Abu-Rabia-Queder & Arar, 2011). Few Arab women succeed in breaking through the "glass ceiling" that restricts their aspirations for social mobility: most live under the male hegemony of Muslim Arab culture that demands their subjection and obedience. In addition they are members of a minority group living under Israeli Jewish majority rule (Halperin-Kaddari, 2003).

Traditional Muslim Arab society's decision-makers fight to retain male hegemony. Recognizing the power of education to motivate change processes or to conserve traditions and values, these conservative forces seek greater involvement and confrontation in the schools, in an attempt to control their children's education (Arar & Oplatka, 2012; Halperin-Kaddari, 2003).

The above theoretical analysis indicates that the gender context in Muslim Arab high schools in Israel is structured by interaction between three levels:

1. Islamic religious and Arab social values and culture (the macrolevel) —seemingly in transition from patriarchal society to weakened patriarchal control
2. Overt and covert policies and learning programs within the school (the mesolevel) (Francis, 2010) and Arab society's perceptions of the school's status.
3. Students' and teachers' individual personal values, personalities, perceptions and motivations (the microlevel).

The Research Field: School Profile

"Al Mawardi" school (fictitious name) is a state senior-high school, established ten years ago and serves approximately 500 students. It is positioned in a relatively large rural village, with a population of less than 10,000. Young people (0–18 years) constitute 56.5% of the population, which exceeds the national proportion of young people in the Arab population (47% 0–18 years). Students mainly belong to low socioeconomic strata, the average monthly wage per household being NIS3, 950 ($987) compared with a national Arab average wage of NIS 4,700 ($1,174). There is a low proportion of self-employed parents (12%) in comparison to their proportion in the general Arab population (18%) (Khamaise, 2009).

Girls constitute 65% of the students, since many of the village's boys are defined as weak achievers and streamed to vocational high schools at the end of Grade 9 (junior high). The school includes theoretical, theoretical-technological and humanistic theoretical streams and remedial classes. The proportion of girls in science and technology classes (including chemistry, physics and biology, software engineering and communications) (61%) resembles their overall percentage in the school. The school is considered a medium size school, 40 teachers are employed there, 57% females and 42.5 % males. All teachers have academic qualifications. A large proportion of the teachers (46%) hold a second academic degree .In 2010, 56%, of students were eligible for matriculation certificate (for girls—68.3%), this percentage is 18 % above the average of success among Arab schools in Israel (Khamaise, 2009).

METHODOLOGY

This ethnographic case study aimed to clarify discourse on equity and social justice in an Arab Muslim senior-high school in Israel, investigating perceptions of teachers (including the principal) and students concerning (1) the way that the school constructs discourse concerning equity and social justice, especially in respect to gender, (2) the students' learning contents and (3) the construction of Muslim male and female teachers' behaviors in their natural environmental reality.

The research relied on data collected during my continued presence in the studied school during the academic year 2009/2010, where I served as an organizational counselor invited by the school and with its consent to document educational processes. At first I was received by the staff with suspicion, but they soon saw me as part of the school scenery. This process of acceptance was boosted by the principal's support and the service that I was able to supply both to the management, the homeroom teachers and students. In order to prevent any role or ethical conflict, from the study's inception, I presented the research themes to the school principal, and obtained his permission to record the research process, promising to maintain the anonymity of the school and its staff or students. As noted, an ethnographic approach guided data-collection (Wolcott, 2002) and an interpretative paradigm was employed to clarify the expression of equity and social justice in the school's different contexts (Sharan, 1998). Three main data-collection tools were used, according to order of appearance:

1. Observations: 32 open observations were conducted over a period of 8 months in the school's classrooms and playgrounds. The researcher recorded these observations in a research diary on a daily basis.
2. A focus group interview was conducted with a group of eight students in Grade 11 (four males and four females). This year group was selected mainly because they had already chosen their majors and they were in the process of preparing for college. The sample was chosen by their grade coordinator following research observations, choosing participants to provide deeper understanding concerning their class interaction, different majors and dress styles, especially that of the girls. The group discussion focused on environmental, social and biological development issues during adolescence, factors that shape perceptions and behavior. Emphasis was given to themes that arose during the observations of the school and especially in the two classes from which the group was selected.
3. In-depth open interviews were held with the school principal, school counselor, a grade coordinator and a homeroom teacher. Each interview lasted from 1.5 to 2 hours, held at the interviewee's chosen location and time. The objective was to clarify issues raised by the students during the observations and focus group and to triangulate data from all three sources to reinforce their validity (Sharan, 1998).The interviews focused on the school staff's perceptions of the school reality. Among the questions raised were: "tell a private external inspector about the school"; which types of activity characterize the school?"; "which figures determine the types of action?" The interviewees were also asked clarifying questions such as "could you give me an example of that?"

The qualitative data gathered from these tools were analyzed with a comparative method (Patton, 1990) and sorted according to the following three levels of analysis.(1) Islamic religious and Arab social values and culture (the macrolevel) (2) Overt and covert policies and learning programs within the school (the mesolevel) (Francis, 2010) and Arab society's perceptions of the school's status and (3) Students' and teachers' personalities, individual personal values, perceptions and motivations (the microlevel).

FINDINGS

Initial analysis offered multifaceted perspectives on the status of social justice in the regimes of this school and challenged simplistic notions. The findings detailed below relate to school climate and pupils' inclusion, the gendered curriculum is exposed, demonstrating how it reflects the values and norms of the surrounding Muslim traditional society, also, indicating tension between the pressures for achievements versus concern for students. These findings expose the overt declarative policies and discourse that this authority promotes to influence the students' perceptions towards equality and equity and a covert program that strives to maintain patriarchal norms and culture. This situation differs from that of schools in settings committed to social justice, where students, parents and staff all see diversity as something positive and enriching and this policy is reflected in both the overt and covert school culture (Sapon-Shevin, 2011).

School Climate and Students' Inclusion

Students' affiliation to a school is defined by the extent to which they sense that they belong to its social milieu, within their class and the school community (Francis, 2010). The findings indicated that the students want to belong, to be identified with central groups yet girls and women teachers may be pushed aside from the main school discourse, so that acceptance of the "other" is not a natural part of the school discourse.

The observations in the school clearly indicated differences in students' affiliation; boys tended to sit together in groups. Some of them explained that they needed to belong, to feel protected, for example the boy student Rabia:

> You need to be connected. There are bisexual cliques in our class, but outside of the school you can only be connected with boys. This gives you friends on whom you can rely in the case of problems.

In the staff lounge, men and women were also separated: most of the female teachers who wore traditional dress sat at the sides, despite their numerical superiority over male teachers. Reem, a female grade coordinator with more modern dress, felt isolated:

> I cannot sit with them, so I sit with the secretary, they make remarks about my dress, even within my earshot, that is what I am and so I prefer to keep a distance from them.

Nevertheless Reem described a process of change concerning the girl students' social relations:

> There is a change in norms, consciousness is growing, there is more freedom of speech and communication between the girls and their parents. They

go out, participate in the school's education projects and in university and return home at late hours in the evenings.

In contrast to Reem, Aiman, a homeroom teacher actually felt that traditional cultural norms still dictated school reality:

> I think that there is still a traditional mentality that leadership is something masculine. It is not acceptable to choose a girl [as a leader], even if she is talented. Girls have an emotional attribute, they try to influence things for the benefit of the boys, and they respond more to the boys' requests.

The principal explained how Arab social norms dictate relationships in the school and often leave the school impotent due to external interference:

> Everything that happens in the school is interpreted in terms of extended family. There is no such thing as individualism. The cousins' phenomenon still prevails, that's the way things are determined in the school yard. If something happens during the recess, they form a group immediately and then there's also reinforcements waiting for them outside the school that try to break in. If a girl has a male cousin he will be responsible for her in school.

Yet it also appeared from the findings that to a large extent, the school constitutes a source of social empowerment for the girls, distant from patriarchal supervision. They experience success in their studies, make social relationships and for some this is a sanctuary where they can act more freely (Khattab, 2006). The girls' high school studies actually open up the possibility of distancing themselves from the traditional society of their homes, delaying marriage age and enabling the development of personal and gender identity based on academic achievements, allowing them to develop future aspirations for an active influential position in society (Khattab, 2006).

The female homeroom teacher Aiman noted the weakening of patriarchal traditions in Arab society, although only to a certain point.

> A large proportion of the parents know about everything. The daughter usually tells her mother that she has been talking to a particular boy; there is open discussion between the daughter and her mother. Today parents often accept the principle of inter-gender relations at this age until they encounter a particular problem, then they treat it most aggressively.

Despite the gap that exists between the culture of the students and that of the adults, and despite the school's inconsistent consideration of gender equality (noted below), the school constitutes a place where the girls can experience a certain amount of freedom and contact with the other sex. This process, as it was observed, constitutes part of the change in Arab Muslim society in Israel.

Gendered Curriculum

"Recognition," as described by North (2008), is reflected in cultural proficiency's core standard of valuing diversity and the need for educators to provide both a formal and a hidden curriculum that at least reflects the cultural groups in the school. The concept of "redistribution" is recognized as the limitation of privilege and entitlement, averting system oppression and prompting educators to examine and address inequitable educational practices (Lindsey et al., 2011).

Although messages conveying values and power do not always receive clear recognition, they are unconsciously associated with and form the content of school discourse and activity. This phenomenon is known in the relevant literature as the "hidden curriculum" (Apple, Au, & Gandin, 2009) and in the present context is well described in the school principal's explanation concerning the issue of gender construction in the school. Saed explained that it was school policy to promote equality between the sexes but noted:

> Students often understand that the predominant language discriminates against one of the two sexes at school, but this is not really our intention. Some of the teachers may use this language that represents the outside society; they don't notice their gender cataloging or the differentiation that they make.

This testimony indicates that a hidden curriculum reflecting society's values influences the school reality. In other words, the teachers' sometimes unconscious behavior towards either of the two sexes is gendered and eventually becomes fixed as the accepted behavior. This behavior constitutes part of society's social construction of gender, and a gap is formed between the school's declared egalitarian intentions and what actually happens in daily scholastic practices, influenced by the outside culture.

The principal felt there was a discrepancy between the school's intentions to promote egalitarian values and what actually happened in practice under the influence of the environment. Evidence of the principal's egalitarian intentions was given by Reem (the grade coordinator), describing the work of the school principal:

> I see for example that when girl students who do not succeed academically, the principal does everything so that they should stay in school. He has a

tendency to protect those girls who are at the bottom of the grades scale; every school tries to protect them in order not to exclude them.

However from the female coordinator's remarks it can be seen that the principal's consideration is nevertheless ambivalent: "he does everything" that can be expected from a principal but "we explain things to him" [if his acts are viewed as inequitable decisions or practices].

Like the principal, Abed the male chemistry teacher also had a positive view of girls' academic potential:

The girls invest more in their studies, they ask, take an interest and some of them in the science classes are convinced that their studies are an opportunity But it bother me to discover that they often help them [the boys] and hand them their homework. As if they were obliged to help them.

Indeed powerful social conventions influence the girls as was evidenced when the educational counselor, Wafa, attempted to register the students to different streams at the start of Grade 10:

I explain how important it is to choose a stream that fits their achievements, but they refuse most forcefully to turn to streams such as electronics or software engineering. Its difficult to alter their perceptions that these are professions only for men, and to convince them that today women are integrating within these or other technological professions.

Afaf, a traditional female student in Grade 11 in the science stream noted that there is less representation of the girls in social activities. When asked why this happened, she unhesitatingly answered:

I'm a religious woman who dresses in a modest fashion that gives me a modest appearance in the community, I was educated to be like this and this is the way I am expected to behave, so I avoid demonstrative behavior or public exposure.

The words of Afaf, Abed, and Wafa indicate the perpetuation of traditional gendering in the school, questioning the relevance of more modern social perceptions. The school had not succeeded in altering the power of social conventions over the male and female students' attitudes and behaviors. Most teachers do not see the discussion of the issue of equality between the sexes as part of their role and prefer to neglect it, accepting it as part of the hegemonic structure of their society despite their more liberal socialization during their academic training (Francis, 2010).

In the observations, it was difficult to find relations between boys and girls in the school yard, since this aroused criticism. The very fact that boys and girls study together in a Muslim Arab high school sometimes endangers the continuation of the traditional girls' education, when parents suspect that such contact deviates from the norms of their home or society.

Rami, one of the male students, indicated that the girls often hid their interaction with the boys from their parents:

> The girls are academically the best in Grade 12. What occupies them 24 hours a day is to find a partner, but it's important that their parents shouldn't know. They have all the necessary tools, a mobile phone, Messenger, chats, Facebook, but their parents don't know about it all.

The above evidence indicates to what extent the school has become an arena for empowering education for Muslim girls, providing them with access to the resource of knowledge and to a discourse of rights that she may not see at home, where she may have a lesser status than her brothers or in the public sphere where she is not expected to appear and is not represented. Yet it also indicates that traditional inequitable norms and behaviors continue to persevere within the school.

Promoting a Discourse of Achievements Rather Than Equality

Previous studies indicate that the Arab-Muslim school is largely achievement-oriented (Khattab, 2006; Mazawi, 1999), a grades economy philosophy predominates and efforts are focused on improving grades. Efforts to create a climate of egalitarianism and concern are pushed to the side (Arar & Abu-Asbah, 2013).

School staff stressed a discourse of achievements. This was suggested as the justification for the school management avoiding promoting women teachers to key positions, since women were seen as focusing on care and concern for students at the expense of efforts to improve achievements. Previous studies such as that of Metcalf and Linstead (2003) also found that women were excluded from organizational discourse and from positions of authority in the school in other more "Western" societies (Skrla, 2000).

Criticism of these policies was voiced by the grade coordinator, Reem:

> Male teachers are usually given jobs because of their seniority, although they have no connection with a particular job. It's true that they can stay in the afternoons more easily than women, and it's not nice to harm them. But what interferes is that everything is measured by achievements, everyone is constantly running, when you talk about the humane aspect of our work its seen as cushioning, being soft ... achievements are primary. In our culture

our husbands expect us to come home early to our homes and not to work late with other men and this prevents our promotion.

The findings indicated that there are two different discourses within the school. Many female teachers including the educational counselor express a discourse of care and concern in contrast to the male teachers who emphasize achievements (Noddings, 2003). In an educational institution that emphasizes a discourse concerning achievements, the efforts of the educational counselor, to promote a feminine discourse of shared experience, support and concern for students are met with resistance (Fletcher, 2001). Additionally, the aspirations of female teachers for promotion meet resistance because they cannot compete with the hours that male colleagues invest and because their feminine leadership style is seen as impeding the aspiration for student achievements. Nevertheless, there are some visible buds of reciprocal assistance between male and female teachers and some attempts to take an interest in students' lives especially among novice female and some male teachers.

Disourses Clash

Contemporary scholars often consider social justice as an egalitarian status entailing citizens having an equal share in terms of access to and distribution of resources, entitlement, and representation and also having an equal voice (Garratt & Forrester, 2011).

In the observations I witnessed tension between the prevailing hegemonic school discourse and students' efforts to alter their reality. This was evident in the girls' alteration of their external appearance and identity from conformity to Islamic traditional values to Western more modern values. Raunek, a girl in Grade 12 defended this new trend:

> In high school girls are occupied with their appearance, although there are more girls wearing scarfs in the school scenery, it's more a matter of style than an aspiration to be religious. Some of them are pleasing their parents, wearing scarfs and closefitting dresses, shirts; it looks fashionable, while her picture on her cell phone or Facebook appears without a scarf.

Thus the girls employ a strategy of partial acquiescence complying with their parents' expectations, yet undergoing a quiet transformation in their self-perception. They do not need to directly confront religious values and norms regarding the need for religious appearance in the public sphere and yet they manage to adapt this appearance to accord with modern values. Rawan, a female student explained:

Today, the scarf is part of the New Look including make-up and care for your face from a very young age, when I was their age we never touched our eyebrows, its different today ... make-up is fashionable now, parents' control is weakened, my mother is the same mother but her supervision and control is not the same. As a result of social pressure parents' control over their children has weakened.

Wafa, the educational counselor described girls' empowerment and students' attempts to change their reality:

Our society has opened up; parents do not have such a strong tendency to push the girls into engagement for marriage from an early age. Many of the girls become engaged and the engagements are broken. They tend to reject engagement claiming that they need to study and are busy.

The Internet constitutes a means for communication between boys and girls, which adults who wish to maintain traditions cannot control. It broadens and varies the communication channels, some supervised that studying in a mixed gender school opens.

Reem, the grade coordinator also explained how girls' high school education counters social expectations for early marriage:

The percentage of girls aspiring to higher education is growing. This influences the percentage of engagements. I remember that when I was in Grade 11, the norm was to be engaged already at this age. Today, we try to introduce the issue of family life surreptitiously; we try to impart sex education.

To conclude, it was evident that the students hold different views regarding the impact of Arab society's values and culture in the shaping of their gender reality. However, there are still gendered distinctions in the school.

CONCLUDING REMARKS

The investigation of discourse on equity and social justice in an Arab-Muslim high school in Israel found that several factors hinder discourse and praxis that would promote social justice.

1. There was apparently a hidden curriculum in the school that contradicted the principal's declared goal of imparting values of equality and social justice (Smith, 2012). Some of the teachers still felt that some types of educational activity are more suitable for boys than girls (Fuller, 2011). They therefore failed to promote equitable change that might undermine the existing patriarchal culture of

their society maintained by the hidden curriculum. Message and practices concerning gender appeared to differ at different levels of the school society: the macrolevel (the sociocultural values and norms of the management) and the microlevel (individual values and norms of the students). Nevertheless, various members of the school staff did feel that their role included helping to modify the existing male hegemony in their society with a stronger role for women (Khattab, 2006; Shah, 2010) including the principal (Theoharis, 2009). This can be seen in the inclusiveness of the learning program: the emphasis on academic achievements for both boy and girl students. However, in the absence of organized educational action and a specific school program, tension continues to exist between the aspirations for gender equality and existing cultural values, impeding the advancement of egalitarian schooling (Apple et al., 2009; Francis, 2010).

2. Directed intentional policy and action is necessary to relate to the needs of the individual student. Despite the activities of both male and female younger teachers who exhibit more care and concern for the students, both boys and girls, there is still little concern for the individual's welfare and a lack of dialogue between teachers and pupils (Noddings, 2003), so that there is little change in the school's structure and organizational culture which remains dominated by a masculine hegemony and culture (Fletcher, 2001; Francis, 2010; Grogan & Shakeshaft, 2011; Skrla, 2000). The Arab school mostly promotes a "grades economy," although it is noteworthy that the girls have considerable academic success within this culture (Arar & Abu-Asbah, 2013).

3. The lack of collegial dialog between the teachers often leads to a clash of expectations, so that the school usually promotes a masculine orientation, faithfully representing and maintaining the surrounding Arab Muslim hierarchical and authoritarian society (Arar & Oplatka, 2011; Shah, 2010; Shapira, Arar, & Azaiza, 2010).

4. Another element affecting the school is a gradual change toward a more equitable reality in the school's Arab community. Often it seems that the school's covert traditional rhetoric and the students' more modern practices lead in different directions (Garratt & Forrester, 2012; Wong, Lam, & Ho, 2002). It appears to be difficult to lead school policy in a particular direction when the surrounding community is not involved in or does it support the process. When teachers tackle challenging issues of social justice and inclusion through their curriculum or their classroom policies and practices, they also need to know they will have administrative support (Smith, 2012). Teachers would be able to introduce greater

social justice and equity if they knew they had support to treat the
students differently in order that their opportunity for success is
equalized (Lindsey et al., 2011)

During adolescence, both boys and girls are occupied with their external appearance (Weaver-Hightower, 2009). Traditionally, the family has
served as a convenient space for inculcation of social and religious norms,
with specific implications for gender, and the family has often constituted
a space of oppression (Smith, 2012). In contrast the contemporary Arab
school in Israel allows Muslim girls a space beyond the total control of the
home (Renold & Allan, 2006; Wong et al., 2002).

Additionally the exposure of Arab Muslim youth to the values and norms
of the majority Jewish society with its Western orientation and to the international world of the mass media (Arar & Shapira, 2012) whether during
their studies or outside the school walls has weakened patriarchal control
of the adolescents daily lives (Khattab, 2006).

It is concluded that the school transmits conflicting messages concerning
the issue of social justice and equity. On the one hand the school claims to
represent modern culture and to strive to provide equality of opportunity
for all students. This message is reinforced by messages that the Muslim
youth absorb from mass communication and from encounters with Jewish
culture. Western modern values encourage a discourse of achievement
and gender equality. On the other hand, Muslim society still largely main-
tains traditional norms and male hegemony in the covert school culture.
According to Theoharis (2009) principals need three critical dispositions if
they are committed to creating inclusive, socially just schools: (1) A global
theoretical perspective. They should understand that school inclusion is
related to other issues of social justice. Issues of oppression, marginalization in minority ethnic society and other forms of exclusions must be at the
center of their understanding. (2) A bold imaginative vision (3)Embracing
a sense of agency. Attention should be given to alternatives to streaming
and efforts should be made to include inclusion of all students within a
shared school community with a zero indifference policy.

The evidence presented here concerning the interplay between the
school's learning programs and prevalent social perceptions in Arab society
and the students' experiences in the studied school raises several questions
concerning the role of the Muslim school in training a new generation for
inclusion in postmodern society. It is concluded that there is a need for
empathetic educators-students dialog, a need to listen to the voice of the
younger generation, and to address the challenge of Muslim Arab society's
social norms in order to promote more egalitarian perceptions and practices. Adopting the dispositions described by Theoharis (2009) might help
those Muslim school principals who wish to create a more equitable society

within their schools to realize their aspirations. The findings emphasize the need to produce a balanced learning program that will oblige the school to commit itself to education for equity and social justice both in the school curricula and daily teaching and learning interactions.

REFERENCES

Abu-Rabia-Queder, S., & Arar, K. (2011). Gender and higher education in different national spaces: Palestinian students in Israeli and Jordanian universities. *Compare, A Journal of Comparative and International Education, 41*(3), 353–370.

Apple, M., Au, W., & Gandin, L. A. (2009). *The Routledge international handbook of critical education.* New York, NY: Routlege.

Arar, K., & Abu-Asbah, K. (2013). Not just location: Attitudes and perceptions of education system administrators in local Arab governments in Israel. *International Journal of Educational Management, 27*(1), 54–73.

Arar, K., & Mustafa, M. (2011). Access to higher education for the Palestinians in Israel. *Education Business and Society: Contemporary Middle Eastern Issues, 4*(3), 207–228.

Arar, K., & Oplatka, I. (2012). Gender debate and teachers' constructions of masculinity vs. femininity of school principals: The case of Muslim teachers in Israel. *School Leadership & Management, 6*(4) 1–16.

Arar, K., & Shapira, T. (2012) "I am leading a quiet revolution": Women high-school principals in the traditional Arab society in Israel. *Journal of School Leadership. 5*(22), 853–874.

Blankstein, A. M., & Houston, P. D. (Eds.). (2011). *Leadership for social justice and democracy in our schools.* Thousand Oaks, CA: Sage.

Chapman, C., & West-Burnham, J. (2010). *Education for social justice: Achieving well-being for all.* London, England: Continuum.

Central Bureau of Statistics (2009). *Statistical Abstract of Israel 2008.* Population estimates by population group, 2.1. Jerusalem: CBS. Retrieved from: www.cbs.gov.il/shnaton60/st02_01.pdf

Connell, R. (2005). *Masculinities.* Cambridge, England: Polity Press.

Fletcher, J. (2001). *Disappearing acts: Gender, power and relational practice at work.* Cambridge, MA: Mets Press.

Francis, B. (2010). Re-theorising gender: Female masculinity and male femininity in the classroom? *Gender and Education, 22*(5), 477–490.

Fuller, K. (2011, July). *Learning gendered leadership: A case study of leadership apprenticeship.* Paper presented at *BELMAS Annual International Conference,* Wybston Lakes, England.

Garratt, D., & Forrester, G. (2012). *Education policy.* London, England: Continuum.

Golan-Agnon, D. (2006). Separate but not equal: Discrimination against Palestinian Arab students in Israel. *American Behavioral Scientist, 49,* 1075–1084.

Grogan, M., & Shakeshaft, C. (2011). *Women and educational leadership.* San Fransisco, CA: Jossey-Bass.

Halperin-Kaddari, R. (2003). *Women in Israel: A state of their own*. Philadelphia, PA: University of Pennsylvania Press.

Hey, V., & Bradford, S. (2004). The return of the repressed? The gender politics of the emergent forms of professionalism in education. *Journal of Education Policy, 19*(6), 691–713.

Khamaise, R. (2009). *The book of Arab society 3*. Jerusalem: Van Leer Institute. [Hebrew]

Khattab, N. (2006). Social capital, student's perceptions and educational aspirations among Palestinian students in Israel. *Research in Education, 68*, 77–88.

Lindsey, R., Lindsey, D., & Terrell, R. (2011). Social justice focusing assets to overcome barriers. In A. M. Blankstein & P. D. Houston (Eds.), *Leadership for social justice and democracy in our schools* (pp. 25–44). Thousand Oaks, CA: Sage Publications.

Mazawi, E. A. (1999). Concentrated disadvantage and access to educational credentials in Arab and Jewish localities in Israel. *British Educational Research Journal, 25*(3), 335–370.

Metcalf, B., & Linstead, A. (2003). Gendering teamwork: Re-writing the feminine. *Gender Work and Organization, 10*(1), 94–119.

Noddings, N. (2003). *Caring: A feminine approach to ethics and moral education*. Berkeley, CA: University of California Press.

North, C. (2008). What is all this talk about "social justice"? Mapping the terrain of education's latest catchphrase. *Teachers College Record, 110*(6), 1182–1206.

Patton, M. Q. (1990). *Qualitative evaluation methods* (2nd ed.). Thousand Oaks, CA: Sage.

Renold, E., & Allan, A. (2006). Bright and beautiful: High achieving girls, ambivalent femininities and the feminization of success. *Discourse: Studies in Cultural Politics of Education 27*, 547–573.

Sapon-Shevin, M. (2010). *Because we can change the world: A practical guide to building cooperative, inclusive classroom communities*. Thousand Oaks, CA: Corwin.

Sapon-Shevin, M. (2011). Zero indifference and teachable moments: School leadership for diversity, inclusion and justice. In A. M. Blankstein & P. D. Houston (Eds.), *Leadership for social justice and democracy in our schools* (pp. 145–168). Thousand Oaks, CA: Sage.

Shah, S. (2010). Re-thinking educational leadership: Exploring the impact of cultural and belief systems. *International Journal of Leadership in Education, 13*(1), 27–44.

Shapira, T. Arar, K., & Azaiza F. (2010). Arab women principals' empowerment and leadership in Israel. *Journal of Educational Administration, 48*(6), 704–715.

Sharan, M. (1998). *Qualitative research and case study applications in education*. San Francisco, CA: Jossey-Bass.

Skrla, L. (2000). The social construction of gender in the superintendency. *Journal of Education Policy, 15*(3), 293–316.

Smith, E. (2012). *Key issues in education and social justice*. London, England: Sage.

Theoharis, G. (2009). *The school leaders our children deserve: Seven keys to equity, social justice and school reform*. New York, NY: Teachers College Press.

University of London. (2009). *Effective pre-school and primary education 3-11 Project (EPPE 3–11). A longitudinal study funded by the DfES (2003–2008). Promoting equality in the early years*. Report to The Equalities Review by Institute of Education, Department for Education and Skills, University of London.

Wade, R. (2007). *Social studies for social justice: Teaching strategies for the elementary classroom*. New York: Teachers College Press.

Weaver-Hightower, M. (2009). Masculinity and education. In M. Apple, W. Au, & L. A. Gandin (Eds.), *The Routledge international handbook of critical education* (pp. 163–176). New York, NY: Routlege.

Wolcott, H. (2002). Ethnography or educational travel writing. In Y. Zou & E. H. Trueba (Eds.), *Ethnography and schools* (pp. 27–48). New York, NY: Rowman & Littlefield.

Wong, K. C., Lam, R., & Ho, L. M. (2002). The effects of schooling in gender differences. *British Educational Research Journal, 28*(6), 827–423.

CHAPTER 9

GENDER, ISLAM, AND REFUGEE STATUS

Possibilities For Negotiating Hybrid Identities and Contesting Boundaries In Digital Spaces

Delila Omerbašić

ABSTRACT

In this chapter, the author examines some challenges that young Muslim women who are resettled as refugees experience in Western spaces, such as the United States. In particular, the ways in which Muslim women and refugees are discursively constructed as weak and homogeneous are considered. Feminist postcolonial theory is used to problematize the dominant discourses about what it means to be a young Muslim woman with refugee status by considering the intersections of gender and religion with race, class, age, ethnicity, nationality, and language. In addition, the author argues that it is

Growing Up Between Two Cultures: Problems and Issues of Muslim Children, pp. 207–233
Copyright © 2014 by Information Age Publishing

important to consider how historical and political contexts intersect to better understand the ways in which power functions to include and/or exclude Muslim women resettled as refugees in various global spaces. Finally, the chapter highlights creative possibilities that exist in collaborative Third Spaces, such as digital spaces, through which young Muslim women can negotiate their hybrid identities and interrupt some of the deficit-oriented discourses through which they are discursively constructed.

> Every voyage can be said to involve a re-siting of boundaries. The traveling self is here both the self that moves physically from one place to another, following 'public routes and beaten tracks' within a mapped movement; and, the self that embarks on an undetermined journeying practice, having constantly to negotiate between home and abroad, native culture and adopted culture, or more creatively speaking, between a here, a there, and an elsewhere. (Trinh, 2010, p. 27)

Thousands of young people resettle as refugees in the United States each year as a result of forcible displacement due to war, conflict, or other forms of persecution in their home countries. There are more than 15.2 million people who are classified as refugees according to the 1951 Convention Relating to the Status of Refugees; its 1967 Protocol; and/or the 1969 OAU[1] Convention Governing the Specific Aspects of Refugee Problems in Africa (United Nations High Commissioner for Refugees [UNHCR], 2010).[2] According to these protocols, refugee status is granted to any person

> who is outside his or her country of nationality or habitual residence; has a well-founded fear of persecution because of his or her race, religion, nationality, membership of a particular social group or political opinion; and is unable or unwilling to avail himself or herself of the protection of that country, or to return there, for fear of persecution. (UNHCR, 2007, p. 6)

A small percentage of those who are granted refugee status are able to resettle into third countries, frequently in North America and Europe. United States and Western European countries, which worked together to develop the initial definitions of refugee status, also have some of the most stringent refugee admissions and asylum policies (Grewal, 2005). Each year, the United States sets a "ceiling" that limits the number of refugees who will be accepted for resettlement. For fiscal year 2012, the ceiling was set to 76,000 people (Bruno, 2012) and 58,000 people were resettled (Negash, 2012). The top ten countries of origin for those resettled included Bhutan, Burma, Cuba, Iraq, Somalia, the Democratic Republic of Congo, Iran, Eritrea, Sudan and Ethiopia (Negash, 2012).

Refugees and asylum seekers are often forced to leave their homes, without control over their ultimate destination (Mosselson, 2006; Trinh, 2010). In addition, refugees who resettle in Western countries arrive with minimal, if any preparation and knowledge of that country's language, culture, and environment (Strekalova & Hoot, 2008; Suárez-Orozco & Suárez-Orozco, 2001). Following resettlement, refugee support organizations, such as the International Rescue Committee (IRC), provide immediate support to families who are beginning to establish new lives. Shortly following the initial resettlement, formal and informal educational institutions serve as a key point at which students and their families who were resettled as refugees begin their adaptation to a new home (Adams & Shambleu, 2006).

In migration that results from persecution, experiences vary greatly based on gender along with ethnicity, race, language, class, religion, and other factors (Hyndman, 2010), thus it is crucial to recognize the heterogeneity that is produced through these intersections. While refugee studies and refugee education literature frequently highlight the national origins of particular refugee groups, little attention is paid to the differences that exist within those national groups, and particularly in relation to gender and religion. For example, although official numbers are not reported, many of those who are resettled are Muslim, such as for example Rohingya Muslims from Burma or many Oromo Muslims from Ethiopia, in addition to those from overwhelmingly Muslim countries, such as Afghanistan, Iran, Iraq, Somalia, and Sudan. Therefore, it is important to consider the experiences of those who are resettled as refugees with a consideration for how their experiences intersect with their faith. Furthermore, although gender impacts the experiences of displacement and resettlement in critical ways, it remains understudied (Hyndman, 2010), resulting in a need for an increased focus on gender in refugee and displacement studies.

The goal of this chapter is to bridge these important aspects of forced migration, focusing particularly on the ways in which Islam and gender intersect to shape the experiences of youth following resettlement to the United States. Specifically, I examine some challenges that teenage Muslim women who are resettled as refugees experience in Western spaces, such as the United States. In particular, I examine the ways in which Muslim women and refugees are discursively constructed as weak and homogeneous. I use feminist postcolonial theory to problematize the dominant discourses about what it means to be a Muslim woman with refugee status by considering the intersections of gender and religion with race, class, age, ethnicity, nationality, and language. In addition, I argue that it is important to consider how historical and political contexts intersect with spaces prior to displacement and following resettlement to better understand the ways in which power functions to include and/or exclude Muslim women in various global spaces. Lastly, I focus on the creative possibilities that exist in Third Spaces, and particularly digital spaces, through which young Muslim women who are resettled as refugees can negotiate their hybrid identities and interrupt the deficit-oriented discourses through which they are discursively colonized.

MUSLIMS IN THE UNITED STATES

While some Muslims in the United States are recent immigrants and resettled refugees from various locations across the globe, others have been in the United States for generations. The actual number of Muslims in the United States is not known, because the census data or the U.S. Immigration Services do not take religion into account (Pew Research Center, 2007). A 2007 report by the Pew Research Center estimates that around 65% of Muslims living in the United States are immigrants, primarily from the Middle East, and include at least 68 countries around the world. While reasons for immigration vary, around 20% of those who immigrated to the U.S. did so to escape some form of persecution. Around 20% of Muslims in the U.S. are native born, more than 50% of whom are African American. Although there are no official statistics on the percentage of Muslims who are resettled as refugees, many refugees have origins in overwhelmingly Muslim countries, such as Afghanistan, Iraq, Iran, Sudan, and Somalia, while others experienced displacement due to persecution based on their religion.

As the demographic estimates indicate, it is important to consider that Muslims in the United States are not a homogeneous group and are a very diverse population. In addition to national origin, diversity also exists in language, class, gender, social and historical experiences, as well as traditions of spirituality (Moore, 2005). As Jen'nan Ghazal Read (2008) notes, there is a great range in terms of religious devoutness among Muslims in the United States,

> Some are religiously devout, some are religiously moderate, and some are non-practicing and secular, basically Muslim in name only, similar to a good proportion of U.S. Christians and Jews. Some attend a mosque on a weekly basis and pray every day, and others don't engage in either practice. (p. 39)

Thus it is important to recognize the multiple ways in which those who are Muslim engage with their spirituality in their daily lives. Furthermore, diversity exists in the Islamic traditions practiced; while the majority of the

Muslims in the United States are Sunni, around 20% affiliate with the Shia tradition (Pew Research Center, 2007).

Although Islam has been one of the major religions in the United States for many years, following the attacks on September 11, 2001, Islam and Muslims have become the focus of national surveillance (Ladson-Billings, 2004). After 9/11, Muslims in the U.S. have become portrayed as dangerous: "Ideologically represented as a threat since 9/11 'they'—Muslim Americans—have been watched, detained, deported, and invaded in order to protect and save 'us'" (Sirin & Fine, 2007, p. 151). Many Americans view Islam in a negative light, frequently relating it to terrorism and oppression (Gorski, 2006). Moreover, those with a Middle-Eastern background in particular have become "widely perceived as culturally alien, [and] may be treated as Other if not Enemy" (Wingfield, 2006, p. 255). More than a quarter of Muslims surveyed by the Pew Research Center (2007) reported experiencing various forms of othering and discrimination, while a significantly higher number worried about the ways in which Muslims are singled out in government policies.

The ways in which Muslims are portrayed in U.S. discourses differ based on gender. While Muslim men tend to be represented as terrorists in dominant mainstream U.S. discourses and popular media, Muslim women are represented as weak, uneducated, and oppressed. The primary symbol that is used to arbitrarily support these claims is the *hijab*. Although many (48%) Muslim women do not wear any head covering, as reported by The Pew Research Center (2007) study, for those who choose to wear it, the hijab represents a visible symbol that one is Muslim. This often impacts the experiences of Muslim women who make the choice to wear it (Sirin & Fine, 2007). As Ajrouch (2004) notes, the hijab serves as a discursive symbol that presupposes oppression in the mainstream, white, American discourses, which do not recognize the variety of reasons why Muslim women in the U.S. wear it.

Muslim Refugee Youth in the United States: Educational Intersections and Challenges

For Muslims who resettle as refugees to the United States, negative gendered representations of Islam compound with the misrepresentations of the refugee experience in the adaptation process. Adaptation is an ongoing process in which a person learns to negotiate personal, societal, and institutional cultures and norms (Anderson, Hamilton, Moore, Loewen, & Frater-Mathieson, 2003). Upon arriving into a new country, the adaptation process begins as families seek to access essential resources needed for survival, like shelter and food (Bolloten & Spafford, 1998). The process is complicated by racism, isolation, marginalization, a negative context of reception, and pressures to learn a new language and obtain self-sufficiency as quickly as possible (Bolloten & Spafford, 1998; Jones & Rutter, 1998; Loewen, 2004; Warriner, 2007). Given that previous skills and education are typically not valued in Western contexts, refugee families are often able to only secure low-skilled jobs, regardless of prior education, training, skills, and knowledge (Li, 2008a).

These compounded misrepresentations have a particularly negative impact on youth who experience them in schools and other educational contexts in the process of adaptation. Youth adaptation frequently takes place in school contexts (Anderson et al., 2003; Hamilton, 2003; Mosselson, 2006). However, schools are often underprepared to support resettled students (Dooley, 2009; Li, 2008a, 2008b; Roxas, 2011) and lack contextualization of their experiences within race, religion, politics, and power (Abu El-Haj, 2002). Within schools, young people who are resettled as refugees ideally have opportunities to learn about their new societies and cope with any negative experiences from their pre- and transmigration experiences in a safe and supportive environment.

Preferably, the adaptation process should be reciprocal, where schools, families, and students adapt to each other's norms (Anderson et al., 2003). However, literature illustrates that students and families often face negative receptions in school contexts, including discrimination, racism, and devaluation of their knowledge (Adams & Kirova, 2006; Li, 2008a; Roxas, 2011). Their linguistic and cultural wealth and the identities negotiated based on that wealth are often disregarded and devalued. Consequently, children "who have lived through difficult episodes in their lives" are at times treated "as objects of correction and remediation" (Campano, 2007, p. 54), incapable of completing grade-level work (Dooley, 2009), and not deserving of opportunities to voice their educational goals and concerns (Li, 2008b; Roxas, 2011). Furthermore, as schools lack an integration of critical understanding of religious diversity, schools may be particularly unwelcoming for those youth who are Muslim. As Abu El-Haj (2002) writes, "it is Islam that is posited as most culturally Other, inimical to 'Western' values and traditions" (p. 309). In this process, young Muslim women in particular are perceived as uneducated and oppressed, especially if they wear head covering (Ajrouch, 2004; Sirin & Fine, 2007). These constructions illustrate that resettled students who are often Muslim are represented as an "Other" whose strengths, knowledge, and potential are often devalued.

(MIS)REPERESENTATIONAL BOUNDARIES

Contemporary youth are always in motion, either physically through travel and migration, or virtually in digital spaces (Bucholtz & Skapoulli, 2009; Dolby & Rizvi, 2008). These active movements serve as contexts for youth's identity negotiation processes, which are always situated within various global systems of power. For those who have moved and relocated geographically, such as displaced youth who resettle in Western countries, the notion of belonging to a "home" extends through multiple spaces and is complicated with the possible return to one's original home place (Brah, 2005; Dolby & Rizvi, 2008). In these global contexts, the identity negotiation process is further impacted by the intersecting categories of gender and religion.

Adolescence is a central period in which youth begin to negotiate their identities, situated in complicated power relationships and sociohistorical contexts of local and global spaces (Erikson, 1985). During this time, youth begin to experience tensions between how they define themselves in relation to how they are defined and represented by their families, immediate communities, and the broader society (Ajrouch, 2004). The difficulties presented for identity negotiation for resettled youth are typically evident in interaction with the established boundaries that support Western, White, male, and Christian normativity, which minimizes the contributions, experiences, and knowledges of those who are not authorized within those categories. For example, many young Muslim women resettle into a context that often frames them as uneducated, weak, and oppressed, while also not recognizing the various ways in which this deficit-based framing may intersect with their identity negotiation processes.

Representations of refugee women and girls in some scholarly literature often reflect those prevalent in dominant discourses, as illustrated in mass media. A simple Internet search for a "refugee woman" or "refugee girl" returns thousands of similar portrayals and images—sad, helpless, crying, and often described as such in accompanying texts. In addition, many of the women and girls in the images are wearing a veil, which to many Western non-Muslims represents a symbol of oppression (Ajrouch, 2004). These images illustrate the way refugee women are written about in academic and mainstream literature, where minimal attempts are made to disrupt their monolithic construction. While their national origin (e.g., Sudanese, Somali, Afghan) is frequently cited in these representations, limited attention is paid to how multiple intersecting factors such as ethnicity, religion, socioeconomic status, language, social histories and legacies of power, including imperialism, colonialism, and other forms of structural oppression in these broader societies, have shaped individual women's experiences as refugees.

These representations illustrate the discursive context which young Muslim women resettled as refugees enter following resettlement, which undoubtedly intersects with their complex identity negotiation processes. At the same time, these young women may also have to negotiate the boundaries of their own culture and faith. As Sirin and Fine (2007) illustrate in their study of Muslim youth in the United States, gendered expectations for behavior and appearance are central factors in experiences of adolescent Muslim youth. They write, "Islam sets very different standards for girls and boys ranging from the way they can dress to the way they can socialize, and we could certainly hear Muslim youth feeling the pressure for standard setting and enforcement, especially for how Muslim females should behave and dress" (Sirin & Fine, 2007, p. 159). Similarly, in her study of high school Muslim girls from Yemen, Loukia Sarroub (2005) found that young women felt comparable pressures to meet expectations for particular ways of behaving.

While these studies indicate that religion can shape the experiences of young Muslim women through surveillance and behavioral expectations, it is imperative to critically approach these findings. These studies represent findings from very specific contexts, and it must be noted that within each exist variations in how young women experience their identities in relation to their religion, culture, and lived experiences. There is no unitary Muslim women's, or girls', experience, and there are variations based on social, political, and historical contexts and understandings of Islam, as well as each individual woman's and girl's interpretations within those contexts. Thus, the challenge for young Muslim women, and particularly those who are resettled as refugees, is to negotiate their identities within expectations and (mis)representations which intersect with complex boundaries and historical contexts of their homes prior to migration and their homes following resettlement.

To better understand these complex experiences and boundary negotiations of adolescent Muslim refugee women, feminist postcolonial scholars offer useful perspectives. As Loomba (2005) indicates, postcolonial theoretical perspectives allow for an analysis of global colonial legacies, which are "articulated alongside other economic, social, cultural, and historical factors" (p. 22), and which have shaped people's lived experiences in relation to colonialism in various ways around the world. Specifically, postcolonial theory is concerned with representation, difference, memory, and history (Bhabha, 2004; Gandhi, 1998), focusing on the issues of "authenticity, representation, and the status of the self" (Moore-Gilbert, Stanton, & Maley, 1997, p. 43). Many postcolonial theorists focus on disrupting the colonial legacies that perpetuate negative discursive representations of those who are deemed to exist in direct contrast to the White, Christian, Western world.

Feminist postcolonial theory, specifically considers gender as an important focus point in these disruptions, highlighting the ways in which women are positioned globally, by taking into account multiple intersections that include race/ethnicity and class (Loomba, 2005). Loomba (2005), Mohanty (2003), and Hegde (1998) foreground the heterogeneity of women around the globe, which aligns with a critical perspective on the experiences of young Muslim women who were resettled as refugees in the United States. In particular, these scholars point not only to the gendered nature of lived experiences, but also to frequent discursive colonization through (mis) representations of the so-called Third World Woman as a homogeneous construction who is "victimized, tradition bound, and passive" (Hegde, 1998, p. 281). Mohanty argues that a legacy of colonialism is a continued discursive colonization and production of the "Third World woman"— she is weak, a victim of her supposedly backward society and patriarchy (within her society), and generally a monolithic construction. Mohanty further indicates that this homogenized "Other" woman is represented in "universal, ahistorical splendor" (p. 41), as backward, uneducated, illiterate, and unaware of her depressed and backward condition, her rights, and her possibilities.

Within this construction of the third world woman are the constructions of a refugee woman and a Muslim woman, who are represented as victims who are vulnerable and suffering. Often, refugee and Muslim women are portrayed as victims of patriarchy. However, through the othering process and discursive colonization, patriarchy in non-Western spaces is criticized, without acknowledgement of the various ways in which Western actions influenced patriarchy around the globe. In particular, patriarchy in pre-dominately Muslim societies is portrayed as especially oppressive, without any recognition of the ways in which Western colonialism and more recent political interventions influenced the establishment of highly patriarchic social structures. Furthermore, through mainstream representation of "other" forms of patriarchy, the Western form is portrayed as invisible and nonexistent. This ensures continued oppression, marginalization, and discursive colonization of women, and particularly women of color and Muslim women, in Western spaces.

Feminist postcolonial theory provides theoretical tools to examine how women are not granted agency and recognition for ways in which they are actively working against various forms of oppression, marginalization, and misrepresentations. This perspective helps disrupt this homogeniza-tion and the discursive boundaries created between the First World/Third World, recognizing instead that women's experiences differ and are often shaped by various intersections of social, historical, and political contexts (Loomba, 2005). Furthermore, this theoretical perspective offers ways to take into consideration the historical factors that intersect with the oppressive social structures across the globe.

HYBRID IDENTITIES

In *Elsewhere, Within here: Immigration, Refugeeism and the Boundary Event*, postcolonial feminist theorist Trinh T. Minh-ha (2010) considers the possibilities that exist in various spaces to interrupt boundaries and discursive dichotomies in productive ways. She draws attention to the hybridities that result from intersections of complex lived experiences, social contexts, and embodied histories, which illuminate dynamic similarities and interconnections among seemingly disparate spaces. To better understand identity negotiation of young Muslim women who resettle as refugees, it is important to consider various contextual intersections that form hybridity of identity in this negotiation process.

Migration that results from persecution is typically marked by displacement from one's home, temporary settlement in another country, and for a small percentage of the global refugee population, resettlement in a third country, such as the United States. As Trinh (2010) points out, terms like (re)settlement imply a level of stability, of starting over, but do not take into account the challenges experienced in the new social, historical, and political contexts of the countries in which new diasporic communities are formed. James Clifford (1994) writes that diasporas are communities of "displaced peoples who feel (maintain, revive, invent) a connection with a prior home. This sense of connection must be strong enough to resist erasure through the normalizing processes of forgetting, assimilating, and distancing" (p. 310). Diaspora implies a distance from a homeland, along with possible imaginative constructions and memories, feelings of estrangement in the new home, and a possibility of return. People are often united by the experience of living in a diaspora, which encapsulates both positive and negative experiences:

> Experiences of loss, marginality, and exile (differentially cushioned by class) are often reinforced by systematic exploitation and blocked advancement. This constitutive suffering coexists with the skills of survival: strength in adaptive distinction, discrepant cosmopolitanism, and stubborn visions of renewal. Diaspora consciousness lives loss and hope as a defining tension. (Clifford, 1994, p. 312)

Thus, although strength is gained through community participation and survival while facing cultural erasure through assimilation, experiences of diaspora are always further complicated by oppression based on race, ethnicity, gender, religion, and class across multiple contexts.

Postcolonial feminist Avtar Brah (2005) argues that it is important to historicize the experiences of diaspora to account for experiences prior to resettlement, but also to recognize the circumstances of arrival. It is essential to consider the ways in which power functions to include and/ or exclude people in their new contexts, including and extending beyond the diaspora communities. More specifically, we need to consider how power intersects with race, gender, class, age, religion, ethnicity, language, and so forth, within each community, as "all diasporas are differentiated, heterogeneous, contested spaces, even as they are implicated in the con-struction of a common 'we'" (p. 618). Thus, for example, in the broader Somali diaspora, we have to recognize the multiple ways in which power is distributed within that community, such as the distinctions that are formed based on gender or class prior to displacement. Similarly, we have to con-sider how racialization and racism intersect with this diasporic journey, as well as different oppressions and privileges based on gender within these various social spaces. Brah helps further the understanding of how colo-nial legacies function to simultaneously advocate for assimilation for those who are resettled into Western spaces, while at the same time furthering their otherness through discursive and physical monitoring and control. Because of these different positions and locations, the meaning of diaspora and diasporic identities is not static and there exist many heterogeneous experiences and hybrid identities in various diasporic communities.

Brah (2005) points to the importance of identifying "a position of multiaxial locationality" (p. 628), which accounts for various physical or imagined locations. She writes that this position represents "locationality in contradiction—that is, a positionality of dispersal; of simultaneous situatedness within gendered spaces of class, racism, ethnicity, sexuality, age; of movement across shifting cultural, religious and linguistic boundaries; of journeys across geographical and psychic borders" (p. 628). This concept provides an important orientation for helping understand how young Muslim refugee women negotiate their identities within diverse systems and legacies of power, pointing specifically to the ways in which identities are hybrid, multiple, and flexible.

Considering diasporas as spaces that nurture hybridity is productive, in contrast to a conceptualization of diaspora as a space in which social prac-tices and power relationships are replicated based on the groups' original homes. In this process, hybridity is produced through language, which bridges the experiences of previous homes with the new locations (Trinh, 2010). In hybrid spaces, in which various social, political, and historical contexts intersect, language shapes identities that are consequently hybrid and always shifting and changing.

This understanding of hybridity is supported by sociocultural perspec-tive on identity in which identities represent enactments of socially and historically situated selves: "people take selves and subjectivities with them from space to space and relationship to relationship … they enact a particular version of self that is appropriate to a time, space, relationship, or activity" (Lewis & Moje, 2003, p. 1983). From this perspective, identities are not enacted all at once; instead they are always in process and enacted in accordance to particular social practices, representing a "self in practice" instead of a "self in essence" (Holland, Lachicotte, Skinner, & Cain, 1998, p. 32). Thus, identities represent enactments and understandings of self, which are always connected to lived experiences and social practices within a particular time and space.

Hybrid identities, and more specifically, their enactments, are intersected with personal agency. Lewis and Moje (2003) write that agency "can be thought of as the strategic making and remaking of selves; identities; activities; relationships; cultural tools and resources; histories" (p. 1985) through language. Agency is then enacted through language to shape behaviors that are situated within particular understandings and enactments of self. But, as Hegde (1998) notes, it is always important to pay attention to ways in which power intersects with the potentiality of agency through enactments of identities. Thus, we need to be cognizant of the various ways in which power intersects with agency, and identity enactments, as well as the possibility that the intentions of agency and identity enactments are recognized in practices (Lewis, Enciso, & Moje, 2007). For example, as illustrated previously, a particular type of Muslim and "refugee woman" is discursively produced in dominant discourses based on a deficit-oriented perception of her global social, political, and historical location, experience with persecution, and political status. While many women do live in challenging and life-threatening conditions, their numerous strategies for survival under these conditions are not recognized in dominant discourses (Mohanty, 2003). Therefore, it is important to disrupt homogenizing discourses by considering the ways in which young Muslim women who were resettled as refugees enact identities.

Oikonomidoy (2009) reports selected findings from a qualitative study she conducted with seven Muslim Somali refugee girls attending a U.S. high school, focusing on development of an academic identity within a global context and illustrating how identities are impacted by local and global contexts. She finds that these identities are defined by "complexity, hybridity and absence of clear boundaries" (p. 23). In particular, the author highlights academic identity formation within the intersecting contexts of microlevel processes, which take place on the school level, and macrolevel processes, which take place on the societal and global levels. Oikonomidoy finds that the students in her study had a very strong sense of identity, as well as pride in their cultural heritage and belonging. She further shows that immigrant and refugee identities are not static, but are flexible and influenced by micro- and macrolevel contexts, which include past, present, and anticipated experiences.

On the microlevel, Oikonomidoy (2009) shows that schools play a key role in influencing refugee students' adaptation process, as this is where they spend the most time interacting with the cultures of their new country. The challenge becomes when the schools are unprepared to meet the needs of refugee students, while perpetuating curricular models that are based on White Eurocentric values and conceptualizations. These educational models are often exclusionary to immigrant and refugee students and thus have a negative impact on their academic identity negotiation. Thus, the author indicates that it is important that schools are supportive of diverse cultures, ethnicities, and languages of students who are often not reflected in mainstream curricula. On the macrolevel, students' identities were shaped by their position in the global context. The young women had homes and lived experiences in several countries—Somalia, Kenya, and the United States. Consequently, as they moved between these spaces, they carry their ways of knowing and living into new contexts, which shapes their hybrid identities. As they adapt to the life in the United States, Oikonomidoy shows that their identities were impacted by their prior experiences and a sense of belonging to more than one place. Although the students were members of different ethnic groups in Somalia, their shared sense of belonging to Somalia fostered a pan-Somali identity in the United States.

As many refugees, including those in Oikonomidoy's (2009) study, imagine the possibility of returning home in the future, it is important to understand the conceptualization of a global identity and the notion of education within a "global flexible space" (p. 35). More specifically, Oikonomidoy notes that educators need to employ "approaches that transcend local and national borders and recognize flexible ways of belonging" (p. 35). In such a way, educators can disrupt the dichotomies of "us" and "them," or "home culture" and "host culture," and create spaces that shift from "our" schools (Szente & Hoot, 2007) to spaces that provide comfort to a multitude of hybrid identities.

While Oikonomidoy's (2009) study illustrates the contexts that impact identity negotiation, it also shows that students enact agency in order to position themselves in particular ways in their new homes. To conceptualize how agency is performed with identity enactments, the concept of *making worlds* will be helpful (Holland et al., 1998). This concept illustrates the dynamic nature of identities as well as the creative potential that identity enactments carry. It relies on Vygotsky's (1978) conceptualization of play:

> Just as children's play is instrumental in building their symbolic competencies, upon which adult life depends, so too social play—the activities of "free expression," the arts and rituals created on the margins

of regulated space and time—develops new social competencies in newly imagined communities. (p. 273)

Agency as enacted through creativity and play in social practices, creates possibilities for change. For example, playfulness exhibited through imagined identities, which may be expressed through digital literacy practices, can create possibilities for different types of future identity enactments.

CONTESTING BOUNDARIES IN DIGITAL "THIRD" SPACES

Youth who have been resettled as refugees in the U.S. are members of the broader transnational population of those who "have moved bodily across national borders while maintaining and cultivating practices tied —in varying degrees—to their home countries" (Hornberger, 2007, p. 325). Diasporic communities, particularly those that resulted from forcible displacement, are frequently located around the globe and maintained through connections that are becoming increasingly digital, such as through the Internet and interactive video games. In recent years, the accessibility and popularity of online gaming practices has significantly increased, creating possibilities to creatively negotiate hybrid identities and contest discursive boundaries. Games such as Assassin's Creed are particularly popular with young people and illustrate how the concept of *making worlds* (Holland et al., 1998) intersects with creativity and hybrid identities in creative digital spaces. For example, the Assassin's Creed series of games attempts to represent particular periods in history, including religious wars in the Middle East and the intricate politics of the Italian Renaissance. The architecture and graphics are beautiful, serving as background to violent plot lines of these games, which is evident in the promotional statement by Ubisoft, the games' developer: "*The setting is 1191 AD. The third crusade is tearing the holy land apart. You, Altaïr, intend to stop the hostilities by suppressing both sides of the conflict. You are an Assassin, a warrior shrouded in secrecy and feared for your ruthlessness*" (Ubisoft, 2008, para. 2–3, emphasis added). While the historical context of the games is noteworthy, the experience of playing the game as an individual who is situated in particular historical, political, and social practices is particularly interesting.

Echoing Bakhtin (1981) in their critical review of the first installment of the game, Seif El-Nasr, Al-Saati, Niedenthal, and Milam (2008) argue that game play experience is heteroglossic, or multivoiced—meaning that game play is situated in multiple voices that give meaning to one's personal experiences in relation to her social and political histories, which impact present and future actions. One of the authors, Maha Al-Saati who identifies as Middle Eastern and from Saudi Arabia reflects on her game play experience:

> Walking towards the city of Jerusalem evoked much emotion; my heart beats as I approach. As I hear the chanting of the monks, the sounds of the church bells, I know I am closer to this magical city—this place of conflict. As I reach Jerusalem, I listen carefully; perhaps I can hear the sound of an Athaani piercing through the skies. To many people of the Monotheistic religions, Jerusalem is a holy land. To go there, is a journey of a lifetime, a dream, perhaps they would want to fulfill at one point in time. For a Middle-Easterner, wandering through the Assassin's Creed game world might be purely driven by nostalgia, in the hope of identifying with the elements of the past. I was in it to explore a heritage many, like me, have deemed lost. (p. 1)

This example illustrates that Al-Saati engages with the Assassin's Creed gaming space in a very personal and embodied way. While authors Seif El-Nasr and Al-Saati, who identify as Middle Eastern, experienced nostalgia in relation to the words, sounds, and accents in the game, their experience differs from those of their co-authors who identified as Western, whose experience focused more on the architecture, the game play tactics, and the overall ambiance of the game. The hybridity of Al-Saati's identities and the multiple locations that she embodies simultaneously, in the East and the West, is brought to light through this gaming experience. This example illustrates that identity enactments within various social practices, such as game play, are situated in relation to the meanings produced within dynamic and intersecting global and local contexts of geographic and virtual spaces.

Dominant discourses typically do not engage with the ways that identities can be negotiated through digital media, such as video games. In fact, these discourses often focus on the allegations that video games, and particularly those with violent content, may have a negative impact on one's identity, behavior, or attitudes. The recognition of ambiguity, multiplicity, and hybridity is often not granted to these social practices in mainstream conversations. However, digital media, including video games, online discussion groups, social media websites like Facebook and YouTube, and communication tools such as Skype and ooVoo provide spaces in which hybrid identities can be negotiated, while contesting various boundaries created by dominant social and cultural discourses.

The mainstream dominant discourses that portray refugees, refugee women, and Muslims in monolithic and deficit-based ways are frequently reflected in the media. These dominant discourses and media representations intersect with the identity negotiation process of adolescents who may identify as Muslim women with refugee backgrounds. While macrolevel relations construct and discursively produce people in different ways, Canagarajah (2004) argues that on the local level people can "resist, modify, or negotiate" these impositions through language (p. 268). Thus, although linked with various systems of historically situated forms of power, language acts to create new possibilities and new ways of interacting with and through power. Consequently, with increased proliferation of digital media and social networks, young people have opportunities to show how they negotiate their identities with and against these dominant discourses that surround them through language and literacy in digital spaces. Literacy practices in these digital spaces allow young Muslim women who are resettled as refugees to contest the boundaries that are established for them, and enact their identities in hybrid ways, drawing upon experiences from home, from their diasporic communities, as well as the broader society in which they live. The online spaces provide opportunities to creatively test out new roles, ideas, and attitudes, while engaging with a broad range of lived experiences.

In recent years, scholars have been focusing on examining the link of technology and transnationalism in global diasporas to consider the possibilities for political action and identity negotiation that exist in digital spaces. These studies indicate that technology is an important element in the lives of displaced people around the world. For example, in his study of Iranian websites, Sharam Khosravi (2000) notes, "While 'return' does not seem to be realized by Iranians in diaspora, 'virtual return' has become a reality for many of them. Iranians have found a homeland in the homepages" (p. 13). Digital spaces enable the negotiation of identity and belonging to a home among people who currently reside in various global locations.

For refugee women and girls in particular, transnational digital spaces are particularly important as they link their social, cultural, linguistic networks that have been impacted through forced migration, while allowing for their own active expression of who they are. Siddiquee and Kagan (2006) conducted a study with six refugee women living in the United Kingdom who are from different countries in Africa in order to understand the impact of technology on their lives after resettlement. They found that technology reduced loneliness and feelings of isolation among the women: "it allowed to recuperate some of their fragmented (due to war of political unrest) social support networks" (p. 196). The women communicated with friends and family around the world and shared images, such as photographs, which helped maintain and rebuild connections with others. This was also helpful for those women who had lower literacy skills—sharing images enabled them to communicate and maintain relationships with others even without having to read/write extensively. The women also relied on the technology in order to access information, such as news from their home countries, as well as information about their new contexts, such as finding housing, employment, and career development courses. In this way, they maintained transnational social networks and connections through digital literacy.

In addition to providing ways to bond with family and community members around the world through negotiation of physical boundaries, digital spaces also allow opportunities for negotiation of discursive boundaries in which diverse knowledges, experiences, and histories are bridged through hybrid identity enactments. Bernal (2006) writes about the Eritrean diaspora and the uses of technology for political engagement through an online community. She writes, "Eritrean websites have fostered the emergence of counter-publics and spaces of dissent where unofficial views are voiced and alternative knowledges are produced" (p. 176). Similarly, Brinkerhoff (2012) found that members of the Tibetan diaspora found a place where they can discuss and voice their political opinions freely on a website called "TibetBoard." The website's creator indicates: "Tibetan people, because of the traditional system, we don't speak openly all the time because of the situation, so that's my purpose. I want people to talk about anything, like politics, without boundary and also have fun" (p. 86). These studies illustrate the important possibilities created through online spaces for community building as well as identity negotiation through technology.

Although these studies do not engage with Muslim participants specifically, examining spaces that bridge Muslim and immigrant/refugee experiences illustrates similar examples. For instance, the website Somalia Online provides a digital space for a community of Somalis around the world. The locations of people who participate in this online community include Canada, Somalia, the United Kingdom, and the United States. The participants use English and Somali languages to communicate around topics that range from politics, religion, and gender issues, such as discrimination of Muslim women in Western spaces based on their choice to wear the hijab.

In addition to online forums and discussion sites where people from global diasporas can gather and negotiate their experiences as well as their identities, social networks like YouTube, Facebook, and Twitter provide similar opportunities. For example, youth along with adults frequently download music videos from their home countries on YouTube. In addition to downloading music, they also take part in the music video comment boards where discussions range from politics, religion, and gender issues. As McGinnis, Goodstein-Stolzenberg, and Saliani (2007) write, "These online sites are the author's spaces—to create, to write, to voice opinions, and to explore their identities" (p. 288) and "to create texts around local, national, and global issues that are important to them" (p. 289).

These examples reflect a trend in digital literacy, which illustrate youth participation in social networks that focus on particular interests, along with various forms of digital communication (Trinh, 2010). As Mills (2010) finds in a review of literature, youth tend to create spaces that allow them a greater level of authorship through collaborations with other youth. In these collaborative spaces, young people create and develop content, "hybridize textual practice" (p. 256), such as for example blogging or combining languages, and often gather in what Gee (2012) calls "affinity spaces," which represent "sharing of knowledge and expertise based on voluntary affiliation around a common interest or goal" (p. 258). This illustrates that digital literacy practices are comprised of more than just technical tools, such as for example smart phones and tablets, but include what Lankshear and Knobel (2007) call the "new ethos stuff." The new ethos contributes to broadening the understanding of the new organizational principles for meaning-making. It represents a privileging of

> participation over publishing, distributed expertise over centralized expertise, collective intelligence over individual possessive intelligence, collaboration over individuated authorship, dispersion over scarcity, sharing over ownership, experimentation over "normalization," innovation and evolution over stability and fixity, creative-innovative rule breaking over generic purity and policing, relationship over information broadcast, and so on. (p. 21)

As such, digital technology has provided the technological tools that support a dynamic new ethos in literacy practices, which is collaborative and decentralized. As these spaces are produced collaboratively, they represent a form of Third Space, which recognizes hybridity, flexibility, and contradiction, while at the same time working to shift or disrupt boundaries, such as those of dual and dichotomous Western and non-Western identities.

Focusing on the creative possibilities that exist in Third Spaces, such as digital spaces, shows ways through which young Muslim women can negotiate their hybrid identities and interrupt the deficit-oriented discourses through which they are discursively colonized. As Sheehy and Leander (2004) note, "space is a product and process of socially dynamic relations. Space is not static—as in metaphorical images of borders, centers, and margins—it is dynamically relational" (p. 1). Conceptualizing space as active and relational allows us to consider the ways in which it is imbued with social and political struggles, along with possibilities to contest boundaries and imposed dichotomies.

Edward Soja (2004) calls for an understanding of space as shaped by, while also shaping social practices, encouraging readers to recognize that we are all "spatial beings" (p. 1), and as such, we need to increase our "consciousness of spatiality" (p. 2). In doing so, we need to think about space in different ways and recognize it as dynamic and relational, meaning that space exists in a dynamic relationship with social and historical contexts. Based on Lefebvre's (1991) concepts of perceived, conceived, and lived spaces, Soja (1996) develops relational concepts that he calls First-space, Secondspace, and Thirdspace. He argues for a radical, or critical postmodern epistemological perspective to understand the relations that exist between these spaces, taking into account how elements from various epistemological perspectives contribute to the broadening of our spatial consciousness. He refers to this as a "both/and also logic," which allows for creative theoretical conceptualizations of hybrid epistemological perspectives (p. 5). He views this as an essential component to understanding the notion of Thirdspace, which does not neatly align with the "real" or "imagined" discourses of Firstspace and Secondspace. Instead, he writes, Thirdspace allows us to develop a new "mode of thinking about space that draws upon the material and mental spaces of the traditional dualism but extends way beyond them in scope, substance, and meaning" (p. 11). Thirdspace thus allows for combinations of thinking about space, its similarities as well as contradictions all at once.

While conceptualizing space as relational with places, histories and social practices, we also need to consider the political conditions that underlie particular meanings and interpretations of space, such as for example in relation to nations, nationhood, and belonging. As Moje (2004) illustrates, these political conditions can be reflected in identity enactments through literacy practices, as spaces "shape and reflect the social, ethnic, identity, and literate practice of the youth who moved through them" (pp. 15–16). She thus encourages us to consider "spatial and temporal identities" as "versions of self that are enacted according to understanding of and relations in different spaces and time periods" (p. 17). Therefore, considering space as relational reflects not only the social and historical contexts of that space, but is also the relationship with the social identities that intersect those contexts through social practices and various forms of power.

Considering space as relational, hybrid, and always productive, allows us to conceptualize the creative possibilities that exist for young Muslim women who were resettled as refugees to negotiate their complex, hybrid identities in digital spaces. This framework broadens the representation of women, and especially women whose bodies, memories, and/or histories are located in non-Western spaces (Hegde, 1998; Loomba, 2005; Mohanty, 2003), foregrounding the heterogeneity of young displaced women who were resettled as refugees in the United States and who identify as Muslim. As mentioned earlier, the frequent discursive colonization takes place through (mis)representations of the so-called Third World Woman as a homogeneous construction who lacks knowledge, strength, and self-awareness. It is crucial to disrupt this homogenization, recognizing instead that women's experiences differ and are often shaped by the intersections of gender with race, ethnicity, religion, culture, socioeconomic status, and location (Loomba, 2005). The ways in which these various intersections are negotiated are often reflected in digital spaces, which allow for creative negotiations of hybrid identities that privilege multiplicity instead of dichotomy.

IMPLICATIONS FOR EDUCATION PRACTICE

In youth experiences with forced migration, education represents a constant among other connections and resources that have been lost (Bolloten & Spafford, 1998; Dachyshyn, 2008; Mosselson, 2006). Although students resettle with many different backgrounds and experiences, schools represent locations where student diversity comes together (Campano, 2007; Pipher, 2002). Unfortunately educational experiences in formal educational institutions are not ideal for students following resettlement. Schools are often not sufficiently prepared to adequately serve the needs of the diverse population of students with refugee experiences, as well as Muslim students. In particular, students' diverse ways of knowing along with the multiple ways in which they negotiate the hybridities of cultural belonging, adaptation, and various representational discourses are seldom recognized and supported. This is challenging, for young Muslim women in particular, because as Sirin and Fine (2007) write,

> When one's social identity is fiercely contested by the dominant discourse either through formal institutions, social relationships, and/or the media, one of the first places we can witness psychological, social and political fallout is in the lives of young people. (p. 151)

In their adaptation process, adolescent Muslim women who were resettled as refugees have to learn to adjust to a life in a different culture, and also to negotiate and contest the ways in which they are minoritized and discriminated against based on their cultural backgrounds and gender in the new society. Youth, and particularly adolescents, live and embody these negotiations. They find spaces and "make worlds" (Holland, et al., 1998) in which these intersections can be negotiated and performed, which need to be recognized and validated in schools. Thus it is important for educators to work with their students and learn about the resources and cultural wealth that students draw upon in their daily lives.

Bucholtz and Skapoulli (2009) write, "it is in local spaces and communities that identities are tried out, embodied, and adapted in order to be made coherent" (p. 2). As "subjects in motion" (p. 1), students are moving across linguistic, global, and virtual spaces to create a variety of meanings (McGinnis et al., 2007). One way to improve the educational experiences of young Muslim women who were resettled as refugees is to incorporate these movements in their digital experiences through which they negotiate their hybrid identities into the classrooms. This can be accomplished by providing opportunities for Third Spaces in classrooms, which engage with complex lived experiences, identities, and knowledges of youth. For example, Gutiérrez, Baquedano-López, and Alvarez (2001) show how using a cultural historical perspective to focus on the development of "joint activities" can foster collaborative and co-produced learning in Third Spaces. They write that learning is not an individual endeavor, but instead is a socialization process that accounts for the individual and her/his interpersonal relationships within a community. In learning contexts, these socializations exist in what they call communities of learners or communities of practice, in which activities are strategic and purposeful, collaboration is normalized, and language and literacy are considered transformational. Moreover, these communities of learners draw on the concept of hybridity as a resource for learning, where "participants draw from their own as well as each other's linguistic and sociocultural resources to collaborate in problem-solving activities" (p. 126). This work provides an example of the transformative possibilities of collaborative spaces in which normalized dominant discourses and practices can be disrupted through enactments and nurturing of hybrid identities (Gutiérrez, 2008).

Being a young woman who is Muslim and resettled in the United States as a refugee can be a challenging experience due to the multitude of boundaries and (mis)representations imposed on her lived experiences. As youth adaptation frequently takes place in schools, it is important to create educational spaces that affirm and value diverse hybrid identities that bridge multiple intersections of lived experience, knowledge, sociopolitical contexts and histories, and recognize the hybrid identities that young people enact. Instead of positioning students as "Muslim" or "refugee," it is important to recognize additional ways in which students may define themselves, along with the ways in which their lived experiences shape their identity negotiation. Providing possibilities for production of Third Spaces that recognize the heterogeneity and multiple ways in which youth participate in such spaces in their lived experiences is important. Spaces that foster enactments of hybrid identities provide critical opportunities for disrupting dichotomous constructions and representations of youth.

As Mills (2010) illustrates, youth from diverse ethnic and socioeconomic backgrounds take part in digital literacy practices, which often foster collaborative meaning-making. This is supported by a Pew Internet and American Life (Lenhart & Madden, 2005) report that indicates, regardless of socioeconomic backgrounds, race, ethnicity, and education levels, youth across the U.S. engage in digital literacies to create and consume content online. There are small variations in the types of literacy and frequency depending on availability of high speed Internet, but youth generally engage in online activities through computers and other digital devices such as smartphones.

Although many students participate in digital production of spaces in out of school settings, which allow for negotiations of their hybrid identities, it is important to provide opportunities for students to engage with such spaces in formal educational settings. To do so, educators must work *with* students and collaboratively determine which spaces would be meaningful and productive given the intersections of their social, historical, and cultural contexts.

In addition to working to engage with students' diverse ways of knowing and being, teachers also need to recognize the many learning tools that students use in their daily lives. This may present a challenge, as formal educational institutions often limit access to various technologies or applications, such as for example smartphones and social media sites. However, learning and meaning-making takes place in various ways, many of which are rapidly changing and evolving. While most people do not have access to very fast Internet in their homes, or several computers and multiple other digital devices, they may share one computer, utilize cell phones or music players, or access digital technology through libraries, community centers, and schools. Recognizing the variety of tools and opportunities for access is important if digital literacy, in all of its variations, is going to be meaningfully incorporated in classrooms. Therefore, educators need to work with students to learn about the resources they use, or would like to use, such as various digital technologies and applications.

Incorporating ways in which students learn outside of classroom through digital technology can provide meaningful opportunities for content-based learning that draws on students' resources and wealth of knowledge. For example, students can engage in social studies topics by drawing on their own experiences in various contexts and with various technological tools. Collaborative learning opportunities in the classroom will also allow students to engage with nondominant perspectives in content areas, which can foster critical understanding of social issues and inspire action-oriented social-justice projects. For example, through digital projects, students can identify issues and challenges they face in their daily lives, such as for example discrimination for wearing the hijab, and analyze them within local/global social, historical, or political contexts. With teachers and classmates, they can work to create content that addresses those concerns, such as for example blogs, animations, and online discussions, which illustrate hybrid identities and complex, context-situated experiences. It is also important that such projects serve a particular purpose, such as promoting learning and discussion that can lead to opportunities for action and contribute to social transformation. By engaging with the production of such spaces, educators can support in greater depth the hybrid identity negotiation and meaning-making through digital literacy. Collaborative learning opportunities in Third Spaces will lead to a development of better educational strategies for all youth, including those with Muslim and refugee backgrounds and experiences, which affirm, value, and nurture complex identities and ways of knowing, and which offer potentials for socially transformative practices.

NOTES

1. Organization of African Unity
2. In addition to 15.2 million refugees, this number also includes internally displaced persons (IDPs; 27.1 million), and asylum-seekers (~1 million). According to UNHCR (2010), IDPs are "individuals who have been forced to leave their homes or places of habitual residence, in particular as a result of, or in order to avoid the effects of armed conflict, situations of generalized violence, violations of human rights, or natural- or human-made disasters, and who have not crossed an international border," while asylum-seekers include "individuals who have sought international protection and whose claims for refugee status have not yet been determined" (p. 23).

REFERENCES

Abu El-Haj, T. R. (2002). Contesting the politics of culture, rewriting the boundaries of inclusion: Working for social justice with Muslim and Arab communities. *Anthropology & Education Quarterly, 33*(3), 308–316.

Adams, L. D., & Kirova, A. (2006). Introduction: Global migration and the education of children. In L. D. Adams & A. Kirova (Eds.), *Global migration and education: school, children, and families* (pp. 1–10). Mahwah, NJ: Lawrence Earlbaum.

Adams, L. D., & Shambleau, K. (2006). Teachers', children's, and parents' perspectives on newly arrived children's adjustment to elementary school. In L. D. Adams & A. Kirova (Eds.), *Global migration and education: School, children, and families* (pp. 87–102). Mahwah, NJ: Lawrence Earlbaum.

Ajrouch, K. J. (2004). Gender, race, and symbolic boundaries: Contested spaces of identity among Arab American adolescents. *Sociological Perspectives, 47*(4), 371–391.

Anderson, A., Hamilton, R., Moore, D., Loewen, S., & Frater-Mathieson, K. (2003). Education of refugee children: Theoretical perspectives and best practices.

In R. Hamilton & D. Moore (Eds.), *Educational interventions for refugee children* (pp. 1–11). London, England: RoutledgeFalmer.

Bakhtin, M. M. (1981). *The dialogic imagination: Four essays* (M. Holquist, Ed.). Austin, TX: University of Texas Press.

Bernal, V. (2006). Diaspora, cyberspace and political imagination: The Eritrean diaspora online. *Global Networks, 6*(2) 161–179.

Bhabha, H. K. (2004). *The location of culture.* New York, NY: Routledge.

Bolloten, B., & Spafford, T. (1998). Supporting refugee children in East London primary schools. In J. Rutter & C. Jones (Eds.), *Refugee education: Mapping the field* (pp. 107–123). Staffodshire, England: Trentham Books.

Brah, A. (2005). Diaspora, border and transnational identities. In Lewis, R. & Mills, S. *Feminist postcolonial theory: A reader* (pp. 613–634). New York, NY: Routledge.

Brinkerhoff, J. M. (2012). Digital diasporas' challenge to traditional power: the case of TibetBoard. *Review of International Studies 38*, 77–95.

Bruno, A. (2012). *Refugee admissions and resettlement policy.* Washington, DC: Congressional Research Service.

Bucholtz, M., & Skapoulli, E. (2009). Introduction: Youth language at the intersection from migration to globalization. *Pragmatics, 19*(1), 1–16.

Campano, G. (2007). I will tell you a little bit about my people: Narrating immigrant past (pp. 52–71). In *Immigrant students and literacy: Reading, writing and remembering.* New York, NY: Teachers College Press.

Canagarajah, S. (2004). Multilingual writers and the struggle for voice in academic discourse. In A. Pavlenko & A. Blackledge (Eds.), *Negotiation of identities in multilingual contexts* (pp. 266–289). Buffalo, NY: Multilingual Matters.

Clifford, J. (1994). Diasporas. *Cultural Anthropology, 9*(3), 302–338.

Dachyshyn, D. M. (2008). Refugee families with preschool children: Adjustment to life in Canada. In L. Adams & A. Kirova (Eds.), *Global migration and education: Schools, children and families* (pp. 251–262). Mahwah, NJ: Lawrence Erlbaum Associates.

Dolby, N., & Rizvi, F. (2008). *Youth moves: Identities and education in global perspective.* New York, NY: Taylor & Francis.

Dooley, K. T. (2009). Homework for refugee middle school students with backgrounds marked by low levels of engagement with English school literacy. *Literacy Learning: the Middle Years*, 1–9.

Erikson, E. 1985. *Childhood and society.* New York, NY: Norton.

Gandhi, L. (1998). *Postcolonial theory: A critical introduction.* New York, NY: Columbia University Press.

Gee, J. P. (2012). *Social linguistics and literacies.* London, England: Routledge.

Gorski, P. C. (2006). Beyond propaganda: Resources from Arab film. *Multicultural Education, 13*(3), 56–59.

Grewal, I. (2005). *Transnational America: Feminisms, diasporas, neoliberalisms.* Durham, NC: Duke University Press.

Gutiérrez, K. D. (2008). Developing a sociocritical literacy in the third space. *Reading Research Quarterly, 43*(2), 148–164.

Gutiérrez, K., Baquedano-Lopez, P., & Alvarez, H. (2001). Literacy as hybridity: Moving beyond bilingualism in urban classrooms. In M. de la Luz Reyes & J.

Halcón (Eds.), *The best for our children: Critical perspectives on literacy for Latino students* (pp. 122–141). New York, NY: Teachers College Press.

Hamilton, R. (2003). Schools, teachers, and the education of refugee children. In R. Hamilton & D. Moore (Eds.), *Educational interventions for refugee children* (pp. 83–96). London, England: RoutledgeFalmer.

Hegde, R. (1998). A view from elsewhere: Locating difference and the politics of representation from a transnational feminist perspective. *Communication Theory, 8*(3), 271–297.

Holland, D., Lachiocotte, W., Skinner, D., & Cain, C. (1998). *Identity and agency in cultural worlds*. Cambridge, MA: Harvard University Press.

Hornberger, N. (2007). Biliteracy, transnationalism, multimodality, and identity: Trajectories across time and space. *Linguistics and Education, 18*(3–4), 325–334.

Hyndman, J. (2010). Introduction: The feminist politics of refugee migration. *Gender, Place and Culture, 17*(4), 453–459.

Jones, C. & Rutter, J. (1998). Mapping the field: Current issues in refugee education. In J. Rutter & C. Jones (Eds.), *Refugee education: Mapping the field* (pp. 1–12). Staffodshire, England: Trentham Books.

Khosravi, S. (2000). www.iranian.com An Ethnographic Approach to an Online Diaspora. *ISIM Newsletter, 6*, 13.

Ladson-Billings, G. (2004). New directions in multicultural education. In J. A. Banks & C. M. Banks (Eds.), *Handbook of research in multicultural education* (pp. 50–65). San Francisco, CA: Jossey-Bass.

Lankshear, C., & Knobel, M. (2007). Sampling "the new" in new literacies. In M. Knobel & C. Lankshear (Eds.), *A new literacies sampler* (pp. 1–24). New York, NY: Peter Lang.

Lefebvre, H. (1991). *The production of space*. Oxford, England: Blackwell.

Lenhart, A., & Madden, M. (2005). *Teen content creators and consumers*. Washington, DC: Pew Internet & American Life Project.

Lewis, C., & Moje, E. B. (2003). Sociocultural perspectives meet critical theories. *International Journal of Learning, 10*, 1979–1995.

Lewis, C., Enciso, P., & Moje, E. B. (2007). Introduction: Reframing sociocultural research on literacy. In C. J. Lewis, P. Enciso, & E. B. Moje (Eds.), *Reframing sociocultural research on literacy: Identity, agency, and power* (pp. 1–14). Mahwah, NJ: Lawrence Erlbaum Associates.

Li, G. F. (2008a). Being Sudanese, being Black. In *Culturally contested literacies: America's "rainbow underclass" and urban schools* (pp. 93–126). New York, NY: Routledge.

Li, G. F. (2008b). Crossing cultural borders in the United States: A case study of a Sudanese refugee family's experiences with urban schooling. In L. D. Adams & A. Kirova (Eds.), *Global migration and education: School, children, and families* (pp. 237–249). Mahwah, NJ: Lawrence Earlbaum.

Loewen, S. (2004). Second language concerns for refugee children. In D. Moore (Ed.), *Educational interventions for refugee children* (pp. 35–52). London, England: Routledge.

Loomba, A. (2005). *Colonialism/postcolonialsm*. London, England: Routledge.

McGinnis, T., Goodstein-Stolzenberg, A., & Saliani, E. C. (2007). "indnpride": Online spaces of transnational youth as sites of creative and sophisticated literacy and identity work. *Linguistics and Education, 18,* 283–304.

Mills, K. A. (2010). A review of the "digital turn" in the New Literacy Studies. *Review of Educational Research, 80*(2), 246–271.

Mohanty, C. T. (2003). *Feminism without borders: Decolonizing theory, practicing solidarity.* Durham, NC: Duke University Press.

Moje, E. B. (2004). Powerful spaces: Tracing the out-of-school literacy spaces of Latino/a youth. In K. M. Leander & M. Sheehy (Eds.), *Spatializing literacy research and practice* (pp. 15–38). New York, NY: Peter Lang.

Moore, J. R. (2005). The role of Islam and Muslims in American education. *Curriculum and Teaching Dialogue, 7*(1 & 2), 155–165.

Moore-Gilbert, B. J., Stanton, G., & Maley, W. (1997). *Postcolonial criticism.* London, England: Longman.

Mosselson, J. (2006). *Roots & routes: Bosnian adolescent refugees in New York City.* New York, NY: Peter Lang.

Negash, E. (2012). Office of Refugee Resettlement: The Year in Review—2012. Washington, DC: Department of Health and Human Services. Retrieved from http://www.acf.hhs.gov/programs/orr/resource/orr-year-in-review-2012

Oikonomidoy, E. (2009). The multilayered character of newcomers' academic identities: Somali female high-school students in a US school. *Globalisation, Societies and Education, 7*(1), 23–39.

Pew Research Center. (2007). *Muslim Americans: Middle class and mostly mainstream.* Washington, DC: Author.

Pipher, M. (2002). *The middle of everywhere: The world's refugees come to our town.* New York, NY: Harcourt.

Read, J. G. (2008). Muslims in America. *Contexts, 7*(4), 39–43.

Roxas, K. (2011). Tales from the front line: Teachers' responses to Somali Bantu refugee students. *Urban Education, 46*(3), 513–548.

Sarroub, L. K. (2005). *All American Yemeni girls: Being Muslim in a public school.* Philadelphia, PA: University of Pennsylvania Press.

Seif El-Nasr, M., Al-Saati, M., Niedenthal, S., & Milam, D. (2008). Assassin's Creed: A multi-cultural read. *Loading, 2*(3), 1–32.

Sheehy, M., & Leander, K. M. (2004). Introduction. In K. M. Leander & M. Sheehy (Eds.), *Spatializing literacy research and practice* (pp. 1–14). New York, NY: Peter Lang.

Siddiquee, A., & Kagan, C. (2006). The Internet, empowerment, and identity: An exploration of participation by refugee women in a community internet project (CIP) in the United Kingdom (UK). *Journal of Community & Applied Social Psychology, 16,* 189–206.

Sirin, S. R., & Fine, M. (2007). Hyphenated selves: Muslim American youth negotiating identities on the fault lines of global conflict. *Applied Development Science, 11*(3), 151–163.

Soja, E. W. (1996). *Thirdspace: Journeys to Los Angeles and other real-and-imagined spaces.* Malden, MA: Blackwell.

Soja, E. W. (2004). Preface. In K. M. Leander & M. Sheehy (Eds.), *Spatializing literacy research and practice* (pp. ix–xv). New York, NY: Peter Lang.

Strekalova, E., & Hoot, J. L. (2008). What is special about special needs of refugee children? Guidelines for teachers. *Multicultural Education, 16*(1), 21–24.

Suárez-Orozco, C., & Suárez-Orozco, M. M. (2001). *Children of immigration.* Cambridge, MA: Harvard University Press.

Szente, J. & Hoot, J. (2007). Exploring the needs of refugee children in our schools. In L. D. Adams & A. Kirova (Eds.), *Global migration and education: school, children, and families* (pp. 237–249). Mahwah, NJ: Lawrence Earlbaum.

Trinh, T. M. (2010). *Elsewhere within here: Immigration, refugeeism, and the boundary event.* New York, NY: Routledge.

Ubisoft Entertainment. (2008). Assassin's creed. Retreived from http://www.ubi.com/US/Games/Info.aspx?pId=6307

United Nations High Commissioner for Refugees. (2007). *The 1951 refugee convention: Questions & answers.* New York, NY: Author.

United Nations High Commissioner for Refugees. (2010). 2009 Global trends: Refugees, asylum-seekers, returnees, internally displaced and stateless persons. New York, NY: Author.

Vygotsky, L. S. (1978). *Mind in society: The development of higher psychological processes.* Cambridge, MA.: Harvard University Press.

Warriner, D. S. (2007). "It's just the nature of the beast": Re-imagining the literacies of schooling in adult ESL education. *Linguistics and Education, 18*(3), 305–324.

Wingfield, M. (2006). Arab Americans: Into the multicultural mainstream. *Equity and Excellence in Education, 39*, 253–266.

CHAPTER 10

STEPPING IN AND OUT OF WORLDS

Bosnian Muslim Girls' Narratives About Cultural and Religious Identity Construction

Lisa Hoffman

ABSTRACT

This chapter features narratives of adolescent Bosnian Muslim women who came to the United States as refugees following the Bosnian War in the 1990s. Each of the women featured in this chapter considers herself to be socially and culturally proficient both within immigrant Bosnian and mainstream U.S. cultures; each is also academically successful and professionally ambitious. In their own words, the young women relate their lived experiences in U.S. culture and their processes of acculturation and identity construction. The analysis highlights the conceptions and reconstruction of cultural and religious identity among these women, who all identify themselves as ethnically Bosnian and religiously Muslim. Narratives and analysis also discuss

Growing Up Between Two Cultures: Problems and Issues of Muslim Children, pp. 235–259
Copyright © 2014 by Information Age Publishing

the role of race, language, and cultural distance in the women's identity construction process.

Each adolescent woman idealizes a bicultural identity in which she is able to step between both Bosnian and U.S. cultural worlds. The women describe various degrees of success with this cultural code-switching and explain their processes of highlighting or downplaying their religious and cultural identity in various social situations. While their experiences in U.S. schools and social contexts vary, all the women are conscious of various influences on their religious and cultural identities and ascribe personal agency to their bicultural identity construction.

"One thing about being Bosnian is that you will always be Bosnian. That's who you are ... I'm Bosnian because I was born in Bosnia."

"What does it mean to be American? I don't know."

"I never think you should lose your culture. That's something you should always preserve. But, you shouldn't have a closed mind.... Take the best from what I have and apply it to who I am.... Am I Bosnian, am I American?... Whatever. Whatever you want to call me, call me, but I'm a product of everything I've been through."

Many factors affect the experience of immigrants growing up between two cultures. These may include religion, race, ethnicity, language, family history and dynamics, cultural distance, and numerous other sociological and psychological factors. This chapter provides a glimpse into the lived experiences and conceptions of identity among adolescent females who came to the United States as refugees from Bosnia and Herzegovina (commonly called Bosnia). Each student identifies herself as Bosnian Muslim (sometimes called Bosniak[1]) in ethnicity and Muslim in religion.

This chapter presents findings of a broader study by highlighting and analyzing narratives from five young women, all of whom live in "Parksburg," a pseudonymous city in the southeastern United States. These five young women represent families both from educated and uneducated, urban and village backgrounds in Bosnia. Their families all fled their homes due to the Bosnian War in the 1990s.[2] Each began elementary school in the former Yugoslavia, arrived in the U.S. during school years, and was either in postsecondary study or nearing high school graduation at the time they shared their narratives about their experiences.

These women are "success stories" within their community in academic achievement and professional career goals. They function socially both in mainstream U.S. society and in the local Bosnian community, though they vary in their comfort levels in each community. They have all mastered the English language and are able to express themselves with ease and articulation as well or better than many native speakers their age. They are also each capable of reflecting on their cultural influences and experiences through the lens of several years in their host country yet significant childhood memories from their home country; this perspective of looking back several years after their initial immigration experience grants these women a reflective view that might differ from that of immigrants who are struggling more acutely with the trauma of relocation or war. While these young women are not all comfortable or satisfied with the cultural identity they now assign to themselves or with how "bicultural" they consider themselves, they each recognize and speak comfortably about the construction of cultural identity.

"Our species thinks in metaphors and learns through stories," wrote anthropologist Mary Catherine Bateson (1994, p. 11). Narrative methodology—or "stories lived and told" (Clandinin & Connelly, 2000, p. 20)—provides a vehicle to acknowledge and delve into the significance of these women's stories of immigration and the construction and reconstruction of their identities (Bell, 2002). Because this chapter features a large amount of quoted narrative, the words of these young women are presented in italics in order to set them apart within the text.

IDENTITY BETWEEN TWO WORLDS

How we identify ourselves *to* ourselves is as important as how we identify ourselves to others, according to Holland, Lachicotte, Skinner, and Cain in *Identity and Agency in Cultural Worlds* (1998):

> People tell others who they are, but even more importantly, they tell themselves and they try to act as though they are who they say they are. These self-understandings, especially those with strong emotional resonance for the teller, are what we refer to as identities. (p. 3)

An individual's *cultural identity* encompasses how the individual relates to members of a group who share a common language, history, and understanding of the world (Norton, 1997). *Identity construction* refers to how an individual negotiates a sense of self within the larger social world. Previous research with refugees and immigrants has addressed the changing sense of self, and a growing body of literature explores *bicultural identities* (Benet-Martínez & Haritatos, 2005; Chen & Sheldon, 2012; Darder, 1995; Kanno, 2003; Marks, Patton, & Coil, 2011).

I refer to identity as constantly constructed, rather than developed in stages. Relating questions of identity directly to those dealing with different cultural contexts, Trueba (2004, pp. 87–88) argues that immigrants manage to acquire and maintain different identities "that coexist and function without conflict in different contexts simultaneously." Experimenting with different identities is seen as a natural part of the cultural adjustment process for immigrants (Ainslie, 1998; Ritivoi, 2002). Resulting multiple identities may be viewed as "a powerful instrument that facilitates adaptation to new sociocultural environments, new roles, and different circumstances" (Zou, 2002, p. 251). For immigrants, assuming different identities "come[s] naturally and permit[s] them to function in multiethnic and multicultural environments" (Trueba, 2004, p. 88). This assumption of multiple identities is in fact "a significant new cultural capital" allowing immigrants to function in varied cultural worlds (Zou, 2002, p. 251).

Other researchers see troubling effects of immigrants' construction of multiple cultural identities. Gee (1996) argues that multiple identities may cause conflict within and around students, if students feel that society—represented by the school—seeks to co-opt their cultural identities. In this case, students may develop a school-related identity which exists in opposition to the native, cultural identity supported by family and community contexts. When this occurs and one identity is associated with beliefs which inherently devalue another identity held by the same student, the student may feel pressure to adopt an oppositional stance toward one of the conflicting identities (Monzó, 2002).

Bicultural Identity Formation

How is cultural identity constructed among individuals who move across two separate cultural worlds? LaFromboise, Coleman, and Gerton (1993, p. 399) claim that "it is possible for an individual to have a sense of belonging in two cultures without compromising his or her sense of cultural identity." This bicultural competence has also been labeled "acculturation," "additive assimilation," "transculturalism," or "cultural integration" (McBrien, 2005, p. 331).

While bicultural identities can be constructed to allow movement across cultural worlds, moving across cultures can cause stress and conflict and bicultural individuals must process conflicting cultural demands and expectations (Benet-Martinez, Leu, Lee, & Morris, 2002). Some researchers on bicultural identity suggest that having a strong identity connection to a culture—even if it is to the home culture—can help immigrants become bicultural because the feeling of belonging to a culture and peer group helps individuals feel psychologically grounded and willing to explore a second culture as well (LaFromboise, Coleman, & Gerton, 1993). The act of negotiating a bicultural identity has been called the "cultural frame switching effect" in the field of psychology (Hong, Morris, Chiu, & Benet-Martínez, 2000).

While some bicultural individuals have constructed "compatible" cultural identities by which they access both cultural frames of reference with ease, other individuals' bicultural identities can be described as "oppositional" because they tend to react to being in one cultural situation by comparing it with their other cultural identity (Benet-Martínez et al., 2002). Bicultural individuals whose identities are oppositional and not integrated still identify with both cultures. At the same time, "they are highly aware of the discrepancies between the mainstream and ethnic cultures and see these discrepancies as a source of internal conflict"; as a result, they dissociate the two parts of their identities and function as "either ethnic or mainstream" but not both at the same time (Benet-Martínez et al., 2002, n.p.).

Religious Identity

As conceptions of ethnic identity and racial identity held by other cultures may differ from common U.S. conceptions and definitions, so also does the conception of religious identity differ across cultures. In cultures in which identification with a particular religion is seen as tantamount to identification with one's ethnic group, religious identity and cultural identity are very closely linked (Milligan, 2003). In such cultures, adherence to a religious identity may be seen as an integral part of belonging to a cultural or ethnic group. In the case of Bosnian Muslims, for example, religious identity and ethnic identity are both so central to cultural identification that they comprise the name by which the cultural group is known ("Bosnian Muslim," until the name "Bosniak" was adopted in 1994). Even when religious and cultural identities are closely associated, though, they are not identical or interchangeable. While a statement of religious identity may indicate a particular ethnic heritage for some cultural groups, on another level it serves as a "broad marker of cultural affiliation" that reflects an identification with a larger religious community that extends beyond one's ethnic group to other religious adherents from around the world (Milligan, 2003, p. 474). Therefore, Bosnian Muslims are connected with Arab Muslims through religious identification, for example, though their cultural identities differ in many other ways.

One reason religious identity is a significant factor among Muslim young people is the negative stigma many Americans have toward Muslims due to associations with fundamentalist extremism and terrorism (McBrien, 2005). When religious identity—and the interconnected cultural identity—is the subject of stereotypes and discrimination, adjustment to a new culture can be affected (McBrien, 2005; Mosselson, 2009).

Cultural Distance

The process of constructing identities across and between two cultural worlds is affected by the cultural differences between the native culture and the host culture. The term "cultural distance" refers to the relative similarity or difference between the two cultures in which an immigrant has lived (Berry & Sam, 1997; Furnham & Bochner, 1982). For these young women who have moved to the United States from an Eastern European home culture, the cultural distance they cross is smaller, metaphorically speaking, than the culture gap might be for immigrants coming from a non-Western culture. Historical cultural linkages between Europe and North America extend to strong cultural influences and similarities in worldviews. Cultural distance is therefore another significant factor in the process of acculturation for immigrants.

FIVE YOUNG WOMEN IN TWO WORLDS

Quotes and a brief description will introduce each young woman in this narrative study.

Jasmina

"I wanna keep my culture, you know, I don't want to become American. I mean, an American citizen, but I still wanna be Bosnian and stuff."

After her father was killed in the war in Bosnia, Jasmina (pronounced "Yas-MEE-na") settled in Parksburg with her mother and siblings only after first moving to Croatia, Germany and Chicago. Like many other Bosnians who lived in a second country before permanent resettlement, she had already become accustomed to German language and culture and had no desire to come to the United States. Jasmina attended schools with many other Bosnian students, and all of her close friends during and since high school are Bosnian.

These strong Bosnian influences do not mean Jasmina is separated from American popular culture, though. When I first met Jasmina at a mosque during an *iftar* meal for the Bosnian community during Ramadan, she dressed modestly and her hair was covered by a scarf. When we later met in the library of her university, however, she wore style-conscious designer jeans and a fashionable hairstyle and makeup. Yet Jasmina's concern with U.S. fashion does not necessarily indicate a lifestyle mirroring that of a native-born American teenager. Even while she does not want to be singled out as an immigrant by her U.S.-born peers, Jasmina is proud of what she identifies as Bosnian customs, such as living with her parents until she marries, and describes herself as an observant Muslim by her observance of dietary laws.

In her self-description, Jasmina claims a strong Bosnian Muslim cultural, linguistic, ethnic, and religious identity: "*I definitely want to pass it on to my kids and stuff.*" When asked if she thought many Bosnian youth were not keeping her culture, she replies, "*Definitely, yeah. Like, you know, I mean, like going out with an American and getting married to them and stuff. I would never do it. It's not that I have anything against Americans. I don't think I could, just because there's so much difference, you know. Like the religious difference.*"

After completing high school, Jasmina earned a scholarship to a well-regarded private university. Her future goals include returning to Bosnia to learn more about her home culture and to help in the country's economic development.

Lajla

"*I went through my phase … the Americanized phase.*"

Lajla (LAY-la) attends a local community college and lives and works with her parents in their family business. Lajla's sweatshirt-and-jeans appearance belies her strong attachment to both her Muslim religious observances and Bosnian customs. Lajla describes her life in the United States thus far as a process of "Americanizing and returning" to a Bosnian identity. She described this process as a back-and-forth negotiation between cultures rather than a process of focusing on both cultures simultaneously:

> *High school, like I adapted so quickly, like, my parents were scared. [Laughs.] Like, I forgot Bosnian…, In high school, like I was already, I barely had any sort of an accent. I observed that Bosnians with [strong accents got] laughed at. So like all my friends were Americans, especially my freshman year, like I didn't have any Bosnian friends.*

Lajla reports assimilating so completely in school that her name was the only feature revealing her heritage. Lajla's cultural identity formation is influenced strongly by her proficiency in English and lack of a Bosnian accent, which she mentions often as allowing her to pass as native-born and "White." She considers this an advantage she has over many other immigrants.

Later in high school, Lajla became interested in exploring her linguistic and cultural heritage. "*The whole like greeting each other by a kiss. Like, we got a lot of attention for that…. When I started [greeting girl friends with a kiss], people were like, 'What you doing?' [I said,] 'I'm just gettin' involved in my culture!'*" [Laughs.]

Lajla's self-described "return" to her Bosnian cultural identity included socializing with Bosnian friends more than American friends. She was inspired by a family trip to Bosnia to try to regain proficiency in Bosnian language and currently speaks Bosnian "more now than ever." She has a Bosnian boyfriend, as dating is common in the Bosnian community, and she is quick to point out that she would only date a Bosnian. However, Lajla also describes being torn between aspects of two cultures and not feeling completely at home in either of them—a cultural dilemma common among children of immigrants (Suárez-Orozco & Suárez-Orozco, 2001). Her narratives describe a tension between her desire for the freedom of driving a car, which she describes as unusual for women in her family, and her determination to keep Muslim dietary laws and to continue improving her Bosnian language skills. This tension shapes the cultural identity she is constructing to incorporate both Bosnian and American values.

Dina

"They're saying like, 'Where you from?' [I say,] 'I'm from Europe!'"

"Or sometimes [I say], 'Bosnia.' They'll be like, 'Where's that at?' 'Europe.' 'Oh, okay. I wanna go to Europe someday.' 'Yeah, me too!' [Laughs.]"

Dina's lifestyle is more conservative and traditional than that of the other girls. With an undertone of complaint, she states that her parents are more traditional than other Bosnian parents, not letting her go out with friends or date. Dina is one of only two Bosnian students in her nursing vocational program in high school; all her other classmates are African American. Dina's English includes speech elements common to African American Vernacular English, and she highlights her Bosnian heritage to differentiate her from nonimmigrant White Americans: "*Sometimes I be joking around, like, 'Don't be saying that, cause I'm white,' you know [when classmates make jokes about white people.] They like, 'You not white. You Bosnian. That doesn't apply to you.' [Laughs.] 'Okay. Even better.'*"

Dina reports that most of the Bosnian peers at her school did not enter a career program, and that many are academically unmotivated and many male Bosnian students drop out of her high school. Making academic and social choices based on an eventual career goal rather than the path of her Bosnian peer group may have placed her in a somewhat separate social world within high school—and thus led to her socializing with mostly U.S.-born classmates rather than other Bosnian-born classmates. Dina has consciously acknowledged and accepted this trade-off as a price to be paid for following her career goals. She considers herself very Bosnian and socializes mainly with family members when not in school.

Selma

"I don't know if it's just like nostalgia or something. But [some other Bosnians] are not really willing to assimilate completely, you know? This is like, deliberate. This is like, 'We are better and we don't need to be Americans,' or whatever ... I don't see anything wrong with assimilation. Taking the good of every culture."

After completing an English for Speakers of Other Languages (ESOL) program at a public school upon arriving in the United States, Selma enrolled in a private prep school with the help of teachers who sought scholarships for her. While this schooling choice opened up a number of educational opportunities, it also separated Selma from Bosnian peers attending public schools. As a college student, Selma now considers her Bosnian language proficiency weak and describes being uncomfortable in gatherings with other Bosnians. She shares that she does not have close Bosnian friends and is ignorant of Bosnian pop culture and the interests of her Bosnian peers.

While Selma describes her language loss as a source of regret, she describes her religious knowledge and devotion as strong. Of all the participants, Selma is the most active in religious observances. She attends mosque regularly and participated in mosque-based religious education as a child. Notably, seeking out both mosque-based weekly prayer and religious education classes involved Selma's parents going outside of the Bosnian community and participating in religious community experiences with non-Bosnian Muslims. Selma is also the most knowledgeable of Bosnian history and cultural arts, likely due to the influence of her educated family. This family and religious heritage is separate from her personal social life, though. When Selma meets new people, she identifies herself as being "from here" rather than as Bosnian.

Hana

"[When people ask,] I'd say 'I'm Bosnian.' I still do even though I'm a [U.S.] citizen. It's something I consider myself. You know, I'll never be an American, even though I am on paper."

Hana describes herself as shy and not inclined to share personal information freely—including information about her cultural and religious background. She has the option of "passing" as a native-born American due to her lack of a Bosnian accent in spoken English. She describes herself as Muslim but quickly says she does not mention her religious identity to coworkers in order to avoid misunderstandings or get into political discussions.

Despite Hana's ability to easily pass as a native-born American and her reticence to mention her religious identity, Hana makes the effort to identify herself as Bosnian when she does choose to describe her cultural identity. She separates her national identity in terms of citizenship from her cultural identity and chooses to use only the Bosnian label: *"My personality was basically formed [in Bosnia.] It's not like I don't identify [with Americans], of course I do, but I always, whenever people ask me, I say I'm Bosnian."* While some other participants described their cultural identity as a "back-and-forth" maneuver between two cultural worlds, or as a melding of aspects of both cultures, Hana has chosen to identify herself only as Bosnian.

THEMES OF GROWING UP BETWEEN TWO CULTURES

Personal Agency in Identity Construction

[Immigrating] makes you reevaluate who you are. 'Cause when you're safe in your own surroundings, like, it doesn't really matter. Every day kind of passes by, and you're just feeling the same thing you've been feeling since you were born. And now here, you're kind of isolated, and you want to get to know really who you are, I think.
—Selma

Each of these young women's narratives reflects the significance of choosing one's own identity labels. These women adopt a variety of approaches to the classic immigrant dilemma of retaining or adopting new cultural identities. In each case, however, they display agency and active reflection as they describe their identity in terms of practices they consciously value, behaviors they choose, and identity labels they self-select. For example, Hana describes a split between personal and official identity and minimizes her official national identity in order to hold onto the personal cultural identity she most values. Lajla is attempting to adopt as much of a Bosnian identity as possible and her social and cultural practices reflect that desire. Jasmina points to two separate cultural identities she wants to maintain. Common among all of the young women, though, is their description of identity as personally and internally constructed. None of the women spoke of their identity primarily in terms of how others see them or how their family describes itself.

The Ideal of Biculturalism

Narratives reveal that cultural identity construction is future-oriented in some cases and past-oriented in other cases. Some of the women describe themselves in terms of who they have been in the past, and some view themselves in terms of who they would like to be in the future. Lajla's feeling of not being Bosnian enough influenced her desire to become more Bosnian, which in turn influences her use of the label "Bosnian" to signify the identity she wants to attain. Her self-selected identity label represents her ideal cultural identity as much as her evaluation of the identity she has currently constructed. Sfard and Prusak (2005) call this "designated identity," by which an individual narrates "stories believed to have the potential to become a part of one's actual identity" (p. 18). In this way Lajla's cultural self-identification signifies the cultural identity she strives for in the future. On the other hand, self-selected labels may also point toward an important connection with the past. For example, Hana's self-selected cultural identity label indicates a connection she wants to keep with her cultural and national heritage: *"I'll never be an American, even though I am on paper."*

While not every participant is able to effectively "step in and out of" both U.S. and Bosnian social fields to the extent she would like, each participant holds bicultural competence as an ideal and constructs her cultural identity in light of that goal. Despite their differences, each of these young women want to construct a cultural identity that will allow them to fully function in mainstream U.S. society while simultaneously retaining a connection to their families and the local Bosnian Muslim community. The ability to downplay their cultural heritage, religious identity, and linguistic identity in school and work situations is one desirable component of the cultural identity they have constructed. When they are around other Bosnians, however, Bosnian linguistic and cultural competence is desirable. Visits back to Bosnia and even the identification label "Bosnian" play significant roles in cultural identity construction.

Stepping In and Out of Two Cultures

The ability of these women to step in and out of Bosnian culture fits LaFromboise, Coleman, and Gerton's (1993) description of biculturalism as having two internalized cultures that can guide attitudes and behaviors. This cultural dance between the two cultures constructed in a bicultural identity also bears similarities to the linguistic act of "code-switching," which refers to the ability to switch between languages to address the requirements of the conversation. In effect, these students assign importance to "cultural code-switching" competence in Bosnian and American social situations. For example, even though Hana speaks about herself as Bosnian only, she also states that she "passes" as a U.S.-born American at work, does not generally identify herself as Bosnian to peers, and has no intention of returning to Bosnia. While she personally identifies her cultural identity as Bosnian and rejects an "American" cultural identity, she chooses to step in and out of two cultures in order to be perceived differently in different social realms.

Valuing the Option of "Passing" as Nonimmigrant

Immigrants may have many different reasons for wanting to "pass" as nonimmigrants in mainstream American culture. Immigration is a volatile political issue, and foreign-born youth may want to avoid the often pejorative labels assigned to immigrants. Immigrants may want to avoid Americans' invocation of stereotypes about other cultures, ethnicities, or religions. Refugees who dealt with traumatic experiences of war and flight from a homeland may wish to avoid questions about their experiences. To an adolescence mindset in which fitting in with peers is of paramount importance, foreign-born young people may simply not want to be singled out as different from other classmates. Social protection, pain from past experiences, and a desire to "fit in" are all possible reasons for wanting the option of "passing" as nonimmigrants.

Lajla, Selma, and Hana all report that they like being able to "pass" as nonimmigrant when they would prefer not to enter into conversation about their cultural background. While they state they are not ashamed of their Bosnian heritage, they usually identify themselves as being "from Parksburg" to people they do not know.

The other two women, Dina and Jasmina, have retained Bosnian accents, making "passing" as nonimmigrant less feasible. For Dina, sounding "European" sets her apart from White (Anglo) Americans among her African American classmates, a distinction she prefers. She is the only participant in a predominantly non-White social situation and, notably, the only one who was not interested in being able to pass as nonimmigrant White at certain times. Her accent highlights her heritage, and differentiating herself from White nonimmigrants is desirable to her. Dina's experience is an important reminder that the experience of immigrants in schools differs in each local context (Ellis & Almgren, 2009)—and in this case, from school to school within the same community. Jasmina, on the other hand, explicitly admits that she would like to have the option of passing as nonimmigrant in some social situations, although she is fiercely proud of her Bosnian heritage. She says she is generally initially perceived as be nonimmigrant White: *"Once I open my mouth they notice. But from all else they would never tell."* Jasmina has gone to great efforts to try to eliminate her accent in order to be able to "pass" more successfully when she so chooses.

Racial identification is a significant part of these women's acculturation experience, and each of the women (except Dina, as stated above) perceive the ability to "pass" as a racially White nonimmigrant as desirable. Unlike Muslims from many other ethnic backgrounds, Bosnian Muslims are recognized as ethnically White by white Americans due to their skin color and Slavic facial features. These young women relate explicitly that their ability to "pass" as a nonimmigrant White Americans gives them real social advantages and more options in controlling how they are perceived within U.S. society. White racial identity in the United States is connected to "institutionalized power and privileges that benefit White Americans" (Chubbuck, 2004, p. 303). This social reality, commonly called "White privilege" (Hytten & Adkins, 2001), was perceived by and mentioned by each one of these women although they did not use that terminology. *"We don't look like terrorists, you know?"* Hana said almost apologetically as she tells how her Bosnian Muslim identity is not visually apparent. *"I'm pretty sure that me having a pretty positive immigrant experience here is due to the fact that I'm White. I really believe that. Because if I was lookin', you know, Arab or, you know, anything else, I think I would run into more—sort of—[pause]—[whispering] I don't know."* Although Hana states she is proud of her ethnic and religious heritage, she notes the social risks of revealing her religious and linguistic background and values being able to hide those at will, depending on the social situation.

Each of the five young women noted that American peers are often oblivious to cultural and ethnic differences that are not racialized.[3] Within the Bosnian community, ethnicity is a significant topic, due to the ethnic divides of the war in the former Yugoslavia. However, ethnicity in Bosnia is not connected to "race" as perceived in the United States. (While Serbs, Croats, and Bosniaks describe themselves as different both ethnically and religiously, all three groups are Slavic Europeans perceived as "White" in the United States.) One of the ironies of racial essentialism in the U.S. is that ethnic and racial differences that are most real to immigrants are often erased in the popular American mindset, so newcomers may be seen by mainstream Americans differently than they have ever seen themselves (Rong & Preissle, 1998).

In discussing identity labels, none of the women wanted to be identified as a "refugee" or identified on the basis of the war that led to their moving to the United States. Each woman also said she avoids talking to Americans about the circumstances that led to her coming to the United States. *"I don't feel like getting into the whole thing,"* Selma said, referring to war and fleeing her home country. Another key reason for avoiding such discussions is Americans' ignorance about Bosnia, according to the participants. *"A lot of people thought that Bosnia was in Africa,"* sighed one participant. Consequently, *"a lot of Bosnian students used that as, 'Oh, look how dumb they are, why should we [bother].'"* In addition, the identity label "refugee" carries a connotation of being disadvantaged or needy or perhaps pitiable, one participant explained, any of which would be inconsistent with these women's perception of their own circumstances and their preferences of how others perceive them.

Religious Identity Constructed as a Private Identification

Although each of the young women in this study identified herself as Muslim, each also reported that she did not volunteer her religious affiliation unless asked explicitly. Lajla stated that she felt more Bosnian than

American and "tried to be" more Bosnian than she had been when she was younger; when asked about religion, though, she simply paused for a while and finally said, *"The Muslim thing, no one ever knew that until I would like mention it."*

Hana described her decision to "pass" in the religious mainstream as a reaction to hostility against Muslims in post-9/11 U.S. culture:

> *In college and in my work, you know, I don't really tell the people what's my ... basically you're just surrounded by Christianity right now. Everywhere you turn, everything revolves around Christianity. Everything. So I don't say, like, I don't go up to people and say, "I'm a Muslim." But if they ask me I tell them. And then all of them get surprised or think that I'm just, you know, making it up or whatever. But it's always like, "Really?" you know, "Why didn't you tell me that?"*

Jasmina also mentioned that she does not volunteer her religious identity, but emphasized that she does not deny it when questioned. (Note also how she equates ethnic and religious heritage in her narrative.):

> *I mean, we're like, Bosnian people by religion, but even when, um, 9/11 happened in school, nobody said anything about it.... [One] Bosnian girl, she, she just said that in one of her classes, after saying that she was a Muslim, she said her teacher treated her differently and stuff. So then, after that she doesn't really want to say—like, she has another class, and in that class she doesn't really want to say she's a Muslim, like, she just says she doesn't have a religion. Which I think is really dumb. Like, I would NEVER do that. I think however bad my experience is, or was, I would never deny my religion. Ever. I don't know what she is thinking.*

Religious Identity and Religious Observance

The young women's expression of strong religious identity does not necessarily correlate with their observance of religious practices. Lajla and Jasmina, in a three-way conversation, speak about religious identity by invoking religious observances they practice in their homes. They both describe religious standards about food as an expression of religious observation which is meaningful to their families in the United States:

Jasmina: *Usually Bosnian women don't cover [their heads]. I mean, that's just not a part of our culture. Even back in Bosnia, girls don't cover. Just grandmas. A lot older than us. [Laughs.]*

Lajla: *I don't know. We have less of the Middle Eastern impact on Bosnia. We have more of the European. With Germany right there and Italy. But it's weird. I was telling Jasmina the other night, like, other than like my family, Jasmina's family's the only ones that*

*like, really cherish the like little Muslim things, like going to the
mosque on a regular basis.... Like me and my sister, and [Jas-
mina's] sister and another girl are really the only ones who don't
eat pork. The rest of them are like, "Well, I'm hungry, you know,
and the pizza's right there." So that's like four or five Bosnians out
of like thirty Muslims.*

Researcher: *Well, would they have done that in Bosnia or do you think that's
because they were here?*

Jasmina: *I think it's just 'cause they moved to the United States and just
'cause they're not in Bosnia, and they don't have a lot of Bosnian
people around them, looking at them, they just say it's okay. Probably 'cause there's so many Americans here and everyone's eating
pork they're like, why don't we, you know?*

Lajla: *That was like a big thing for us. In my family, the pork issue. Our
parents were protective to make sure you ask what you're eating,
don't eat it if there's nothing else.*

Jasmina: *It's definitely up to the parents like to raise the generation like....
My little brother, I don't remember what grade he was when we
moved to the United States, but like, he is so big on not eating
pork. Like, I mean, when my mom buys stuff, he will double check
the package. [Laughs.] Really!*

Lajla: *My brother, I remember in elementary school, he was in fifth grade
and he had lunch before me. And he would, on our way we'd pass
each other, and he would tell me, "You can have this and have
that." I swear! He's really strict on that.... Our parents didn't
speak English much, so, you know, he'd check.*

Lajla and Jasmina's descriptions of their brothers double-checking their
parents' food choices suggests that in addition to being significant for
religious reasons, keeping dietary standards became a signifier connecting
younger generations to traditions and observances of their homeland, in
addition to a connection to their religious identities.

Dina attributes a moral value to religious observance which she sees
lacking in other Bosnian families in Parksburg. She comments on several
occasions about children's disobedience and rebellion once they have come
to the United States. In the following narrative, she links those behavioral
shifts with a change in religious observance and the moral climate of the
community: *"That's why I think some, a lot of parents, a lot of children I mean,
are out of order. Cause in Bosnia, every, like, every Friday we went [to mosque], and
every Saturday we went. And all the days you can go in there. Keeps you in order.
But here ... [shakes head]"*

It should be noted that although Dina attributes moral value to going to a mosque and observing religious practices, she mentioned at another time that neither she nor her parents go to mosque or practice regular prayer. Of the five women introduced here, only Selma and her family visit a mosque on a weekly basis; they also attend a religious education program at a mosque. Yet of all the women, Selma reports feeling least connected to the Bosnian community. Lajla and Jasmina attend mosque activities held in conjunction with Ramadan and said they observed the Ramadan fast on some days. Dina and Hana did not describe observance of any religious ritual nor attendance at religious events held in connection with either other Bosnians or Muslims from other ethnic backgrounds. This is despite Dina's report that she and her family only socialize with other Bosnians. The variations in observance highlight that among women in this study, adherence to religious practices is not connected with the degree of connection with the local Bosnian community or with claiming Bosnian cultural or religious identity.

Construction and Reconstruction of Religious Identity in the United States

Although each woman mentioned that she did not volunteer information about her religious identity to Americans around her, each woman also mentioned a strengthening of religious identity within their families after the Bosnian War and after immigration to the United States. Selma reported her sense of religious identity developing and strengthening in the United States more than it would have in Bosnia:

> When I came here, I had to like, I was developing my identity as a person 'cause I was so young. But then also, I had never gone to mosque before, because prior to the war, we were not religious. Like, I never had gone to mosque in Bosnia. So here, we were taken to this mosque [the Arab-American Mosque], and that was like my first real experience with religion, and with learning Arabic, and learning what the Quran is, and all that. So that kind of came as part of being an American. [long pause] Which is interesting that like the political situation in your own country, like, influences what happens when you come to America. Cause then, you know, you might have the freedom to—or the opportunity to practice something that you didn't even do in your own country.

Selma's observation that "prior to the war, we were not religious" indicates an important element of religious identity to most of the women: the strengthening of religious identity within the U.S. These changes in development of religious identity after moving to the U.S. have been studied among other Muslim immigrant groups as well (Duderija, 2007). In some cases, the increase in religious observance and the increased significance of religious affiliation to cultural identity construction is a result of the religiously divided war as well as a result of immigration. Jasmina says, for example, "*Before the war, my mom wasn't really religious. And after the war happened, she became really religious.*"

The reconstruction of religious identity as Muslim may coincide with increased pride in ethnic heritage. Bosnians "have to differentiate themselves," Selma says. "They have been discriminated against, so now they're going to reevaluate their identity. Now they're really Bosnian, and they really are proud of that heritage." Selma explains how she views the relationship between religion, culture, history, war, and Bosnian identity:

> *If you go to Bosnia, you will see people, young girls and old ladies, covered. Here, not really. There's one lady that married a Lebanese guy, she might cover once in a while. But it's not really, we're not very, um, fundamental in, like, the way we interpret Islam. Because, like, we were conquered by Turks like 500 years ago. So, it's like, it's more of a tradition than a religion, really. And it's really after the war that we really went back to our roots and, like, started appreciating who we are and, like, redefining ourselves. Because the war, you know, kind of makes you reconsider…. It's weird. I mean, we had mosques in Bosnia, and I'm sure a lot of like older people went, I don't know. But my parents never took me. It was a Communist country before that, you know.*

Selma's narrative reveals identity construction taking place on several levels—both in the global arena and locally in Parksburg. According to her description, refugees are not the only ones reconstructing their cultural identities with a changing role for religious and ethnic identity. Instead, the changing religious identity is happening simultaneously for Bosnians in the postwar years, both in the Bosnian homeland and the Diaspora.

Selma's comment about Islam being "more of a tradition than a religion" for Bosnian Muslims reflects her perception of the interconnectedness of ethnic and religious identity. It also reveals the difference she observes between the religion that is tied to ethnic identity and the religious observance she has learned and practiced since coming to the United States and attending a mosque. Selma states she learned about Islam at the local majority-Arab mosque, which is attended by more observant Muslims from the Middle East, rather than learning about her religious heritage from other Bosnians, who have historically been less religiously observant.

Cross-Cultural Religious Identity and Cultural Distance

While Selma's religious identity has been strongly influenced by Muslims in her community from other ethnic backgrounds (particularly at the majority-Arab mosque), the other women reported not interacting with refugee or immigrant students from other cultural backgrounds, regardless of religious affiliation. When asked about her Somali Muslim classmates in high school, Jasmina says, *"Honestly, I never really asked anyone … I saw the movie* Black Hawk Down. *I'm guessing [her Somali classmates' arrival to the U.S.] has something to do with that. But honestly I don't know…. People will think I just moved over here just 'cause, you know. They don't know the real reason behind anything. I don't really know or care about the real reasons of others."* In Lajla's case as well as Jasmina's case, social interactions appear to follow ethnocentric connections rather than religious connections.

Although not every participant spoke in such ethnocentric terms, each woman described her experience as distinct and distant from that of refugees from other countries: *"Most of us Bosnians who came here lived good, good lives before the war … meaning we always had good health care, good education from the beginning, and good nutrition, everything."* Compared to the experience of Somali Muslims, many of whom also attended the same high schools, *"It's kind of like comparing apples and oranges. It's completely different people."* As mentioned previously, the identity label of refugee was undesirable to these women, as was the assumption of an association with refugees and immigrants from other backgrounds.

While this narrative study focused on Bosnian Muslim rather than Somali Muslim youth in the same community, the comments above raise the point of *cultural distance* in bicultural identity construction. Research has shown that students whose home culture is more different than school culture face greater challenges in adjusting to and succeeding in school (McBrien, 2005). Each of these five women commented that their lifestyle in Bosnia was in many ways similar—and in some ways "superior"—to their lifestyle in the United States. Dina and Jasmina noted that the curriculum in their Bosnian schools was far more advanced than in their Parksburg schools, and Selma had more modern conveniences and amenities in her home in Bosnia than in her first apartment in Parksburg. Common remarks include Bosnia being *"Western," "modern,"* and *"more European than Middle Eastern."* In addition to material comparisons to U.S. lifestyles, the women reported other cultural similarities to the United States, such as most of their mothers holding jobs outside the home in Bosnia. Their European background suggests a shorter cultural distance to span between their home culture and host cultures than would be the case for many other immigrant groups. The relatively short cultural distance is another reason why "passing" as (Western) nonimmigrant is more feasible and less personally problematic for these women than it would be for many Muslims from other cultural backgrounds.

Cultural and Social Positioning With Peers

Each of these five young women described the cohesion of Bosnian students within the community into a tight social group. The women differed in the degree to which they socialized with this Bosnian peer group or with American peers, both in high school and in postsecondary studies. Approval or disapproval of the presence of Bosnian cliques varies from woman to woman. Integration in, or distance from, the tightly connected immigrant peer group seems to be closely related to each participant's public cultural self-identification as "Bosnian" or "American." In addition, the degree to which these young women socialized within Bosnian social circles in school related to how strongly they report being connected to the Bosnian community now as young adults. The students who were most closely linked to other Bosnians in school were also those who now follow more traditional Bosnian customs as adults rather than living as their U.S.-born peers. These customs include living with their parents until they marry rather than living in a dormitory or apartment, adopting traditional gender roles such as cooking for fathers and brothers, following traditional restrictions regarding dating, talking about marriage in their future, and stating they would only marry a Bosnian man. Both Lajla and Jasmina stated unequivocally that they would live with their parents until they moved in with their husbands: "It's Bosnian custom," Lajla said. Dina's family followed more traditional gender roles; she had been in charge of cooking for her father and brothers since middle school and was not allowed to date. Selma, Lajla, Jasmina, and Dina all initiated conversations about marriage, which somewhat surprised me given their young ages. While Selma stated that she doubted she could marry a Bosnian man because of how much Bosnian language she has lost, Lajla, Jasmina, and Dina all volunteered that they would only marry Bosnians.

Stepping In and Out of Cultures in School

Regardless of how close each young woman felt to the tight-knit Bosnian peer group, those who related "pulling away" from the immigrant peer group achieved the highest academic success. Students who were most successful academically were willing to separate themselves from the immigrant peer group and take harder classes in which they were often the only nonnative English speaker. One young woman explained it this way: "*A lot of the ones who did go to college sort of had to get away from the Bosnian community and go out on their own, and really concentrate on college. The ones who were really tied to the community, a lot of them didn't go to college.*"

Another participant was more bluntly personal in her confession: *"I ran away from it. It's not like, it's my life, I don't want to be around them or anything, but—I was there, now I'm ready to move on, you know?"*

For decades, the cultural process of schooling (Spindler, 1987) has been identified as having a strong influence on students' identity construction (Nieto, 1996; Rong & Preissle, 1998; Portes & Rumbaut, 2001). U.S. educational history includes many instances of religious minorities being alienated by the Protestant Christian heritage of the U.S. education system (MacDonald, 2004) and of immigrant students receiving inequitable educational opportunities (Gitlin, Buendía, Crosland, & Doumbia, 2003). Hones (2002) reports that inadequate training is often related to teacher misunderstandings of refugee children's cultures and backgrounds. Selma's first schooling experience in the U.S. reflects this ignorance: *"My ESL teacher, I was actually her first Bosnian student. So she had never encountered like, a blond, um, Muslim child, so she was really confused. [Laughs.] She was kind of bewildered by the fact that I was White and blond and also a Muslim. [Laughs].... But she was really good."* The role of teachers in refugee students' adjustment is significant, as Hones and Cha (1999) identify teachers as having central roles in promoting positive adjustment and socialization within U.S. culture.

Each young woman sharing narratives here attended ESOL classes in Parksburg public schools for one year, after which they were mainstreamed into regular classes. Their short stay in ESOL (English for Speakers of Other Languages) classes is likely due to their early age of arrival and corresponding speed of language learning, in addition to their high level of early education within a European school system. years. Each of the women reflected on their ESOL classes as useful and their ESOL teachers as concerned nurturers who encouraged them to interact with their native-English-speaking peers and tackle grade-level academic work with the scaffolding assistance of the ESOL classroom.

These women's school narratives stand in contrast to other research on refugee experiences in which teacher and administrative antipathy toward refugees serve as a major barrier to refugee student adjustment (McBrien, 2005). Each of the five participants complained that many of their Bosnian peers were academically disengaged:

> *A lot of [Bosnian] kids were there because they were forced to be there.... A lot of them had just come from Germany or other places where they had just started flourishing, just started making their friends, and starting to belong in Germany in that social system. And then they were withdrawn from that and put in America. The same thing happened to me.... However I retained that drive to get an education. But, a lot of students I found, Bosnian students, were not as motivated, were not looking for an education. They were just kind of self-pitying themselves. Like, "I don't want to be here. Why am I here? Now I have to go through this again, learning the language and meeting friends."*

Each student reports that the older generation of Bosnians encourages academic achievement among the immigrant youth. Yet for many immigrant youth, cocooning within a clique of fellow Bosnians allows these young people to reject the acculturating, socializing, and academic influence of schools and therefore to resist the reconstruction of their cultural identities through the Americanizing force of schooling. Banding together in a new culture and new school was a way of *"surviving in all this chaos,"* according to Selma. The description of these refugee students' rejection of U.S. schoolwork, peers, and culture resembles Berry and Sam's (1997) "separation" type of cultural identity construction. This "separation" type of acculturation stands in contrast to, for example, Lajla's integration of a bicultural identity through which she feels comfortable embracing ideas and peers from both Bosnian and American cultures.

After their positive ESOL experiences in public elementary schools, these five Bosnian young women attended public or private middle and high schools. The schools attended by the five women in this study were very different in the demographics of the student body, academic rigor of the curriculum, choices of course offerings, economic and physical resources, and socioeconomic status of the surrounding community. In each case, though, the girls' narratives about teachers and the school system were largely positive. Some factors that may contribute to these positive experiences may include increased teacher training and school awareness as more refugee and immigrant students moved into the area, the effect of many of these Bosnian women's efforts to "pass" as nonimmigrant White, and strong emphasis on academic achievement and persistence within their families. As their reports of dropouts among their immigrant peers indicate, the women whose narratives are shared here are not representative of every Bosnian Muslim student in the U.S. These young women consider themselves successful in achieving academic success, in pursuing career goals, and in attaining degrees of bicultural competence. While the stories of their lived experience may not reflect universal experience with U.S. schooling, they shed light on some of the aspects of identity construction undertaken adolescents growing up between two cultures.

CONCLUSION: IDENTITY CONSTRUCTION AND RECONSTRUCTION

Family dynamics, professional decisions, religious commitments, and even visits back to their homeland may all be among the factors that influence how these young women continue to construct their cultural identities past adolescence and into adulthood. Sfard and Prusak (2005) warn that a reified version of an individual's description of identity can act as a self-fulfilling prophecy, in which "the descriptors that outlast action exclude and disable just as much as they enable and create" (p. 16). These narratives capture snapshots of five young women's reflection upon themselves and upon the ways in which they view themselves at a particular moment in adolescence. The process of stepping in and out of cultures, or of straddling cultures, or of living within two cultures, may change with life experiences, maturation, and new work and family roles. The way in which they reflect upon acculturation processes and the ways in which they define themselves religiously and culturally may well change if these young women eventually become parents themselves and present bicultural identities, experiences, and values to another generation. Continued reflection upon cultural identity will likely inform—and be informed by—valued practices, deliberate behaviors, and social relations throughout their adult lives.

NOTES

1. Bosnia and Herzegovina is one of the countries of the former Yugoslavia in southeastern Europe. Bosnian Muslims, or Bosniaks, were officially recognized as a separate people group under socialist Yugoslavia in 1969. Prior to that recognition, both Serbs and Croats had claimed historical ties to this group of people and their territory. Muslims of Bosnia are descended from Christian Slavs who converted to Islam under the Ottoman Empire. While Bosnian Muslims have officially been known as "Bosniaks" since 1994 (and are sometimes referred to as "Bosniacs" or "Muslim Slavs"), no participant in this study ever said any of those terms. Every participant whose narratives appear here identified herself ethnically as simply "Bosnian." When asked for clarification, she described herself as Bosnian Muslim. Following the terminology used by the women themselves, I use the term "Bosnian Muslim" within this chapter.

2. The United Nations High Commission for Refugees defines a "refugee" as an individual who has left his or her home country due to fear of persecution based on political, ethnic, or religious grounds (USA for UNHCR, 2013). While sharp distinctions between refugees and immigrants are not always clear, refugees often have common experiences not shared by other immigrants. For example, refugee families often must leave their homes suddenly and without preparation and live in another country before being resettled permanently in a third country. As a result, arrival in the United States is frequently accompanied by sudden, traumatic, and sometimes unexpected cultural transitions (Haines, 1996).

3. See Torres and Ngin (1995) for a history and analysis of both the term and the phenomenon of "racialization."

REFERENCES

Ainslie, R. C. (1998). Cultural mourning, immigration, and engagement: Vignettes from the Mexican experience. In M. M. Suárez-Orozco (Ed.), *Crossing: Mexican immigration in interdisciplinary perspectives* (pp. 283–300). Cambridge, MA: Harvard University Press and D. Rockefeller Center for Latin American Studies.

Bateson, M. C. (1994). *Peripheral visions: Learning along the way*. New York, NY: HarperCollins.

Bell, J. S. (2002). Narrative inquiry: More than just telling stories. *TESOL Quarterly, 36,* 207–213.

Benet-Martínez, V., & Haritatos, J. (2005). Bicultural identity integration (BII): Components and psychosocial antecedents. *Journal of Personality, 73*(4), 1015–1050.

Benet-Martínez, V., Leu, J., Lee, F., & Morris, M. W. (2002). Negotiating biculturalism: Cultural frame switching in biculturals with oppositional versus compatible cultural identities. *Journal of Cross-Cultural Psychology, 33,* 492–516.

Berry, J. W., & Sam, D. L. (1997). Acculturation and adaptation. In J. W. Berry, M. H. Segall, & C. Kagitcibasi (Eds.), *Handbook of cross-cultural psychology: Social behavior and applications* (Vol. 3, 2nd ed., pp. 291–326). Boston, MA: Allyn & Bacon.

Chen, K., & Sheldon, J. P. (2012). Arab American emerging adults' bicultural identity, acculturation stress, and perceptions of parenting. *Journal of Immigrant & Refugee Studies, 10*(4), 438–445.

Chubbuck, S. M. (2004). Whiteness enacted, whiteness disrupted: The complexity of personal congruence. *American Educational Research Journal, 41,* 301–333.

Clandinin, D. J., & Connelly, F. M. (2000). *Narrative inquiry: Experience and story in qualitative research.* San Francisco, CA: Jossey-Bass.

Darder, A. (Ed.). (1995). *Culture and difference: Critical perspectives on the bicultural experience in the United States.* Portsmouth, NH: Greenwood.

Duderija, A. (2007). Literature review: Identity construction in the context of being a minority immigrant religion: The case of Western-born Muslims. *Immigrants & Minorities, 25*(2), 141–162.

Ellis, M., & Almgren, G. (2009). Local contexts of immigrant and second-generation integration in the United States. *Journal of Ethnic & Migration Studies, 35*(7), 1059–1076.

Furnham, A., & Bochner, S. (1982). Social difficulty in foreign culture: An empirical analysis of culture shock. In S. Bochner (Ed.), *Cultures in contact: Studies in cross-cultural interactions* (pp. 161–198). Oxford, England: Pergamon.

Gee, J. (1996). *Social linguistics and literacies: Ideologies in discourses.* Bristol, PA: Falmer Press.

Gitlin, A., Buendía, E., Crosland, K., & Doumbia, F. (2003). The production of margin and center: Welcoming-unwelcoming of immigrant students. *American Educational Research Journal, 40,* 91–122.

Haines, D. W. (1996). Patterns in refugee resettlement and adaptation. In D. W. Haines (Ed.), *Refugees in America in the 1990s: A reference handbook* (pp. 28–59). Westport, CT: Greenwood Press.

Holland, D., Lachicotte, W., Skinner, D., & Cain, W. C. (1998). *Identity and agency in cultural worlds*. Cambridge, MA: Harvard University Press.

Hones, D. F. (2002). *American dreams, global visions: Dialogic teacher research with refugee and immigrant families*. Mahwah, NJ: Lawrence Erlbaum.

Hones, D. F., & Cha, C. S. (1999). *Educating new Americans: Immigrant lives and learning*. Mahwah, NJ: Lawrence Erlbaum.

Hong, Y.-Y., Morris, M. W., Chiu, C.-Y., & Benet-Martínez, V. (2000). Multicultural minds: A dynamic constructivist approach to culture and cognition. *American Psychologist, 55*, 709–720.

Hytten, K., & Adkins, A. (2001). Thinking through a pedagogy of Whiteness. *Educational Theory, 51*, 433–457.

Kanno, Y. (2003). *Negotiating bilingual and bicultural identities: Japanese returnees betwixt two worlds*. Mahwah, NJ: Lawrence Erlbaum.

LaFromboise, T., Coleman, H. L. K., & Gerton, J. (1993). Psychological impact of biculturalism: Evidence and theory. *Psychological Bulletin, 114*, 395–412.

MacDonald, V.-M. (2004). *Latino education in U.S. history, 1513–2000*. New York, NY: Palgrave.

Marks, A. K., Patton, F., & Coil, C. G. (2011). Being bicultural: A mixed-methods study of adolescents' implicitly and explicitly measured multiethnic identities. *Developmental Psychology, 47*(1), 270–288.

McBrien, J. L. (2005). Educational needs and barriers for refugee students in the United States: A review of the literature. *Review of Educational Research, 75*, 329–364.

Milligan, J. A. (2003). Teaching between the cross and the crescent moon: Islamic identity, postcoloniality, and public education in the Southern Philippines. *Comparative Education Review, 47*, 468–492.

Monzó, L. (2002, April). *English immersion and the politics of identity: An ethnographic study of Latino immigrants*. Paper presented at annual meeting of the American Educational Research Association, New Orleans, LA.

Mosselson, J. (2009). From the margins to the center: A critical examination of the identity constructions of Bosnian adolescent refugees in New York City. *Diaspora, Indigenous, and Minority Education: Studies of Migration, Integration, Equity, and Cultural Survival, 3*(4), 260–275.

Nieto, S. (1996). *Affirming diversity: The sociopolitical context of multicultural education* (2nd ed.). White Plains, NY: Longman.

Norton, B. (1997). Language, identity, and the ownership of English. *TESOL Quarterly, 31*, 409–429.

Portes, A., & Rumbaut, R. G. (2001). *Legacies: The story of the immigrant second generation*. Berkeley, CA: University of California Press.

Ritivoi, A. D. (2002). *Yesterday's self: Nostalgia and the immigrant identity*. Lanham, MD: Rowman & Littlefield.

Rong, X. L., & Preissle, J. (1998). *Educating immigrant students: What we need to know to meet the challenges*. Thousand Oaks, CA: Corwin Press.

Sfard, A., & Prusak, A. (2005). Telling identities: In search of an analytic tool for investigating learning as a culturally shaped activity. *Educational Researcher, 34*, 14–22.

Spindler, G. D. (Ed.) (1987). *Education and cultural process: Anthropological approaches* (2nd ed.). Prospect Heights, IL: Waveland.

Suárez-Orozco, C., & Suárez-Orozco, M. M. (2001). *Children of immigration.* Cambridge, MA: Harvard University Press.

Torres, R. D., & Ngin, C. (1995). Racialized boundaries, class relations, and cultural politics: The Asian-American and Latino experience. In H. A. Giroux & P. Freire (Series Eds.) & A. Darder (Vol. Ed.), *Critical Studies in Education and Culture Series. Culture and difference: Critical perspectives on the bicultural experience in the United States* (pp. 55–69). Westport, CT: Bergin & Garvey.

Trueba, E. T. (2004). *The new Americans: Immigrants and transnationals at work.* Lanham, MD: Rowman and Littlefield.

USA for UNHCR. (2013). What is a refugee? Retrieved from http://www.unrefugees.org/site/c.lfIQKSOwFqG/b.4950731/k.A894/What_is_a_refugee.htm

Zou, Y. (2002). Multiple identities of a Chinese immigrant: A story of adaptation and empowerment. *Qualitative Studies in Education, 15,* 251–268.

PART V

EXPERIENCES OF MUSLIM YOUTHS GROWING UP IN A NON-MUSLIM COUNTRY

CHAPTER 11

THE STRENGTHS AND SKILLS OF CHILDREN

Self-Descriptions of Somali and Local Australian Children

Agnes E. Dodds, Nadia Albert, and Jeanette A. Lawrence

ABSTRACT

In this chapter, we focus on how Somali primary school children describe their personal strengths and school-related skills. They are growing up in relation to both their Somali Islamic heritage culture and the Australian national culture held out to them in their schools.

We used computerized and illustrated paired comparison tasks to investigate the Somali children's self-descriptions. We compared their self-described personal strengths with those of their local (Australian) peers. We also compared Somali and non-Somali self-described strengths and school-related skills with those attributed to them by their parents and guardians.

The findings indicate that most of the Somali children's self-described strengths agreed with those of their local peers, although they described themselves as more brave but less loving. Along with their peers, the Somali

Growing Up Between Two Cultures: Problems and Issues of Muslim Children, pp. 263–289
Copyright © 2014 by Information Age Publishing

children disagreed with their guardians about their strengths and most of their school-related skills. Somali guardian/child pairs agreed with each other but disagreed with non-Somali pairs in indicating that the Somali children were skilled in spelling and maths but unskilled in music. The findings suggest that these Somali children were choosing personal preferences from among the values held out to them by both their Somali heritage and Australian mainstream cultures.

People from Somalia have been resettling in Australia since the 1990s. They mostly arrived as refugees after suffering and displacement in their homeland, in African refugee camps, and in transit. Many of their children are now in primary (elementary) school and encountering the mainstream Australian culture, for some effectively for the first time. These young children often find themselves living in two different "worlds" or cultural contexts with different, sometimes conflicting expectations and norms (Cooper, 2011). We were interested in how Somali children see themselves in relation to their Somali and Australian cultures. We focused specifically on how these children would describe their own strengths and skills in relation to those expected of children in their Somali families and in Australian schools.

Resettlement has often been seen as difficult for Somali people, partly because of the long-term effects of trauma, displacement, and uncertainty, and partly because of their circumstances in Australia (Browne, 2006). Life-style issues that arise during resettlement, for example, are related to their poor employment and housing. They also are often related to the difficulties of practicing the Muslim faith in secular or Christian countries (Buck & Silver, 2012). Muslim cultural practices such as regular prayer, distinctive dress, dietary requirements, and seasonal fasting are now recognized and mostly accommodated in multicultural societies like Australia. Some practices of Somali families, however, seem to be less understood in countries receiving refugees and asylum seekers (e.g., for Finland: Degni, Pöntinen, & Mölsä, 2006; for the United States: Nilsson, Barazanji, Heintzelman, Siddiqi, & Shilla, 2012; for Australia: Renzaho, Green, Mellor, & Swinburn, 2011).

Somali views may differ from Western views about children's responsibilities, gender-related roles, and patterns of behavior inside and outside the home (e.g., Jones, 1998; Mohamed & Yusuf, 2011). As one teacher in the Kenyan camps observed, Somali girls are often kept out of school to assist with household tasks (Buck & Silver, 2012). Another Somali parent told Canadian researchers: "back home, when our children are seven years old, they are grown" (Dachyshyn, 2007, p. 257). These kinds of expectations of children and children's roles can lead to misunderstandings when Somali families encounter mainstream, Western expectations at school.

The kinds of protracted encounters between culturally different ways of thinking and acting that immigrant and minority parents and children experience are usually considered under the label of "acculturation experiences" (e.g., Berry & Sabatier, 2010; Goodnow & Lawrence, 2013; Rudmin, 2003). Acculturation describes the reactions of groups and individuals to protracted meetings between two or more cultures. For newcomer and minority groups it usually relates to how they deal with the ways of thinking and acting belonging to the mainstream culture at the same time that they are dealing with the ways of thinking and acting belonging to their heritage culture. People exhibit different strategies or styles for acquiring, retaining, and/or rejecting one or both sets of cultural values and practices. Integration (involvement in both one's heritage and national culture) is usually considered the strategy that most consistently supports well being in immigrant young people (Berry & Sabatier, 2010).

Acculturation experiences, however, are likely to disrupt family life (Bornstein & Cote, 2006), especially when parents make adjustments to living in two cultures more slowly than their children (Telzer, 2010). Children and young people are constantly challenged to acquire the instrumental skills and expressive values needed to communicate with peers and adults in school and other community organizations. Parents, especially home bound mothers, are under less pressure to adapt to the mainstream (Dorner, Orellana, & Jiménez, 2008). It is not surprising, then, that parent/child acculturation gaps can arise, bringing challenges to a family's traditional values and practices (Fuligni, 2012; Telzer, 2010), and challenges to traditional patterns of family relationships (Kwak, 2003).

Children and in fact, all developing persons who live in the context of two cultures are likely to be experiencing acculturation at the same time that they are experiencing ongoing "enculturation processes." Enculturation describes the experiences by which members of a heritage culture progressively orient their children into their culture's values and practices (Lawrence, Brooker, & Goodnow, 2012; Oppedal, 2006). These continuing enculturation processes do not stop when children and their families meet with other cultures. Both forms of cultural orientation, then, figure in the total developmental experience of any immigrant child (Oppedal, 2006).

From this perspective, it can be seen that the children of Somali refugees growing up in Australia are likely to encounter sometimes conflicting and sometimes overlapping expectations and adult-initiated activities. Their parents follow traditional lines of parenting and work hard to bring them up in traditional ways. Their schools offer alternative ideologies and activities. The task for the children is to learn how to navigate their way through these different sets of cultural perspectives and experiences (Mistry & Wu, 2010). This largely involves children in finding ways to think about themselves and to present themselves in terms of the qualities and skills that allow them to feel comfortable in each culture (Goodnow & Lawrence, 2013).

SOMALI CHILDREN DEVELOPING IN AUSTRALIAN SCHOOLS

Any child's interactions with the social world can be seen in terms of the "goodness of fit" of their navigations through social institutions and the experiences they offer young people (Eccles et al., 1993, p. 93). A good, positive fit occurs when environmental demands and children's expectations and competences are in substantial agreement. Children then feel that they belong, and that they are acquiring the qualities and competences they need to thrive in that environment. They feel "at home" culturally. In contrast, a poor, negative fit occurs when environmental demands and children's competences are out of kilter. Children then are left confused, alienated, or feeling 'not at home' in their cultural environment (Lawrence, Benedict, & Valsiner, 1992; Lawrence et al., 2012).

When starting school, all children encounter some differences between the beliefs and practices accepted at home and the beliefs and practices presented in this new environment (e.g., Entwisle & Hayduk, 1978; Fleer & Hedergaard, 2010). Immigrant children, however, encounter more challenges in school than those faced by their local peers (e.g., Cooper, 2011; Dachyshyn, 2007).

Some school practices, for example, run contrary to Somali parents' religious and cultural values (e.g., sex education and what parents and children see as school-based lax disciplinary practices and loose learning strategies; Degni et al., 2006; Jones, 1998). Some core school subjects such as music and art do not sit well with an Islamic world-view (Ibrahim, Small, & Grimley, 2009). Academic English is an essential foundation for all learning, but English may not be spoken at home. In addition, the transition to using academic English is made particularly difficult by the oral tradition of Somali culture and the fact that the Somali language was not written down until the early 1970s (Clyne & Kipp, 2005).

Some Somali parents seem not to engage easily with their children's schools. Their own interrupted education can add to their difficulty with school expectations that parents will become involved with the school and assist their children with homework and other school tasks (Warsame, 2010). Somali parents traditionally assume teachers will do their work and only be in touch if there is a problem (Hussein, 2011). When they do help with children's learning, Somali parents seem to rely on the formal style of rote learning used in Quranic learning, and that does not agree with the less formal learning tasks and styles usually followed in Western schools (Jones, 1998).

These different sets of cultural and educational practices can leave the children with the task of working out how best to present themselves and their growing skills in their interactions with both their worlds. Oppedal (2006, p. 102), for instance, describes children's abilities to adjust to different sets of adult expectations and demands as "cultural switching." Children are able to adjust to alternating cultural demands much as bilingual children switch forms of language in adaptive responses to surrounding circumstances. In an original study (Dodds et al., 2010) we built on Oppedal's proposal, suggesting that instead of simply reflecting the skills valued by one environment and then another, children develop their own sets of preferences among school-related skills. Some of their preferences reflect Somali concerns, and some school concerns, but the children's constructions are their own.

The acculturation experiences of these Somali children were mostly in relation to their local schools. At the same time, they were being enculturated into their Somali Islamic culture, with a strong community presence in the area. The children were attending two schools in disadvantaged areas of urban Melbourne. The schools invited Mission Australia, a nongovernment organization, to conduct after-school learning and sport programs for the whole school population as the African Pathways Project (a report of related research and interventions is presented in Lawrence & Dodds, 2009). The project was welcomed by the local Imam who attended social events and endorsed the learning and sports programs.

Children's Understanding of Their Competences

Children are quite capable of actively participating in their environments, and making choices among the abilities and norms offered them by adults (e.g., Diesendruck & Markson, 2011; Flynn, 2008). As young as 3 years, for example, they can form rudimentary self-representations of themselves as possessing particular abilities (e.g., "I can ride a bike") or particular psychological attributes (e.g., "I am happy"; Wang, Doan & Song, 2010). By second grade, most children are able to differentiate among their competences and to form judgements about their abilities, although they may tend to inflate those abilities in comparison with the judgments made by teachers (Wigfield & Karpathian, 1991). Towards the end of primary school, however their judgments seem to be more in line with those of their teachers (Nicholls, 1979).

By the end of primary school, boys and girls typically attribute different abilities to themselves. Eccles, Wigfield, Harold, and Blumenfeld (1993), for instance, found that by fourth grade in the United States, boys had stronger beliefs in their abilities in maths, but girls had stronger beliefs in their abilities in reading and music. These early gender stereotypic views are important, because they affect the values students place on some school subjects later in high school (e.g., maths), and also affect their performance in those subjects (Marsh & Ayotte, 2003).

In an unusual cross-cultural study of the self-related abilities and attributes of children between 4 and 9 years, Wang (2004) found that the self-descriptions made by European American children in the United States were different from self-descriptions made by Chinese children in China. While the American children described themselves more in terms of their emotions and personal attributes, the Chinese children described themselves in terms of their relationships and behaviors.

Researching Somali Children's Perceptions and Challenges

Each cultural group is likely to have specific issues and adaptations related to their background and resettlement experiences (Goodnow & Lawrence, 2013). These specifics demand sensitivity and appropriate methodologies on the part of researchers who are seeking to understand a given group's self-perceptions (Goodnow, 2013; Lawrence, Dodds, & Brooker, 2010). Researchers need to be confident that the responses they observe genuinely reflect the group's experiences and ways of thinking and acting, and are not an artifact of inappropriate methods and measures (Schwarz, 2009). They need, for example, appropriate comparison groups to ensure that the patterns in their data can be appropriately attributed to the specific target group and do not simply reflect what any group would demonstrate in that same situation (Fuligni, 2012).

We needed to be assured, for instance, that Somali and local children who shared disadvantaged life circumstances would be able to comfortably report their self-descriptions to researchers (Lawrence et al., 2010). To address that issue, we developed an interactive computer program that allows children and young people to make considered judgments, and to work at their own pace. This program presents children with simple statements and attractive cartoon representations of pairs of strengths and then pairs of school-related skills. The children make choices between pairs. We also needed to be assured that any distinctive patterns of Somali children's self-descriptions would be authentically their own, related to their cultural experiences and commitments rather than being an expression of general disadvantage.

Accordingly, in the original study (Dodds et al., 2010), we obtained evidence of Somali children's self-descriptions of their school-related skills using this paired-comparison task. As a check, we also obtained similar data from two comparison groups. They were a group of local disadvantaged children in the same classes as the Somali children. As a further check, we added a group of local children from a nearby school where families lives in more advantaged circumstances (Dodds et al., 2010; Lawrence & Dodds, 2009). These comparative data allowed us to identify the descriptions of their school-related skills that were specific to the Somali children, for example, owning as their own the school-related skills of maths, spelling and problem solving, and rejecting music and art. The data also allowed us to identify a skill that all three groups owned as theirs (sport) and one that all three rejected as the least among their skills, although their schools had been promoting it (making a speech).

We also pointed out that it would be useful to compare Somali and non-Somali's children's self-descriptions of personal skills not specifically attached to school curricula and procedures. Would cultural differences be greater or less when descriptors were not part of the children's formal education? We suggested it would be important to compare children's self-descriptions with those of their parents. These research strategies would help us to better understand Somali children's preferences.

Accordingly, we added several different sets of analyses for the follow-up research reported in this chapter. Each set of analyses was designed to address the specificity of Somali children's self-description. They involved first comparing the self-described strengths of Somali children with those of local disadvantaged and advantaged groups, and adding that to analyses of their self-described school-related skills. For these analyses we drew on a subsample of the original groups who had completed both a personal strengths task as well as the school-related skills tasks. The second set of analyses involved asking a group of Somali and disadvantaged local parents and guardians to describe their children's strengths and skills using the same response measures as those used by their children. Because we were seeing the parents and guardians in their homes, we took the opportunity to also ask them about their aspirations for their children's education. We expected these different sources of data would help us understand more fully the self-presentations of these Somali children.

SOMALI AND NON-SOMALI CHILDREN'S SELF-DESCRIPTIONS OF THEIR STRENGTHS

Participants for the analyses of children's self-descriptions of their strengths were 90 Grade 5 and 6 children in three subgroups of the original sample

(Dodds et al., 2010). These children had completed the extra task involving paired comparison choices of their personal strengths. Three groups were: (1) 21 Somali children (12 boys, 9 girls), with a mean age of 11.4 years (SD = .94); (2) 40 non-Somali Disadvantaged children (16 boys, 24 girls) from the same schools, with a mean age of 11.6 years (SD = .76); (3) 29 non-Somali Advantaged children from a school in a nearby socially more advantaged area (11 boys, 18 girls), with a mean age of 11.0 years (SD = .80).

Materials and Procedures

Each participant worked on a laptop computer in a one-to-one session with a trained researcher who would offer assistance with typing and navigation through the programs. Most children preferred to do their own typing.

Self-described strengths were presented in a computer program (Lawrence, Campbell, & MacInnes, 2007) as 28 randomly ordered pairs of 8 statements of a personal strength, with each strength demonstrated by cartoon animals in appropriate activities. For example, 'I am a good friend' is illustrated by a bird eating the ticks on the head of a buffalo (St. Luke's Innovative Resources, 2005). The other seven illustrated strengths were: I am brave, happy, loving, I look after other people, I can be trusted, I work hard, and I will try new things. The individual strengths were chosen in consultation with teachers and community workers as suitable for the children's ages and cultures.

For each pair (e.g., I am brave vs. I am happy), the participant was asked "Which of these two best describes your strengths?" For analyses, we gave each strength a score for each child reflecting the number of times it was chosen as a relative personal strength (range, 0–7).

Findings

The Somali, Disadvantaged and Advantaged groups described for themselves similar patterns of relative strengths, with different group mean scores for only two strengths in relation to the group overall mean scores: I am brave and I am loving. On analysis, a 3 group by 2 gender MANOVA with repeated measure of strength (8) yielded two 2-way interactions for strength by group, $F(14, 588) = 1.79$, $p = .04$, $\eta^2 = .04$, and strength by gender, $F(7, 588) = 4.63$, $p = .00$, $\eta^2 = .05$, and a main effect for strength, $F(7, 588) = 9.98$, $p = .00$, $\eta^2 = .11$. The mean strength scores for boys and girls in three groups are shown in Table 11.1.

Table 11.1. Mean Scores and Standard Deviations for Eight Strengths, for Somali, Disadvantaged and Advantaged Boys and Girls

Cultural Group:	Somali		Disadvantaged		Advantaged		
Gender:	Boy	Girl	Boy	Girl	Boy	Girl	
n =	12	9	16	24	11	18	
Strength:							
I am a good friend	4.42	4.00	4.44	4.33	4.55	4.50	c
(SD)	(1.24)	(1.58)	(1.37)	(1.47)	(1.70)	(1.38)	
I work hard	3.92	3.78	4.19	3.17	3.73	3.33	
	(1.78)	(2.05)	(1.72)	(1.37)	(1.74)	(1.72)	
I am brave	3.92	2.78	3.06	3.04	1.91	2.06	a, c
	(1.56)	(2.39)	(1.48)	(1.76)	(1.76)	(1.63)	
I try new things	3.73	3.33	3.97	3.33	3.56	3.71	
	(1.74)	(1.72)	(1.71)	(1.61)	(1.63)	(1.30)	
I can be trusted	3.58	4.89	3.50	4.25	4.00	3.83	b, c
	(0.90)	(1.05)	(1.63)	(1.29)	(1.67)	(1.62)	
I look after others	3.50	4.11	3.62	3.67	3.82	4.11	
	(1.62)	(1.62)	(1.67)	(1.27)	(1.54)	(1.64)	
I am happy	3.08	2.00	4.00	2.50	4.00	3.06	
	(1.24)	(1.00)	(1.51)	(1.64)	(2.15)	(1.77)	
I am loving	1.83	2.89	1.63	3.29	2.64	4.22	a, b, c
	(1.03)	(1.45)	(1.31)	(1.57)	(2.29)	(1.73)	
Mean strength score	3.50	3.50	3.50	3.50	3.44	3.42	
	(0.00)	(0.00)	(0.00)	(0.00)	(0.15)	(0.16)	

Key: a = Interaction for strength by group difference (Helmert contrasts); b = Interaction for strength by gender; c = Strength differs from mean strength score.

As shown in Table 11.1, for I am brave, the Somali group had a mean score that was higher than their mean for all other seven strengths, and it was higher than the comparable mean for the Disadvantaged group, that in turn was higher than the mean of the Advantaged group. The inverse pattern appeared for I am loving. The Somali group had a relatively lower mean score than the Disadvantaged group whose score was relatively lower than that of the Advantaged group.

All 39 boys had a relatively lower mean score than all 51 girls for I am loving, and for I can be trusted. As a total sample, all children had a higher mean score than their overall mean for I am a good friend and I can be trusted, but a lower mean score for I am brave and I am loving.

CHILDREN'S AND GUARDIANS' DESCRIPTIONS
OF CHILDREN'S STRENGTHS AND SKILLS

To compare children's self-descriptions with those of their parents and guardians, we used the responses of 31 child/guardian pairs of 12 Somali children (6 boys, 6 girls) and their guardians, and 19 non-Somali Disadvantaged children (8 boys, 11 girls) and their guardians. Thirty-one parents or guardians completed the same computerized paired comparison tasks as their children, and then made comments about their educational aspirations for their children. This was around half Somali and non-Somali (Disadvantaged) parents or guardians of children in the initial study from two disadvantaged schools. Forty agreed to participate but nine withdrew for a variety of reasons (e.g., moving out of the district, family crises).

Parents or guardians identified themselves as 6 Somali fathers and 6 mothers, and as 2 non-Somali fathers, 16 mothers and 1 grandmother/guardian. It was culturally inappropriate for us to probe for exact relationships to the children, with some refugee family compositions quite complex. As a conservative response then we call all "guardians."

We interviewed the guardians in their homes. A trained Somali worker of the same gender as the guardian interviewed each Somali adult, accompanied by an English-speaking researcher. The Somali workers also interviewed two Somali children who had limited English language. Having a researcher present and participating in all interviews was respectful, and minimized language and interpretive difficulties and any problems with recording the data. Somali parents often involved the researcher in the conversation. They felt comfortable with the interviewers.

We also asked the guardians two specific questions about their aspirations for their children at school: "What do you wish [child] to achieve while at primary school?", "What are your hopes for [child's] education overall, and is there anything you would like them to do after school?"

FINDINGS

Children's Strengths

The cultural groups of Somali and non-Somali child/guardian pairs did not differ in their descriptions of the children's relative strengths. There were differences, however, in the strengths described by all the boys and all the girls compared with those their guardians described for them. On analysis, there was a three-way interaction with strength for child/ guardian role by gender of child, $F(7, 189) = 2.44$, $p = .03$, $\eta^2 = .08$; a two-way interaction for child/guardian role by strength, $F(7, 189) = 6.43$, $p = .00$, $\eta^2 = .19$; and a main effect for strength, $F(7, 189) = 3.66$, $p = .01$, $\eta^2 = .12$. The mean strength scores for children and guardians are shown in Table 11.2. The three-way interaction is illustrated in Figure 11.1.

Table 11.2.   Mean Scores and Standard Deviations for Eight Strengths, for Pairs of Somali and Non-Somali Boys and Girls and Their Guardians

Cultural Group:	Somali				Non-Somali				
Gender, Child:	Boy		Girl		Boy		Girl		
Respondent:	Boy	Guar.	Girl	Guar.	Boy	Guar.	Girl	Guar.	
n =	6	6	6	6	8	8	11	11	
Strength:									
I am a good friend (SD)	4.33	1.50	4.17	2.00	4.88	3.38	4.27	1.18	b
	(1.51)	(2.07)	(0.75)	(1.88)	(0.99)	(2.72)	(1.90)	(1.17)	
I work hard	3.50	3.83	4.17	4.50	3.50	3.38	2.45	4.27	
	(1.87)	(2.64)	(2.14)	(0.84)	(1.93)	(2.20)	(1.70)	(1.95)	
I am brave	4.33	1.83	2.50	3.33	2.75	3.50	3.55	2.64	
	(1.51)	(2.14)	(2.26)	(1.86)	(1.67)	(1.77)	(1.81)	(1.86)	
I try new things	3.50	3.00	2.50	3.00	4.13	3.00	3.64	3.64	
	(1.05)	(2.28)	(1.52)	(1.79)	(1.25)	(2.14)	(1.21)	(1.75)	
I can be trusted	3.50	3.33	5.00	2.33	3.63	3.87	4.36	2.82	a
	(1.05)	(2.34)	(1.27)	(1.63)	(2.13)	(1.89)	(1.12)	(2.09)	
I look after others	3.17	4.50	4.17	5.00	3.88	4.38	3.64	4.82	b, c
	(1.33)	(2.74)	(1.60)	(1.10)	(1.55)	(1.69)	(1.21)	(1.25)	

(Table continues on next page)

Table 11.2.   (Continued)

Cultural Group:	Somali				Non-Somali				
Gender, Child:	Boy		Girl		Boy		Girl		
Respondent:	Boy	Guar.	Girl	Guar.	Boy	Guar.	Girl	Guar.	
n =	6	6	6	6	8	8	11	11	
Strength									
I am happy	3.00	3.33	1.83	4.67	4.38	2.88	3.09	4.45	a
	(1.27)	(1.75)	(0.75)	(1.63)	(1.69)	(1.55)	(1.87)	(1.64)	
I am loving	1.83	2.00	3.50	3.17	1.13	3.63	2.73	4.18	a, c
	(1.47)	(1.80)	(1.05)	(1.72)	(1.13)	(1.60)	(1.62)	(1.66)	
Mean score	3.40	2.92	3.48	3.50	3.53	3.50	3.47	3.50	
	(0.20)	(1.43)	(0.05	(0.00)	(0.09)	(0.00)	(0.13)	(0.00)	

Key: a = Interaction for Strength by role (child, guardian) by gender of child; b = Interaction for Strength by role; c = Strength differs from mean strength score.

The patterns of interaction in Figure 11.1 show that for I am happy, the boys had a higher mean score than girls, but that their guardians' mean scores disagreed. Guardians of the boys gave them a lower mean score than the guardians of the girls gave them.

Boys gave themselves lower scores than girls gave themselves for two other strengths: I am loving and I can be trusted. For I am loving, all guardians agreed with the relative boy and girl differences, but their scores were less extreme for the boys. The overall score for I am loving for the whole sample was lower than the overall mean. For I can be trusted, the boys had a lower mean score than the girls. While the guardians of the boys, however, gave them a score close to the boys' own, the guardians of the girls gave them a much lower score.

The two-way interaction related to the child/guardian role can be seen in Table 11.2. For I am a good friend, all children had a higher mean score than their overall mean, while their guardians gave them a much lower score. For I look after other people, all children had a lower score, although it was close to their overall mean. Their guardians, however, gave them a considerably higher mean score, and the mean score for the whole sample was higher than the overall mean.

Children's School-Related Skills

The cultural groups of Somali and non-Somali child/guardian pairs differed in their descriptions of the children's relative skills in school subjects,
but not in their descriptions of their children's procedural skills. On analysis of subject skills, there were three two-way interactions with subject skill:
for cultural group, $F(6, 162) = 3.36$, $p = .01$, $\eta^2 = .11$; gender of child, $F(4,$
$162) = 2.73$, $p = .02$, $\eta^2 = .10$; and role (child, guardian), $F(6, 162) = 4.28$,
$p = .00$, $\eta^2 = .14$. There also was a main effect for subject skill, $F(6, 162) =$
7.46, $p = .00$, $\eta^2 = .22$. The mean subject skill scores for Somali and non-
Somali groups of boys and girls and their respective guardians are shown
in Table 11.3. The three-way interaction is illustrated in Figure 11.1.

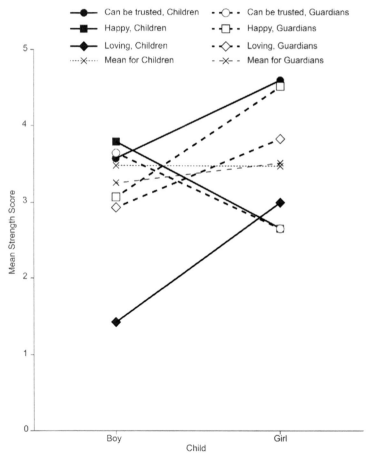

Figure 11.1.   Interaction of strength by role by gender of child.

As shown in Table 11.3, for spelling there was a culture-related inter-action. Somali children and their guardians combined gave the Somali children a mean score that was relatively higher than the mean score that the non-Somali children and their guardians gave the non-Somali chil-dren. Both cultural means were quite high relative to the means for other subject skills. In contrast, for music, the Somali children and their guard-ians combined gave them a much lower mean score than the mean score the non-Somali children and guardians gave them, although the whole sample gave music a lower mean score than the overall mean.

For maths, the interaction was related to gender. The whole set of boys and their guardians from both cultures gave boys a higher mean score in

Table 11.3.   Mean Scores and Standard Deviations for Seven School Subject Skills for Somali and Non-Somali Combined Groups Pairs of Children and Parents, for Boys and Girls

Cultural Group:	Somali				Non-Somali				
Gender, Child:	Boy		Girl		Boy		Girl		
Respondent: n =	Boy 6	Guar. 6	Girl 6	Guar. 6	Boy 8	Guar. 8	Girl 11	Guar. 11	
School Subject Skill:									
Spelling	6.83	8.17	5.83	7.50	3.50	7.63	5.91	4.00	a
(SD)	(2.14)	(4.45)	(2.56)	(4.14)	(2.20)	(3.96)	(3.21)	(3.49)	
Maths	8.33	9.00	5.33	7.33	7.87	9.25	4.55	6.00	b
	(2.94)	(3.23)	(3.88)	(3.67)	(3.80)	(3.15)	(3.48)	(3.95)	
Sport	9.33	6.67	11.00	7.83	10.75	7.00	8.00	6.45	c, d
	(2.88)	(2.16)	(1.27)	(1.47)	(1.49)	(3.89)	(2.65)	(2.54)	
Reading	6.50	8.33	4.83	7.17	4.75	4.88	7.91	9.18	c
	(2.26)	(2.34)	(3.37)	(2.32)	(4.40)	(4.73)	(1.51)	(2.04)	
Writing	6.83	7.17	5.83	7.17	5.88	5.13	5.91	6.18	
	(2.48)	(2.04)	(3.06)	(2.14)	(2.70)	(2.30)	(3.45)	(2.60)	

(Table continues on next page)

Table 11.3. (Continued)

Cultural Group:	*Somali*				*Non-Somali*				
Gender, Child:	*Boy*		*Girl*		*Boy*		*Girl*		
Respondent:	*Boy*	*Guar.*	*Girl*	*Guar.*	*Boy*	*Guar.*	*Girl*	*Guar.*	
n =	*6*	*6*	*6*	*6*	*8*	*8*	*11*	*11*	
School Subject Skill:									
Art	4.00	6.67	8.50	5.50	7.00	5.88	8.45	9.00	
	(2.83)	(3.83)	(4.23)	(3.39)	(3.34)	(3.80)	(3.08)	(2.65)	
Music	1.83	0.67	4.83	2.00	6.25	4.88	5.82	6.09	a, d
	(1.84)	(0.52)	(3.49)	(2.90)	(3.62)	(4.22)	(3.50)	(4.37)	
Mean school subject skill score	6.24	6.67	6.60	6.36	6.57	6.38	6.65	6.70	
	(0.84)	(0.61)	(0.72)	(0.93)	(0.98)	(0.71)	(0.54)	(0.35)	

Key: a = Interaction for subject skill by culture (Somali vs non-Somali children and guardians combined); b = Interaction subject skill by gender (boys vs girls and guardians combined); c = Interaction for subject skill by role (child vs guardian); d = main effect for subject skill, mean differs from overall mean.

comparison with their school subject mean than the whole set of girls and their guardians combined in comparison with their overall mean.

For sport and reading, the interactions were related to role. For sport, all children gave themselves a comparatively higher mean score than all their guardians gave them, and the sample score was higher than the overall mean. For reading, the pattern was the opposite. All children giving themselves a comparatively low mean score, while their guardians gave them a comparatively higher mean score.

On analysis of procedural skills, there were two two-way interactions for children compared with guardians by procedural skill, $F(5, 135) = 11.71$, $p = .00$, $\eta^2 = .30$; and a main effect for procedural skill, $F(5, 135) = 22.73$, $p = .00$, $\eta^2 = .46$. The mean procedural skill scores for children and guardians are shown in Table 11.4.

**Table 11.4,   Mean Scores and Standard Deviations for
Six Procedural Skills, for All Children and All Guardians**

Respondent:	Child	Guardian	
n =	31	31	
Procedural Skill:			
Computers	8.26	5.52	a, b
(SD)	(2.46)	(3.15)	
Working by myself	6.26	3.87	a
	(2.49)	(2.80)	
Problem solving	5.42	9.48	a
	(2.47)	(2.14)	
Conflict resolution	4.35	5.13	b
	(2.44)	(2.19)	
Working in a group	4.77	5.55	
	(2.42)	(2.19)	
Making a speech	3.16	2.65	b
	(3.07)	(2.72)	
Mean procedural skill score	5.37	5.37	
	(0.87)	(0.73)	

Key: a = role (child vs guardian difference); b = main effect for procedural skill, mean differs from overall mean.

As shown in Table 11.4, for two procedural skills: computers and working by myself all children had a higher mean score than their guardians gave them in comparison with their overall means. The whole sample gave children a higher mean score than the overall mean for computers. In contrast, for problem solving, the children gave themselves a comparatively lower mean score than their guardians gave them. For conflict resolution, the whole sample gave the children a lower mean score than the overall mean, although this was a particular emphasis in the schools.

GUARDIANS' EDUCATIONAL ASPIRATIONS FOR THEIR CHILDREN

We coded the guardians' open-ended comments in relation to the two questions about their aspirations for their children. Seven nonoverlapping coding categories were their aspirations for their child's: academic achievement, self-determination, self development, behavior, social involvement, sport, going to university, and the guardians' satisfaction. There was perfect interjudge agreement for guardians' aspirations for primary school, on 49 of 54 codings (91%), and for their overall educational aspirations on 58 of 59 codings (98%). We resolved disagreements by discussion.

The Somali and non-Somali guardians had similar patterns of aspirations for their children while they were in primary school, $X^2(6, 53) = 7.44$, $p = .29$; but different patterns for their children's educational experiences overall, $X^2(5, 59) = 17.59$, $p = .01$. The patterns of the comments made by the two cultural groups of guardians are shown in Table 11.5.

In relation to primary school, most of the comments were about their child achieving academically (100% of Somali, 57% of non-Somali). For example a Somali father (S66) commented in specific terms about his son: "To be good in science subjects and maths, and that is what I have always advised all my children, because I would like that they will be oriented in the technical field for their future." A local non-Somali mother (NS47) said about her daughter and school provisions: "Do the best she can. Take advantage of things there for her. Enjoy learning. Child has always wanted to learn and will put in extra, but needs more facilities and encouragement. They should have programs." Few Somali guardians mentioned their child's self development (e.g., 8% compared with 47% of non-Somalis) and no Somali mentioned a child's self-determination (15% of non-Somalis). Only around 17% of Somalis and 26% of non-Somalis said they were satisfied with their child's performance.

Table 11.5. Percentages of Somali and Non-Somali Parents Making Specific Comments About Their Educational Aspirations for Their Children, with Examples

	Guardians' Aspirations			
Focus of Aspiration:	*In Primary School*		*For Education Overall*	
Cultural Group:	*Somali*	*Non-Somali*	*Somali*	*Non-Somali*
Aspiration for Their Child's:				
Academic achievement	100.0	57.0	91.67	63.15
e.g., *do well, pass everything*				
Self [a]	8.33	47.36	0.0	57.89
e.g., *happy in what he's doing*				

(Table continues on next page)

Table 11.5.   (Continued)

Focus of Aspiration:	*In Primary School*		*For Education Overall*	
Cultural Group:	*Somali*	*Non-Somali*	*Somali*	*Non-Somali*
Aspiration for Their Child's:				
Self-determination [a]	0.0	15.0	0.0	36.84
e.g., whatever he decides to do				
Behavior	8.33	5.26	-	-
e.g., *well behaved*				
Social involvement	16.67	26.31	16.67	0.0
e.g., *mixing with other kids*				
Sports involvement	8.33	21.05	–	–
e.g., *her sport achievement*				
University entry [a]	–	–	66.67	10.52
e.g., *graduate from university*				
Vocational pathway	–	–	25.0	10.52
e.g., *a brilliant engineer*				

Key: a = Somali percentages differ from non-Somali for education overall, adjusted standardized residual > = 2.

In relation to their child's education overall, most comments again were about their child's academic achievement (92% of Somalis; 63% of non-Somalis), and the comments were different in focus. For example, one Somali father (S33) coupled his wish for his daughter's behavior with his wish for her success: "Be good girl, successful, well behaved." A non-Somali mother (NS30) instead coupled school success with happiness for her daughter: "Year 12, be pretty happy—ecstatic—that's the main thing. I don't care after that."

More Somali guardians (67%) specifically mentioned that they wanted their child to go to university or college, compared with only 11% of non-Somalis. For example, one Somali mother (S29) commented that she had special aspirations for her son, "To do very well at school, go to university, not want him to do TAFE (technical college) first, that's ok but not for my kids."

No Somali guardian mentioned their child's self development (58% of Non Somalis); or their child's self-determination (37% of Non Somalis). For example, concerning his daughter, one non-Somali father (NS42) said: "I can't answer until she knows what she wants to pursue, or she'll marry a rich man and not have to work."

DISCUSSION

We set out to use several analyses to explore the self-descriptions made by Somali children who are in Australian primary schools. Although most of these children were born in Australia, their families are still in the process of resettling after trauma and displacement. The children are growing up in multiple worlds (Cooper, 2011) as they move between home, school and other cultural contexts, particularly the local mosque and its community. Each of their cultural worlds holds out to them its particular expectations and resources. Each child in interacting with the different worlds, develops a sense of self in relation to those expectations and resources (Shweder, Goodnow, Hatano, LeVine, Markus, & Miller, 2006).

Children developing within their sometimes conflicting cultural worlds have the task of constructing a working view of themselves and their competences that allows them to feel at home in both their Somali and Australian cultures (Lawrence et al., 2012). They cannot avoid the meeting of the cultures and they are involved in processes of acculturation, whatever position and commitments they may come to form for themselves (Berry & Sabatier, 2010). Even immigrant young people who develop oppositional identities in relation to the mainstream culture, for instance, are responding, albeit negatively, to the pressures of acculturation (Portes & Rumbaut, 2001). These Somali children's parents and guardians also are under some pressure to acculturate, although the accepted wisdom is that the acculturation adjustments of parents usually are slower than those of their children (Telzer, 2010).

The children's acculturation experiences centered around their schools. Several Somali families, for example, were unwilling for their children to play sport with local teams. They were extremely supportive, however, of the inter-school games that the African Pathways project organized. The children were safe. Parents were welcomed. Refreshments were halal. The children were not under outside pressures to adjust, the schools were accommodative of cultural festivals and rituals. There were points of adjustment, however, in the children's environment. Local classmates' birthday party rituals, for example, were challenging, partly because birth dates are either unknown or unmarked in their families. Somali children also did not know the etiquette related to invitations and presents. The values of Somali and Australian ways of life were being offered to the children at the same time. They had ongoing opportunities to develop their own preferences.

We did not confront acculturation or enculturation experiences directly. Instead we chose to treat children's self-descriptions as child-centred indicators of children's constructions of themselves in relation to their worlds of home and school. Apart from the Wang (2004) study, we could find little research directly focused on children's self-descriptions. The self-descriptions, nevertheless, give a reasonable approach to understanding children's formulations of a sense of self. "This is how I see my relative qualities and skills" provides a window on what children own and value about themselves. When we asked for choices among school-promoted skills, we gained some insight into how well a child's sense of self fits with the skills specifically valued in that world. When we added self-descriptions of a more personal kind, and also could add comparative descriptions by parents, we hoped to gain some insight into at least one dimension of the children's home world. We could ask the children to make some relative judgments and choices without using unfamiliar instruments, or materials that were too academically oriented or formal (Lawrence et al., 2010).

The relative emphases that the Somali children conveyed in their self-descriptions were in part similar and in part different from the emphases of their local peers. Being brave was more of a relative strength for the Somali children than for either of the two local groups. Being loving was not. Being loving, in fact, was not overly popular as a self-description for any of the children, and especially not for the boys. For the subsample with guardian responses, guardians agreed with their boys that being loving was not one of their greater strengths. The girls and their guardians, however, gave it a higher place among their girls' strengths, although again it was not particularly popular with the guardians. Although boys saw themselves as relatively happy, girls did not. The guardians, however, did not agree with either boys or girls about their relative happiness. While the boys' guardians saw them as less happy, the girls' guardians saw them as considerably happier.

Boys in all three groups saw themselves as more trustworthy than girls. In contrast, the subsample girls saw themselves as much more trustworthy than their guardians saw them. This was even though, like the children, the guardians prized it as a strength. It is a puzzle as to why these Somali and non-Somali parents did not endorse their daughters' trustworthiness.

Children in all three groups agreed that being trustworthy and a good friend were their greatest strengths. Neither Somali nor non-Somali guardians agreed with their children's descriptions of themselves as good friends. Rather, guardians from both cultural groups placed looking after other people among their children's greater strengths, again disagreeing with their children. The guardians did agree, however, that their children were moderately brave, hard working and willing to try new things.

We did not find Somali versus non-Somali cultural differences for the children's strengths in the child/guardian choices. Instead, we found sample-wide child/guardian differences that were not culturally related, although they were gender related.

It is possible that our set of strengths omitted some of the qualities most valued in Somali culture. Dybdahl and Hundeide (1998), for instance, listed culture-related behaviors that mothers and children in Mogadishu said they valued in children. Mothers included obedience, being helpful and hardworking, going to school and Quran school, and not fighting. Children valued obedience, being helpful, doing household chores, and learning and studying. Perhaps if we had added obedience to our list, we would have seen more cultural differences. The Somali children in our study did not think they worked hard. Although their guardians agreed with them, this could still be a matter of contention. In further work, it would be useful to ask respondents how much value they placed on their chosen qualities and abilities.

Somali and local child/guardian pairs again largely agreed on the children's relative abilities on school-related procedural skills. No one included making a speech and resolving conflicts among the children's greater skills. This was in the face of the teachers' insistence that these were important skills that we should offer in our possibilities. All the children, not only the Somalis, seem to have resisted the school's values in this case. Compared with their guardians, all children saw themselves as relatively more skilled with computers and in working by themselves, but less skilled in problem solving.

It was only in the descriptions of the children's abilities in subjects belonging to the school curriculum that cultural differences emerged. There were two points of difference, and these also involved children and guardians agreeing with each other. Somali child/guardian pairs, compared with non-Somali pairs, saw their children as more skilled at spelling and less skilled at music. The Somali rejection of music showed the influence of traditional Islamic values on both children and guardians (Kahin, 1997; Rutter, 2006). Although music is a subject in Australian primary schools, the Somali children did not see it in the same light as maths and spelling, and their parents certainly agreed with these emphases.

All boys and their guardians saw the boys as more skilled at maths than all girls and their guardians saw them. All children saw themselves as more skilled at sport than their guardians saw them. All children saw themselves as less skilled at reading than their guardians saw them.

Somali and non-Somali guardians valued education highly and most wanted their children to graduate from high school. Non-Somali guardians, however, were more likely to include in their aspirations their child's personal development and abilities to make their own decisions about their educational pathways. More Somali guardians were concerned about their children's academic progress at primary school, whereas more of the non-Somalis were concerned about their children's personal qualities.

When they are considered along with our earlier analyses (Dodds et al., 2010), we suggest, these findings point to a group of young Somali children who are moving toward seeing themselves in ways that are not completely in tune with the cultural values of home, and not completely in tune with the values of their school. This should not be surprising, given the navigational tasks that are naturally involved in all people's exploration and testing of cultural values. Diesendruck and Markson (2011), for example, found that children make judgments among the cultural norms of everyday activities. Quite young children work out which adults to trust (Harris & Corriveau, 2011), and even when following directions, add their own short-cuts to the modelled procedures (Flynn, 2008).

These Somali children see themselves, for example, as having acquired some skills that are valued in their heritage culture, especially maths and spelling (Jones, 1998; Kahin, 1997). They also do not identify among their own skills music that fits less well with Somali Islamic culture (Rutter, 2006). In these patterns of personal descriptions, they are not like their local Australian peers. Their preferred skills, then, are likely to be out of step with some of the curriculum emphasized in their school learning. One school principal from another school, for example, told us she insisted on all children being involved in music classes. Most Somali parents at her school had come to accommodate that requirement. Only one family had withdrawn a child.

Valuing maths and spelling is not likely to create disagreement between Somali parents and their children's teachers. Nor are the Somali parents' high academic aspirations for their children. Misunderstandings, however, may arise even for highly prized accomplishments. Some misunderstandings arise, for instance, when their children are not doing as well at school as their parents had hoped and in some cases expected. Immigrants often come full of hope and aspirations and are disappointed when their children meet the language barrier or different standards, and do not excel.

Parental disappointment then may coincide with the differences in teaching and learning strategies that Jones (1998) found in a small U.K. sample of Somali parents. They felt the schools were not helping their children to progress academically. In interviews with Somali parents, we also were frequently told that the schools were not teaching their children enough maths and spelling, and not setting enough homework in these subjects. Their frustration at what they saw as lax approaches to learning may be attitudes shaped partly by the typical concerns of immigrants for their children to achieve well academically (Fuligni, 2012) and partly by the formalized and rote learning methods they are familiar with in their Quranic learning (Hussein, 2011).

Several gender related differences also may reflect a more traditional cultural perspective, although that would not explain the local guardians' similar views. While not unexpected, these stereotypic attitudes are concerning. Educators have long been alarmed, for example, about the widely held and persistent belief that girls are weaker at maths then boys. Eccles et al. (1993), for example, found that children's estimation of their maths ability was already gender-related in second grade and did not change as the children progressed through primary school. This did not happen for other school skills, for which students changed their appraisals as they moved through school, becoming more or less competent. She argued that this finding could reveal a powerful influence of parental stereotypes.

In summary, the comparative approach we took in our analyses allowed us to tease out some of the specifics of these Somali children's perceptions of their own characteristics and abilities. The child/guardian and gender-related discrepancies could have been interpreted as acculturation gaps (Telzer, 2010) in the Somali families if we had not found similar trends in child/guardian pairs of local non-Somali children. The children from both groups saw their social skills in a more positive light than their parents and guardians. We do not know why parents and guardians think girls are happier than the girls themselves. A child's happiness is difficult to judge. Nor do we know why these girls' guardians did not see them as trustworthy. Of course, we cannot say if the children were more accurate or the parents and guardians. These findings require replication with other Somali and local samples. We are confident, along with other researchers, that primary school children can reflect upon and report on their sense of themselves (e.g., Mason & Danby, 2011).

In other studies with refugee children from this and other cultural backgrounds we found again that refugee and local children could not be distinguished on the basis of their perceptions of their own well-being and abilities (Dodds et al., 2010: Lawrence, Collard, & Kaplan, 2013; Lawrence & Dodds, 2009). The finding that the Somali and local children in the current study did not differ on many of the personal and social skills (especially being a good friend and being trustworthy) suggests that their concerns and interests were not far from each other's.

These Somali children certainly owned different views of themselves than the self-descriptions that would belong exclusively to either Somali or Australian normative views of children's strengths and skills. As they make their way through the messages held out by both cultures, they are developing their own self-perceptions and these are not carbon copies of those of their parents or of their schools. These children are developing a sense of themselves in their multiple worlds.

ACKNOWLEDGMENTS

We wish to acknowledge the support of colleagues from the University of Melbourne and Mission Australia in conducting these studies. Mission Australia provided financial support for this research as part of the African Pathways Project.

REFERENCES

Berry, J. W., & Sabatier, C. (2010). Acculturation, discrimination, and adaptation among second generation immigrant youth in Montreal and Paris. *International Journal of Intercultural Relations, 34*, 191–207.

Bornstein, M. H., & Cote, L. C. (2006). *Acculturation and parent/child relationships: Measurement and development*. Mahwah, NJ: Lawrence Erlbaum Associates.

Browne, P. (2006). *The longest journey: Resettling refugees from Africa*. Sydney, Australia: University of New South Wales Press.

Buck, P., & Silver, R. (2012). *Educated for change? Muslim refugee women in the west*. Charlotte, NC: Information Age Publishing.

Clyne, M., & Kipp, S. (2005). On the Somali language in Melbourne. *Migration Action, XXVII*(1), 19–22.

Cooper, C. R. (2011). *Bridging multiple worlds: Cultures, identities, and pathways to college*. New York, NY: Oxford University Press.

Dachyshyn, D. M. (2007). Refugee families with preschool children: Adjustment to life in Canada. In L. D. Adams & A. Kirova (Eds.), *Global migration and education: Schools, children and families* (pp. 251–262). Mahwah, NJ: Lawrence Erlbaum.

Degni, F., Pöntinen, S., & Mölsä, M. (2006). Somali parents' experiences of bringing up children in Finland: Exploring social-cultural change within migrant households. *Forum: Qualitative Social Research, 7*(3), Art. 8. Retrieved from http://www.qualitative-research.net/fqs/

Diesendruck, G., & Markson, L. (2011). Children's assumption of the conventionality of culture. *Child Development Perspectives, 5.* 189–195.

Dodds, A. E., Lawrence, J. A., Karantzas, K., Brooker, A., Lin, Y. H., Champness, V., & Albert, N. (2010). Children of Somali refugees in Australian schools: Self-descriptions of school-related skills and needs. *International Journal of Behavioral Development, 34*, 521–528.

Dorner, M., Orellana, M. F., & Jiménez, R. (2008). It's one of those things that you do to help the family: Language brokering and the development of immigrant adolescents. *Journal of Adolescent Research, 23*, 515–543.

Dybdahl, R., & Hundeide, K. (1998). Childhood in the Somali context: Mothers' and children's ideas about childhood and parenthood. *Psychology and Developing Societies, 10*, 131–145.

Eccles J. S., Midgely, C., Buchanan, C. M., Wigfield, A., Reuman, D., & MacIver, D. (1993). Development in adolescence: The impact of stage/environment fit. *American Psychologist, 48*, 90–101.

Eccles J. S., Wigfield, A., Harold, R. D., & Blumenfeld, P. (1993). Age and gender differences in children's self- and task perceptions during elementary school. *Child Development, 64*, 830–847.

Entwisle, D., & Hayduk, L. (1978). *Too great expectations: Young children's academic outlook.* Baltimore MD: John Hopkins University Press.

Fleer, M., & Hedegaard, M. (2010). Children's development as participation in everyday practices. *Mind, Culture, and Activity, 17*, 149–168.

Flynn, E. (2008). Investigating children as cultural magnets: Do young children transmit redundant information along diffusion chains? *Philosophical Transactions of the Royal Society: Biological Sciences 363*, 3541–3551.

Fuligni A. J. (2012). Gaps, conflicts, and arguments between adolescents and their parents. *New Directions for Child and Adolescent Development, 135*, 105–110.

Goodnow, J. J. (2013). Refugees, asylum seekers, displaced persons: Children in precarious positions. In G. Melton, A. Ben-Arieh, J. Cashmore, G. S. Goodman, & N. K. Worley (Eds.), *The SAGE Handbook of Child Research* (pp. 339–360). New York, NY: SAGE.

Goodnow, J. J., & Lawrence, J. A. (2013). Cultural contexts and development. To appear in M. Bornstein and T. Leventhal (Eds.), *Children in contexts*. In W. Damon (series ed.) & R. M. Lerner (vol. 1), *Theoretical models of human development. Handbook of child psychology* (7th ed.). New York, NY: Wiley.

Harris, P., & Corriveau, K. H. (2011). Young children's selective trust in informants. *Philosophical Transactions of the Royal Society, 366*, 1179–1187.

Hussein, F. (2011). Charter schools: Choice of Somali-American parents. *Bildhaan, an International Journal of Somali Studies, 11*, 150–163.

Ibrahim, H. H., Small, D., & Grimley, M. (2009). Parent/school interface: Current communication practices and their implications for Somali parents. *New Zealand Journal of Education Studies, 44*(2), 19–30.

Jones, L. (1998). Home and school numeracy experiences for young Somali pupils in Britain. *European Early Childhood Education Research Journal, 6*, 63–72.

Kahin, M. H. (1997). *Educating Somali children in Britain.* Stoke on Trent: Trentham Books.

Kwak, K. (2003). Adolescents and their parents: A review of intergenerational family relations for immigrant and non-immigrant families. *Human Development, 46*, 115–136.

Lawrence, J. A. Benedikt, R., & Valsiner, J. (1992). Homeless in the mind: A case-history of personal life in and out of a close orthodox community. *Journal of Social Distress and Homelessness, 1*, 157–176.

Lawrence, J. A., Brooker, A., & Goodnow, J. J. (2012). Finding a cultural home: In J. Bowes, R. Grace, & K. Hodge (Eds.), *Children, families and communities: Contexts and consequences* (4th ed., pp. 74–88). Sydney, Australia: Oxford University Press.

Lawrence, J. A., Campbell, H., & MacInnes, A. (2007). *Strengths and skills of kids.* Computer program. Melbourne, Australia: The University of Melbourne.

Lawrence, J. A., Collard, A., & Kaplan, I. (2013). Understanding the wellbeing of children: What helps children from refugee, immigrant and local backgrounds feel better. In K. De Gioria & P. Whiteman (Eds.), *Children and childhoods 3: Immigrant and refugee families* (pp. 111–133). Newcastle upon Tyne, England: Cambridge Scholars.

Lawrence, J. A., & Dodds, A. E. (2009). *Developmental research within the African pathways project: A report to Mission Australia on research activities.* Melbourne, Australia: The University of Melbourne.

Lawrence, J. A., Dodds, A. E., & Brooker, A. (2010). Constructing research knowledge with refugee young people: Using computer-assisted techniques. *ISSBD Bulletin, 2,* 26–29.

Marsh, H. W., & Ayotte, V. (2003). Do multiple dimensions of self-concept become more differentiated with age? The differential distinctiveness hypothesis. *Journal of Educational Psychology, 95,* 687–706.

Mason, J., & Danby, J. (2011). Children as experts in their lives: child inclusive research. *Child Indicators Research, 4,* 185–189.

Mistry, J., & Wu, J. (2010). Navigating cultural worlds and negotiating identities: A conceptual model. *Human Development, 53,* 5–25.

Mohamed, A., & Yusuf, A. M. (2011). Somali parent-child conflict in the Western world: Some brief reflections. *Bildhaan, an International Journal of Somali Studies, 11,* 164–173.

Nicholls, J. G. (1979). Development of perception of own attainment and causal attributions for success and failure in reading. *Journal of Educational Psychology, 71,* 94–99.

Nilsson, J. E., Barazanji, D. M., Heintzelman, A., Siddiqi, M., & Shilla, Y. (2012). Somali women's reflections on the adjustment of their children in the United States. *Journal of Multicultural Counseling and Development, 40,* 240–252.

Oppedal, B. (2006). Development and acculturation. In D. Sam & J. Berry (Eds.), *The Cambridge handbook of acculturation psychology* (pp. 97–111). Cambridge, England: Cambridge University Press.

Portes, A., & Rumbaut, R. G. (2001). *Legacies: The story of the immigrant second generation.* Berkeley CA: University of California Press.

Renzaho, A. M. N., Green, J., Mellor, D., & Swinburn, B. (2011). Parenting, family functioning and lifestyle in a new culture: The case of African migrants in Melbourne, Victoria, Australia. *Child and Family Social Work. 16,* 228–240.

Rudmin, F. W. (2003). Critical history of the acculturation psychology of assimilation, separation, integration, and marginalization. *Review of General Psychology, 7,* 3–37.

Rutter, J. (2006). *Refugee children in the UK.* Maidenhead, England: Open University Press.

Schwarz, M. (2009). Is psychology based on a methodological error? *Integrative Psychological & Behavioral Sciences, 43,* 185–213.

Shweder, R. A., Goodnow, J. J., Hatano, G., LeVine, R. A., Markus, H. R., & Miller, P. J. (2006). The cultural psychology of development: One mind, many mentalities. In W. Damon (Series ed.) and R. M. Lerner (Vol. 1), *Theoretical models of human development. Handbook of child psychology* (Vol 1., 6th ed. pp. 716–792). New York, NY: Wiley.

St. Luke's Innovative Resources. (2005). *Strength cards for kids.* Bendigo, Australia: St. Luke's.

Telzer, E. H. (2010). Expanding the acculturation gap-distress model: An integrative review of research. *Human Development, 53,* 313–340.

Wang, Q. (2004). The emergence of cultural self-constructs: Autobiographical memory and self-description in European American and Chinese children. *Developmental Psychology, 48,* 3–15.

Wang, Q., Doan, S. N., & Song, Q. (2010). Talking about internal states in mother-child reminiscing influences children's self-representations: A cross-cultural study. *Cognitive Development, 25,* 380–393.

Warsame, S. (2010). School for all? Home-school cooperation and school development as conditions for supporting Somali children's learning. *Finnish Journal of Ethnicity and Migration, 5*(3), 17–26.

Wigfield, A., & Karpathian, M. (1991). Who am I and what can I do? Children's self-concepts and motivation in achievement situations. *Educational Psychologist, 26,* 233–261.

CHAPTER 12

RELIGIOSITY AND HAPPINESS OF AMERICAN-MUSLIM YOUTHS

An Empirical Study of Faith Maturity and Subjective Well-Being

Chang-Ho Ji

ABSTRACT

This chapter explores the state of personal religiosity and subjective well-being of American Muslim youths and the relationship between these two psychological attributes. Adapting the theory of patriarchal interpretation of Islam and Muslim faith, this chapter also examines the moderating effect of gender between faith maturity and subjective well-being. The samples are taken from 336 Muslim youths age 18–20 in southern California. The results show that American Muslim youths are highly religious as well as relatively happy about their life in the United States. Mature faith is found to increase subjective well-being of the Muslim youths. The moderating-gender effect hypothesis is also supported. Vertical faith maturity is significant in

Growing Up Between Two Cultures: Problems and Issues of Muslim Children, pp. 291–311
Copyright © 2014 by Information Age Publishing
All rights of reproduction in any form reserved.

accounting for the variance in male Muslim youth's subjective well-being, whereas it is the horizontal trait of faith maturity that is more influential in relation to female Muslim youths.

This chapter intends to contribute to the study of Muslim youths in Western countries in two different ways. It first provides an empirical look at the state of religiosity and subjective well-being of American-Muslim youths and the relationship between these two psychological attributes. To this end, the analysis measures religiosity and subjective well-being with valid, reliable, and theory-based psychological instruments. Doing so enhances credibility of the present study as well as offers an opportunity to reassess some conclusions of previous studies on subjective well-being of Muslim youths in Western countries.

Second, this study intends to go one step further by addressing a more theoretical question of whether or not the importance of personal religiosity to subjective well-being varies between the male and female Muslim youths. Are male American-Muslim youths more religious and satisfied with their life than are female American-Muslim youths? Related to this question is whether the linkage between religiosity and subjective well-being differs across males and females among Muslim youths in the United States.

Research of Muslim Religiosity and Happiness

Over the course of the last three decades, happiness has been a popular topic in psychological and social science inquiry. It is commonly defined as a positive state of mind (Argyle, 1987), representing a preponderance of positive over negative affect and as personal content with life as a whole. Not surprisingly, considerable theoretical and empirical effort has been exerted toward understanding the determinants of personal happiness including material well-being (Fischer, 2008), family factors (Amato, 1994), and personality and personal values (Jacob & Brinkerhoff, 1999) among many others.

As part of the inquiry, there has been ample research on the salience of personal religiosity on perceived happiness. One consistent finding derived from these studies is that both inner spirituality and institutional religiousness are significantly and positively correlated with personal happiness (Holder, Coleman, & Wallace, 2010). For instance, review studies by Cohen (2002) and Francis, Jones, and Wilcox (2000) concluded that happiness was significantly associated with church attendance, religious commitment, general spirituality, satisfaction with church activities, religious beliefs, religious identity, religious coping, and attitude toward Christianity, even though published studies did not always report strong correlations (see also Lewis & Cruise, 2006). This view was largely in line with Argyle (2002) who conducted a meta-analysis of 56 religiosity-happiness studies. Also consistent with this array of studies is the investigation into spiritual well-being by Rowold (2011), in which spiritual well-being was found to predict levels of perceived happiness. Knowledge of religion might be the only religious attribute that often fails to substantially correlate with personal happiness and life satisfaction (Holder, Coleman, & Wallace, 2010).

The above studies, however, provide primarily analysis of Christian subjects, most affiliated with Protestant churches. Relatively little research has occurred in relation to Muslims except for a few studies. A first exception lies in the recent effort by Abdel-Khalek (2011) who studied the association between religious belief and perceived life quality of Kuwait Muslim college students. Abdel-Khalek concluded that religious belief would be an important component of self-rated quality of life among Muslim individuals. In a similar vein, Alavi (2007) chose Iranian students and noticed a significant, positive relationship between religious behavior and subjective well-being. A couple of other published studies are resonating with this point of view: Abdel-Khalek (2006, 2007), Baroun (2006), and Abdel-Khalek and Lester (2009).

Yet, most of these Muslims studies are plagued with measurement caveats as they used one or two generic, unreliable items rather than a psychometrically sound inventory in measuring personal religiosity. For example, in Abdel-Khalek's (2011) study, religiosity was operationalized by asking two items: "What is your level of religiosity in general?" and "What is the strength of your religious belief when compared to others?" Despite Abdel-Khalek's assertion for the validity and reliability of such a measurement, it is possible that his research employed a psychologically dubious measure of personal religiosity, thus making his findings difficult to fully accept without further corroboration.

Further, apart from such a measurement concern, no research has ever taken place centering on young Muslim people growing up and living in non-Muslim or Western countries. Research advances made up to now were grounded in Muslim-majority countries. For this reason, noteworthy is a study by Werkuyten and Nekuee (1999) who surveyed Iranian Muslim refugees living in the Netherlands. In view of this study, social discrimination made stronger ethnic identification that had a harmful effect on self-mastery. Lower self-mastery subsequently led to lower subjective well-being. Cultural conflict had a direct negative influence on subject well-being. It also had an indirect effect through self-esteem. Werkuyten and Nekuee, however, were only interested in whether or not and how happiness was dependent on discrimination and cultural conflict. Absent in their study was the salience of personal religiosity in conjunction with perceived happiness, even though religion would play a prominent role in shaping Muslim perception of and attitude toward their life.

In view of qualitative research, Muslims in Western countries live under high levels of isolation, anxiety, fear, and social phobia (Abdo, 2006; Kwan, 2008; Salzbrunn, 2012; Thun, 2012). They are portrayed in the literature as experiencing higher prejudice and more hate crime than any other minority group. This assertion would be taken particularly seriously for young Muslims granted that adolescents and college-age young adults often represent one of the most vulnerable population groups in terms of stress and depression (Khuwaja, Selwyn, Kapadia, McCurdy, & Khuwaja, 2007). Similarly, Tindongan (2011, pp. 72–73) contended that young American-Muslims are especially worrisome because they not only have to "encounter [developmental] difficulties as they grow into adulthood" but also face a very "rough terrain of obstacles" in their American school due to the September 11 event. In support of this claim, opinion surveys show that, compared to other religions, Islam is indeed viewed less favorably by most American people (Altareb, 1996).

Notwithstanding this array of qualitative studies, we still lack empirical data about the subjective well-being of young Muslims in Western countries. We as yet know little about how religious Western-Muslim youths are and what influence Muslim faith exerts on subjective well-being of these young Muslims. This chapter attempts to fill these research gaps by referring to a quantitative data set from college-age Muslim youths in the United States.

Faith Maturity and Subjective Well-Being

The present chapter refers to faith maturity in assessing personal religiosity. To begin with faith maturity, in the psychology of religion literature, faith maturity typically addresses "the priorities, commitments, and perspectives" of "a person of vibrant and life-transforming faith" across most religious traditions (Benson, Donahue, & Erickson, 1993, p. 2). It applies to religious traits and experiences of different religions, depreciating denominational, economic, social, and racial specificity (Ji, 2004). The concept centers on the value, process, and behavioral facet of personal religion, giving more weight to how beliefs are held rather than to what is believed by religious people and communities. In line of this reasoning, the Faith Maturity Scale was developed by Benson, Donahue, and Erickson (1993) with the broad framework that mature faith involves both one's personal relationship to God (vertical faith maturity) and one's connection with others that is exhibited through altruistic sentiments, community involvement, and concern for social justice (horizontal faith maturity) (Hui, Ng, Mok, Lau, & Cheung, 2011; Ji, 2004; Sanders, 1998).

Faith maturity is known to help individuals cope with psychological adjustment as well as life- and work-related distress (Harrowfield & Gardner, 2010; Salsman & Carlson, 2005); it is also reportedly predictive of personal involvement in religious activities and youth ministry (Gane & Kijai, 2006; Hui, Ng, Mok, Lau, & Cheung, 2011). Of the two dimensions, according to Hui and others (2011), horizontal faith has an impressive linkage with social relationship and environmental protection, while its connection with other criterion variables such as religious practice is not as strong as that of vertical faith. This finding was replicated by other studies as well (Garland, Myers, & Wolfer, 2008; Ji, Pendergraft, & Perry, 2006; Sanders, 1998; Sherr, Garland, & Wolfer, 2007). Based on this differential pattern of relationship, Hui and others contended that a mature and balanced religious life should contain a horizontal facet of faith maturity in addition to the vertical dimension to transcend the self by concern for humanity and community.

Building on the faith maturity literature, this chapter examines the degree to which faith maturity affects subjective well-being of college-age Muslim youths in the United States. As stated above, the significance of religiousness within personal perception and experiences of happiness is distinctive and well-documented in the literature. Religious people, regardless of their religious background, tend to report greater happiness (Diener, Tay, & Myers, 2011; Hackney & Sanders, 2003; Koenig & Larson, 2001) and also exhibit fewer psychological problems such as depression, anxiety, and substance abuse (Koenig & Larson, 2001; Ji, Perry, & Clarke-Pine, 2011; Waite & Lehrer, 2003).

By the same logic, I anticipate that the higher faith maturity American-Muslim youths have, the greater subjective well-being they will manifest. Faith maturity is closely associated with intrinsic religiosity and doctrinal orthodoxy, which are conducive to high levels of subjective well-being (Ji, 2004; Newton & McIntosh, 2010; Salsman & Carlson, 2005; Wong-McDonald & Gorsuch, 2004). Accordingly, it would be logical to expect that increased faith maturity leads to increased subjective well-being among Muslim youths in the United States.

Gender Differences

With respect to gender differences, my hypothesis is that female American-Muslim youths are more religious than their male counterparts. The gender gap in personal religiosity is well established in psychology of religion, which Sullins (2006) described as one of the most consistent findings in the religiosity literature. A variety of accounts have been offered to explain this phenomenon from a biological explanation (Miller & Stark, 2002; Stark 2002) to a socialization-based power-control theory (Collett & Lizardo, 2009). The biological theory claims that gender differences in propensity toward risky behavior is at the heart of religious disparity between men and women. The power-control theory, on the other hand, contends that socioeconomic status, education, and patriarchal versus egalitarian family background and structure determine the nature and extent of male and female religiousness.

This chapter, following the dominant view, expects to find a gender gap in faith maturity between male and female Muslim youth in the United States. Religious differences between men and women in Muslim countries seem to be rather clear: women are found to be more religious than men on most measures of personal religiosity (Gonzalez, 2011). For Muslim immigrants, as for those in Muslim home countries, Islam is a salient foundation of their personal, ethnic, and cultural identity regardless of the level of acculturation (Britto & Amer, 2007). The nature and extent of Muslim commitment to their religion found in home countries reportedly remain more or less the same among Muslim immigrants to Western countries (Diehl, Koenig, & Ruckdeschel, 2009). In some cases, religious conventionalism becomes even more distinctive for second generation young Muslims. If such is the case, the gender-religion linkage noticed in Muslim countries is likely to be persistent among Muslim youths growing up and living in the United States.

Turning to subjective well-being, this chapter estimates the moderator effect of gender on the importance of faith maturity to subjective well-being. I expect to find empirical support for the following gender-variance hypothesis: the affirmative effect of vertical faith on subjective well-being is more distinctive among male American-Muslim youths, whereas horizontal faith is more influential in relation to female American-Muslim youths.

My hypothesis originates in a patriarchal interpretation of Islam and Muslim tradition. According to Hopkins (2006, p. 337), studies on masculinity in traditional Islam have reached "a critical mass" in the related literature, strongly agreeing that Islam, in general, is characterized by patriarchal interpretation of Allah, the Koran, and its religious teachings. Moreover, popular Islam not only places significant weight on Allah's patriarchal image but prompts Muslim men to develop appropriate gender roles, authority, leadership, and other masculine attributes following the model of Allah in its conventional religious interpretation (cf. Afary, 2009; Bonate, 2006; Kazemi, 2000). Accordingly, associated with Allah and his power, young Muslim men may perceive Islam and the male deity as effective discourses for them by which they find the meaning of their life, alleviate stress and depression, and enhance self-satisfaction, which together in turn conjure up the increase of overall subjective well-being.

In contrast, the dominant interpretation of Islam and Allah as being patriarchal and masculine might work as an obstacle for young Muslim women, in particular those living in the United States and Western countries, when they depend on vertical faith to foster positive thoughts and subjective well-being. Instead, female Muslim youths would turn to the horizontal aspect of religious faith that promotes a caring and bonding relationship with other people and service to humanity. The affective and human-relational dimension of religious faith has often been identified as salient among women in patriarchal religions because women in such religious environments are commonly denied access to religious consummation other than via deference to male leadership (Jacobs, 1984; Wright & D'Antonio, 1980). This differs from men who have a capacity for and means of approach to authority, power, and leadership that yield critical incentives for them to stay in and promote the religion. In this vein, it is my expectation that female American-Muslim youths tend to rely on the horizontal aspect of faith to enhance their subjective well-being, while male Muslim youths are inclined to the vertical relationship and submission to Allah and his power and control for personal happiness and fulfillment.

METHODOLOGY

Samples

The sample was comprised of 336 Muslim youths age 18–20 who were affiliated with two Muslim youth organizations and three public- and private-college student associations in southern California. For possible survey research, I initially contacted 19 Muslim college student associations, youth organizations, and mosques in the region through local Muslim informants, students, college professors, and research associates. Five of the 19 organizations agreed to participate in the research after reviewing the questionnaire, including two youth organizations with the condition that only those aged 18 years old or above would be surveyed.[1] There were roughly a total number of 600–650 youths in those participating organizations. The questionnaire was then administered with their leaders' support and endorsements, via internet and site visitation to their various religious and social gatherings.

The participants averaged 9.54 years of residence in the United States ($SD = 3.75$), and 48.35% were identified as women. Just over half of the sample (51.19%) belonged to one large public university student association, while the rest were rather evenly spread over one small public university student association (11.31%), one private university student association (13.39%), and two youth organizations (10.42% and 13.69%). Male samples came from four of the five organizations (except for one youth organization); female samples represented all the five organizations. Participants were also asked to report educational background: 18.75% were high school students and 81.25% undergraduate college students.

Variables

The dependent variable in this chapter was drawn from the Satisfaction with Life Scale, one of the most popular self-report measurements of subjective well-being. This five-item inventory has been frequently used (e.g., Ayyash-Abdo & Alamuddin, 2007; Werkuyten & Nekuee, 1999; Zhang & Leung, 2002) since its development and validation by Diener, Emmons, Larsen, and Griffin (1985). The test developers claimed the inventory was designed to gauge the extent of "global satisfaction" that an individual has toward his or her life.

For the analysis, as presented in the upper tier of Table 12.1, the 7-point five items were subject to factor analysis using the principal axis factor method and varimax rotation, which indicated that they measured a single construct of personal subjective well-being. Scale reliability was assessed by computing Cronbach alpha: the estimate was .61. The five items were averaged to measure subjective well-being.

With respect to the predictors, the 7-point Faith Maturity Scale was used to measure faith maturity (Benson, Donahue, & Erickson, 1993). The original inventory consists of 12 items reportedly measuring two components of vertical and horizontal faith maturity. For the study, 8 of the 12 items were selected to cut the length of the survey questionnaire and to increase the response rate of the participants. The eight items were then subject to factor analysis using the principal axis factor method and varimax rotation, which gave two factors explaining 61.33 % of the total variance. The lower tier of Table 12.1 presents the results of the factor analysis by item. As can be seen in the table, both factors were comprised of four items each. A first factor was dominated by the items measuring personal relationship with Allah, which was named Vertical Faith Maturity. The other factor was labeled Horizontal Faith Maturity. It was associated with the items on the relation with other people and responsibility for the world. Cronbach alpha values for the two factors were .68 and .73, in the order given. The mean

Table 12.1.   Summary of Items and Factor Loadings for the Satisfaction With Life Scale and the Faith Maturity Scale

	Factor Loading	
Item	1	2
The Satisfaction with Life Scale		
The conditions of my life are excellent.	.90	
I am satisfied with my life.	.89	
So far I have gotten the important things I want in life.	.76	
If I could live my life over, I would change almost nothing.	.67	
In most ways my life is close to my ideal.	.64	
The Faith Maturity Scale		
I have a real sense that Allah is guiding me.	.76	.15
I feel Allah's presence in my relationships with other people.	.76	.29
I feel life is filled with meaning and purpose.	.76	.13
The things I do reflect a commitment to Allah.	.69	.29
I give significant portions of time and money to help other people.	.19	.77
I show that I care a great deal about reducing poverty in my country and throughout the world.	.26	.74
I feel a sense of responsibility for reducing pain and suffering in the world.	.20	.69
I seek out opportunities to help me grow spiritually.	.08	.60

Note. $N = 336$.

scores of the corresponding four items were computed for the Vertical and Horizontal Faith Maturity scores.

In addition to faith maturity, I included a couple of control variables relevant to the prediction of subjective well-being: gender, education, years of residence in the United States, and the organizations that the participants were affiliated with.[2] The happiness literature reports the salience that gender and education have on the prediction of subjective well-being (Kageyama, 2012; Lacey, Kierstead, & Morey, 2012; O'Brien, 2008). On the other hand, the length of stay in the United States was reported by

Khuwaja, Selwyn, Kapadia, McCurdy, and Khuwaja (2007) to inversely correlate with sociopsychological stress and depression. For the present analysis, the gender and education variables were coded a value of 1 when participants were identified as male and in college education, and zero for female and in high school. Of the five participating organizations, the public university student association that produced the largest sample size served as the reference category in dummy coding.

RESULTS

Descriptive Analysis

Table 12.2 summarizes descriptive statistics of faith maturity and subjective well-being. The mean well-being score was 4.37, one equivalent to 62.43% of the possible maximum score. This finding indicates the American-Muslim samples as a whole feel relatively happy about their overall life condition.

Table 12.2.   Descriptive Statistics and Gender Differences in Faith Maturity and Subjective Well-Being

	All Sample		Female		Male		
	M	SD	M	SD	M	SD	t (333)
Vertical Faith Maturity	6.04	.99	6.15	1.00	5.92	.96	2.24**
Horizontal Faith Maturity	5.74	.98	5.87	.99	5.63	.95	1.99**
Subjective Well-Being	4.37	1.05	4.63	1.12	4.13	.93	4.40*

Note. $*p < .01; **p < .05.$

Regarding faith maturity, the participants reported higher levels of vertical faith maturity than horizontal faith maturity. The mean vertical faith score equaled 86.29% of the maximum score, which was slightly greater than the 82.00% for horizontal faith. Notwithstanding this hiatus, the Muslim participants should be portrayed as quite religious on both dimensions of faith maturity.

Next, the scores of faith maturity and subjective well-being were subjected to tests of statistical significance in order to compare the male and female participants. As given in the right column of Table 12.2, significant differences appeared in both faith maturity and subjective well-being. The female participants scored significantly higher than the males on the vertical and horizontal faith scales. Also, higher levels of subjective well-being were found from the female respondents.

Hypothesis Testing

To begin with the entire sample, the coefficients for the faith maturity variables in Table 12.3 show that the increase of both vertical and horizontal faith was linked with the growth of subjective well-being. The square of the partial correlation coefficient for vertical faith indicated that it explained 4% of the variance of subjective well-being. This ratio was greater than the 2% for horizontal faith, positing that vertical faith was more influential in predicting subjective well-being than was horizontal faith.

Table 12.3. Regression Analysis Summary for Faith Maturity and Demographic Variables Predicting Subjective Well-Being

	B	SE	$r+$
Constant	.19	.94	
Age	–.01	.01	–.01
Male	.02	.12	.01
College Education	.36**	.18	.11
Youth Organization A	.31	.17	.05
Youth Organization B	1.30*	.29	.38
Private Univ. Student Assoc.	1.31*	.31	.25
Public Univ. Student Assoc. A	.06	.18	.02
Vertical Faith Maturity	.22*	.18	.19
Horizontal Faith Maturity	.13**	.06	.13
R Sq. / Adj. R Sq.	.25 / .23		
F (df)	12.04* (9, 325)		

Note. *$p < .01$; **$p < .05$; +r = partial correlation coefficient; categorical variables: gender (0 female++, 1 male), education (0 high school++, 1 college), organization (1 youth organization A, 2 youth organization B, 3 private university student association, 4 public university student association A, 5 public university student association B++); ++reference group.

As to the control variables, one distinctive finding lies in the significant effects of the Muslim organization dummy variables. Two organizations stood out with significantly higher levels of subjective well-being as compared to the reference student association. They were affiliated with either a suburban area or private university known for economic wealth, high housing prices, and high tuition and education fee. The socioeconomic aspect of the city and college might be the source of the variance from the reference student associations. In addition, the college student respondents reported higher scores on subjective well-being than did the high school students. Yet, gender and years of residence in the United States were not statistically significant in accounting for subjective well-being, which stands at odds with previous studies asserting that gender and years of residence are significant in predicting happiness and depression of Muslim youths (Kageyama, 2012; Khuwaja, Selwyn, Kapadia, McCurdy, & Khuwaja, 2007).

Having considered the entire sample, I next considered the moderating effects of gender on the relationship between faith maturity and subjective well-being, as expressed by my research hypothesis. To test this hypothesis, the American-Muslim participants were grouped according to gender. The results reported in Table 12.4 offer strong empirical support for the expectation that the relationship between religiosity and subjective well-being varies between the male and female Muslim participants. For the male respondents, vertical faith was positively associated with subjective well-being, explaining 11% of the total variance, which was an impressive explanatory power. Horizontal faith, however, was not significant. Reversely, horizontal faith significantly contributed to the growth of the female participants' subjective well-being with an explained variance of 5%, while vertical faith was of little help in predicting subjective well-being.

DISCUSSION

Faith Maturity of Muslim Youth

The present study shows that college-age American-Muslim youths are quite religious when measured by vertical and horizontal faith maturity. The participants, on the average, have reported horizontal and vertical faith scores corresponding to 82% and 86% of the maximum score, respectively.

Compare these proportions with those I previously acquired from evangelical college students in southern California (Ji, 2004). These Christian college students had a mean vertical and horizontal score equivalent to 54% and 67% of their respective highest score. A nationwide survey of Protestant youths reported an average horizontal and vertical faith score of 60% and 74% of the maximum score (Ji, Pendergraft, & Perry, 2006). Salsman

Table 12.4. Estimating the Moderating Effects of Gender on the Relationship Between Faith Maturity and Subjective Well-Being

	Male			Female		
	B	SE	r+	B	SE	r+
Constant	.63	1.04		−.62	1.72	
Age	−.01	.01	−.07	−.00	.01	−.02
College Education	.37	.21	.17	.50	.34	.12
Youth Organization A	.51	.72	.12	.41	.33	.10
Youth Organization B				1.43*	.20	.50
Private Univ. Assoc.	.94*	.35	.21	1.42*	.31	.35
Public Univ. Assoc. A	−.20	.20	−.08	.57	.31	.15
Vertical Faith	−.32	.09	−.33	.16	.09	.14
Horizontal Faith	−.01	.09	−.01	.21	.08	.22
R Sq. / Adj. R Sq.	.19 / .17			.31 / .27		
F (df)	5.04* (7, 165)			8.41* (8, 153)		

Note. *$p < .01$; **$p < .05$; +r = partial correlation coefficient; categorical variables: gender (0 female++, 1 male), education (0 high school++, 1 college), organization (1 youth organization A, 2 youth organization B, 3 private university student association, 4 public university student association A, 5 public university student association B++); ++reference group.

and Carlson (2005) studied college student in Kentucky: the horizontal and vertical faith mean scores of their participants were parallel to 53% and 61% of the maximum scores. Compared to the ones from the present Muslim samples, these ratios from non-Muslim youths are smaller in size by 15–25 percentage points. This finding may postulate that American-Muslim youths are more religious relative to their Christian counterparts.

Regarding gender differences, the present data suggest that female American-Muslim youths are more religious than male American-Muslim youths, particularly in vertical faith. That females are more vertical and horizontal in faith maturity than males is aligned with the previous findings of Hui and his colleagues (2011). Here, non-Muslim females reported significantly higher faith maturity scores than did males by four percentage points, which is compatible with the four-percentage-point difference from the present Muslim samples. This congruity posits that the pattern of gender difference in faith maturity might be persistent across Islam and other religions.

Subjective Well-Being of Muslim Youth

Equally germane to the present study, the Muslim participants are noticed to be relatively happy and satisfied with their current life condition. They have reported an average subjective well-being score that corresponds to about 65% of the possible maximum score on the scale. In addition, the female participants are found to feel significantly more content with their life than do the male samples.

Are American-Muslim youths particularly unhappier relative to their non-Muslim counterparts in the United States? The test development chapter by Diener, Emmons, Larsen, and Griffin (1985) would be a useful source to address this. Their subjects were 176 non-Muslim college students at the University of Illinois for whom the researchers used a total score of 5 items on the 7-point scale. The participants yielded a mean total score of 23.5, one equal to 67% of the maximum total score. Accordingly, I have calculated my American-Muslim participants' total subjective well-being score by summing their ratings of the five items on the same 7-point scale. The Muslim students report a mean total score of 21.73 with $SD =$ 5.26, which is parallel to 62% of the maximum score. The difference is statistically significant, t (335) = –6.17, $p < .001$.

This observation finds support from other subjective well-being studies. Pavot, Diener, Colvin, and Sandvik (1991) employed 136 college students and reported a mean total score of 24.49. Two additional studies took place in the Midwest. Coutinho and Wooley (2004) surveyed 157 college youths at a Midwestern university; Oishi, Diener, Suh, and Lucas (1999) measured subjective well-being of 121 University of Illinois students. Another study was conducted by Utsey, Ponterott, Reynolds, and Cancelli (2000) with reference to 213 African American college students from several regions in the United States. The average scores for these three studies were 24.54, 23.36, and 20.67, in the order given. Notice that three of the four scores are significantly greater than the 21.73 for my Muslim students with t (335) = –9.62, t (335) = –9.79, and t (335) = –5.68. All comparisons are significant at $p < .001$. The only exception pertains to the African American students studied by Utsey, Ponterott, Reynolds, and Cancelli (2000): the present Muslim samples exhibit higher levels of subjective well-being than the African American group, t (335) = 3.70, $p < .001$.

Put together, the above discussion suggests a small gap in subjective well-being between college-age American-Muslim and non-Muslim youths. Possibly, Muslim youths are slightly less happy compared to non-Muslim youths: the score differences between the two groups range from 5% to 7% of the maximum total measurement score. For this reason, it is important to recall that the Muslim participants' subjective well-being is higher than the one for African American college students, an ethnic group that remains at a more pronounced social, educational, and economic disadvantaged status in many areas than White Americans. The difference is about 3% of the maximum score.

This is to say that college-age American-Muslim youths are relatively happy, and in extent, their subjective well-being is measured somewhere between those of White and African American youths. There seems to be no evidence in the present data to assert that Muslim youths in the United States are particularly discontented with their life condition. My suggestion finds further support from an earlier study on the acculturation and stress of young female Muslim immigrants to the United States (Khuwaja, Selwyn, Kapadia, McCurdy, & Khuwaja, 2007). In this study, the authors found only moderate levels of depression and stress among the participants, levels compatible with those for non-Muslim American female youths. A study of older immigrants yielded the same conclusion with respect to depression among Muslim adults in the United States (Abu-Bader, Tirmazi, & Ross-Sheriff, 2011). About half of the American-Muslim adults reported depression, yet it was at best average or moderate when its mean score was placed on the entire depression scale. This level of depression is rather typical of other new immigrant adults to the United States as well (e.g., Kim, Sangalang, & Kihl, 2012).

Religiosity in Subjective Well-Being

As to the role of religiosity in subjective well-being, the results support the research hypothesis and the majority view in the literature that emphasizes the importance of religion to subjective well-being. In the present data, as faith maturity of American-Muslim youths increases, the extent of their subjective well-being increases, which holds for both vertical and horizontal faith. That is, for American-Muslim youths as a whole, vertical faith engenders personal happiness in much the same way as horizontal faith maturity prompts subjective well-being.

At the same time, however, it is equally important to note that the relationship between religiosity and subjective well-being may differ between male and female Muslim youths in the United States. Vertical faith is significantly and positively related to the satisfaction that the male Muslim youths have toward their life. Vertical faith represents the so-called conventional form of Muslim religiosity that promotes a close relationship with Allah and total dependence on his divine power. The affirmative influence of this form of traditional Islam may be exclusive to the male Muslim youths. According to the present data, it does not relate to the subjective well-being of the young female Muslims.

This result may support my assumption that the mechanism that faith maturity affects subjective well-being of American-Muslim youths varies with gender. Vertical faith contributes to the increase of the male Muslim youths' subjective well-being, but it is horizontal faith that is key to the subjective well-being of the female Muslim youths. This gender variation, in my view, might be explained by the patriarchal presentation of Allah in popular Islam, one ushering female American-Muslim youths to the horizontal dimension of Islam to find meaning and utility for personal life and happiness.

Ideally I would have liked to test the gender-moderator hypothesis outside of the United States including the Middle East and Central Asia where Muslims constitute the majority of the populations. European countries with Muslim immigrants would also offer another interesting case in which to test the hypothesis. Unfortunately, such parallel studies of non-American settings have yet to be conducted. Nevertheless, the current example of the college-age Muslim youths of the United States provides some initial support for my theory and a direction for future studies.

CONCLUSION

The present study provides interesting insights into the religiosity and subjective well-being of college-age Muslim youths in the United States. Contrary to popular perception, Muslim youths might be relatively happy about their life in the United States. At least, I could not find clear evidence indicating that they are particularly unhappy with or frustrated at their current life condition, which stands in contrast with former qualitative studies that have often portrayed American-Muslim youths as unhappy, depressed, and at-risk. In addition, the data suggest that American-Muslim youths are highly religious in both vertical and horizontal faith maturity. They report a strong and intimate personal relationship with Allah and accept horizontal-faith values like service to neighborhood and humanity and acts of justice and mercy as salient in their religious belief. Likewise, American-Muslim youths are possibly more religious than their non-Muslim counterparts, even though a direct comparison was beyond the present study.

The results also reveal that mature faith is conducive to subjective well-being of Muslim youths in the United States. Religious faith seems to be a valuable psychological asset for American-Muslim youths to live a happy life in the United States. Concurrently, I also need to be attentive to the interaction between faith maturity and gender. Vertical faith maturity is significant in accounting for the variance in the male Muslim youth's subjective well-being, whereas it seems to be the horizontal trait of faith maturity that prompts happiness among the female Muslim youths. Put differently, gender tends to moderate the relationship between personal religiosity and subjective well-being of American-Muslim youths.

NOTES

1. The original intent of the present study was to study Muslim adolescents and high school students in the survey research area. Regretfully, this plan was modified to focus only on college-age Muslim youths because most of the contacted organizations, including all the local mosques, refused to participate in the research. In addition, it was quite difficult, if not impossible, to get individual parental approval and consent for their children to join the research.
2. Some readers might be interested in a comparison between Shia and Sunni Muslims. But I decided to eliminate the related item from the questionnaire based upon the request from the surveyed organizations and student associations. One informant said that the vast majority of the respondents were Sunni Muslims with roughly 10% being affiliated with Shia Islam.

REFERENCES

Abdel-Khalek, A. M. (2006). Happiness, health, and religiosity: Significant relations. *Mental Health, Religion, & Culture*, *9*, 85–97.

Abdel-Khalek, A. M. (2007). Religiosity, happiness, health, and psychopathology in a probability sample of Muslim adolescents. *Mental Health, Religion, & Culture*, *10*, 571–583.

Abdel-Khalek, A. M. (2011). Religiosity, subjective well-being, self-esteem, and anxiety among Kuwaiti Muslim adolescents. *Mental Health, Religion & Culture*, *14*, 129–140.

Abdel-Khalek, A. M., & Lester, D. (2009). A significant association between religiosity and happiness in a sample of Kuwaiti students. *Psychological Reports*, *105*, 381–382.

Abdo, G. (2006). *Mecca and main street: Muslim life in American after 9/11*. Oxford, England: Oxford University Press.

Abu-Bader, S. H., Tirmazi, M. T., & Ross-Sheriff, F. (2011). The impact of acculturation on depression among older Muslim immigrants in the United States. *Journal of Gerontological Social Work*, *54*, 425–448.

Afary, J. (2009). The sexual economy of the Islamic republic. *Iranian Studies*, *42*, 5–26.

Alavi, H. R. (2007). Correlatives of happiness in the university students of Iran (a religious approach). *Journal of Religion and Health*, *46*, 480–499.

Altareb, B. Y. (1996). Islamic spirituality in America: A middle path to unity. *Counseling & Values*, *41*, 29–38.

Amato, P. R. (1994). Father-child relations, mother-child relation, and offspring psychological well-being in early adulthood. *Journal of Marriage and Family*, *56*, 1031–1042.

Argyle, M. (1987). *The psychology of happiness*. London, England: Methuen.

Argyle, M. (2002). Religion. In M. Argyle (Ed.), *The psychology of happiness* (pp. 164–177). New York, NY: Routeledge.

Ayyash-Abdo, H., & Alamuddin, R. (2007). Predictors of subjective well-being among college youth in Lebanon. *Journal of Social Psychology*, *147*, 265–284.

Baroun, K. A. (2006). Relations among religiosity, health, happiness, and anxiety for Kuwaiti adolescents. *Psychological Reports*, *99*, 717–722.

Benson, P. L., Donahue, M. J., & Erickson, J. A. (1993). The Faith Maturity Scale: Conceptualization, measurement, and empirical validation. *Research in the Social Scientific Study of Religion*, *5*, 1–26.

Bonate, L. J. K. (2006). Matriliny, Islam, and gender in northern Mazambique. *Journal of Religion in Africa*, *36*, 139–166.

Britto, P. R., & Amer, M. M. (2007). An exploration of cultural identity patterns and the family context among Arab Muslim young adults in America. *Applied Development Science*, *11*, 137–150.

Cohen, A. B. (2002). The importance of spirituality in well-being for Jews and Christians. *Journal of Happiness Studies*, *3*, 287–310.

Collett, J. L., & Lizardo, O. (2009). A power-control theory of gender and religiosity. *Journal for the Scientific Study of Religion*, *48*, 213–231.

Coutinho, S. A., & Woolery, L. M. (2004). The need for cognition and life satisfaction among college students. *College Student Journal*, *38*, 203–206.

Diehl, C., Koenig, M., & Ruckdeschel, K. (2009). Religiosity and gender equality: Comparing natives and Muslim migrants in Germany. *Ethnic and Racial Studies*, *32*, 278–301.

Diener, E., Emmons R. A., Larsen, R. J., & Griffin, S. (1985). The Satisfaction with Life Scale. *Journal of Personality Assessment*, *49*, 71–76.

Diener, E., Tay, L., & Myers, D. G. (2011). The religion paradox: If religion makes people happy, why are so many dropping out? *Journal of Personality and Social Psychology*, *101*, 1278–1290.

Fischer, C. S. (2008). What wealth-happiness paradox? A short note on the American case. *Journal of Happiness Studies*, *9*, 219–226.

Francis, L. J., Jones, S. H., & Wilcox, C. (2000). Religiosity and happiness: During adolescence, young adulthood, and later life. *Journal of Psychology and Christianity*, *19*, 245–257.

Gane, B., & Kijai, J. (2006). The relationship between faith maturity, intrinsic and extrinsic orientations to religion and youth ministry involvement. *Journal of Youth Ministry*, *4*, 49–64.

Garland, D. R., Myers, D. M., & Wolfer, T. A. (2008). Social work with religious volunteers: Activating and sustaining community involvement. *Social Work*, *53*, 255–265.

Gonzalez, A. L. (2011). Measuring religiosity in a majority Muslim context: Gender, religious salience, and religious experience among Kuwaiti college student, a research note. *Journal for the Scientific Study of Religion*, *50*, 339–350.

Hackney, C. H., & Sanders, G. S. (2003). Religiosity and mental health: A meta-analysis of recent studies. *Journal for the Scientific Study of Religion*, *42*, 43–55.

Harrowfield, R., & Gardner, D. (2010). Faith at work: Stress and well-being among workers in Christian organizations. *Journal of Psychology and Christianity*, *29*, 208–217.

Holder, M. D., Coleman, B., & Wallace, J. M. (2010). Spirituality, religiousness, and happiness in children aged 8–12 years. *Journal of Happiness Studies*, *11*, 131–150.

Hopkins, P. E. (2006). Youthful Muslim masculinities: Gender and generational relations. *Transactions of the Institute of British Geographers*, *31*, 337–352.

Hui, C. H., Ng, E. C. W., Mok, D. S. Y., Lau, E. Y. Y., & Cheung, S. (2011). "Faith Maturity Scale" for Chinese: A revision and construct validation. *International Journal for the Psychology of Religion*, *21*, 308–322.

Jacobs, J. (1984). The economy of love in religious commitment: The deconversion of women from nontraditional religious movements. *Journal for the Scientific Study of Religion*, *23*, 155–171.

Jacob, J. C., & Brinkerhoff, M. B. (1999). Mindfulness and subjective well-being in the sustainability movement: A further elaboration of multiple discrepancies theory. *Social Indicator Research*, *46*, 341–368.

Ji, C. C. (2004). Faith maturity and doctrinal orthodoxy: A validity study of the Faith Maturity Scale. *Psychological Reports*, *95*, 993–998.

Ji, C. C., Pendergraft, L., & Perry, M. (2006). Religiosity, altruism, and altruistic hypocrisy: Evidence from Protestant adolescents. *Review of Religious Research*, *48*, 156–178.

Ji, C. C., Perry, T., & Clarke-Pine, D. (2011). Considering personal religiosity in adolescent delinquency: The role of depression, suicidal ideation, and church guideline. *Journal of Psychology and Christianity*, *30*, 3–15.

Kageyama, J. (2012). Happiness and sex difference in life expectancy. *Journal of Happiness Studies*, *13*, 947–967.

Kazemi, F. (2000). Gender, Islam, and politics. *Social Research*, *67*, 453–474.

Kim, B. J., Sangalang, C. C., & Kihl, T. (2012). Effects of acculturation and social network support on depression among elderly Korean immigrants. *Aging & Mental Health*, *16*, 787–794.

Koenig, H. G., & Larson, D. B. (2001). Religion and mental health: Evidence for an association. *International Review of Psychiatry*, *13*, 67–78.

Khuwaja, S., Selwyn, B. J., Kapadia, A., McCurdy, S., & Khuwaja, A. (2007). Pakistani Ismaili Muslim adolescent females living in the United States of America: Stresses associated with the process of adaptation to U.S. culture. *Journal of Immigrant & Minority Health*, *9*, 35–42.

Kwan, M. (2008). From oral histories to visual narratives: Re-presenting the post-September 11 experiences of the Muslim women in the USA. *Social and Cultural Geography*, *9*, 653–667.

Lacey, H., Kierstead, T., & Morey, D. (2012). De-biasing the age-happiness bias: Memory search and cultural expectations in happiness judgments across the lifespan. *Journal of Happiness Studies*, *13*, 647–658.

Lewis, C. A., & Cruise, S. M. (2006). Religion and happiness: Consensus, contradictions, comments and concerns. *Mental Health, Religion, and Culture*, *9*,

213–225. Miller, A. S., & Stark, R. (2002). Gender and religiousness: Can socialization explanations be saved? *American Journal of Sociology, 107,* 1399–1423.

Newton, A. T., & McIntosh, D. N. (2010). Specific religious beliefs in a cognitive appraisal model of stress and coping. *International Journal for the Psychology of Religion, 20,* 39–58.

O'Brien, C. (2008). Sustainable happiness: How happiness studies can contribute to a more sustainable future. *Canadian Psychology, 49,* 289–295.

Oishi, S., Diener, E., Suh, E., & Lucas, R. E. (1999). Value as a moderator in subjective well-being. *Journal of Personality, 67,* 157–184.

Pavot, W., Dienner, E., Colvin, C. R., & Sandvik, E. (1991). Further validation of the Satisfaction with Life Scale: Evidence for the cross-method convergence of well-being measures. *Journal of Personality Assessment, 57,* 149–161.

Rowold, J. (2011). Effects of spiritual well-being on subsequent happiness, psychological well-being, and stress. *Journal of Religion and Health, 50,* 950–963.

Salsman, J. M., & Carlson, C. R. (2005). Religious orientation, mature faith, and psychological distress: Elements of positive and negative associations. *Journal for the Scientific Study of Religion, 44,* 201–209.

Salzbrunn, M. (2012). Performing gender and religion: The veil's impact on boundary-making processes in France. *Women's Studies, 41,* 682–705.

Sanders, J. L. (1998). Religious ego identity and its relationship to faith maturity. *Journal of Psychology, 132,* 653–658.

Sherr, M. E., Garland, D. R., & Wolfer, T. A. (2007). The role of community service in the faith development of adolescents. *Journal of Youth Ministry, 6,* 43–54.

Stark, R. (2002). Physiology and faith: Addressing the "universal" gender difference in religious commitment. *Journal for the Scientific Study of Religion, 41,* 495–507.

Sullins, D. P. (2006). Gender and religion: Deconstructing universality, constructing complexity. *American Journal of Sociology, 112,* 838–880.

Thun, C. (2012). Norwegianness as lived citizenship: Religious women doing identity work at the intersections of nationality, gender and religion. *Nordic Journal of Religion & Society, 25,* 1–25.

Tindongan, C. W. (2011). Negotiating Muslim youth identity in a post-9/11 world. *High School Journal, 95,* 72–87.

Utsey, S. O., Ponterott, J. G., Reynolds, A. L., & Cancelli, A. A. (2000). Racial discrimination, coping satisfaction, and self-esteem among African Americans. *Journal of Counseling & Development, 78,* 72–80.

Waite, L. J., & Lehrer, E. L. (2003). The benefits from marriage and religion in the United States. *Population and Development Review, 29,* 255–275.

Werkuyten, M., & Nekuee, S. (1999). Subjective well-being, discrimination and cultural conflict: Iranians living in the Netherlands. *Social Indicators Research, 47,* 281–306.

Wong-McDonald, A., & Gorsuch, R. L. (2004). A multivariate theory of God concept, religious motivation, locus of control, coping, and spiritual well-being. *Journal of Psychology and Theology, 32,* 318–334.

Wright, S., & D'Antonio, W. (1980). The substructure of religion: A further study. *Journal for the Scientific Study of Religion, 19,* 292–301.

Zhang, L., & Leung, J. (2002). Moderating effects of gender and age on the relationship between self-esteem and life satisfaction in mainland Chinese. *International Journal of Psychology, 37,* 83–91.

CHAPTER 13

"THAT'S NOT WHAT I WANT FOR MY CHILDREN"

Islamic Schools as a Parental Response To Childhood Experiences of Mainstream British Schooling

Farah Ahmed

ABSTRACT

This chapter builds on Ahmed (2012) where I presented findings from a small-scale qualitative study that looked at home-schooling Muslim mothers who have developed an alternative education approach to mainstream British schooling called *Shakhsiyah Education*. Their work has led to the establishment of two small schools and Islamic teacher education courses to generate culturally coherent provision for Muslim children. Their motivation is in part a response to their own experiences as immigrant or second-generation Muslim children who attended mainstream British schools during the 1980s and 1990s. I present their concerns and motivations in some depth and go on to present their discussions on their hopes and ambitions for their own children and the challenges they have identified to generating culturally

Growing Up Between Two Cultures: Problems and Issues of Muslim Children, pp. 313–338
Copyright © 2014 by Information Age Publishing
All rights of reproduction in any form reserved.

coherent education for their children in the British context. Through presenting the insider voices of these women, this chapter will contribute to the discourse by providing both adult and children's perspectives as a group of Muslim women engage in reflexive discussion about their experiences as children, as parents and as teachers.

INTRODUCTION

This chapter presents some insider voices from the experiences of British Muslims growing up between two cultures. I aim to let these voices speak for themselves by presenting their own words, with minimal editing, in the hope that such a narrative presentation will qualitatively enhance the discourse taking place in other chapters in this book. I do not present a review of existing literature or attempt to offer a comparison with other research; instead I apply the concept of "naturalistic generalization" (Stake & Trumbull, 1982) as an appropriate mechanism for sharing small-scale qualitative case-study research. I offer up these specific insider voices to enhance the overall empathetic understanding of readers of this book through the vicarious experience of reading narrative accounts given by participants.

The Study—Muslim Mother-Educators Who Founded and/or Work in Islamic *Shakhsiyah* Foundation (ISF)[1]

The data presented here was collected during a small-scale qualitative study conducted in 2009–2010. The study was designed to explore the views of a group of home-schooling Muslim mother-educators who have developed an alternative education approach to mainstream British school-ing called *Shakhsiyah Education* (Personalized character education). Their work has led to the establishment of two small schools and Islamic teacher education courses with the aim of providing culturally coherent education for Muslim children. The objective of the study was to explore participants' understanding of the theory of *"Shakhsiyah Education"* as a culturally coher-ent alternative for their British Muslim children, and their attempts to implement this theory in their schools. *Shakhsiyah Education* refers to the fundamental aim of Islamic education as development of human personal-ity and the necessary synthesis of classical Islamic pedagogy with modern approaches as a means to realize holistic human development. Limitations of space do not allow for expositions of curricula used in the schools or detailed debate about the personal perspectives expressed by this group of women as given here. Findings from this study related to holistic Islamic

Education have already been published (Ahmed, 2012), and an analysis of the methodology used in this study can be found in Ahmed (2013).

In Ahmed (2012) it was noted that because the context of the study became highly politically charged due to false media allegations about the schools coinciding with the study, participants discussions became decidedly personal. It had already been anticipated that participants own experiences of growing up between two cultures may have a bearing on their motivation; but in the new climate, this issue became a focal point of many of the initial discussions that participants engaged in. Despite my involvement as an insider-researcher, as a founding member of the schools, and my awareness of my own personal motivations; I had not realized how much my colleagues' motivation was also linked to childhood experiences of British mainstream schooling. Their discussions explored their concerns and motivations in some depth as well as the hopes and ambitions they have for their own children. This was in addition to the discussion about the strengths of and challenges they face in generating a culturally coherent education. Through presenting an analysis of these mothers' views, this chapter will contribute to this book by providing both adult and children's perspectives as the participants speak about their experiences as children and as parents and teachers.

The majority of participants in the study were immigrant or second-generation Muslim children who attended mainstream British schools during the 1980s and 1990s (see Table 13.1).

Table 13.1 demonstrates that this is a diverse group of women, half of whom are in mixed-race marriages. As such they are aware that they are not simply navigating their identity and lives between two cultures but rather at the interface of multiple cultures. Their discussions as given below illustrate that what they hold in common is a deep commitment to an Islamic identity unifying all their other identities (Ahmed, 2012). This is their solution to being Muslim in Britain.

In relation to childhood experiences, 4 of the 10 participants immigrated to the United Kingdom during their early primary years; three were born in Britain and attended primary education here, another three immigrated as adults and have school age children in U.K. schools. As participants' personal experiences had not been the subject of the study they were reported as a side issue to findings as presented in Ahmed (2012); this chapter provides an opportunity to explore the impact of these personal experiences on their motivation for involvement in Islamic *Shakhsiyah* Foundation (ISF) in more depth. It looks also at their claims about *Halaqah*.

> *Halaqah* is a spiritual circle-time instituted by Prophet Muhammad in his *tarbiyah* (education) of early Muslims; it is conducted purely orally with students and teacher sitting in a circle on the floor. An integral part of

Table 13.1. PLEASE CAPTION TABLE

School-Leaders Halaqah Pseudonym	Age Range	Country of Origin	Approx Length of Time in Britain	Marital Status/ Background of Husband	No. of Years in Teaching/ Education Teaching Qualification	No. of Years in ISF or Home-Schooling Group	No. of Children	No. of Children Who Have Attended ISF
Farah (Researcher)	35–40	Pakistan	30 years	Married Husband of Mixed race Turkish - Pakistani	16 years PGCE	12 years	3	3
Aisha	35–40	Pakistan	Born in Britain	Married Husband Convert from Seychelles	16 years PGCE	12 years	8	7
Khadija	35–40	Kenya-East African Asian	26 years	Married Husband Pakistani Origin	12 years no Teaching Qualification	7 years	5	5
Salma	35–40	Iraq	17 years	Married Husband Iraqi	12 years no Teaching Qualification	12 years	3	2
Hafsa	35–40	Pakistan	Born in Britain	2nd Marriage Husband Convert West-Indian Origin	11 years no Teaching Qualification	9 years	4	4

(Table continues on next page)

Table 13.1. (Continued)

School-Leaders Halaqah Pseudonym	Age Range	Country of Origin	Approx Length of Time in Britain	Marital Status/ Background of Husband	No. of Years in Teaching/ Education Teaching Qualification	No. of Years in ISF or Home-Schooling Group	No. of Children	No. of Children Who Have Attended ISF
Zaynab	20–25	Congo Convert to Islam	20 years	Married Husband Ghanaian Origin	2.5 years no Teaching Qualification	2.5 years	1 (Under 3 years old)	0
Kulthum	35–40	Pakistan	5 years	Married Husband Pakistani Origin	12 years no Teaching Qualification	3 years	3	3
Ruqayyah	25–30	Pakistan	23 years	2nd Marriage Husband Pakistani Origin	3 years no Teaching Qualification	2.5 years	2	2
Fatimah	20–25	Pakistan	Born in Britain	Married Husband Pakistani Origin	9 months no Teaching Qualification	2 years (Previously worked as School Administrator)	0	0
Maryam	35–40	Indian/ Yemeni	13 years	Married Husband Indian/ Yemeni	6 years no Teaching Qualification	2.5 years	2	0

317

traditional Islamic education, *halaqah* continues to be core practice in Muslim cultures. *Halaqah* is credited with transformation of personalities, empowerment of individuals and communities through a social-justice agenda, and the development of Islamic intellectual heritage, including sciences, arts and mysticism (Zaimache, 2002). The format varies immensely and can be transmission-based/teacher-led or dialogic/student-led. It can also be a collaborative group effort. The "curriculum" or content is open, but the paradigm is an Islamic worldview and the frame of reference is the Islamic revealed texts, that is, the Qur'an and Sunnah (sayings of the Prophet). (Ahmed, 2012)

Halaqah is used in *Shakhsiyah* Schools to provide a dialogic forum within an Islamic spiritual context. These oral discussions provide children with a space to explore their identities and address real and complex issues that they face growing up as Muslims in Britain.

Data Analysis and Presentation of Findings

To address these concerns of this chapter, I had to engage in new data analysis. I read through transcripts again and isolated text which is related to

1. personal childhood experiences and narrative connected to growing up challenges of parenting/teaching between multiple cultures
2. the use of halaqah in ISF to address perceived challenges in growing up between multiple cultures
3. expressions of ambitions and desires for their own children
4. personal motivations for their work as educators

This recoding enabled a refocusing of my reading of the data from understanding the workings of *Shakhsiyah Education*, to the challenges around growing up and parenting as Muslims in Britain. A remarkable amount of personal narrative was identified, highlighting a number of key unifying beliefs that emerged out of these personal experiences which participants then explored. I have summarized these below in three sections, using a collective first-person voice to emphasize the remarkable consistency in the narratives given by individual participants.

1. Childhood Experiences

a.   Mainstream schooling led to double identities, as children we didn't fit into school and led different lives at school and at home. There was also disconnect with our parent's cultures, at the time we felt that they didn't understand us.

b.   Supplementary religious education did not meet our needs due to adults' lack of knowledge of our secular-liberal educational experiences in the British context.

2.   Challenges of parenting/educating in the West

c.   That's not what we want for our children.

d.   Our children are confused when growing up between multiple cultures, this created stress and pressure for them as they try to fit in.

e.   Muslim children can lose confidence and become ashamed to be themselves. Teachers in mainstream schools are not able to deal with their needs.

f.   There are a lot of internal issues that Muslim adults struggle with; children need to be supported through these.

3.   Overcoming these challenges—Generating culturally coherent dialogic education

g.   We believe that a culturally coherent holistic education rooted in classical Islamic culture will provide a continuity of experience for our children between home and school.

h.   We believe this will give them a secure identity and the confidence to fully participate in wider society as adults, whilst still being true to themselves, their Islamic beliefs, values and practices.

i.   We believe that the cornerstone of our work is *halaqah* and that this culturally coherent pedagogy enables children to explore their own identities, belief systems and difficult and controversial issues. *Halaqah* provides a safe space for critical dialogic thinking and develops emotional resilience.

j.   We believe that *Shakhsiyah Education* is a credible alternative educational model that meets the needs of our children and other Muslim children. We believe that synthesizing classical Islamic education and modern curricula and pedagogy through thematic learning based around *Halaqah* will give children the best of both worlds, preparing them for the educational, technological and multicultural realities of the modern world whilst retaining their Islamic identity.

I present these perspectives in more depth below beginning with childhood experiences and moving on to adult beliefs and motivations.

1. Childhood Experiences: Narratives of primary education in mainstream British schooling:

Personal Narrative

> *"To be lonely, is to be among men who do not know what you mean"*
> *—Isaiah Berlin*

In discussing participants' personal experiences, I begin with an account of my own, which had featured in my reflective work during the course of the study. At the time I was considering the usefulness of a secular-liberal education for Muslim children in relation to their personal autonomy. I was asking questions such as, is secular-liberal education the only way forward in a diverse society? Does it cater for children from other cultural traditions? Like my colleagues, my personal experience of secular-liberal education had been negative; I felt it limited my development of "self" and identity and therefore autonomy. I felt pressurised, caught between cultures, struggling to define myself. The effects of this are difficult to explain to someone who has not experienced the moral superiority of secular-liberal education from an outsider's perspective.

In the late 1970s, I arrived in this country aged five and was immediately enrolled into school. My earliest school memory is of children calling me and my sister "stupid," as we did not understand them when they tried to talk to us. A number of years of deep confusion followed, as I attempted to relate to a completely new language and culture. I remember not having any clear sense of "self" throughout my primary years as my inner world was almost paralyzed by confusion in my external world. I knew I didn't "belong" and other children recognized this, leaving me socially isolated. I therefore had ample time to realize there was something "wrong," but as a child lacked the tools to understand why.

My most meaningful educational experiences were rare instances where I could relate to the subject matter, for example reading a novel about immigration in English. At other times I was frustrated but helpless in the face of cultural prejudice from teachers. I travelled three miles to the nearest secondary girls school which had a high proportion of Muslim and Hindu girls, whose parents wanted single-sex schooling for their daughters. Well-meaning teachers crafted lessons to liberate us, organizing debates about arranged marriages, at least once a year. By the time we were fifteen, teachers could not understand why most of us were unconvinced by their arguments; why we demonstrated mild amusement at their efforts, and rejected "liberation," We enjoyed our close, supportive family life and valued "arranged marriage" is part of this culture. Unlike our teachers, we did not see our culture as inferior, in need of modernization or Europeanization.

In 1990, I went from the comfort of multicultural Brent in North London to study philosophy at the University of Bristol; among an undergraduate cohort of mainly White students lacking experience of other ethnicities. Education again became an isolating experience. I struggled to communicate meanings I was making from my cultural perspective. At the time I accepted all these experiences as a natural consequence of being a Muslim in a different culture. I am using "culture" to mean, values and practices arising from a specific worldview.

1. Participants' Narratives of Childhood Experiences

There are similarities between my experiences and those of my colleagues.

a. Mainstream schooling led to double identities, as children we didn't fit into school and led different lives at school and at home. There was also a disconnect with our parent's cultures; at the time we felt that they didn't understand us.

In their *Halaqah* group, school leaders described the tensions they faced as Muslim children in British mainstream schools and their relationships as children with their parents.

Aisha: No, no I'm not saying they (the primary years) are not important except that at that point you don't address certain turmoil, but in the secondary years you're more engaged with yourself, ... when the emotions ... and you actually start wondering well what is my purpose in my life? What am I doing? And ... obviously, we ... went to mainstream schooling and had the home environment as well and we were given different morals (at home) and society was giving another (set of) morals and we had to get through the mess and make choices by ourselves, because our parents didn't understand because they never had that issue. They never had to face that turmoil, so we were in this phase of turmoil for a long time where you're sifting through which morals; you know personally, which type of morals you are willing to take on.

Khadija: Constant dilemmas, constant dilemmas

Aisha: Yeah and it's only when, I know for myself the clarity came when I (came to) Islam and thought no! ... that makes sense, the clarity of purpose is there and I know from what Allah ... has given us and ... (because He) created the world and this is our purpose and that just did it for me.

Hafsah: ... we're saying that we lived one lifestyle ... we had double identities basically.

Aisha: We did have parallel (identities), yeah we did.

Hafsah: One lifestyle at home, another at school, but then what we did at home was to please the people at home and what we did at school was to please the people around us at school.

Salma: You didn't live for yourself, to please yourself?

Hafsah: No

Aisha: But you didn't know where you were, that was the turmoil!

Hafsah: No because you didn't understand, you didn't have a direction, you didn't have a focus. You didn't have an understanding ...

Khadija: No because I thought he (Dad) didn't understand me or understand my friends or understand my school.

School leaders discussions present their experience of having to deal with double identities as children as a powerful motivation for seeking out a different kind of education for their own children; a powerful motivation that led them initially to become home-educators. Their discussions also include conceptual and pedagogical doubts about the aims and structures of British mainstream schooling which although arising partly from Islamic beliefs and Islamic educational principles are not directly connected to their childhood experiences and so have not been included here.

b. Supplementary religious education did not meet our needs due to adults' lack of knowledge of our secular-liberal educational experiences in the British context.

Hafsah discusses her experiences of attending the local Mosque (Masjid) after school and contrasts this to *Halaqah*. This is picked up by the others who conclude that children have questions that Mosque teachers are not equipped to answer and indeed don't want to address. This discussion was in the context of contrasting Mosque lessons with *Halaqah* as used in *Shakhsiyah* schools.

Hafsah: ... how is this Halaqah different? I mean I went to a Masjid as a child and ... basically we played when the Imam wasn't there, we got hit with a stick when he was there and you just got up to mischief and Masjid was this place to get up to mischief so we stopped going to the Masjid and my Dad brought us back home … he had his own way of doing things but anyway we did have the discussions and sitting down and doing the dhikr and what have you and I remember that more than the Masjid. I remember those discussions (with my Dad). And when I … (became an) adult … and was questioning things that (the discussions) probably made me think about Islam and go towards (Islam) more than if I (had) just learnt from the Masjid.

Khadija: I think if you go to a Masjid when you're a child, if you are sitting in a dars (lesson) then you're not allowed to (ask) questions from the Imam. If you ask how do you know Islam is the right religion, how do you know there is Allah, why should I listen to … the Qur'an, then you get slapped or you know a beating with a stick or how dare you question … your religion, whereas in the Halaqah we can ask these questions and I think the child is also confident they'll get an acceptable answer, an answer which will satisfy their curiosity whereas in the Mosque these questions are never answered so you have these doubts, these suspicions which lingered on and for some people it caused confusion and you know they went astray, but for some people … they stayed on the right path.

Hafsah: Could it be because the people actually teaching in the Masjid couldn't connect with us living in this society?

Khadija: I think that generation was different because the generation in those days, for example … my own Dad, when he would say Islam is the right deen (way of life) and not the other religions I still had doubts. I wasn't satisfied by his answer even though I knew the stories of all the Prophets and I knew the stories of the Seerah (Life of Muhammad). (Although) he (Dad) knew everything because he's written books mashaAllah, I read them, but his answers didn't satisfy my curiosity. I wanted more and I didn't get it.

Hafsah: What you're saying, … it's not giving them information; it's giving them information but then allowing them to stop and think about the information and to question that information. I mean I'm just thinking about when I questioned this (her belief in Islam). I never questioned it as a child, never.

Salma: You're afraid to question it, that's the main thing.

Hafsah: No, (I never thought about questioning) because (of) the way I was taught … but then (in my) late teens, early twenties when I had my first child I started to question and think about, what is the reason for all this…. But I think for me to have had that answer at an early age … what I was looking for in life … and to have (had) the understanding … it would have made me a lot stronger growing up. But I wavered from one thing to another and I was never strong enough … for my identity really …

Hafsah goes onto speak about the needs of Muslim children, that they need the space to question their beliefs but in a supportive Muslim environment where adults understand the children's needs.

Hafsah: And that's the wrong way to do it (not allowing children to ask questions) because if you start putting that fear … I got to an age where I was like 'do I want to be Muslim then?' and these are the questions the children will start to ask – "do I want to?" This is what it's like and this is what does happen…. So it … it has to be done (children have to be allowed to question their beliefs) and this is where maybe other settings are going wrong doing it in that way (not providing a space for questioning).

Khadija: … that's what I'm saying. For our generation or children who are still in the dars (lessons) in the Mosque, look at who's teaching them …? Look at it from their (Mosque teacher's) perspective. They think these children nowadays are rude or disobedient and you know rebellious, how dare they question! Whereas our objective (in Shakhsiyah schools), our objective, our view towards these children asking us these questions, we think it's a positive thing that children in Halaqah are debating and asking and questioning and thinking and pondering but if you go somewhere else the teacher doesn't expect this behavior from children.

Aisha: This is why, you know, we are talking about the whole child because we can't take a segment of them and just nurture that, because they would be lopsided like we were … what did we have Islamically? We didn't have any concepts. We just knew that we had to go to Madrasah, we had to learn this and once we've learnt that then that's it, then we're Muslims. You know, depending on how … where you were and how well informed your parents were and had the time (to spend) with you, coming from abroad. So I think what we're trying to do is really stick to the traditions of Islam to actually beautify the Deen for them so they see it in its whole picture, not just look at memorizing the Qu'ran or just look at Salah (prayer) ... we're really trying to give them tools for life and that's what schooling is about if you understand it as the tarbiyah (education) of Islam. It's the tools for life isn't it?

Schoolteachers also discussed childhood school experiences and issues of identity. They too identify this as a motivation for bringing their own children to *Shakhsiyah* schools.

Zainab: I grew up, well I was born in Congo but I grew up here in the U.K. and I went to a state school ... I found that okay ... (but) having come from abroad and then coming into a school in a Western country, obviously I found it really difficult. I was an EAL student and I think maybe at the time as well there wasn't much provision made for EAL students ... I enjoyed the experience somewhat but then I think at the time I wasn't Muslim so I mean I saw things in a different sort of perspective and you just sort of.... You just got on with it ...

Fatimah: Were you Christian before?

Zainab: Yeah, yeah I was Christian before. So I saw things from a different angle to how I do now. So yeah you just got on with the school routine. You generally enjoyed it but obviously there was always the stuff like you know bullying. You learnt bad manners, you know at the age of seven I learnt words that I really shouldn't have ... but you thought that this was the norm ... and you didn't really know any better.... For me personally it was really different because I was non-Muslim at the time ... and I see things differently now that I'm Muslim, ... the school experience was okay but your needs weren't completely catered for, and also I remember the fact that your personality wasn't built, you know by the teachers. You were just sort of taught subjects, (they didn't) have a connection with you or just build you as a person.... They just sort of taught what they taught and that was it.

Ruqayyah: Like (in) a robotic manner.... My school experience ... I was born in Pakistan and I came to this country when I was about seven and I felt quite lost. I don't feel as though

I got the support that I needed. In primary school I felt lost and then it's like that same thing just carried on in secondary school … it's like our identity … it's like I felt as though my identity didn't mean much, you know…. It's like it was buried. I felt as though my identity was buried and school was … it was like a robotic system of trying to get the lessons out of the way if you like … you know home was where Islam was … that's where the culture was but school was just where I wasn't able to show that I'm a Muslim, you know, I wasn't (able to show) my identity.

Fatimah: You wanted to blend in, isn't it?

Ruqayyah: Yeah

Fatimah: We were never taught about Islam in school. I'd never … I don't remember ever being taught Islam. I think there was one topic that we learnt about Islam and that was … slaughtering of animals.

Kulthum: Okay (this is said sarcastically)

ALL LAUGH

Fatimah: That's what it was, the slaughtering of animals, that's all we were taught.

Kulthum: (I went a to a convent school, in a Muslim country) … we did History, we did Geography, we did all the subjects. It was never linked to Islam. I never knew my Islamic history as such before I started teaching here. And … when you just don't know about your heritage you do have some sense of low self-esteem …

Fatimah: … when we were younger we didn't get all (of) this … I remember my parents saying "oh pray, pray, pray" and it never used to make any difference to me because I was like "why?" and they never used to explain to why because there's not enough time. I'm one of seven so Mum's always had her hands full.

Ruqayyah: You know I remember when my Mum was teaching me how to pray Salah, I was very little and she goes to me "okay you pray this many Fardh and you pray this many Sunnah." I said "what's Sunnah?" and I remember Mum's like "Sunnah." Yeah but what is Sunnah and I remember getting so frustrated and my Mum, the poor thing, wasn't able to …

Ruqayyah expresses her frustrations as a child that her mother did not understand that basic Islamic terms like *Sunnah* need explaining to children in the west. Whereas in Muslim societies these are common terms that children would pick up naturally, in the west many of these terms need careful explanation.

2.   Challenges of parenting/educating in the West

c.   That's not what we want for our children.

Participants go on to discuss their concerns about their own children.

Ruqayyah: (when you're in a State school) … you're blending in to school (culture), you're not being reminded that you're a Muslim but I'm so blessed…. I feel so blessed that my children are getting Islam at home and at school, and that is the reason why I struggled to take them out of the state system because in the state system I was constantly struggling…. Their own identity isn't even solid and yet here they are being taught, you know, how to go to these different routes, or how to take these different routes and this is why …

Fatimah: It's true! It's confusion for them isn't it?

Ruqayyah: … it's so much confusion you know. It confuses the child so much and this is why I struggled to take them out of that system and to bring them here and I feel so blessed that my children are here. It is such a struggle.

Maryam, whose children attend a State school, discusses the importance of consistency between home and school environments for young children.

Maryam: You know that's what we're missing in the English (State) school. My daughter goes (to a State school). She's in a good school but (she doesn't appreciate Islamic values) … She was telling me that she was getting angry at her sister the other day and I said that we have to show sabr (patience and humility) and just the word sabr, if you say it one of our children in (Shakhsiyah) school (even in the) nursery, they understand…. She is 11 years old and I'm telling her (to) show sabr and she didn't even want to stay still, just for me to finish … I had to raise my voice, sit her down, sit with her together because what she's getting in the school is not linking with what I'm doing it at home. But over here the Halaqah really relates to what they will be practising at home, the Halaqah really reflects it (their home culture).

d.   Our children are confused when growing up between multiple cultures; this creates stress and pressure for them as they try to fit in.

> **Aisha:** One of the positive things about the children learning through Halaqah ... it raises the self esteem, confidence, vision, purpose, all of these things it puts them into perspective for them.

> **Salma:** I think it's the main thing for our children is to be proud to be Muslim (because) when they are in a Muslim school they feel it is normal but when they go, later on in their life, to be in the other community, like when they're in a school or college or university (we hope) they wouldn't hide and all the time (need to be) defending themselves ... they have to know how to talk, and learn how to stand up for themselves and be proud about themselves and if you don't establish this at a young age ...

> **Aisha:** Then it's about identities isn't it? Establishing positive identities!

> **Salma:** Otherwise they will melt in the community and they will forget who they are.

e.   Muslim children can lose confidence and become ashamed to be themselves. Teachers in mainstream schools are not able to deal with their needs.

Aisha talks about the lack of understanding amongst teachers in mainstream schools.

> **Aisha:** ... the fact that now you know we're doing teacher training ... we're extending our hands out to ... anybody really, anybody, even if it was a non-Muslim who decided they wanted to come along to the ... teacher training course because they want to get perspective for their teaching so that they can really cater for their communities, because you will find lots of schools in London have got nearly 100% or 99.9% of Muslims in their schools so those teachers in those schools need to understand their students.

> **Hafsah:** State schools?

Aisha: Yeah state schools.

Aisha goes onto describe the frustrations felt by Muslims when trying to express their own identity.

Aisha: Can I give you a perfect example. I'll give you a perfect example … there's a family we knew (who) were going on Hajj (pilgrimage). Now you would imagine you know that BA (British airways) has lots of Hajj flights. When the agents booked them they booked a section, a third of the plane for their group for a whole Hajj flight. Now we went (to) drop off (the family). There are different types of Hajj okay. There are certain types of Hajj you're in Ihram (dress of a pilgrim) when you leave your home. Now how many centuries have Muslims being living here? Hajj flights are happening all the time. When we went to drop off this family there were two people … they're sort of just vetting, looking at passports and everything (before you go to check-in) and the disgust on their face at looking at the Muslims dressed in the two loin cloths. (Muslims) who are going to this spiritual journey, an obligation from Allah and they've left all their belongings behind, so (it's) a very spiritual time for them. They've made their intention, they left everything behind, all their worldly (goods) and if they die on this path then they're really, you know, people of the Jannah (paradise). Okay. There you have these two people and they just look so off. They looked really negative, they were almost like sneering at the people dressed in their loin cloths and this … this really upset me and you know I was with my husband and … I really, really and if it happened to me again I would go and speak to them but I wanted to go up to them and say to them 'do you understand what is happening here? Do you know what's going on…. (Why) is it that the element of understanding isn't there from people when it comes to Muslims and even (of) our rituals? If you go to somewhere like Whitechapel, the Bangladeshi community, that's how they live. They wear their Lunghis and you know Kameez over the top. This is their identity. (Just) like you have the punk rocker or the girl in the mini (skirt) down the street and that's fine, and that doesn't get sneered at but the Muslim identity is often sneered at and this is a very important issue. It all comes back to (is the reason for) the insecurities of the Muslims at large and this is why then they feel like "oh we've got to protect our children because there's too many negativities around."

Hafsah: You know what's coming out for me from this is when we're looking at community cohesion … the Muslims are trying so hard to create this community cohesion but from the other side it's not happening. It's a one-way …

f.   There are a lot of internal issues that Muslim adults struggle with; children need to be supported through these.

Participants are also aware of internal issues and tensions within the Muslim community. These too are considered to be important when providing a culturally coherent education. However they feel solutions to this must come from the Muslim community itself.

Khadija: When we talk about Muslim community … people, sometimes immediately refer it to as the Pakistani Muslim community but when we talk about Muslim community we're actually talking about Muslims from different backgrounds, cultures, languages, traditions coming from different parts of the world. So discussing community cohesion within the Muslim community and between the Muslim community and other communities; we need to understand the mindset of the people we're talking about because it's very easy to say this is how we should be and this is what we do but when everyone has got their own ideas and their own ideologies and their own, you know, sets of beliefs. Regarding the Muslim community we have different sects inside the community if I can use that word. You have some Muslims who think that living inside this, in this country means adhering wholeheartedly to the laws and regulations and schools, education system of the country and even if that means compromising your own religion. We have another group you could say which think it's okay to adhere to some rules of the country including the education system while still keeping your own cultural traditions and beliefs and values and then on the other side we have still a third group of people which think that no we should forsake everything that this country has to offer whilst living in this country and stick only to the laws given to us by Allah and if that means home schooling or a family is stopping children from going to the high street or public places or mixed work situation. So when we discuss community cohesion I think it's … we have to understand that there are different … there is a varied mindset in here and who are we talking to and who are we talking on behalf of when we talk about this.

Participants discuss some contentious issues from their own ethnic cultures as well as intrareligious differences. Participants are aware of intrareligious differences but approach the problem through referencing early Islamic practices. Much of this conversation revolves around racism. They have found that Islam rejects racism and this has been grasped as a solution to identity issues. They now see their identity as not about color or nationality but about a belief system or worldview, a worldview that rejects racism and nationalism.

Hafsah: People … they connect Pakistani and Islam together and then say because we're Pakistani we hate this culture, we don't want to be Pakistani and if this is the way it (Islam) is we don't want it.

Salma: But they are ignorant. Well they are ignorant. They thought that the culture is Islam but Islam's totally different from culture

Hafsah: I came to a point in my life when I questioned and I said you know what, if this is what Islam's about do I want to be Muslim and that's when I started on the journey of questioning what Islam is and looking at it for myself and seeing that the difference here is immense because being a Muslim and being Pakistani is totally different and that's when everything started to fit in place and it all clicked. Prior to that there was no thought behind it.

Later the discussion turns to a new notion of constructing a "British Islam," participants discuss their own households, many of which involve mixed-race multicultural marriages. They want to give their children an Islam based multicultural worldview, not a "British Islam."

Hafsah: What is British Islam? That's what I'd like to know.

Salma: Muslims are kind of anywhere and everywhere and they don't mind living anywhere as long as they obey they (have) obedience to Allah

Aisha: If anything I think we're reviving the actual truth and basis of a unified Islam for all, for everyone, for anyone, for (all) mankind like Allah decreed it. That is our essence.

Hafsah: See if we look at British Islam so does that mean you can be … you have to be British to be a Muslim. It's not right. It doesn't work does it?

Aisha: I think that these concepts are nonsensical because they just don't fit with if you … what is this? British Islam, then (do) we start doing you know Afghani Islam …

Hafsah: But that's promoting nationalistic views again isn't it?

Aisha: (Or is it) just saying I say La illaha illaAllah Muhammadur RasoolAllah (testament of Islamic faith) and I eat chips as well. I mean come on … does it mean to say that I say La illaha illaAllah Muhammadur RasoolAllah and I like fish and chips because … and is that now saying I'm a British Muslim.

LAUGHTER

Aisha: This is the thing, I'm sorry it does not make sense, in my house it's just so multicultural it's unbelievable.

Hafsah: Yeah, yeah same thing in mine Aisha.

Later, Khadija talks about the importance of a way forward.

Khadija: And parents and the community should see the school as a vehicle to bringing the Ummah (Muslim community) together and moving forward so we're not working alien to them, we're part of the community but we're just, we're going ahead. There's no point Muslims just bickering amongst ourselves and complaining about this system and that system and this and that and our hardship and our struggles and there has to be a way forward. There has to be something going ahead and if the community realizes that this school is set up with this objective to take this, the current children … our future Ummah, the future generation with leadership skills and with a vision for the future and a vision for unity and overcoming these obstacles and divides between Muslims and non-Muslims then I think we are meeting our targets and goals because this is what our aim is.

3. Overcoming these challenges—Generating culturally coherent dialogic education

g. **We believe that a culturally coherent holistic education rooted in classical Islamic culture will provide a continuity of experience for our children between home and school.**

Maryam: You know that's what we're missing in the English (state) school. My daughter goes (to a State school). She's in a good school but (she doesn't appreciate Islamic values) ... She was telling me that she was getting angry at her sister the other day and I said that we have to show sabr (patience and humility) and just the word sabr if you say it one of our children in (Shakhsiyah) school (even in the) nursery, they understand.... She is 11 years old and I'm telling her show sabr and she didn't even want to stay still, just for me to finish the ... I had to raise my voice, sit her down, sit with her together because what she's getting in the school is not linking with what I'm doing it at home. But over here the Halaqah really relates to what they will be practising at home, the Halaqah really reflects it (their home culture).

Kulthum: There's one particular girl, she came to my class. She's a new girl, and she actually (left her old) school because she was unhappy so we obviously, you know, catered to her needs and I was extra careful in handling (her) because she was very quiet but you know now that she has actually started talking, she's beginning to talk and she's beginning to make friends and her mother said previously that she has never made a friend in all these years and she is in Year 4 now so she's quite old considering that. So I think (this) school really helps children in a lot of ways other than just their studies. So these things are definitely positive.

Ruqayyah: ... the children take away something very, very important here. They take away the fact that Islam is something that we are with every step of the way... this Deen is a way of life, ... no matter what we do, we have to link it back to Islam and if it is (not) taught like this ... you would find that children they might grow up thinking okay, this is my life and put Islam on a back seat if you like and will treat it as something on the side

h. **We believe this will give them a secure identity and the confidence to fully participate in wider society as adults, whilst still being true to themselves, their Islamic beliefs, values and practices.**

Aisha: We are not trying to educate them (children) in isolated cocooned fashion. That isn't our intention, that isn't what the school's about. We want them to be confident Muslims for the future and that means understanding the world around them but also relating them to it and being involved in it to the point where of course their principles are not affected and they protect their Islam.

Ruqayyah: That's what we give them I think ... we give them a lot of confidence in themselves, in their Islam whereby you know, Allah knows best, but they wouldn't have got that really actually, probably not got that in a state system

Aisha: You know you've got to evaluate yourself, you've got to check yourself ... the conscience ... We've got that with us and it is inclined to do good but there's always the two options at any crossroads or any decision that needs to be made and I think the Halaqah gives a strength of character ... we want our children ... (to) have the courage of their convictions. And if you truly say that (I am) a Muslim, then we have to live by those principles and have the courage to stand up for them and to stand by them, be steadfast and remain firm on them. You can't do that if you don't have the understanding. Therefore you just come full circle round (to Halaqah). Halaqah is pivotal in shaping their personalities, shaping their understanding, shaping their mind, shaping their heart, their inclinations, their love of things and that just is fluid. It goes into all the other lessons and everything that we do at the school and I just think that's got to be one of the most important things of what we do.

Khadija: (My children who have now left Shakhsiyah schools), they work well as part of a group and you know not forgetting that they've all gone into non-Muslim schools so their friends or their class peers may include Muslims, non-Muslims from different cultures yet they're able to hold their own personality together and withstand all sorts of and different types of peer pressure, the children are still able to remember that, you know, they're Muslims at the end of the day and they've got certain objectives in life and that should not be compromised however great the pressure is. I think that's just giving an example of my own children but looking at other children who've left the school also you can see this as a theme for all of them.

i.   **We believe that the cornerstone of our work is *halaqah* and that this culturally coherent pedagogy enables children to explore their own identities, belief systems and difficult and controversial issues. *Halaqah* provides a safe space for critical dialogic thinking and develops emotional resilience.**

> **Aisha:** I think our Halaqah has a real cutting edge approach is because it nurtures children's different aspects, so it's their social needs, their emotional needs, their intellectual needs, even being able to self-reflect. I mean I haven't seen anywhere that children at that age are able to reflect and question their own thinking which is quite, if you know Blooms, it's quite a high order thinking skill to actually question (yourself) or even question another person…. It's the same thing with the Halaqah. You're teaching children to do that but in a very basic, ground roots level but then slowly building on it and that instills a certain amount of clarity as well…. Halaqah is focal because we are nurturing these children, their Shakhsiyah (personal character), their spirituality, their intellectual mind, their understanding, their knowledge … so that they can be positive people for the future but with a strong Islamic identity and understanding, a clear understanding of what their mission in life is and where they want to reach and I think that is in a nutshell what the school's about…. And I also think one of the nice things about Halaqah is that children actually feel that you're listening to them and I think that's so important because we always say it's not about the teacher talking, it's about giving the chance to children. You know children have this thing about "oh but you're not listening to me Mama" or "you're not listening to me teacher." No at that time, I feel like you're saying this is our time together but it's also your time for you to say how you feel and this is really, really important. I mean people pay for therapy these days, you know, but you know we're doing it from reception class where the children feel they can express themselves. I mean you won't have confused, angry, you know, complicated individuals Insha'Allah because they've been able to express their problems or even their misunderstandings or, you know, how they feel.

> **Aisha:** So there's a fine line, you know, between directing and guiding and forcing or even completely staying silent like we say about, you know, in the Halaqah where you're, as a

teacher you have to keep inputting. You're very important to what's going on there.

Salma: … the impact of the Halaqah, you can see it at home… I have a daughter who was here and (now she's in) high school and you can see the difference in her behavior and how mature (is her) thinking and she understands the concept of talking, expressing herself in a polite way and in a way that … she wouldn't make people around her angry or upset but she will express herself freely and in a way that people understand her…

Hafsah: It's the oracy, it's that confidence.

j. **We believe that *Shakhsiyah Education* is a credible alternative educational model that meets the needs of our children and other Muslim children. We believe that synthesizing classical Islamic education and modern curricula and pedagogy through thematic learning based around *Halaqah* will give children the best of both worlds, preparing them for the educational, technological and multicultural realities of the modern world whilst retaining their Islamic identity.**

Zaynab: … putting whatever the theme is, Africa or whatever… throughout all the subjects so that they …

Ruqayyah: It enriches it a lot more.

Zaynab: They experience (the theme) in many different ways, in math, in science. They experience it in many different ways and (the learning) links with the children and … the teaching (is) a lot more practical … a lot more on trips, doing practical work, kinaesthetic learning. It should be that way … and it makes it more real for them …

Ruqayyah: And they're a lot happier.

Zaynab: … when we were doing bones, everything was linked to the skeleton so at Year 4 level they were actually able to learn the names of the different bones which they're not supposed to but you know through songs they were able to construct the skeleton, label (bones), … what happens to the bones, when does ossification take place, all these very, very difficult words which are literally secondary level they were able to learn these …

Kulthum: and write poems about the bones and … it reinforces … all that really helps thematically. It does work but as long as you're skilled at it … I think it's the best way of teaching.

CONCLUSION

This chapter has explored the views and experiences of a specific group of Muslim women; a group that has a clear Islamic identity, and is actively seeking out a way of manifesting that identity whilst living in Britain. These women's narratives have much in common, four of them immigrated into Britain during their primary years and dealt with the challenges that this involves. Those who were born here also disclose similar narratives; one participant who grew up in a Muslim majority country but attended a convent school also describes a similar experience of a split identity and feeling that her home culture was not valued.

These experiences are clearly a motivation for their work as are their concerns about their own children's educational experience. The issue of children's education which is occupying many Muslims in Muslim minority countries is being addressed by these women and mothers through developing a holistic Islamic education for their children. This education they perceive as appropriate for the British context but is characterized by an Islam based multiculturalism which also encourages respect for intrareligious, interreligious dialogue and dialogue with the host society. They have rejected ethnic or nationalistic forms of Islam in their journey in exploring their own identity. This rejection of home-country identification also leads to a rejection of a "British Islam." These women appear to see themselves as global citizens living in a multicultural world; they are working through intercultural and intrareligious differences by seeking out early Islamic teachings and practices.

They recognize that these issues are very personal and very complex and they recognize the need for children to be supported in their own individual journeys. They see their use of the traditional Islamic pedagogy of *Halaqah* as a means to offer this support to Muslim children in a globalized world where Islam is often presented in the negative. This deep commitment to *Halaqah* and the strong claims they have made about *Halaqah*, that is, that it is pedagogy that encourages a form of autonomy within the Islamic context are now being explored through further research.

REFERENCES

Ahmed, F. (2012). Tarbiyah for Shakhsiyah (educating for identity): Seeking out culturally coherent pedagogy for muslim children in Britain. *Compare: A Journal of Comparative and International Education, 42*(5), 725–749. doi:10.108 0/03057925.2012.706452

Ahmed, F. (2013). Exploring Halaqah as research method: A tentative approach to developing Islamic research principles within a critical "indigenous" framework. *International Journal of Qualitative Studies in Education.*

Stake, R. E., & Trumbull, D. J. (1982). Naturalistic generalisations. *Review Journal of Philosophy and Social Science, 7*(1&2), 2–10.

Zaimache, S. (2002). Education in Islam: The role of the mosque. *Muslimheritage. com.* Retrieved from http://www.muslimheritage.com/topics/default.cfm?Tax onomyTypeID=101&TaxonomySubTypeID=19&TaxonomyThirdLevelID =134&ArticleID=220

AUTHOR INDEX

SUBJECT INDEX

ABOUT THE AUTHORS

Heba Abuzayyad-Nuseibeh is a doctoral candidate in Curriculum and Instruction with an emphasis in Adult Education at the University of South Florida (USF). Her cognate is in Research and Measurement. She received the Graduate Certificate in Evaluation from USF. Heba is a former lecturer at Al-Quds University in Palestine teaching business courses for Information Technology (IT) students. While completing her dissertation, Heba is teaching "Equity in Schools and Workplace" course for undergraduate level students at USF. She is also a graduate assistant at USF's department of Adult, Career, and Higher Education helping to convert face-to-face courses to online versions. Her research interests are in distance learning, online learning communities and intercultural competency. You may contact Heba at pearla.az@gmail.com

Farah Ahmed is a visiting research associate at the Center for Research and Evaluation in Muslim Education at the Institute of Education, University of London. She has a BA hons in philosophy, MEd in educational research and is currently a PhD candidate at the University of Cambridge. Her research interests are developing culturally coherent Islamic research models and classical Islamic pedagogy and its implementation in contemporary contexts. Her PhD is looking at the use of Halaqah (Islamic dialogic circle-time) to develop autonomy in Muslim children. Farah has been active in Muslim education for 20 years and is a founder of Islamic Shakhsiyah Foundation where she currently works as director of education. The foundation runs two primary schools and is developing a holistic Islamic education programme for Muslim children in a western context, including curricula, resources and teacher education courses.

Nadia Albert is the Northern Territory Program Coordinator for the National Association for Prevention of Child Abuse and Neglect, Nightcliff, Northern Territory, 0814, Australia. She completed her honors thesis in psychology in 2007, as part of her bachelor of arts/social work at the University of Melbourne. Nadia has practiced as a social worker in both hospital and community settings with families and children. Nadia has worked as a program manager for programs focused on strengthening communities' capacity to adapt and implement Respectful Relationships programs.

Lesliee Antonette is Professor Emeritus and Past Director of the Northeastern Pennsylvania Writing Project Stroudsburg at East Stroudsburg University of Pennsylvania, located in the Pocono Mountains of Northeastern Pennsylvania. She and is currently Owner/Consultant of LA Consulting, which designs custom Professional Development programs based on Antonette's OPEN model of learning and Writing to Engage Diversity (WED) strategies for both K-16 educational institutions and businesses across the country.

Alexis Ball, MS, MFA, is a Research Analyst & Field Coordinator, Northern Illinois University, Office of Research, Evaluation, and Policy Studies. Alexis Ball worked as a bilingual teacher in Mexico City and an English as a second language reading teacher in Chicago and has worked extensively with diverse populations, including Muslim students and families. She completed a Master of Visual Arts at UNAM in Mexico City and a M.S. Ed. in Literacy Education and is completing her Ed.D. in Literacy Education. Her experiences abroad and with diverse communities in the Midwest region of the United States have contributed to her passionate belief in serving multilingual/multicultural learners through student-centered, creative, informed, and targeted programming based on high quality research.

Mayra C. Daniel, EdD, is an associate professor, Northern Illinois University Department of Literacy Education. She is a native of the island of Cuba who immigrated with her family to the United States at the age of 10 in order to escape communism. Having been in the role of "the other" as a new immigrant, she understands the many challenges faced by culturally and diverse students when they begin life in an unfamiliar school system that does not offer culturally sensitive pedagogy. She believes the strength of any nation lies in the cultural, religious, and linguistic diversity of its citizens. Her world-view is that teachers who reach out to students and their families will eliminate the cultural mismatch that so often interferes with and prevents academic success.

Agnes Dodds is an associate professor of medical education in the Melbourne Medical School at The University of Melbourne, Victoria, 3010, Australia. Her background is in education and educational psychology. Her research interests are in the developmental experiences of young people, and her current projects include studies of the development of medical students, and the school-related experiences of refugee children.

Rumjahn Hoosain is honorary professor of psychology at the University of Hong Kong. His interests are in cognitive psychology, including psychological aspects of the Chinese language, bilingualism, and multicultural education.

Lisa Hoffman is assistant professor of graduate studies in education at Indiana University Southeast in New Albany, Indiana. She teaches courses in research, curriculum, and working with English language learners. Her research interests include acculturation processes of immigrant children and families, educational needs of refugee families, educational opportunities for gifted and talented English learners, and teacher professional development and action research.

Kathleen P. King, EdD, is professor and chair of the Department of Adult, Career and Higher Education at University of South Florida in Tampa, FL. Kathy's major areas of research and expertise include transformative learning, leadership, faculty development, distance learning, instructional technology, and diversity. The International Continuing and Adult Education Hall of Fame recognized Dr. King's outstanding contributions to adult and higher education with her 2011 induction. As an award winning author who has published 22 books, she is also a popular keynote and conference speaker, mentor, and professor.

Jeanette Lawrence is an honorary associate professor in developmental psychology at The University of Melbourne, Victoria, 3010, Australia. Her Ph.D. is from The University of Minnesota. Jeanette's research interests are in personal and social development across the life-course. She has current studies in child protection, court processes, procedural justice for young people, and the developmental experiences of young people, especially refugees and students. She has expertise in research methods of data-collection including computerised techniques.

Delila Omerbašić was born and raised in Sarajevo, Bosnia & Herzegovina, and moved to Philadelphia, PA in 1994. She received a bachelor's degree in economics (2001) and master's degrees in liberal arts (2004) and education (2008) from the University of Pennsylvania. Currently, she is a PhD candidate in education, culture and society (ECS) at the University of Utah. Her research interests include literacy practices, digital multimodal literacies, and refugee education. She is currently working on her dissertation and focusing on how several young women who were resettled as refugees engage with multimodal literacy practices in digital spaces. This study is grounded in critical sociocultural theory of literacy and draws on elements of postcolonial feminist theory, postmodern geography, and cultural studies. The goal of the study is to better understand how language is used in digital spaces for complex negotiations of identity, agency, and various social dimensions of power. This research, which builds on the emerging literature on digital experiences of transnational youth, is being conducted at a local refugee community center and will be completed in summer 2013.

Hasan Nuseibeh is a PhD candidate at the University of South Florida in the Department of Information Systems and Decision Sciences. Mr. Nuseibeh joined the University of South Florida after winning the Fulbright Scholarship for foreign students. Before that he worked as an instructor at the college of business teaching business, management information systems and computer courses at Al-Quds University in Jerusalem. He was also the information systems director at the president's office at the same university. His current research interests include social networks and the effects of cloud computing technologies on organizations.

Osman Özturgut is currently an assistant professor of doctoral studies at the University of the Incarnate Word, San Antonio, Texas, United States. Dr. Özturgut has worked in the field of international and comparative education for over a decade. He has been an administrator and faculty member in various higher education institutions in Turkey, China, and the United States. He has conducted research in China, South Korea, Japan, Turkey, South Africa, and the United States. He is an expert in international and comparative higher education, cultural competency, and leadership studies with numerous publications and presentations in these areas and conducted many workshops.

Shifa Podikunju-Hussain was born in Kerala, India. The youngest of seven children, she has lived in India, Brunei and Singapore before coming to the United States for higher education. She earned her doctorate degree in counselor education, specialization in school counseling from the

University of Florida in 2008. She worked as a school counselor for 8 years in the Alachua County Public Schools system in Gainesville, Florida. Since 2009, she has worked as an assistant professor of School Counseling at Indiana University Southeast in New Albany, Indiana. Her research interests include acculturation issues of immigrant and refugee families, working with Muslim families in K-12 schools, and the education and cultural competence training of school counselors and educators as an emerging field in Southeast Asian secondary education.

Hafiz Printer is an educator within the Ismaili-Muslim community. A deep interest in identity and understandings one's place in society led him to study both history and psychology at the University of Toronto. He continued his education earning a bachelor of education from the University of Toronto, followed by a double master's in education and Islamic Studies from The University of London in collaboration with the Institute of Ismaili Studies. He has also had a rich variety of teaching experience from working with street youth in Kolkata to teaching in London, Essen, Toronto and Vancouver.

Farideh Salili is honorary professor in the Department of Psychology at the University of Hong Kong. Her research interests are in cross-cultural differences in student learning and motivation, bilingual learning, and multicultural education.

Deborah A. Stiles is a psychologist, researcher, and professor specializing in understanding and helping young adolescents from many countries. She has been conducting multi-method, multistage research with adolescents living in Norway and Singapore since the 1990s. The word "with" adolescents is used instead of "on" adolescents because Dr. Stiles seeks to understand how youth see their world and so she always involves adolescents in the interpretation of the results of her investigations. She works at Webster University, an international university that has campuses on four continents, but is based in St. Louis, Missouri, United States. At Webster University she is professor and coordinator of applied educational psychology and director of Intercultural Research Consultants in the School of Education.

Lara Tahoun is a first generation Egyptian American Muslim born to immigrant parents. She taught secondary English in Egypt for 5 years, and has built on this experience by completing over 40 hours of graduate credits in teaching and cultural diversity in an American Public School classroom. Lara was a guest presenter at RAWI's (Radius of Arab American Writers) 2007 Her paper, "The High Price of Pancakes: The Politics of

Publishing for the Arab American Writer" demonstrates the subtle and exclusionary nature of the publication of works by American Muslim writers. Ms. Tahoun now lives in East Stroudsburg, Pennsylvania where she raises two, second generation American Muslims who both participate in the American Public School system while maintaining their cultural/ religious identities. In a word, create a culturally competent world.

CPSIA information can be obtained at www.ICGtesting.com
Printed in the USA
BVOW02s1344150315

391669BV00003B/7/P